MW00387278

King Arthur and
the Goddess of the Land

King Arthur and the Goddess of the Land

The Divine Feminine in the *Mabinogion*

Caitlín Matthews

Inner Traditions
Rochester, Vermont

Inner Traditions International
One Park Street
Rochester, Vermont 05767
www.InnerTraditions.com

Copyright © 2002 by Caitlín Matthews

All rights reserved. No part of this book may be reproduced or utilized in
any form or by any means, electronic or mechanical, including photocopying,
recording, or by any information storage and retrieval system, without
permission in writing from the publisher.

Library of Congress Cataloging-in-Publication Data
Matthews, Caitlin, 1952–
   King Arthur and the goddess of the land : the divine feminine in
the Mabinogion / Caitlín Matthews.—2nd ed.
       p. cm.
   Rev. ed. of: Arthur and the sovereignty of Britain. 1989.
   Includes bibliographical references and index.
   ISBN 0-89281-921-9 (pbk.)
   1. Mabinogion. 2. Arthurian romances—History and criticism.
3. Tales, Medieval—History and criticism. 4. Tales—Wales—History
and criticism. 5. Mythology, Celtic, in literature. 6. Femininity of god
in literature. 7. Kings and rulers in literature. 8. Great Britain—In literature.
9. Goddesses in literature.   I. Matthews, Caitlin, 1952–. Arthur and the
sovereignty of Britain. II. Title.

PB2273.M33 M36 2002
891.6'631—dc21

                                                       2002010771

Printed and bound in the United States at Lake Book Manufacturing, Inc.

10 9 8 7 6 5 4 3 2 1

This book was typeset in Legacy with Aon Cari as a display font

For my dear John:
until the finding and founding of the Court of Joy,
my true companion.

*But right good stories he knows, such as that none could ever
be aweary of hearkening to his words.*

THE ELUCIDATION

Contents

Preface to the Second Edition

The myths of our own land and ancestry speak more deeply to our condition than do the myths of other lands. I was raised on classical mythology, but it was not until I found a copy of the *Mabinogion* in the school library that I began to understand what a treasury of native mythology waited to be explored. Here were stories that shot through my being with the brilliance and velocity of meteors. Living closely attuned to the land of Britain meant that I had a deeper sense of what these stories were telling. It was like hearing and comprehending the complex motifs of a vast symphonic work.

My adult life has been spent pursuing the themes and concepts of Celtic mythology, which have their own distinct patterns. They intertwine the universal archetypal themes of honor, heroism, and adventure with very native concerns about the fulfillment of one's *geasa,* or soul obligations, with initiatory encounters with empowering otherworldly beings, and with the preoccupation of service to and guardianship of the sacred land. To me, these themes are not ancient motifs of a long-dead race, but rather the living song of a vibrant people, a song which I strive to sing in my turn.

It is my great pleasure to continue the Myth Book of Britain, begun in *Mabon and the Guardians of Celtic Britain*. In *King Arthur and the Goddess of the Land* the source of the Arthurian legends is revealed and the relationship between Arthur and the Goddess of Sovereignty is explored. I hope that readers will come to appreciate the stories of the *Mabinogion* as the mythic soil in which the Arthurian legends seeded and to understand the wider mythic context of Celtic and British tradition. As with *Mabon*, this volume is also fully revised and updated.

Like Macsen Wledig, who dreamed of the lady in the chair, may the Goddess of Britain, Lady Sovereignty, welcome you to the shores of these stories, that you may begin your own quest.

Preface to the First Edition

He was dubious of much that these poets
asserted though they were indeed most skilled
artists and remembrancers and conservators
of the things of the Island, yet he suspected that
they tended to be weavers also of the fabulous
and were men over-jealous of their status,
and secretive touching their traditio, but then,
after all, their disciplina was other than his
and this he knew for certain that whatever else
they were, they were men who loved the things
of the Island, and so did he.

DAVID JONES, *THE SLEEPING LORD*

The collection of texts known as the *Mabinogion*, which Lady Charlotte
Guest first published in English in 1849, has perhaps suffered most
because of its name. Those unfamiliar with the riches that the title
obscures might respond, "the Mabi-*what?*" as they pass over seemingly

unpronounceable Welsh names and remote traditional stories appearing to have lost their motivation or purpose. However, the *Mabinogion* is a veritable treasury well worth exploration.

It has long been valued by Arthurian scholars who have quarried its stories for early references to King Arthur. It has never left Welsh oral tradition and is a prime source of British mythology and folklore. It is likewise an important link to the ancestral British mysteries. For though these stories were first transcribed in the twelfth century, they arise out of a lively storytelling tradition and bear remarkable traces of earlier beliefs and myths.

The *Mabinogion* falls into five distinct categories, which may be summarized as follows:

1. The Four Branches *(Pedeir Keinc y Mabinogi):* the stories of "Pwyll, Prince of Dyfed," "Branwen, Daughter of Llyr," "Manawyddan, Son of Llyr," and "Math, Son of Mathonwy," which form the *Mabinogion* proper and which are drawn from the earliest mythological levels.

2. The pseudo-histories of "Lludd and Llefelys" and "The Dream of Macsen Wledig," which concern traditions about King Lud and the emperor Magnus Clemens Maximus.

3. The stories relating to the Dark Age Arthur: "The Dream of Rhonabwy" and "Culhwch and Olwen."

4. The romances that depict the more medieval end of the Arthurian tradition, which are paralleled by the stories told by the French storyteller Chrétien de Troyes: "Owain" or "The Lady of the Fountain," "Gereint and Enid," and "Peredur."

5. "Taliesin" ("Hanes Taliesin"), which is not properly part of the *Mabinogion,* but which Lady Charlotte Guest included in her collection.

In *Mabon and the Guardians of Celtic Britain*[111] I have already dealt with the Four Branches and "Taliesin" as well as commenting on "Culhwch and Olwen." In this volume I intend to comment fully on the remaining stories, following the same general process as before. Although *King Arthur and the Goddess of the Land* can be read as complete in itself, there will necessarily be references to *Mabon and the Guardians of Celtic Britain* where points of comparison arise.

Like the texts that comprise the Bible, the stories of the *Mabinogion* are all derived from different ages and storytellers. The more I study them, however, the more certain I am of their interconnected nature. I am less concerned here with the literary merits of the *Mabinogion* and the historicity of its sources than with revealing the mythological subtext that links the proto-Celtic Arthur with the medieval king. Such an exploration is necessary so that those who are unable to research the sources and parallel texts for themselves may have an appreciation of the mythic subtext underlying the later stories of Arthur, which, though clothed in medieval dress, draw upon myths and themes of the Celtic Otherworld for their inspiration.

In *Mabon and the Guardians of Celtic Britain* I traced the cult of the goddess Modron's son through the earliest stories of the *Mabinogion*. In this volume my intention is to reveal the Goddess herself in her specific guise of Sovereignty, which is how the Irish title of the Goddess of the Land, *flaitheas* or lordship, is commonly translated. The Goddess of the Land and her many representatives seem to me to stand at the very center of Arthurian legend. Indeed, every story within this book is concerned with political sovereignty—who rules the land most effectively—or with the prime figure of the land, the Celtic Goddess of Sovereignty herself, and her relationship with the king, who ultimately derives his sovereignty from her.

The known and unknown storytellers of the Matter of Britain unconsciously inherited what the early poet-seers and sibyls knew: Motifs of wasteland and Wounded King, cauldrons that give life, sacrificial kings whose heads are borne on mystical dishes, wronged maidens, and misguided knights all lie at the heart of the matter.[115] The empowerment of the king by Sovereignty has become subsumed in the Grail quest, while the surrounding lore has fallen into a morass of courtly love and chivalric adventure.

In this book we will discover the relationship of Arthur, the undying king, to Sovereignty, Goddess of the Land, through the medium of the related texts of the *Mabinogion*. It will be revealed that the mystical marriage of Arthur Pendragon to Sovereignty animates the core of the Matter of Britain, a myth which continues to have its own life. Buried within the narratives, stories, and pseudo-histories of the *Mabinogion* lie the clues to this relationship. Through reference to these stories and their Celtic and early European parallels, we will see how the gifts of the Goddess of Sovereignty and the behavior of her kings weave their recurring themes in the myths of Britain.

The theme of Sovereignty and king was unconsciously conveyed by storytellers of both oral and literary traditions throughout the Middle Ages at a time when the Celtic concept of the Goddess of the Land had begun to lose its strength and resonance. The great Goddess of Sovereignty survived, subsumed in countless fays and otherworldly characters, especially as Morgan le Fay, who, as sister to Arthur, reclaimed many of the earlier images, and who featured in stories tracing the hunting of Sovereignty's beasts and in tales about the finding of the hallows, the Goddess's treasures.

Although readers may find jumping-off points for feminist or psychological discussion, we should remember that the *Mabinogion* is not about everyday folk and their everyday scenarios. These are powerful myths drawing upon ancient themes. In uncovering these stories, we must behave like visiting anthropologists and allow the protagonists in them to behave in their own way without imposing our modern values and motivations upon their actions. It follows that the more we visit these myths and meet their inhabitants, the sooner we will understand them.

As a mere mythographer, my role is to guide the puzzled reader through these complex tales with some degree of clarity, to supply parallel sources for study and comparison, and, most important, to instill a love of Britain's native traditions into her people and her sympathetic admirers, for in the tide of time, our understanding is crucial to the survival of these traditions. It is our guardianship and handling of them that will influence their transmission to people not yet born.

Acknowledgments

Due acknowledgment must be made to the myriad scholars whose translations have made so many texts available to me for study and comparison; without their endeavors, this book would never have been started.

My special love goes to John Matthews, who has put up with my invasion of his pitch with great good humor. I thank him for bringing to my attention texts I'd never heard of and pointing out connections that I might well have missed.

To Professor Gearóid Ó Crualaoich of the Department of Irish History, University College, Cork, for his helpful advice on the appearance of dragons in Irish literature, as well as to his colleague Professor Padraig Ó Riain, for the possible relationships between Nennius and the *Echtra Airt*, grateful thanks.

To Wolfe van Brussel for listening, and to Mildred Leake Day for her enthusiastic support; I need friends like you! Special thanks to Karl Mullner for his help in translating the story that appears in chapter 9. To R. J. Stewart, many thanks for enabling me to expound on the material of chapter 2 in his Life of Merlin course in March 1987 at Hawkwood College, Stroud.

To Kathleen Herbert, a true faery godmother, who has helped me in matters Saxon and encouraged me in matters Arthurian. To Chesca Potter for her illustrative genius.

Grateful acknowledgment is made to Agenda Editions for permission to reproduce extracts from *The Roman Quarry* and *Kensington Mass* by David Jones and to Faber and Faber Ltd for extracts from *The Anathemata* and *The Sleeping Lord* by David Jones.

how to Use This Book

I am well aware that more than one interpretation can be made of each of the stories cited in *King Arthur and the Goddess of the Land,* as in *Mabon and the Guardians of Celtic Britain.* It has been my endeavor to let the stories speak for themselves wherever possible. My task has been to reveal the hidden layers beneath each of these medieval stories and to juxtapose parallel texts from the proto-Celtic and post-Celtic periods that have served as sources for each.

That being the case, I have followed the same method as in *Mabon and the Guardians of Celtic Britain.* Each of chapters 2–7 includes a short synopsis of the story discussed, but this should not be substituted for a complete reading of the text, for which you will need your own copy of the *Mabinogion.* In each synopsis you will find parenthetical numbered references that correspond directly to the numbered commentary which follows in each chapter. Within the commentary are references to other stories and major themes either preceding or following it.

This explorative study is intended as a workbook to be used as an adjunct to your own reading and research. For your discovery, or rediscovery, a full list of texts and other source works appears in the bibliography, which is indexed in numerical order and cross-referenced with numerals in superscript found throughout chapter 1 and in each subsequent chapter's commentary. When mentioning a topic already addressed in *Mabon and the Guardians of Celtic Britain,* for easy reference I have cited where the original discussion can be found—e.g., *Mabon,* chapter 6.

In the case of chapters 5–7, the synopses are considerably shorter than each tale merits; but these romances are so extensive that I have had to restrict the retelling in order to concentrate on the commentary. Each of these romances, however, merits a book on its own, and for each there has been much I have been unable to discuss due to lack of space.

Throughout the book I have adopted the simple expedient of capitalizing the word *Sovereignty* when discussing the Goddess of the Land; when *sovereignty* appears in lower case, it refers to the political rule of the land.

It should be noted that different editions of the *Mabinogion* do not always agree as to detail and that the romances in particular reveal many variants. I have chosen to work from Jeffrey Gantz's translation because this edition is most widely available at the time of this writing.

For an overview of the major themes outlined in this study, please refer to the appendix, The Wheel of the Year: King and Goddess.

A Guide to Welsh Pronunciation

The following is a rough guide for those who do not speak Welsh but wish to pronounce the names in these stories with some degree of authenticity. Welsh, though it looks full of impossible clumps of consonants, is pronounced as it is written, unlike its less logical neighbor, Saesneg (English).

1. The vowels, both long and short, are roughly equivalent to Italian sung vowels, with the exceptions of:

    u   as in *ill*, or French *tu* (e.g., Pered'ur: Pere'dir)

    w   as in look (e.g., Ca'dwr: Cad'oor)

    y   in monosyllabic words and final syllables of
          multisyllabic words, as in *pin* (e.g., Rhyd: Hri'id)

---

y   the definite article *y* and in first syllables of multisyllabic words, such as the *u* in *but* (e.g., Cynon: Kun'on)

2. Diphthongs are logically pronounced:

     ai, ei, ae   as in *wine* and *pint* (e.g., Owain, Gereint, and Gafaelfawr: O'wine, Ger'ynt, and Gav-ile'vawr)

     wy   as in French *oui* (e.g., Rhonab'wy: Hrona'booee)

     aw   as in *out* (e.g., Ef'rawg: Ev'roug)

     oe   as in *boil* (e.g., coed: coid)

3. Consonants are pronounced as in English with the following exceptions:

     c   is always hard as in *cake* (e.g., Cai: Kie)

     ch   is aspirated *kh* as in Scottish *loch* (e.g., Gwal'chmai: Gwalkh'my)

     dd   is voiced *th* as in *there*, not as in *thin* (e.g., Lludd: Hlith)

     f   is voiced *v* as in *vet* (e.g., Gwenhwy'far: Gwenhooe'var)

     ff   is *f* as in *fat* (e.g., Fflur: Fler)

     g   is hard *g* as in *gate* (e.g., Glewlw'yd: Gleooloo'eed)

     ll   is *hl*; if you raise the blade of the tongue to the roof of the mouth behind the tooth ridge and blow "huh," this roughly approximates the sound (e.g., Llefel'ys: Hlevel'is)

     r   is slightly trilled

     rh   is *hr*; the *r* is slightly trilled (e.g., Rhy'awdd: Hri'owth)

     th   is as in *thin* (e.g., Arthur: Arthir)

4. The stress falls on the penultimate syllable of a multisyllabic word or on the first syllable of a two-syllable word.

1
Arthur and the Matter of Britain

If his forehead is radiant like the smooth hill in the lateral light, it is corrugated like the defense of the hill, because of his care for the land and for the men of the land.

DAVID JONES, *THE ROMAN QUARRY*

And Sovereignty said to Niall: "And as you saw me ugly at first but at last beautiful, even so is royal rule. The land cannot be won without battles, but in the end everyone finds that sovereignty is both beautiful and glorious."

"ECHTRA MAC ECHACH MUIGMEDOIN"

The Fame of Arthur, Undying King

Arthur lives in the imagination and soul of the people. He is the focus and burning glass for many aspirations, combining the heroic endeavors of the pagan world with the spiritual chivalry of Christian Europe. Arthur's grave, as the early Welsh poems *Englynion y Beddau* (Stanzas on the Graves) tell us, is an unthinkable sepulchre; he has not died but dwells in Avalon—he will come again. The legends in which he figures have currency among both the very simple and the very wise because of the Arthurian world's immediacy in human terms and because its stories operate on many levels.

The Matter of Britain, as the stories of Arthur are called, is a very subtle blend of stories, history, traditions, and beliefs; its followers are likewise various—literary critics, medievalists, and folklorists mingle with those who like the stories for their own sake. There are others for whom Arthur has become a cult figure. He is hero and god,[120] a being whose identity is worthy of assuming within the confines of a war game or role-playing scenario,[147] a model which psychologists can apply to patients' unconscious functions, and an inspiration to mythographers and metaphyscians.[47, 86] Arthur is the stuff of epic film, novel, and enduring mythic heroism.

This Arthurian mystique has been copiously studied and extrapolated. Despite the protestations of rationalists that evidence for the historical Arthur is thin on the ground, the argument that he did exist will not go away. Reverence for Arthur has at various times assumed a semi-mystical fervor which scholars have found distasteful, for to them it surpasses the respect properly due to someone whom they regard as a literary invention and it teeters on the verge of the downright heretical. How has this come about?

The medieval literary corpus of Arthurian stories that most of us know is only one stratum of the excavation in question. If we look deeper, the literary evidence becomes thinner, but what does exist reveals quite a different picture of Arthur. One existing source is the *Mabinogion,* which, though first written down between 1100 and 1250 C.E., was the product of a rich oral tradition and preserves a portrait of Arthur and features of his career that might baffle someone familiar with the great king only through late-medieval sources.

For a start, Arthur was not a noble king based on the Norman or Plantagenet model; he was a warlord surrounded by his war band which was not above a little cattle-raiding or pig-reiving, according to the Welsh Triads.[38] In texts like Geoffrey of Monmouth's *History of the Kings of Britain,*[10] Arthur performs his own deeds rather than sending one of his knights to carry them out on his behalf. We are continually struck, however, by the way in which Arthur seems to move effortlessly between the earthly realms and the Otherworld, for he seems at home in both.

And here, perhaps, we are at the root of the mystery, for Arthur blends skillfully into a mythological hinterland which is even now only just being comprehended. His power to excite reverence or mystical fervor is due in no small part to his connection with and relationship to deeply rooted mythological archetypes arising from the land of Britain. While it was "almost a miracle if he could extract a tear at a pious reading or discourse," St. Ailred of Rievaulx wrote of an unnamed novice in 1141 C.E., it is no wonder that this novice "had frequently been moved to tears by fables which were invented and dissembled concerning an unknown Arthur"[92]—for the consciousness of that time more easily swarmed with native and familiar archetypes than with those propounded by St. Ailred and his fellow clerics.

In the same way in which saints stepped into the shoes of native deities, so the medieval King Arthur replaced the earlier proto-Celtic Arthur, who was in turn a resonance of a mythic archetype of ancestral memory. Mythic identities, like suits of clothes, are changed or appropriated easily. In *Mabon and the Guardians of Celtic Britain*[111] I attempted to show how one mythic motif percolated through British tradition to take in figures as diverse as Arthur, Bran the Blessed, and Mabon himself. In this volume my intentions are to show another kind of mythic archetype, that of Sovereignty, the Goddess of the Land, for it is through her that Arthur earns much of the supernatural reverence surrounding him. His association with her and her representatives will be detailed in chapter 10.

Arthur's reputation seems, from medieval accounts, to be based solely on his Round Table knights and their exploits and on his notable birth and passing into Avalon. In fact, Arthur's is a submerged reputation based on deeds and exploits whose traces can be discovered in extant early literary sources. In these episodes, such as the "Preiddeu Annwfn" (The Spoils of Annwfn—*Mabon*, chapter 6), in which we see him traveling in his ship, *Prydwen*, to steal the empowering symbols known as the hallows, he is dressed in his mythic guise, fulfilling an ancient, redemptive action in order to return balance to the land of Britain. In doing so, Arthur is the earliest Grail winner, establishing a pattern that is followed by Perceval, Bors, and Galahad in the later texts.

While these early exploits have been expunged from literary sources, for the most part, Arthur's begetting, birth, and passing remain as clear indications of his once mythic stature. His life follows the criteria laid down by Celtic storytellers who told tales of the separate incidents in the hero's life: his mysterious conception and birth, his fosterage and obscure childhood, his timely recognition and empowerment, his otherworldly journey, his confinement or illness, and his mysterious death.[12, 137] These features continued to be emphasized even in medieval sources.

The story of Arthur's conception provides an interesting parallel to the usual scenario of the mythic hero as offspring of both an earthly parent and an otherworldly parent. According to Geoffrey of Monmouth,[10] Arthur is conceived in Igraine by the expedient of Merlin's transformation of Uther into the semblance of Gorlois, Igraine's husband. Although Uther is an earthly father, the fact that he appears to Igraine through the means of otherworldly shapeshifting makes him more than human at that point. A similar set of circumstances applies to the conception of Galahad (see chapter 3).

Arthur is not raised by his natural parents, but is fostered in the traditional Celtic way by Sir Ector, according to Malory.[25] Layamon, on the other hand, tells of Arthur's fostering by the Lady Argante, queen of the faery.[43] Arthur is recognized as Uther's son and the rightful king by his act of pulling the sword from the stone.[10] He journeys to Annwfn in order to win the hallows, which will heal the land and empower him.[111] His enfeeblement and disempowerment are the result of his separation from Gwenhwyfar (Guinevere); he does not die, however, but is borne to Avalon to be healed of his wounds.[11] Such a mythic framework can be constructed using the most available of medieval texts, such as those by Geoffrey of Monmouth and Sir Thomas Malory. What becomes clear is that Arthur is more than mortal, though how much more may be debated. William Blake, whose own mythic instinct was sure and uncanny, was in no doubt:

> The giant Albion was Patriarch of the Atlantic; he is the Atlas of the Greeks, one of those the Greeks called titans. The stories of Arthur are the acts of Albion, applied to a Prince of the fifth century, who conquered Europe, and held the Empire of the world in the dark age, which the Romans never again re-covered . . . And all the fables of Arthur and his round table; of the warlike naked Britons; of Merlin; of Arthur's conquest of the whole world; of his death, or sleep, and promise to return again . . . All these things are written in Eden.[53]

Whether in Eden or the Otherworld, the fame of Arthur is undying, rooted deeply in the mythic beginnings of our race. Whether Dark Age battle leader or medieval king, mortal or demigod, Arthur is primarily Guardian of Britain. And the acts of Arthur are indeed those of Albion and thus of Britain, for Albion is one of the land's ancient names. Arthur's story and its place in our mythic history became the core of Europe's first literature. It is a story that has been embellished beyond belief, served up to kings and noblewomen, pored over fervently in secret by clerics, and recited openly by *trouvères* and troubadours alike. This story was the Matter of Britain.

The Matter of Britain

King Arthur and the Knights of the Round Table offered considerable scope for the medieval storyteller. Indeed, one might say that the

Matter of Britain was the first soap opera: No matter how many times it was boiled, there was always a new variation to be served. That these variations may have been borrowed from other, non-Arthurian sources has been one of the major concerns of Arthurian scholarship. Such findings usually discount the oral tradition, but that is where we must make our beginning.

We can only guess at the extent of Arthur's fame before the writings of Chrétien de Troyes in the second half of the twelfth century. Certainly at this time Arthur and his court inhabited the oral rather than the literary tradition and were probably best known among the British (who were in the process of becoming the Welsh, being called *wealas,* "foreigner," by their Saxon neighbors) and the Bretons, who were expatriate Britons living in northwest France. Traces of the colonization of Brittany can be found in the story of Macsen Wledig (see chapter 3). If it had not been for the Bretons, it is unlikely that Arthur and the Matter of Britain would have had such a literary impact on Europe, for their storytellers drew directly on the shared British and Breton oral tradition and were responsible for the transmission of many stories into French literary tradition.

In the course of time, literary tradition cross-fertilized oral tradition throughout Europe. It is one such cross-fertilization that has given us the Arthurian romances of the *Mabinogion,* which will be discussed in detail in chapters 5–7. "The Lady of the Fountain," "Gereint and Enid," and "Peredur" are all paralleled in Chrétien de Troyes's *Yvain, Erec and Enid,* and *Perceval.* In a book of this size it is impossible either to explore fully the nature of the parallels or to provide the full critical apparatus needed for such a study, although references will certainly be given here, if only briefly. Readers whose interest leads them into this vast field may consult the bibliography, where details of critical works are given. Those who are sufficiently interested might do well to read Chrétien's stories[7] and draw their own conclusions.

I am well aware that this field is strewn with scholarly reputations, the owners of which have chauvinistically supported their national legends and literary traditions. The fact remains that there is insufficient evidence to state categorically either that Chrétien's stories predate those of the *Mabinogion* or vice versa. I personally hold that both were derived from a then-existent and now-defunct oral tradition, and that the texts we read today show traces of cross-fertilization.[115] We have no knowledge of how numerous or how widespread were the storytellers, *conteurs*, and trouvères throughout Europe. All that we can be sure of is their influence on literary tradition. Additionally, links between Wales and Brittany are certain. The existence of even one Breton or British storyteller-turned-conteur at the court of Marie de France would account for a great deal of the familiar content of Chrétien's work. Certainly Marie, great-granddaughter of the first trouvère, William IX of Aquitaine, would have drawn court storytellers of all kinds and traditions.

Whether Chrétien's writings preceded the *Mabinogion* or were drawn from a common source, he undoubtedly worked from one that was firsthand rather than from a chain of oral tradition because the similarities between the texts are too close, though Chrétien's text is polished and courtly and rationalizes the otherworldly happenings while the *Mabinogion* has less polish and is more concerned with showing otherworldly events and their impact on the earthly realm.

An oral tradition reaching far into the past informed the Matter of Britain. Both British and Irish storytellers drew on a common fund, particularly of characters "which were once shared among all Celtic peoples and moved about freely among them, to be appropriated [not only] to different heroes as local and national interests dictated—to King Conchobar mac Nessa, Cú Chulainn, and Fionn Mac Cumhail and the heroes who surrounded them in Ireland—but [also] to Arthur and to his attendant warriors in Britain."[56]

These common Celtic and proto-Celtic themes (those adopted from existing native beliefs) were inherited by the expositors of oral tradition, who "gave to the storytellers in Celtic countries the immense repository of imaginative, colorful, and even fantastic story themes on which their high reputation was based, and which proved to have such a rare attraction for foreign audiences.[56]

We should not be surprised to find that the Matter of Britain was wholeheartedly adopted in Europe and that the majority of Arthurian romances are to be found written in French. Norman French, the language of the Norman kings, who were the greatest political unit in Europe, was a language and culture that overlaid that of France, Brittany, and Britain in the twelfth century. Storytellers needed patronage from the well-to-do, and to wealthy courts they undoubtedly went. And while poets and storytellers still exercised their ancient function in benighted parts of Wales and Brittany, their role became increasingly anachronistic as Europe began to open up. Movements of clerics, appointments of bishops, and the establishment of monasteries throughout Europe under the leadership of St. Benedict brought learning to the wealthy as well as provided the skill for the transcription of oral stories and their transmission in written form. As the professional errant storyteller became an established part of French courts, the Matter of Britain began to take shape.

In his commentary on the prophecies of Merlin in Geoffrey of Monmouth's *History of the Kings of Britain,* a twelfth-century cleric, Alain of Insulis, wrote:

> What place is there within the bounds of the empire of Christendom to which the winged praise of Arthur the Briton has not extended? Who is there, I ask, who does not speak of Arthur the Briton, since he is but little less known to the peoples of Asia than to the Bretons, as we are informed by our palmers who return from the countries of the East. The Eastern peoples speak of him as do the Western, though separated by the breadth of the whole Earth.[92]

Arthur became, in short, the hero of medieval Europe. This view was at odds with that held by native Britons, for whom Arthur became an emblem of national resurgence: the king who would come again to rescue his people from the yoke of foreign oppression. Even among the Bretons this myth was a living tradition in the twelfth century:

> Go to the realm of Armorica, which is lesser Britain, and preach about the market places and villages that Arthur the Briton is dead as other men are dead, and facts themselves will show you how true is Merlin's prophecy, which says that the ending of Arthur shall be doubtful. Hardly will you escape unscathed, without being whelmed by curses or crushed by the stones of your hearers.[92]

Arthur lived on in a land that had been colonized more than seven centuries earlier by expatriate Britons who settled in Brittany after fleeing from the social and political upheavals of fourth and fifth century Britain. However significant Arthur may have been as an instrument of propaganda during the centuries of Saxon and Norman incursion, Britons had no doubt about one thing: As one early Welsh manuscript, *Llyfr Gwyn Rhydderch*, chauvinistically states about Britain's sovereignty, "no one has a right to this island except only the nation of the Cymry, the remnant of the Britons, who came here in former days from Troy."[51] Whatever else this statement implies, the fact is clear that Britons looked back farther than Arthur for their inspiration. Troy loomed large, though how greatly it figured before the writings of Geoffrey of Monmouth is not entirely clear.

According to Geoffrey, Brutus, the great-grandson of Aeneas, came to Britain and established his lineage there. On what basis is this pseudo-history (others would call it a fable) founded? Virgil's *Aeneid* has seldom been out of the hands of readers since its composition in the first century B.C.E. It tells of the founding of Rome and was therefore a tool of Roman expansion. The continued popularity of the *Aeneid* rests on the fact that it has often been the first book from which *latimers,* or translators, con their Latin; its intrinsic qualities as a racy story and its poetic composition have recommended it to many. The *Aeneid* and the *History of the Kings of Britain*[10] are virtually contiguous; as a sequel to the *Aeneid,* Geoffrey's chronicle vaunts the Roman and Trojan antecedents of Britain's kings. But was this the only source for the idea that Britons were descended from the remnant of Troy's survivors?

Taliesin, the semi-mythical seer-poet, reveals himself to be a prophet of the Britons by means of his poetic omniscience:

> *Oh! what misery*
> *Through extreme of woe, prophecy will show*
> *On Troia's race!*
>
> *A coiling serpent*
> *Proud and merciless*
> *On her golden wings,*
> *From Germany.*
>
> *She will overrun*
> *England and Scotland*
> *From Lychlyn sea-shore*
> *To the Severn.*
>
> *Then will the Brython*
> *Be as prisoners,*
> *By strangers swayed*
> *From Saxony.*
>
> *Their Lord they will praise,*
> *Their speech they will keep,*
> *Their land they will lose*
> *Except wild Walia.*
>
> *Till some change shall come,*
> *After long penance,*
> *When equally rife*
> *The two crimes come.*

Britons then shall have
Their land and their crown
And the stranger swarm
Shall disappear.

All the angel's words,
As to peace and war
Will be fulfilled
To Britain's race.[23]

He speaks here, of course, of the incursion of the Saxons. But his first few words align him with the remnant of Troy as if he were that legendary race's prophet (see *Mabon,* chapter 7). "Hanes Taliesin" may not be accurately dated to before Geoffrey of Monmouth's time, but certainly this passage seems to be connected to the tradition concerning Merlin's release of the two dragons, which is documented in *History of the Kings of Britain.*[10] It is part of a mythos that looks to its ancestral roots, whether real or imaginary. Furthermore, we should not overlook the preponderance of genealogies that arose during the centuries of Saxon and Norman rule, wherein British poets and clerics recited or transcribed their patrons' illustrious lines, invariably linking them to a Roman, Arthurian, or saintly lineage. Inventing ancestors is not a new game, but how much is genuine remembrance?

It has been suggested that Geoffrey's *History* is Britain's version of the Irish *Book of Invasions.*[51] The *Lebor Gabala Erenn* [8] tells the history of many raids made upon Ireland. It was compiled over a vast period of time, incorporating many ancient traditions and linking them to Biblical ancestors. In this book we read of the descent of the Irish from the peoples of Greece, Egypt, and Spain, the lands which lay along the route traveled by the invading tribes that settled in Ireland. Such claims have been dismissed as false and misleading—akin to Geoffrey's fabrications. But there is now reason to suppose that this tradition was not so far wrong.

The origins of the myths of a race are hard to trace but are usually tenaciously attached to their tradition: Errors of detail are common, but general report may occasionally have grains of truth. If the Irish could trace their ancestry to Greece, it is equally possible for the British to have a tradition that spoke of Trojan forebears. It is known that Geoffrey borrowed from Nennius's *British History*,[28] but Nennius himself drew upon all kinds of manuscripts and traditions which are no longer available to us. Geoffrey further said he was indebted to Walter, Archdeacon of Oxford, for the loan of "a very ancient book written in the British language," of which his *History* was but a translation. Of such books—long since vanished—scholars are very properly suspicious. We will never know, but it is possible that this lost book might indeed have been the *British Book of Invasions*, couched in the same language and based upon the Irish model.

Whatever the truth of the matter, there was a homegrown myth that rivaled the Trojan one: that of Arthur, who repelled the incursion of the Saxons and who, after a necessary period during which Britain would suffer untold wrongs under the Saxon yoke, would come again to restore Britain to her former greatness. Such nationalistic myths have little place in our time. We are reminded so by Daniel Defoe, who wrote in his satire *Jure Divino* that

> *Our Ancestors obtain'd the Kingdom thus,*
> *And left the ill-got Recompense to us;*
> *The very Lands we all along enjoy'd,*
> *They ravish'd from the People they destroy'd.*[101]

Since the mapping of the human genome, myths of racial purity and dominance have been blown out of the water: We are all kindred to each other many times over. The Goddess of Sovereignty has her own methods of assessing worthy champions for her empowerment. They may be rich or poor, noble or of common stock, British or of another race—but they will be right for the land if she chooses them. Only her champions recognize the true nature of the land, who is the mother of us all.

The name of the game, the subtextual energy of the Matter of Britain, is about sovereignty: Who holds the land and by what mystical right? Only those kings and invaders are successful who draw their empowering emblems and mystique from the deep mythical framework of the land. For us to appreciate how Arthur and the related champions of Britain in the *Mabinogion* truly function, we need to investigate the role of kingship and its relationship to the land.

The Calling of the Kings

The *Mabinogion* is a primary document in the Matter of Britain. It draws on the earliest mythic archetypes of both pseudo-history and the cross-fertilization between stories from the British oral tradition and French romances. Each one of the stories discussed in this book shows a hero or champion who is battling for sovereignty of one kind or another. Lludd must overcome three dreadful scourges which ravage his country (chapter 2); Macsen seeks a woman revealed in his dreams and succeeds in becoming the ruler of Britain (chapter 3); Rhonabwy is despondent about the state of his native Wales, but his dream reveals a combat for another kind of sovereignty between Arthur and Owain (chapter 4); Owain becomes the king of an otherworldly realm (chapter 5); Gereint's story reveals a complex relationship among several characters who strive for sovereignty on many levels (chapter 6); while in Peredur's adventures the empowering symbols of sovereignty are sought and found (chapter 7). How each of these characters achieves his aim will be shown in successive chapters, but in some way or other they are all either appointed champions of kings or archetypal kings themselves.

Each may justifiably be called a either a king or a champion because each is accountable to Sovereignty, the Goddess of the Land. But we must not take the medieval notion of kingship as our model here; Arthur and his knights and champions, as well as the other mythical kings, are drawn from an entirely different frame of reference. In order to understand the nature and complexity of Sovereignty's relationship with the king, we must examine the basis of Celtic kingship.

The rites of kingship retain a magical and mystical significance even in our own time. The distillation of ages of tribal ritual still raises an atavistic shudder in some of us as we watch the British coronation ceremony today. It is difficult to express in words just what causes such a primitive reaction within us, but it is clearly connected to the way in which the monarch is presented as the representative of the tribe to both the people and to the otherworldly guardians of the land.

The modern coronation rite of course harks back to a more deeply moving and atavistic rite in which a king was married to the land. Irish texts speak of the *banais rigi,* or the "wedding of the kingship."[70] This was a ritual particularly upheld within the Celtic nations. It is possible that:

> [i]n the elder days, when the succession passed through the female line, the Sovereignty resided in the person of the queen, who, as high priestess, was also the reincarnation of the Great Earth Mother and chose from among her warriors a man to mate with, lead her war band, and after the cycle of seven years, become the king—sacrifice and die to ensure fertility for the soil and prosperity for the tribe.[158]

We will see in the succeeding chapters just how this ancient understanding lies hidden within the stories of the *Mabinogion,* as well as in the Arthurian legends. Matrilinear considerations are still visible in, for instance, Mordred's attempts to win Arthur's throne. Arthur is Mordred's father, while Arthur's sister—a role variously filled by Anna, Morgan, or Morgause, depending on the traditions we draw upon—is Mordred's mother (see chapter 10). We will also see how the insult to Gwenhwyfar—which occurs in "Owain," "Gereint and Enid," and "Peredur"—dishonors the land, for Gwenhwyfar is Arthur's sovereignty in the flesh. For this reason the role of queen's champion is a prime honor at Arthur's court. Both Gereint and Peredur take this part, while Lancelot succeeds them in the French romances.

The wedding of the kingship held strong mystical connotations. In this ceremony the king was mystically conjoined with his kingdom through either stepping into the sacred footprint of the ancestor or being raised up by his tribe to sit upon the inauguration stone, a symbol of the land. Such a stone can be seen at Dunadd in Strathclyde, Scotland, where the Gaelic kings of western Scotland were "made." Another famous stone was the Lia Fal at Tara in Ireland, which would cry out under a destined king. By these ceremonial means the king aligned himself with his sacred ancestors and simultaneously established a contract with the ground beneath his feet. The anvil into which the sword of kingship is thrust in later traditions of Arthur is merely an extension of the royal king-making stone: Only the rightful king may draw it out. It is a supreme example of the kingly marriage with the land. And later still, in John Boorman's film *Excalibur* (Orion, 1981) the imagery of sword and cup is superimposed in such a way that the answer to the question "Whom does the Grail serve?" becomes "The land and the king are one." We will see in chapters 7 and 9 how the Grail is but one of the hallows guarded by Sovereignty and wielded by the rightful king or champion.

Late survivals of the wedding of the kingship were recorded in the twelfth century, the time when the major Arthurian and Grail texts were transcribed. Giraldus Cambrensis recorded one such in his *Irish Itinerary*, where he described the inauguration of a king of Ulster:

> When the whole people of that land has been gathered together in one place, a white mare is brought forward into the middle of the assembly. He who is to be inaugurated embraces the animal before all, professing himself to be a beast also. The mare is then killed immediately, cut up in pieces, and boiled in water. A bath is prepared for the man afterwards in the same water. He sits in the bath surrounded by all his people and all . . . eat of the meat of the mare which is brought to them. He quaffs and drinks of the broth in which he is bathed [by] dipping his mouth into it.[60]

Here Sovereignty is represented by the white mare, which, as we saw in chapter 2 of *Mabon*, is the totem of the Goddess of the Land as represented by both Rhiannon and Epona. The Indian Vedic *asvamedha* ritual, in which a queen symbolically mates with a dead stallion, has a close cultural overlay with the rite that aroused Giraldus's clerical distaste.[130]

But not all survival rituals of this kind employed sacred bestiality. In 1170 Eleanor of Aquitaine decided to inaugurate her son Richard—the future Lionheart—as Duke of Aquitaine. She arranged a symbolic marriage between him and St. Valéry, the legendary martyr and patroness of the district. The saint's ring was placed on Richard's finger "in solemn token of his indissoluble union with the provinces and vassals of Aquitaine."[100]

Marriage and kingship are very similar contracts. While there is harmony and mutual respect between the partners (husband and wife, in the case of marriage; king and land in kingship), both marriage and reign are likewise harmonious. But when love is withheld or abused, the contract is severed. Throughout the Grail legends it is this very relationship between land and king that is crucial to the story, for the land and its bounty are interwoven with the destiny of the rightful king. When the contract is fractured, fertile land becomes wasteland.

According to bardic lore, the spiritual duties of a king were strictly entailed: If his rule was just, then his land and people were fertile and content, as this ancient Irish text relates:

> So long as he preserves justice, good will not be lacking to him, and his reign will not fail . . . By the Prince's justice, every right prevails and every vessel is full during his reign . . . By the Prince's justice, fair weather comes in each fitting season, winter fine and frosty, spring dry and windy, summer warm, with showers of rain, autumn with heavy dews, and fruitful. For it is the prince's falsehood that brings perverse weather upon wicked peoples and dries up the fruit of the earth.[146]

This statement may remind us of Lerner and Loewe's musical *Camelot*, in which Arthur praises the climate of his land where the seasons are marked by ideal weather conditions.

There are plenty of examples in Celtic literature of an unfruitful land caused by a wrongful or unjust king, as we will see in chapter 2, where Vortigern's reign is discussed. Although Lludd himself is a good king, his kingdom suffers under three plagues, each wreaking devastation, and he must find a solution. Sometimes the perturbation is much deeper, an enduring evil left over from a past age which no king has yet rectified or appeased. Such is Lludd's problem, and Manawyddan's, too, in the Third Branch of the *Mabinogion* (*Mabon*, chapter 4). Sometimes the forces of the land are out of alignment because the king's wife is an unworthy representative of Sovereignty, such as Conn's Otherworld woman, Becuma (see chapter 2). Their marriage is not a true union and the land reflects this imbalance by failing in milk and grain.

The king's union with the land, the Goddess of Sovereignty, is a very special one characterized by an exchange of energies and powers: The king swears to uphold his land and people and to be true to them, while Sovereignty gives him otherworldly gifts enabling him to keep his oath. At its base, the Celtic concept of Sovereignty is related to the Middle Eastern concept of wisdom as Sophia, who consorts with kings as the creative and wisdom-bestowing mystic woman appearing in the form of either an angelic presence or an earthly woman. Solomon and Sheba are the prime example of this king-Sophia paradigm. In British symbolism, Arthur and one of Sovereignty's representatives, such as Gwenhwyfar, exemplify the similar king paradigm.

Arthur's relationship with Sovereignty is an extraordinary one, for not only does he relate to otherworldly and earthly women who represent some aspect of the Goddess, but also his role extends to selecting knights of his court, his champions, who similarly relate to the figures of Sovereignty. These knights are usually those closely related to Arthur by blood, such as his nephews and cousins, Gwalchmai (Gawain), Gereint, Culhwch, Goreu, and Owain.

This practice of Arthur may be more clearly understood if we look once more at the customs of Celtic kingship. Royal primogeniture was not introduced into Britain until the time of the Norman kings. Celtic kingship was elective, the successor being drawn from suitable candidates within one royal clan whose members claimed a common ancestor. The king chose and appointed his successor, or *tanaiste* (literally, "second"), during his own lifetime. The choice was made with the approval of the clan's elders and ensured the succession in the event of the king's sudden death. In Ireland such an appointment was made at a great gathering of the people known as a *feis,* or assembly, so that the whole clan knew who the tanaiste was. It is perhaps significant that Gereint, Culhwch, Goreu, Owain, and others are publicly honored by Arthur during such an assembly. Arthur also leaves his court for the express purpose of finding his appointed champions, Owain, Gereint, and Peredur.

Part of the king's contract with Sovereignty was outlined by the number of *geasa* (singular *geis*) laid upon him by men of wisdom at the beginning of his reign. A *geis* is a prohibition or obligation binding an individual on pain of the loss of honor. A king might not lose honor, for doing so not only diminished his authority but also mystically harmed the land. Breaking a geis implied fracturing the contract between king and land. In an Irish story concerning Arthur, "Echtra an Mhadra Mhaoil" (The Story of the Crop-Eared Dog), Arthur says:

> Good people . . . there are many geasa upon me, and one of them is to convene the chase of the Dangerous Forest at the end of every seventh year. If the chase should prove favourable for me the first day, to leave the forest; if not, to stay the second day, and the third concerning the hunt. And I shall not break my geasa . . . for he is a person without prosperity who breaks his geasa.[135]

This chase is emblematic of Arthur's seven-year agreement with Sovereignty, which must be ratified in order for his reign to continue. As we will see in chapter 6, the chase for the white hart is part of this tradition and is one of the rare occasions when Arthur himself engages in the action of the story.

One of Arthur's famous geasa surviving into medieval memory was never to eat until a wonder had appeared before him; and the best-known tale about the proving of this geis is "Sir Gawain and the Green Knight."[31] We are already familiar with a similar geis: that upon Pwyll to climb to the top of the Mound of Arberth, whereupon he might see a wonder or be wounded (*Mabon,* chapter 2).

The double-edged nature of geasa hinges upon the capacity for selflessness of the person who has received them. As long as a king who has been given geasa lives harmoniously with his contract and serves his people, he is king in truth; but there usually comes a moment when he must decide between his own interests and keeping his geasa or his contract with Sovereignty. This usually takes the form of a life-or-death decision, such as when Cú Chulainn is invited to eat a roasted dog by the Morrighan in the "Táin bó Cúaligne": His geasa include an obligation to accept food when it is offered to him and a prohibition against eating dog's flesh because the dog is his totemic beast. He eats the meat and accepts the consequences, but his contract as Ulster's champion is at an end.[171]

At all times the king is bound to uphold the law, which is most binding upon him:

> The king must have patience, self-government without haughtiness, speak truth and keep promises; honour the nobles, respect the poets, adore God; keep the Law exactly without mercy. Boundless in charity, care for the sick and orphans; lift up good men and suppress evil ones; give freedom for the just, restriction for the guilty. At Samhain (November 1, Hallow-mas) he must light the lamps and welcome the guests with clapping. He must appear splendid as the sun in the Mead Hall.[158]

So goes an instruction of Cormac mac Airt, known as the Irish King Solomon and famed for his laws and noble institutions of learning, but this might well be a description of Arthur in his great hall, the most resplendent of kings in that supposedly Dark Age, the king who shines yet in the hearts and imaginations of many as the upholder of Light against Dark. But there are few to mark the nature of his union with the land, and that is the underlying purpose of this book; for, as mentioned in chapter 1 of *Mabon and the Guardians of Celtic Britain,* this will enable us to call forth the Pendragon and to name the land, correctly identifying that aspect of Sovereignty which is appropriate to our time.

The Goddess of the Land

The Goddess of Sovereignty has long been acknowledged by scholars to be an intrinsic part of the Celtic world—she is viewed as a literary type or an ancient survivor of pre-Christian times. As we examine the evidence for this, we may be astounded to find that, far from being a cultural cliché or an abstraction, the power of the living Goddess is paramount. She appears in many guises: as an otherworldly maiden whose beauty dazzles; as a bountiful queen bestowing the gifts of the land upon her people; as Dark Woman of Knowledge, *cailleach,* or Loathly Lady who appalls with her ugliness—but not for long. The dark aspect of the Goddess is but the last waning crescent, which will turn to a new moon in the twinkling of an eye to reveal her as Princess of beauty, youth, and gladness.

Each of our stories shows how she interacts with the protagonists of a tale: She may appear to heroes and kings, urging them on to find her gifts or to champion her cause; she may assume the shape of a mortal woman, becoming an exemplar of the Goddess; or she may use many earthly women in one story so that each aspect of the Goddess is manifested.

Although the feminine deity had been officially expunged from Christian worship or lodged in the niche reserved for the Blessed Virgin, she did not vanish from the consciousness of a people who had revered her at stream and in grove from the dawn of time. Goddesses haunted the medieval imagination, as a glance at any text will testify. While Europe may have been nominally Christian, believers evidently approached the new expression of deity with images drawn from their own native mythic traditions. Times change but stories endure. The Goddess passes into the shape of Sovereignty and into many other guises which I have not discussed in this book. She becomes as well the personification of the land.

The Goddess of Sovereignty is primarily the *anima mundi,* the feminine spirit of the earth beneath us, who in many different countries assumes an appearance as a *juno loci* with a set of symbols appropriate to her cult. The first localized cults of the Blessed Virgin were built upon this understanding, giving us "Our Lady of" this or that place. Every country has its own Sovereignty, emblematic of that country's political identity. Britain's prime symbol once appeared on the common penny as Britannia, a personification first portrayed on Roman coins of the conquest period, showing Britain arrayed with the spear, shield, and mural crown of Minerva, goddess of wisdom. This symbolic representation, once in everyone's pocket, now appears only on the British fifty-pence piece.

Yet examples of Sovereignty in British tradition are often difficult to discern. In our discussion of the Sovereignty themes in the *Mabinogion,* the reader will notice that I have frequently resorted to Irish texts to explicate the text in question. There is a good reason for this: Although British—what we would now call Welsh—tradition embodied and preserved a good deal of evidence for Sovereignty, this occurred mainly in the oral tradition only and has been subsequently lost. The Irish tradition—in which poets and storytellers merged almost imperceptibly with that other professional class, the Christian clerics—preserved both an oral and a written tradition, which, for reasons of geographical isolation and other cultural effects, have come down to us in a nearly complete body of lore. The loss of a parallel Welsh tradition is partially made up for by the preservation and transmission of British stories in Breton and French traditions, from which they emerged to form the Matter of Britain. "Whatever the reason may have been," says the respected scholar Rachel Bromwich, "there can be no doubt of the great value for comparative purposes of early Irish literature"[56]

Glenys Goetinck has rightly pointed out that "for many scholars 'Celtic origin' and 'Irish origin' have become synonymous. Welsh tradition has been regarded as . . . a channel through which Irish legends filtered to the continental romancers."[74] The *Mabinogion* does preserve a truly British tradition, which, though it is paralleled frequently in Irish tradition, does not necessarily draw directly upon it. We must posit a common heritage, remembering that the cultural norm was dictated by a professional class of poets and storytellers highly trained in transmitting classified information by way of their arts. Their stories would have provided a common store of tradition in imagery and song, which would have been as potent, if not more so, than the media culture that is common in our own time on both sides of the Atlantic.

If we consider the evidence within the *Mabinogion* that is discussed in this volume and in *Mabon and the Guardians of Celtic Britain,* as well as in the parallel and comparative stories in the commentaries, we can seen that expressions of the Divine Feminine did not suddenly cease in early Romano-British culture, but that in the post-Celtic period they developed in a totally new way, spreading organically by means of the oral tradition into the deep levels of mythic consciousness. When a deity steps down from a shrine and is seemingly exiled from its cult, two things may happen: That deity either gradually fades from memory or becomes newly enshrined in the hearts of the people. This is what happened to Sovereignty as the skill of storytellers enhanced beyond the scope of local cult her function as the bestower of wisdom and power. It is astounding that a few localized aspects of the great Earth Mother of primitive belief should have melded together and survived to form one of the major figures not only of Celtic and Arthurian tradition but also of the redemptive Grail legends—yet this is what happened. The foundation mysteries of the Goddess underlie the Matter of Britain, as does the Succession of the Pendragons, with all its ancient resonances of earlier beliefs.

The most clearly defined portrayal of Sovereignty is found in early Irish literary tradition, where she is called Eriu, Ireland herself. A late-fourteenth-century poem by Gofraigh Fionn Ó'Dálaigh addressed to

his future patron, Tadhg Mainistreach, Lord of Desmond, shows us
Eire as the Goddess of Sovereignty awaiting her true husband:

> *Patience awhile, O Eire!*
> *Soon shalt thou get a true spouse.*
> *He is not yet a grown man,*
> *O Eire, thou home of comfort.*
> *O smooth plain of Usneach,*
> *fair Temhair of Da Thi,*
> *I know him who shall wed thee,*
> *a hero child whom thou shalt love.* [102]

The Goddess of the Land awaiting a worthy consort was a well-
established theme by the time of this poem, but the Irish had achieved
a high degree of skill in portraying Sovereignty as the consort of kings,
as we find in the following story, "Echtra Mac Echach Muigmedoin"
(The Adventures of Eochaid Muigmedon's Sons). It concerns primarily
Niall of the Nine Hostages, who was a historical high king of Ireland
from 379 to 405 C.E. I give the fullest synopsis of this story because it
establishes a primary source for Sovereignty's relationship with the king.

The Adventures of Eochaid Muigmedon's Sons

King Eochaid Muigmedon has four sons by his wife, Queen Mongfind.
He also has a concubine called Cairenn Casdubh, a captive from Alba,
who gives birth to Eochaid's son Niall beside a well. Cairenn is subsequently forced into slavery by Queen Mongfind and has to abandon
her child. Niall is found by a wandering poet, Torna Eces, who fosters
him until the boy is nine and has long golden hair. Eochaid recognizes
his son formally at court and Niall's first deed is to clothe his mother
in the royal purple, bringing her toil to an end.

When the time comes for Eochaid to appoint his tanaiste, he
sends all five boys to the smith Sithchenn, who is also a druid and
prophet. On order to test the boys to see which one should become
king, he sets fire to his smithy and stands by to see what the boys will

do. The four eldest boys rush into the flaming smithy and bring out a chariot that is being repaired, a vat of wine, some weapons, and a bunch of kindling; but Niall brings out the anvil, the tongs, bellows, and hammers—all the tools of the smith's craft—so that Sithchenn's choice fell upon him.

Queen Mongfind is dissatisfied with this outcome and demands another test. The boys are then armed as men and are sent off hunting to see how they will fare. They kill a boar and set up a fire but they are soon very thirsty. In turn each of the four elder boys goes in search of water, but each one encounters the same hideous hag who guards a well from which she allows none to drink save the one who kisses her. In turn, each flees. Last, Niall himself arrives and sees her:

> [E]very joint and limb of her, from the top of her head to the earth, was black as coal. Like the tail of a wild horse was the gray bristly mane that came through the upper part of her head-crown. The green branch of an oak in bearing would be severed by the sickle of green teeth that lay in her head and reached to her ears. She had a middle fibrous, spotted with pustules, diseased, and shins distorted and awry. Her ankles were thick, her shoulder blades were broad, her knees were big, and her nails were green.[171]

Niall agrees not only to kiss her but to lie with her as well. When he kisses her he finds that:

> ... there was not in the world a damsel whose gait or appearance was more lovable than hers! ... Plump and queenly forearms she had; fingers long and lengthy; calves straight and beautifully coloured. Two blunt shoes of white bronze between her little, soft-white feet and the ground. A costly full-purple mantle she wore, with a brooch of bright silver in the clothing of the mantle. Shining pearl teeth she had, an eye large [and] queenly, and lips red as rowanberries.[70]

Amazed, Niall asks who she is and is told, "Lordship is mine; O King of Tara, I am Sovereignty." She commends him for his perseverance in the face of her ugliness and invites him to drink of the well, bidding him not to give his brothers anything to drink until they acknowledge him as his father's tanaiste. And so Niall becomes high king, reigning long and prosperously, as does his line after him.

In this, one of many king-making stories in which Sovereignty appears, we note that she is primarily a transformative goddess, changing from hag aspect to maiden, renewed by Niall's acceptance of all that kingship entails. It is this very element of transformation from hag to maiden that helps us track the parallel developments of Sovereignty within British and Arthurian tradition. Niall's success is dependent upon many factors, not least of which is his early boyhood deed of freeing his mother from slavery. There are many elements in this story that are strongly reminiscent of the story of Rhiannon and Pryderi. Even the poet Torna Eces, "thunder knowledge," who fosters Niall, is strikingly similar to Teyrnon Twrf Liant, "lord of the raging sea." The hag's horselike hair may also indicate a parallel with Rhiannon (*Mabon,* chapters 2 and 4).

By freeing his mother from servitude, Niall has already set in motion the transformative chain of events that will make him king. His action of seizing the anvil is also significant, especially if we recall the sword-in-the-stone motif, which establishes Arthur's kingship likewise through a competitive test. Perhaps the part of this story that is most indicative of Sovereignty's empowerment is her guardianship of the well. Invariably Sovereignty gives her cup only to the rightful kingly candidate or champion. In this, as we will later see, she is the prototype of the Grail Maiden. More important, she is the guardian of the hallows, those otherworldly empowering elements that underlie the regalia of the king-making ceremony. The hallows—often formalized into the spear, the sword, the cup, and the cauldron, though appearing in many variations—may not be handled by any save the rightful king or most worthy champion. In the test or quest by which they are found, Sovereignty often assumes her guise of hag, although she is by no means restricted to that role.

The transformative Goddess of Sovereignty is a unique feature in Irish and British tradition, rarely encountered elsewhere in such a profusion of expressions, except perhaps in Indian and Tibetan traditions, where aspectual qualities of single deity are often manifest as different entities rather than as one archetype. This same method of understanding deities and inner archetypes was once commonplace in the proto-Celtic era but is no longer so in an age when the concept of *deity,* whether male or female in expression, has become virtually featureless and two-dimensional, and therefore totally absent from the consciousness of many people.

In order to help the reader conceptualize the features of Sovereignty in a very generalized sense, figure 1 lists the names, aspects, functions, and characteristics of Sovereignty as they appear in this book. They are by no means the last word and should be considered only as a rough guide. Sovereignty is too subtle and transforming a goddess to be pinned down and decoded definitively. She chooses her own methods of making herself known and may use more than three aspects to reveal herself, as indeed she does in "Peredur" (see chapter 7). There is even a case for her appearing in four aspects, if one considers the evidence of the Arthurian legends in which the admonitory Black Maiden, who shares all the features of the cailleach except age, is a transitional figure between the hag and maiden aspects. The Black Maiden presents an aspect of the Goddess identifiable to anyone familiar with Celtic mythology: that of the woman warrior who often acts as bodyguard or resourceful companion to the champion, as Luned does for Owain in "Owain," also called "The Lady of the Fountain" (see chapter 5).

The "emblematic colors" in figure 1 are derived from a number of textual sources which comprise a familiar set of details corresponding to all the outlined aspects. The woman who possesses all these colors in her appearance—she is white of skin, red of cheek and lip, black of hair—is the ideal woman over whom the champion languishes. She may appear in a dream or, as in Peredur's case, the champion may see these three colors in vivid juxtaposition and so envision a dream

	Maiden Aspect	Mother/Foster Mother Aspect	Hag/Cailleach Aspect
Aspect of Royal Rule	princess	queen	queen mother
Appearance	beautiful maiden	royal woman	hag or Black Maiden
Emblematic Color	white	red/white	black or black and white
Function	She invites	She empowers	She guides and warns
Empowering Drink	the red drink of lordship	the milk of fostering	the dark drink of forgetfulness
Title in the Grail Legends	Grail Maiden or Grail bearer	queen of the hallows	Grail messenger
Other Titles	Flower Bride	Sovereignty	Loathly Lady, Dark Woman of Knowledge

Figure 1. The shape of sovereignty

woman. This ideal woman is none other than Sovereignty, who combines all these colors and their symbolic qualities within her own person. It is not insignificant that these three colors are also those of the alchemical processes by which radical changes manifest the most precious gold.

The warrior woman embodiment of the Black Maiden may be said to combine the colors black and white, which are frequently represented by the chessboard of combat, another emblem of the land or of Sovereignty herself. The Black Maiden fulfills the role of tutor in some of the stories, as Luned does for Owain (see chapter 5). She may also be the challenger—which is how the Black Maiden appears to Peredur (see chapter 7). In all her forms, this role can be traced throughout Celtic literature, from the women warriors who teach the hero battle skills—such as Scathach in the story of Cú Chulainn—to the satirists, such as Morrighan in the story of Cú Chulainn.[88] The Black Maiden battles hard to bring her protégé to self-knowledge and responsible action; in many ways she is an active champion of Sovereignty and corresponds to the male figure identified here as the Provoker of Strife, an archetype fulfilled by Iddawg, Efnissien, and Cai in "The Dream of Rhonabwy," "Branwen, Daughter of Llyr," and the romances, respectively. These men are troublemakers in whom we can perceive the role of Sovereignty's guardian (see chapter 8).

Sovereignty is not merely a passive archetype, some kind of negative cypher whose sole purpose is to empower kings and heroes. As a goddess and through her human representatives she exists in her own right and actively promotes, obstructs, or dismisses her chosen candidates. She and her elect continually modify and develop their relationship; as the essential quality of the land personified, Sovereignty has the right to change her mind and frequently does so. Even Arthur himself is not exempt from her strictures.

Arthur's brilliant early career is mostly overshadowed in later texts by his own seemingly passive stance as a king who does not hazard his own person, but who sends out his knights instead. As we shall see in chapter 10, his inability to retain Gwenhwyfar (Guinevere) is a symptom of the kingly relationship with Sovereignty. His enmity with Morgan is similarly significant. The demise of the Round Table fellowship is nothing less than the reordering of the land in Britain under a new regime, according to Sovereignty's decision. There is purpose, then, in the frequent inclusion by medieval storytellers of a set-piece dream in which Arthur meets the Goddess as Fortuna, upon whose wheel he has been both elevated and abased.[3, 25]

The point at which the historical and mythic concepts of Arthur meet and merge is perhaps best seen and understood in the undying king's defense of Britain. Arthur's timely welding together of the scattered kingdoms of Britain to form a bulwark against barbarian invaders thrusts him into prominence. But he is only one of many such defenders dating back before Bran the Blessed, whose head was buried at the White Mount in London to prevent invasion—a talismanic burial, which, say the triads, Arthur abhorred because he wished to fulfill this role alone, and which he undid through his supervision of the lamentable disinterment of the head of Bran.[38]

Vortimer, the erstwhile king of Britain and Vortigern's son, similarly asked for his body to be dismembered and buried at the ports to defend Britain from Saxon invasion.[38] Even earlier than Vortimer was Constantius Chlorus, the imperial commander of Gaul, who, in the late third century C.E., routed the usurping Allectus, murderer of the British emperor Carausius (whose seamanship, ironically, had effectively defended Britain from foreign invasion). Constantius Chlorus was subsequently active in restoring Britain and in strengthening its borders. His defeat of Allectus was marked by the striking of a golden medallion; on the reverse of his portrait appears a kneeling woman, the spirit of London herself, welcoming his appearance, and the legend *Redditor lucis aeternae,* "restorer of the eternal light." This tradition seems to have been borrowed from currency of Carausius, whose coins call him *Restitutor Britanniae,* "restorer of Britain," and hail him *Expectate veni,* "come, awaited one."[49]

If Arthur ever found time to strike such coins himself, none has survived, yet these titles might well be used to refer to him, for he deserved them as much as, if not more than, Constantius or Carausius for his defense of Britain's sovereignty. Historical tradition affords Arthur the title *Dux Britanniarum,* the old Roman military appellation given to those who defended the northern frontiers, and Nennius attests to many battles that Arthur fought in Britain's defense, notably the eighth battle, which "was in Guinnion fort, and in it Arthur carried the image of the holy Mary, the everlasting Virgin, on his shield."[28]

Geoffrey of Monmouth, calling on this tradition, gives his own version of this incident, placing it at the Battle of Badon: "And across his shoulders, a circular shield called Pridwen, on which there was painted a likeness of the Blessed Mary, Mother of God, which forced him to be thinking perpetually of her."[10]

British tradition was not slow to afford Arthur the status of a Christian king and emperor whose defense of his realm was but an extension of his defense of Christendom. But though the two passages above have been disputed in that Nennius's text implies that Arthur carried the Virgin's image on his shoulder rather than his shield (due to a confusion between two old Welsh terms, *ysgwyd*, or "shield," and *ysgwydd*, or "shoulder"), if we consider Geoffrey's singular slip in confusing *Prydwen*, Arthur's ship, famed from long British usage, with his shield, we find an interesting implication: The meaning of *Prydwen*, the name of Arthur's ship, may unlock for us the true relationship of Arthur to the land of Britain in a more mystical sense. *Prid, pridd*, or *pryd* may mean, variously, "dear," "earth," or "beauty." The suffix *wen*, from *gwen* or *gwyn*, means "white" or "blessed," so that *Prydwen* might signify the "white or blessed earth." Prydein is, of course, one of the names of Britain. Perhaps beneath the writings of Nennius and Geoffrey we may discern Arthur's true championship of the Lady of Britain, the indwelling Goddess and Sovereignty of the Land on whose defense Arthur's thoughts were perpetually set.

According to ancient tradition, it was in the ship *Prydwen* that Arthur sailed to gain the empowering hallows of Sovereignty, receiving them from the Underworld of Annwfn—a feat which, says the poet Taliesin, caused him to wear a "mournful mien," for out of three ships full of men, only seven men returned from that place. It is precisely because of his care for and his defense of the blessed earth of Britain and its Sovereignty that Arthur is remembered. This duty separates him from other men and incorporates him into Britain's landscape. As the poet David Jones wrote: "if his forehead is radiant like the smooth hill in the lateral light, it is corrugated like the defence of the hill, because of his care for the land and for the men of the land."[84]

2
Lludd and Llefelys

Britons then shall have
Their land and their crown,
And the stranger swarm
Shall disappear.

"Hanes Taliesin"

Do not permit your sword hilt to fall into the
hands of the one of the Coraniaid, for misfor-
tune would befall; like Lludd who destroyed
the poison, you are the supplier of holy water
to our nation.

Lewys Mon to his patron
(medieval Welsh poem)

The Testing of Lludd

In the first story of this discussion we find all the necessary ingredients for our study: kingship, Britain's sovereignty, and otherworldly manifestations of disorder and challenge. All of these factors feature in the testing of Lludd in his new role as king. The story is short and simple and relates the adventures of Lludd, king of Britain, and his attempts to rid his kingdom of three plagues which threaten his sovereignty.

As will become clear, the function of the Wondrous Youth is paramount in both our story and the parallel and source texts that accompany it. This is the role of the young Merlin, for example, who, as Emrys, confounds Vortigern's magicians (see the section Sovereignty's Son on page 44). Perhaps, in some lost original of our story, Llefelys acted in a similar way to support and vindicate his brother's kingship. It is likewise in such a mode that Taliesin helps his young patron Elphin at the court of King Maelgwn (*Mabon,* chapter 7).

The incident of the dragons is paralleled in Geoffrey of Monmouth's *History of the Kings of Britain,*[10] in which Britain's sovereignty is represented by the red dragon—still the national emblem of Wales. It is likewise the device or totemic beast of the greatest line of kings, the Pendragons, and is ultimately the representative beast of Sovereignty herself. In the evolution of the Arthurian legends we continue to accumulate traditions relating to the dragon. One of the more intelligent treatments of this theme is found in John Boorman's film *Excalibur,* in which not only is Merlin the arch dragon-priest, attached in a prophetic and magical role to King Arthur, but also the land of Britain itself is understood to be animated by the spirit of the dragon. When the king is wounded (by the adultery of Guinevere and Lancelot), Merlin is deactivated on the magical levels and the land is rent; the powers of the dragon are no longer safely channeled through the roles of king and priest but are loose to wreak havoc in the kingdom. Wasteland, unnatural rites, and weak kingship result.

We must view the dragons in "Lludd and Llefelys" in a similar light. The emblematic beast of Britain—the red dragon—does battle with the foreign dragon. Both Taliesin in his poetry[177] and Merlin in his prophecies[150] speak at length about this combat and its consequences for the people of Britain. The overcoming of the red dragon by the white will ensue, say Merlin and Taliesin, followed by a return of Britain's primacy, before the ending of the world. For those interested in pursuing the historical, allegorical, and mythological meanings of the prophecies of Merlin, they are dealt with exhaustively in R. J. Stewart's book *The Prophetic Vision of Merlin*.[150]

Synopsis of "Lludd and Llefelys"

(1) Beli the Great had three sons, Lludd, Caswallawn, and Nynnyaw, as well as a fourth, Llefelys. Lludd reigns after his father and has rebuilt London as his chief fortress. Llefelys has married the king of France's only daughter and has become king of that country in his turn.

(2) Three plagues fall upon Britain: (3) First, the Corannyeid arrive, who are able to overhear anything that is uttered in the kingdom, which means they cannot be overthrown; (4) second, a scream ensues every May Eve which robs men of their strength and causes women to miscarry, children to become mad, and animals and soil alike to become barren; and (5) finally, the king's court is mysteriously robbed of its provisions. (6) Seeking his brother's advice, Lludd sets off for France very secretly. Llefelys meets him in mid-ocean with his own fleet. To avoid the Corannyeid overhearing, Llefelys counsels that they speak only through a bronze horn. But whatever each says is misunderstood by the other. Llefelys has the horn washed out with wine, which removes this contrary set of spirits. He then advises his brother on how to deal with each of the plagues.

Lludd returns to Britain and implements his brother's advice. (7) He summons all his people together with the Corannyeid, mashes with water the insects which Llefelys has given him, and throws the water over the assembly. It destroys the Corannyeid but leaves the British unharmed. (8) He then measures the length and breadth of the island to discover its center, which is found to be Oxford. There a pit is dug; in it is placed a vat of mead and over it is laid a silk sheet. Two dragons then begin fighting there. When they are tired, they sink down onto the sheet in the form of piglets, drink up the mead, and fell asleep. They are immediately bundled into the sheet, locked in a stone chest, and buried in Snowdon, the most secure part of the kingdom. This ends the screaming on May Eve. (9) Last, Lludd himself prepares to stay up all night and catch whoever has stolen his court's provisions. He has a tub of cold water ready to immerse himself in if he should feel sleepy. Soon he sees a heavily armored man enter with a basket into which he has placed all the stolen food. They struggle and Lludd overcomes his adversary, making him grant restitution and service of the king for ever afterwards. So were the three plagues overcome and so was peace restored to Britain.

Commentary

(1) Tradition credits Beli with many descendants. He is none other than Beli Mawr (the Great), ancestor of the Welsh princes, whom Geoffrey of Monmouth calls Bellinus. Tradition also credits Beli with marrying Anna, the cousin of the Virgin Mary. In the triads Beli is called the father of Arianrhod. Lludd is none other than King Lud, who, in the *History of the Kings of Britain*,[10] renamed Trinovantum as Caer Lud. In our story Lludd is indeed named again as the founder of London, as Caer Lud afterwards became. Ludgate, near modern Fleet Street, still bears his name. Statues of him and his brothers appear on the porch of the church of St. Dunstan-in-the-West on Fleet Street. Llefelys is the Welsh name for Clovis, the Merovingian king of the Franks, a historical contemporary of Arthur born c. 465 C.E. He is incorporated into this story as a foil for Lludd and appears nowhere else in Welsh tradition.

Caswallawn appears in "Branwen, Daughter of Llyr" as the oppressor and usurper of Britain and one responsible for its enchantment (see note 2 below). Nynnyaw, or Ninian/Nennius, plays no part in our story, although Geoffrey credits him with a hand-to-hand combat with Julius Caesar in his *History*.[10] The many muddled genealogies that stem from Beli Mawr speak of a Nwyfre, father of Lliaws, who is married to

Beli's daughter, Arianrhod. As this would make Lliaws the son-in-law of Beli, do we have here a possible explanation for Llefelys, who nowhere else appears as a son of Beli? The names Nynnyaw and Nwyfre are sufficiently similar to cause this confusion, but the names Lliaws and Llefelys sound very similar as well. Llefelys is credited with gaining a very favorable match in the unnamed daughter of the king of France. He seems to have taken on the role of Wondrous Youth in this story (see note 6, below).

(2) The enchantments of Britain are a perennial theme in oral and early literary tradition. Two specific instances spring to mind in the context of this story: the enchantment that falls upon Dyfed in "Manawyddan, Son of Llyr" (*Mabon*, chapter 4), and the wasteland of the Grail legends. In the first of these, a mist covers Dyfed and takes away all living things. It is caused by the otherworldly workings of Llwyd ap Cil Coed, the enemy of Pwyll's family. In the Grail corpus, the wasteland may have one of several causes, the chief of which is the wounding of the king. According to the rules under which Sovereignty operates, a blemished or wounded king cannot rule, and his failure to abdicate is reflected in the land's loss of fertility. In the *Didot Perceval*,[32] however, the wasteland is the fault of Perceval, who sits, unworthy, on the Perilous Seat, thereby causing a mist to descend and a great scream to be heard.

Triad 36 speaks of the three oppressions that come upon Britain. The Welsh word used to describe these is *gormes* (plural *gormesiad*), which denotes "plague" or "foreign oppression" (see note 3, below). The enchantments in this story are thus concerned with the sovereignty of Britain. It is not clear how Lludd's reign should have merited these plagues, for his rule is a fair one with no hint of a rupture in the king's traditional relationship with the land. But, as we will see, these plagues are mainly of otherworldly origin, arising from deep within the land to challenge or test Lludd's kingship.

If we look into the triads and into parallel Arthurian tradition, we will find that similar problems trouble Arthur's career as king. He is described in Triad 26 as pursuing and seeking to destroy an other-worldly pregnant sow called Henwen. It is prophesied that "the Island of Britain would be the worse for her womb-burden."[38] At first the sow gives forth wheat, bees, and barley, but her next offspring are not so beneficial to the Island. She bears three contentious beasts: a wolf cub, an eagle, and a kitten, the last of which grows to become the fearsome Palug Cat eventually killed by Cai.[105]

Arthur also provokes trouble by uncovering the head of Bran the Blessed. While the burial of Bran's head is described as one of three fortunate concealments—for its interment protects Britain from invasion—its disinterment is called one of three unfortunate disclosures in Triad 37. Arthur's hubris in wanting no one but himself to defend Britain causes considerable trouble.

The three fortunate concealments and their reversals, the three unfortunate disclosures, listed as follows, are very relevant to our understanding of Britain's sovereignty:

1. The head of Bran, buried to protect Britain from invasion, is disinterred by Arthur out of hubris.

2. The bones of Gwrthefyr the Blessed (Vortimer), which protect Britain from Saxon oppression, are disinterred by Gwrtheyrn the Thin (Vortigern) out of love for Ronnwen (Renwein, Rowena), Hengist's daughter.

3. The dragons that Lludd buries at Dinas Emrys are disrupted by Vortigern when he attempts to build his tower over their resting place.

Each of these three concealments is clearly intended for the safety of Britain, and in each case it is a king who is responsible for its disruption. We are perhaps unused to conceiving of Arthur as an irresponsible king, but it is possible that Triad 20 can elucidate Arthur's action. In this triad he is called one of three Red Ravagers of the Island of Britain: "But there was one who was a Red Ravager greater than all three: Arthur was his name. For a year neither grass nor plants used to spring up where one of the three would walk; but where Arthur went, not for seven years." This is an indictment indeed, and one which clearly follows the tradition that it is Arthur's rupture with Sovereignty which causes the wasteland.

The acts of a king are never discrete; they have far-reaching repercussions throughout the life of the land and its people. The story of Lludd is too vestigial to establish the causes of the land's three plagues, but we may be sure they are closely related to the nature of his early reign and that, like Arthur, it lies within his strength to put things right again.

(3) The Corannyeid seem to derive from the same source as the Breton faery folk, the Korrigans. These beings are said to be descendants of the female druids, whose spells maliciously interfered with the lives of ordinary people; they robbed families of children, substituting changelings, and worked much petty magic. According to Breton folk tradition, they danced and sang and were not able to stop their singing unless someone passed by and asked a favor. If the passerby was successful, he received a gift; if not, he was afflicted by their enchantment.[109]

Like the Welsh Tylwyth Teg (the fair family), as the faery kind are called, the Corannyeid are omniscient, hearing everything that is uttered. This is partially why all faery peoples are spoken of with great reverence and careful respect, lest they blight the lives of mortals in any way. Of course this omniscient hearing is also a power that Math ap Mathonwy has in the Fourth Branch story of the *Mabinogion* (*Mabon*, chapter 5). Triad 36 tells that the first of the three oppressions upon Britain comprised "the people of the Coraniaid, who came here in the time of Caswallawn, son of Beli; and not one of them went back. And they came from Arabia."[38]

Caswallawn is frequently mentioned in regard to the enchantments of Britain. In "Branwen, Daughter of Llyr" he actually causes destruction himself by usurping Bran's role as king during Bran's absence

from Britain (*Mabon,* chapter 3). Caswallawn, however, is also traditionally known as a rival, along with Julius Caesar, for the hand of a
British princess, Fflur. This lost story is most intriguing and we have
reference to it only in the triads.[163] Because Caswallawn is obviously
associated with the struggle against the Romans, it has been suggested
that although Triad 36 speaks of the "Coraniaid," perhaps the term
should properly be Cesaryeit, the Romans or followers of Caesar.

(4) The scream that sounds over Britain every May Eve has precedents
in British tradition. In "Pwyll, Prince of Dyfed," May Eve, the magical
time without barrier between the worlds, is when Rhiannon loses her
child, Pryderi. In the same story, May Eve is the time when a giant claw
tries to carry off the foals of Teyrnon (*Mabon,* chapter 2). Taliesin also
manifests himself at this magical time.

Similarly, the resounding scream is a recurring motif. When
Culhwch is striving to gain entrance to the hall of Arthur in "Culhwch
and Olwen," he threatens to let out a shout, audible throughout the
kingdom of Britain, that will blight pregnant women with miscar-
riages and render virgins barren. The effect of the dragon's scream in
"Lludd and Llefelys" is as devastating as the Dolorous Blow, which
causes the wasteland in the Grail legends.

The shriek is closely related to other manifestations of Britain's
wronged Sovereignty. In "The Lady of the Fountain," the lady gives a
lamentable shriek when her champion is killed by Owain; it is said to
sound three times, like a triple *ochone,* or keen. A similar shriek is
sounded by Enid in "Gereint and Enid" when her husband is carried in
upon his shield as though dead, and it is only her shriek when Earl
Limwris attempts to rape her that revives the wounded Gereint and
calls him to spring to her defense. In these examples, the Goddess of
the Land's representatives utter the cry that the land itself often makes
in other Celtic contexts.

The wail of the *beansí* (banshee), often heard at the death of certain
individuals, is that of a tutelary spirit of a place or family and is thus

related to the cry uttered by Sovereignty's representatives. More telling, perhaps, is the stone that cries out under the true king in Irish sovereignty stories: the Lia Fal (stone of Fal). This stone is related to the Perilous Seat in Arthurian tradition, the seat at the Round Table that is reserved for the destined Grail winner, who, as we will see, shares in the king's sovereign duty to the land. This stone seat, emblematic of the land, cries out when an unworthy or undesignated knight sits upon it, and indeed does so when Perceval occupies it.[32]

The shriek of the dragon is the voice of the land itself crying out under oppression. We have yet to see just how the Goddess of Sovereignty uses the dragon as one of her many guises (see chapter 9). A discussion of the most obvious parallels to the episode of the dragon's scream, notably the story of Vortigern's tower, follows later in this chapter in the section Sovereignty's Son.

(5) The blighting of Britain is matched in microcosm by the theft from the court of a year's supply of provisions sufficient to feed the king and his retainers—a considerable loss for Lludd. This is the only episode in British tradition to show the bounty of the Grail or cauldron working in reverse (see note 9).

(6) In the following section, where we compare parallel texts, we see that the role of the Wondrous Youth is a paramount feature of these stories. The text of "Lludd and Llefelys" is somewhat at variance with this, save that Llefelys is described as "handsome and wise." In fact, Llefelys does not know why his brother is coming—yet he takes his fleet to meet Lludd and, embracing him, says he knows why Lludd has come. It would appear that he has the ability of the ancient poet-kind, that of *dichetul dichennaib* (see *Mabon*, chapter 7), or spontaneous knowledge, which arises from psychometrically touching his brother.

The Corannyeid or their agents seem to infiltrate the horn through which Lludd and Llefelys discuss the three plagues in what is surely the earliest episode of "bugging" in British history! Llefelys is discerning enough to know the solution and swills out the horn with wine. This is the first time that alcohol is used in this story; later, the dragons are contained only after being rendered drunk. Here, in the misunderstanding caused by the horn, we have perhaps the remnant of the two brothers' contention. We will see that the troublemaking actions of the Corannyeid, which here cause each brother's misinterpretation of the other, are representative of a motif reflected throughout the Sovereignty tradition. In "The Dream of Rhonabwy" we find Iddawg, the Churn of Britain—so called for his propensity to stir up strife—playing much the same role: It is he who bears the offer of a truce from Arthur to Medrawt (Mordred), but delivers it in such a way as to provoke the Battle of Camlann. This character is identifiable within the Sovereignty tradition as the Provoker of Strife, a role that Efnissien in "Branwen, Daughter of Llyr" also fulfills (see chapter 8).

(7) The Corannyeid bear a close similarity to the Saxons of Nennius's account.[28] In this telling Hengist calls a pretended peace summit, which is actually a trap leading to the slaying of all the British delegates. In "Lludd and Llefelys," however, it is the Corannyeid who are overcome. They represent the danger of the archetypal enemy of Britain's sovereignty—the threat of a previous race of overthrown people. Their otherworldly prescience and malevolence remind us strongly of the Fomorians and Fir Bolgs who similarly afflict the Tuatha de Danaan in the Irish mythological cycle.[8]

The measures that Lludd takes to overcome the Corannyeid may have been influenced by two existent traditions, one from the Bible, the other from the *Vita Merlini.* Just as Lludd purges the land of Britain and its people of the Corannyeid, so too does Moses purge the Israelites by grinding the idolized golden calf into powder, scattering the dust on the water, and making the people drink it (Exodus 32:20). In the *Vita Merlini,* Merlin is purged of his madness by drinking from the waters of a new fountain, at which point in the text Taliesin speaks at length about the curative properties of different springs.[11] In both Merlin's and the Israelites' cases the healing waters are harsh and purgative, a symbol of Sovereignty's power manifesting itself through the land. In Celtic heroic tradition, Sovereignty's champion is wounded deeply; his healing is effected by a cailleach, who alternately plunges him into a cauldron of poison and a cauldron of cure—the first one to toughen him, the second to heal him (see note 19, chapter 7).

(8) Llefelys advises Lludd to find the center of Britain and there to prepare the pit for the dragons. Oxford seems an odd sort of center if we are considering the modern map of the British Isles. Lludd's kingdom extends from the Welsh coast to East Anglia, west to east, but for Oxford to be at the center, it can extend no farther from the south coast than up to the Humber. Sacred centers of countries, however, are not necessarily centrally positioned, except in the roughest sense. As Alwyn and Brinley Rees have shown in their *Celtic Heritage,*[137] all the *omphaloi* or sacred stones indicating the center of Ireland's ritual king making are to be found in Meath, where the functions of kingship, learning, and sovereignty are mystically present, making up a series of *temenoi* (sacred enclosures) in which the other four provinces are essentially represented. A similar arrangement exists in modern Britain, where the administrative center is London while its scholastic centers are Oxford and Cambridge.

Triad 37 speaks of Lludd's burial of the dragons as one of the three fortunate concealments and their uncovering in the reign of Vortigern as one of the three unfortunate disclosures. This triad is specifically concerned with the mystical protections by which Britain's sovereignty is safeguarded. The other two concealments are the head of Bran, which, as we saw in chapter 3 of *Mabon,* is uncovered by Arthur, who cannot endure the thought of anyone other than himself serving as Britain's protector; and the bones of Gwrthefyr the Blessed (Vortimer), Vortigern's son.

Vortimer stands against his father and fights off the Saxons. He is, according to Geoffrey of Monmouth,[10] made king by popular demand after Vortigern is deposed, proving himself a champion of Sovereignty by fighting four battles against the Saxons and, at his death, requesting to be buried on the Saxon shore so that "wherever else they may hold a British port or may have settled, they will never again live in this land."[28] Both Nennius and Geoffrey state that his final request is ignored, and that his remains are interred, according to the respective chronicles, either at London or in Lincoln. Triad 37 ignores both accounts and specifically says that Vortimer's remains are buried at the chief seaports of Britain.[38] Further discussion of Vortigern's role and the dragons follows in the next section, Sovereignty's Son.

While the dragons remain airborne, they keep their form, but when they draw near the ground, they turn into pigs, those chthonic creatures that emerge from the Underworld, which, according to "Math, Son of Mathonwy," is their place of origin. During his madness, Merlin addresses his remarks to a pig in the forest of Celyddon:

> *Little pig, be not sleepy,*
> *Terrible tidings come this way . . .*
> *A distant prophet has predicted*
> *That kings of foreign blood-ties—*
> *Gaels and Romans, treacherous Britons,*
> *Will bring ferment to this land.*
>
> *Gaels and Romans, treacherous Britons,*
> *Will bring ferment to this land.*

In this obscure poem (my translation), "Yr Oianau" (The Greetings),[152] the pig seems to represent the dormant spirit of Britain. It would seem that there is a distinct sequence in which the beasts that are emblematic of Britain become dragons when the land is active and pigs when the land is passive.

(9) The stealer of the provisions is described as a mighty magician and as a giant, but he remains unnamed in the story. There are two other

instances in which we can find traces of this last plague. In "Pwyll, Prince of Dyfed," Rhiannon gives Pwyll a bag into which a beggar can place food without ever filling it; only when a gentleman or nobleman puts both feet inside and tells the bag it has had enough will it be full. By this ruse her former suitor, Gwawl, is trapped. Rhiannon's bag is clearly an otherworldly receptacle whose appetite is as capacious as a giant's. Size and shape have different dimensions in the Otherworld, where small things seem large and large things may be small. A second instance that this last plague calls to mind is the hamper of Gwyddno Garanhir, Elphin's father in "Hanes Taliesin." This hamper, one of the Thirteen Treasures of Britain and said to be guarded by Merlin in his retirement on Bardsey Island, delivers food for one hundred after food for one is placed in it.

As we saw in *Mabon and the Guardians of Celtic Britain,* the rightful king or Pendragon needs the empowerment of the Thirteen Treasures or other sacred objects of Sovereignty's regalia in order to be a true king. Arthur goes to Annwfn in his ship *Prydwen* in order to win these objects, including the cauldron, the prototype of the Grail. In "Lludd and Llefelys," Lludd, although in every respect a brave and generous king, has yet to win his kingship from the empowering otherworldly forces of the Goddess of Sovereignty. It would seem probable that the unnamed giant with whom he must wrestle is indeed Gwyddno. That an otherworldly agent is at work we need have no doubt, for the provisions always disappear at night and all watchmen are overcome with deep sleep. Lludd cannot depute any champion to act for him in this enterprise, but keeps watch himself and stays awake by splashing himself with water. He alone must overcome the *gormesiad* (plagues), which are sent almost as tests, in order to validate his kingship.

The overcoming of the three gormesiad is likewise a feature of "Peredur," in which the hero defeats the nine witches of Gloucester, three serpents, and the Black Oppressor, as well as the devastating unicorn, whose horn dries up the waters. And indeed, as we have noted, the resonances between features in "Peredur" and the underlying features of the Grail legends are very strong. When the king is in harmony with his kingdom, the land flourishes; when he is out of union with Sovereignty, the result is wasteland, disorder, and dissension. In this model, however, the one who overcomes these *gormesiad* is the king's nearest companion, his champion or seer-poet whose courageous deeds or prophetic insight enables him to uphold his sovereign's rights in the land by rectifying the imbalances within the kingdom. Such a one is the Grail winner Peredur or the youthful prophet Merlin or Mabon, the youth who stands in the place of Sovereignty's son.

Sovereignty's Son

Reading "Lludd and Llefelys," we cannot but be struck by the obvious parallels between it and Nennius's account of Vortigern's tower.[28] Geoffrey of Monmouth's version of the story of the tower is better known,[10] but there are closer parallels to be drawn to Nennius's earlier account.

In Nennius we read of Vortigern's disastrous career: He is made king by default and sustains his sovereignty—despite the universal disapproval of his people—by inviting the alien Saxons to act as his federal troops. He compounds this enormity by marrying Renwein (called Rowena by Geoffrey), the daughter of Hengist, the Saxon chief. As if this were not enough, Vortigern shows himself lost to reason by marrying his own daughter as well and having by her a son called Faustus.

It follows that when St. Germanus comes to Britain to attend a synod of the British clergy, it is in order to denounce Vortigern and his incestuous kingship. Knowing this, Vortigern instructs his daughter to place Faustus in Germanus's lap and accuse the saint of fathering the child. Undeterred by this accusation, Germanus says to the boy, "I will be your father and will not send you away until a razor, scissors, and comb are given to me and you are permitted to give them to your father after the flesh." The child turns to Vortigern, who is both his father and his grandfather, and bids the king cut his son's hair for him. Vortigern is thus outfaced by his own son and shamed before the synod, who accuse him, rightfully, of incest, and he flees from his court.

Thereafter he goes to Snowdon and tries to build a stronghold, but the tower keeps falling. His druids advise that he find a boy without a father whose blood may be sprinkled on the foundation. His men discover a boy playing at ball who is called fatherless by his rival playmates. The mother is questioned and denies ever having lain with a man. The boy is then brought to the tower and there questions the druids about the foundation of the edifice. They cannot tell what lies there. The boy reveals that there is a lake under the foundation and that two vessels are buried there, but the druids cannot guess what they contain. A cloth lies between them and in it are two dragons, says the boy, one white and the other red. The cloth is the kingdom, the lake is the world, the red dragon is that of Britain, and the white is that of the Saxons. He tells Vortigern to find another stronghold, for he himself will remain in the present one. He then reveals that he is Ambrosius, or Emrys, the Overlord.[28]

Geoffrey closely follows this account, with a few variations, notably the additions of the early chronicler Nennius, who drew on *The Life of Saint Germanus of Auxterre*.[28] This saint did indeed visit Britain, as has been historically attested. In *The Life of Saint Germanus*, Vortigern shows himself to be a perfect example of a bad king: He commits every action alien to the coronation oath of a British king by actively inviting enemies over the threshold and putting them in positions of trust; he commits incest; and he almost reverts to human sacrifice. But there are three youths who stand between him and his "rightful" kingship.

As we have already stated, he is deposed by his people in favor of his son Vortimer, whose heroic deeds against the Saxons earn him eternal popularity but also an early death, allowing Vortigern to resume the throne once more. Vortimer, though called Blessed, is unable to stem the successive waves of invaders with his own sacred burial, which is supposed to act as a safeguard against further seaborne forays. However, he acts as an admirable champion of Sovereignty.

Set against the stalwart Vortimer who redeems his father's deeds is the son born of incest, Faustus, who, due to the patronage of St. Germanus, later becomes a saint. Not only is Vortigern unable to use this sinfully begotten child for his own ends, but in addition his downfall is caused by Faustus. Vortigern has, in effect, no rightful sovereignty at all. He is a usurper who has to be bolstered by his country's natural enemy. Even the tower, his last stronghold, will not remain erect.

It is at this point that we meet the third young man to disrupt his designs—the young Merlin, in this story called Ambrosius or Emrys, who, in Nennius's account, is the rightful ruler. Myrddin (Merlin) Emrys and Ambrosius Aurelianus were frequently conflated among chroniclers who were often reliant on oral tradition alone for their compilations. In the legendary history of Britain it is indeed Ambrosius Aurelianus who succeeds Vortigern as king, but in this version we see Myrddin Emrys as a manifestation of the Pendragon's own priest and prophet. He is able to state exactly what is wrong not only with Vortigern's tower, but also with his reign. The stronghold of Snowdonia is a microcosm of the state of Britain itself.

Emrys, as we learn from subsequent traditions about Merlin, is begotten of a daemon or spirit of the air and his mother, who, like the Virgin, "knows not man." He is an innocent youth, yet full of wisdom. He is Sovereignty's own son, her vindication, and so is never endangered by Vortigern's evil designs. He is destined to reveal the state of Britain and send its unlawful king packing, and he banishes Vortigern with these words:

> "Go forth from this fortress, for you cannot build it, and travel over many provinces, to find a safe fortress, and I will stay here." So the king gave him the fortress, with all the kingdoms of the western part of Britain, and he went himself with his wizards to the northern parts . . . and there he built a city, that is called by his name, Caer Gwrtheyrn.[28]

Vortigern relinquishes sovereignty into the hands of Sovereignty's own son until "the king shall come again," or a rightful Pendragon is inaugurated. Thus Vortigern is thwarted by three young men: his own sons, Vortimer and Faustus, and Emrys.

There is a parallel or possibly a source text from which both this story and that of "Lludd and Llefelys" stem. It comes from the repertoire of the professional Irish poet and was certainly circulating in Ireland before the tenth century, where it was one of 350 stories that had to be learned by the qualified poet. It is the "Echtra Airt," or "The Adventures of Art."

> Conn, King of Ireland took to wife Becuma, an otherworldly woman who had been banished from the Land of Promise by the Tuatha de Danaan for committing adultery with Manannan's son. She was really in love with Conn's son, Art, but preferred to be queen. During their reign neither corn nor milk could be found in Ireland, and Conn called his druids to find the cause of this affliction. They told him that it was because of Becuma that Ireland was barren of food, but that if the son of a sinless couple could be found and slain at Tara, where his blood might be mixed into the soil, then the famine might be averted. Conn travelled to the Otherworld, where he was hosted by Rigru Roisclethan and her husband, Daire Degamra.
>
> Seated in a crystal chair was a youth, Segda Saerlabraid. He befriended Conn and, when he heard about Conn's errand, begged to be allowed to go to Tara with him. For Conn lied, saying that he needed a youth such as Segda in order that he might be bathed in the waters of Ireland and so heal the land. His parents were dismayed and revealed that, among their kind, people never mated unless it was to conceive a child and he was the only fruit of their union. However, Segda and Conn returned to Ireland, after Conn had promised many sureties for Segda's safety.
>
> The druids insisted that their advice be implemented: that Segda should be killed and his blood mingled "with the blighted

earth and the withered trees, so that its mast, fruit, fish and produce" might be increased. Seeing the men of Ireland ready to kill
him, Segda asked to be put to death willingly. Just then a lowing
cow, followed by a woman, came on the scene; she demanded to
know what was happening. She asked the druids to tell her what
was in the two bags hanging from the cow's sides, but they couldn't
tell. "A single cow has come here to save an innocent youth," she
said. "Let the cow be killed and her blood mixed with the soil of
Ireland and on the doors of Tara." When the cow had been killed,
the two bags were examined: inside were two birds—one with one
leg, the other, with twelve. They rose above the host and fought each
other; the one-legged bird being victorious. The druids were still
unable to interpret the meaning of this, and the woman said, "You
[the men of Ireland] are the bird with twelve legs and the little boy
is the bird with one, since it is he who is in the right. Let those
druids of yours be taken away and hanged." Then she told Conn to
put Becuma away, else Ireland would lack a third of its produce. In
a further incident, Art causes the downfall of Becuma by his otherworldly adventures in which he brings back a suitable bride,
Delbhchaem, with whom he ousts Becuma and succeeds to his
father's throne.[171]

This tale is in the forefront of the Irish king cycle and tells of Art,
who actually reigned in the third century. The parallels between this
and both "Lludd and Llefelys" and the story of Vortigern's tower are
remarkable. Ireland suffers affliction as well, though instead of foreign
invaders, it is afflicted with barrenness because of Becuma's unsuit-
ability as a bride (or as a representative of Sovereignty). Like Vortigern,
Conn has a suitably kingly son. Conn's visit to the Otherworld to find
the sinless youth must obviously be likened to the search for Emrys.
Here, however, the boy's mother is significantly called Rigru, "the
queenly one," while her son, Segda, is called Saerlabraid, "noble
speech." We have here a portrait of Sovereignty and her son. In the sub-

sequent episode at Tara, when Segda is about to be killed, he is saved by the cow and the woman, who is none other than Rigru herself come to save her child and reveal where the true Sovereignty of Ireland lies. She refutes the druids, as Emrys does in Nennius's account of Vortigern's tower.

That we are dealing with a parallel text or a text from a common source is evident from the story's use of birds rather than dragons. There is no word for "dragon" or "serpent" in early Irish, except when borrowed from British or Latin tradition. The Gaelic concept of *monster* is that of a water serpent, or *nathair,* though Scots Gaelic tradition supplies us with *nathair sgiathach,* or "winged serpent," as a term for "dragon." The twelve-legged bird here stands not for foreign oppression so much as injustice or lies, a totally false premise on which to establish kingship. The one-legged bird stands for the truth or justice of Sovereignty, whose champion is her own son, Segda.

The Sovereignty motif is, as we have stated, most strongly represented within Irish tradition, where the nature of sacral kingship is ever stressed. The task of dating the three stories is a difficult one. If we examine figure 2, we will see how the evidence falls. The earliest historical character, the legendary King Lud, appears in the latest transcription of these three traditions, while the latest historical character, Vortigern, appears in the earliest transcriptions. The common themes of the stories are set forth in figure 3 for easy reference. The protagonists share the sovereignty theme of Sovereignty in the uncovering of the dragons and the refutation of supposedly wise men by or on behalf of a boy or youth. The stories may stem from a common source now lost to us, but each upholds a remarkable battle for the kingship that reveals the role of Sovereignty's son.

Mabon's profound influence underlying the texts of the *Mabinogion* has already been noted in *Mabon and the Guardians of Celtic Britain,* where we see the characteristics of the Wondrous Youth. Sovereignty's son is Mabon, who is revealed in these related stories as Merlin Emrys, Segda, and perhaps also Llefelys, whose innocence

Historical Character	Reigned	Text	Date of Transcription
Lud	first century B.C.E.	the *Mabinogion*	fourteenth century C.E.
Art mac Conn	c. 220 C.E.	"Echtra Airt"	thirteenth century; pre-tenth century in oral poetic repertoire
Vortigern	425–455 C.E.	Nennius	c. 828–829 C.E.
Vortigern	425–455 C.E.	Geoffrey of Monmouth	c. 1136 C.E.

Figure 2. Common sources of the two dragons of Sovereignty

defends Sovereignty herself. He is shown to be the forerunner of the Pendragon or rightful king in these stories—one who clears the ground in advance by revealing corruption and the causes of the land's disorder.

The Contention of the Two Brothers

"Hanes Taliesin"[23] alludes to a story known as "The Contention of Lludd and Llefelys," which may well have been an earlier title of "Lludd and Llefelys" in the *Mabinogion*. If this is so, it is intriguing, for it suggests a development untouched in our narrative. Lludd and his brother, although kings of Britain and France respectively, confer rather than contend in "Lludd and Llefelys." The twelfth-century bard Llewelyn Fardd also alludes to this lost story: "I am an eloquent lad who is known in the court, like the contention of Lludd and Llefelys."[38] But however well known this story had once been, we no longer possess it.

The stories parallel to "Lludd and Llefelys" fail to hint at such a contention. There is a Welsh folktale, however, that may embody a half-understood fragment of the original. It is significant in that it speaks of two brothers, obviously of Beli Mawr's lineage, who have a seemingly trivial argument about sovereignty. Even more interesting from the

Texts	Beasts	Imprisoned Within	Center	Wise Youth	Parentage	Invaders/ Representatives of False Sovereignty	Cause of Wasteland/ Plagues	True Representatives of Sovereignty
"Lludd and Llefelys"	dragons	stone chest	Oxford	Llefelys	earthly	Corannyeid shout	dragon's	Lludd
Nennius; Geoffrey of Monmouth	dragons	two vessels	Snowdon	Emrys	daemon/ woman	Saxons/ Vortigern invites Saxons to Britain	Vortigern marries his own daughter,	Ambrosius; Pendragons
"Echtra Airt"	birds	two bags	Tara	Segda	otherworldly parents	Becuma's tainted powers	Conn marries Becuma	Art and Delbhchaem

Figure 3. Parallels to "Lludd and Llefelys"

point of view of our discussion is that Arthur himself emerges as right-ful Pendragon of Britain: The folktale mentions the very giant whom Arthur overcomes just before his accession. The tale is retold by John Rhys, who did much field research in nineteenth-century Wales, draw-ing on oral folk memory and traditions prevalent at the time.

There were two brothers who were kings, called Nyniaw and Pebiaw. One moonlit night Nyniaw said to his brother, "See what an extensive field I possess."

"Where is it?" asked Pebiaw.

"There," said his brother, "the whole firmament."

"Well, as to that," said Pebiaw, "see how many sheep and cattle I have grazing in your field."

"Where are they?" asked Nyniaw.

"There, the great host of stars, each of golden brightness, with the moon to shepherd them."

"Well, they shall not graze on my field," replied Nyniaw. And the two kings fought, embroiling both kingdoms and their subjects in terrible war so that they were nearly exterminated.

Rhitta Gawr, king of Wales attacked them because they were obviously both mad. He conquered them and shaved off their beards. But when the other twenty-eight kings of Prydain heard of this treacherous assault, they raised up armies and stood before Rhitta to avenge Nyniaw and Pebiaw. Rhitta conquered every one of them and shaved off their beards, making himself a gigantic cloak into which the beards were decoratively worked.[139]

There is a connection to this folktale in Geoffrey of Monmouth's *History,* where we learn that Arthur never fought a stronger man than Retho (Rhitta), the Giant of Mount Arvaius. Rhitta once requested Arthur to send him his beard so that he might fix it above those of the other British kings whom he had overcome or else to come and fight him in single combat. Arthur slew Rhitta, taking not only his beard but the cloak of beards as well.[10]

The connection between the tale recounted by Rhys and "Lludd and Llefelys" is not immediately apparent, but if we look at the name of Nyniaw, or Ninian, we realize that this is none other than one of Lludd's other brothers, who, according both to the *Mabinogion* and to Geoffrey of Monmouth, is called Nennius.[10] As we have already stated, Llefelys does not appear anywhere as the brother of Lludd or son of Beli except in the *Mabinogion*. Who, then, is Pebiaw? We must remember that in all these stories we are dealing with folk tradition, not the pseudo-respectable chronicles of literary tradition. Pebiaw is obviously an onomatopoeic doublet for Nyniaw, like Jack and Jill of the nursery rhyme, or like some of the risible characters who appear in "Culhwch and Olwen," such as Lluched, Nefed, and Eissiwed (oh, cry, and shriek).

In truth, we might overlook altogether the story of the contentious brothers if Rhitta Gawr didn't figure in it. His reappearance in a separate context in Geoffrey's *History*[10] makes this folktale significant to the sovereignty of Britain. The contention of Pebiaw and Nyniaw is in itself as inconsequential as the sayings of the Men of Gotham in folk tradition, but there are certain elements which, even in this folk story, retain a familiarity from mainstream tradition.

First of all, there is the motif of beard shaving. Rhitta's object in shaving off the vanquished kings' beards is symbolically clear: At one stroke he robs them of their manhood and their sovereignty. We have already encountered this shaving motif in Nennius's account of Vortigern's incestuously conceived son and St. Germanus—admittedly only a parallel to "Lludd and Llefelys," but still close enough to our original story. Further, we recall the many similar shaving incidents in "Culhwch and Olwen" revolving around the vanquishing of a giant (*Mabon*, chapter 6). "Lludd and Llefelys," if it can be found at all in this tangle of similarities, is in such muddy water that we cannot guess at the original transcription.

Second, we find from Rhys's field research that Nyniaw and Pebiaw are changed into oxen for their sins and that they fall into a lake in Cardiganshire,[139] where they are locally called Uchain Pannog, or

"Pannog's oxen." Two contending brothers here become beasts, not dragons or pigs as in "Lludd and Llefelys," to be sure, but an interesting transmogrification nevertheless. A similar tale is told of Twrch Twryth, who plunges into the sea in "Culhwch and Olwen" (see *Mabon*, chapter 6).

The third familiar element is the contest for the sovereignty of Britain, which appears in all versions of the story. In Rhys's Welsh folktale, Rhitta stands in the place of Vortigern and the foreign invaders, taking advantage of the brothers' contention and shaving their beards in order to undermine their manhood and sovereignty, the typical act of a conqueror.

A last familiar connection relates to the *anoethu,* or impossible tasks, which Culhwch has to perform in "Culhwch and Olwen." The sixth task is that he obtain the twin oxen Nynnyaw and Peibyaw, who were once men changed by God as punishment. The implication of this task's difficulty lies in the reconciling of eternally arguing men, now oxen under a single yoke. To create a straight furrow, oxen must pull together. The contention of Nyniaw and Pebiaw in the Welsh folktale is the result of hubris, for theirs is only a mortal kingship whose sovereignty does not extend to the heavens. They are changed into oxen because they each have claimed to own the "oxen," or stars, in the field of the firmament.

There is another tradition in which stars and oxen are paired, as we may see in the rhapsodic acclamation of the Irish poet Amergin on the invasion of Ireland. He asks a rhetorical question:

> *Who brings cattle from the house of Tethra?*
> *Upon whom do the cattle of Tethra smile?*
> *Who is this ox?*[171]

Tethra is an early Fomorian deity of the sea, and "cattle from the house of Tethra" is a poetic kenning for the stars. We are reminded again of "Preiddeu Annwfn" (*Mabon,* chapter 6), in which Taliesin complains about the ignorance of clerics:

They know not whose the brindled, harnessed ox
With seven score links on his collar.

Perhaps we at last have the ability to understand the mystery that is encoded in this folktale of Nyniaw and Pebiaw. In Welsh tradition the seven stars of the constellation of the Plow or Great Bear are known as Arthur's Wain (wagon). The only one who can lay claim to yoke the oxen of the stars is none other than the Mab Darogan, the Son of Destiny, the ruler who puts aside his own affairs in order to uphold the sovereignty of the land (see _Mabon,_ chapter 6). This is the role traditionally assumed by Arthur, who, as a young man in all strata of the Arthurian corpus, unites warring factions and brings them under one yoke in order to expel invaders.

The contention of Nyniaw and Pebiaw is clearly a mythic parable tumbled into folklore. The hubris underlying this story points to the truth that those who fail to defend the land under their charge are destined to be but the servants of the one who upholds Sovereignty. As Nynnyaw and Peibyaw are overcome by Rhitta, so Arthur, as rightful Pendragon, overcomes Rhitta the Giant. Nor does the story rest there; it was considered to be of sufficient importance for Malory to incorporate it into _Le Morte d'Arthur,_[25] in which Rhitta appears as Ryons, king of Ireland, who demands the submission and beard of Arthur. It will be remembered that it is to Ireland that Arthur directs his quest for the cauldron, one among the many treasures of Annwfn which he seeks in "Culhwch and Olwen."

In both the folktale of Nynnyaw and Peibyaw and the story of Vortigern's tower, contention precedes the coming of the Pendragons. In "Lludd and Llefelys," Lludd is established safely in his kingship, having solved the mystery of the three plagues with the help, not contention, of his brother. We would indeed be fortunate if the knotted threads of this story were less tangled, but as it is, we must be content instead to appreciate their colors as they weave through the tales, antecedents and descendants.

The reign of Lludd, or Lud, tells the story of Britain's sovereignty before the coming of the Romans, a lost era of legend. But the Roman occupation, rather than erasing past glories, has instead contributed to legends concerning Britain's kings. It is in such a context that we turn to Macsen Wledig, emperor of the West.

3
The Dream
of Macsen Wledig

. . . our own Elen of the Army-paths . . .
She for whom the Imperator
                                    could not sleep
nor ride out with his comites and duces
                                    . . . nor could he
find solace of his most loved falcon
nor from any venery
                                    which formerly
had been some respite from
the tedium of affairs of state.

DAVID JONES, *THE KENSINGTON MASS*

Britain in Roman Rig

Britain is tenacious regarding its traditions. While it has been properly proud of its native achievements, it has not been slow to turn its defeats into greater victories and capitalize on disaster. This has been nowhere more apparent than in the aftermath of the Roman occupation. The desperate struggle to repel invasion, which typified the early centuries of the first millennium, was modified into either an acceptance of Roman rule or a localized resistance which soon emulated Roman tactics, customs, and standards.

By the time "The Dream of Macsen Wledig" was transcribed in the Middle Ages, Wales had already fought off Saxon incursion and separated itself from the realm of England established by the Saxons. Both Welsh and Saxons had then undergone the further indignity of Norman oppression. But despite the subsequent influences of these new invaders, it was the Romans who gave Britain a new understanding of her sovereignty. The notion of many petty kingdoms being welded together under one empire briefly became fact, an idea on which the legends of Arthur are firmly based. It was from the Roman model that Britain learned to combine its forces effectively. The lesson of Rome gave authority and cohesion to the embattled kingdoms of Wales long after the empire's armies had left her shores up until the Normans imposed their government upon the Welsh princes.

We have only to look at the Welsh genealogies to learn what pride Britain took in her Roman connections. Past glories of imperial ties are reflected in many family lines. But the prime story of Rome's wedding with Britain is best told in "The Dream of Macsen Wledig," in which Britain's sovereignty is overcome in a mystical manner, enhancing defeat and vaunting national pride.

The eponymous hero of this tale, Macsen, is none other than Magnus Clemens Maximus, a Spaniard who had served in the Roman army in Britain and who was proclaimed emperor of the West by the disaffected troops of the previous emperor. In this story he marries Elen, daughter of Eudaf, a Welsh nobleman—but this is only the evidence of legend. That the emperor Maximus did indeed marry a British wife from a noble line is very possible, but history does not name her. In fact, history has little to do with this story, except in a rather circuitous way.

What has come down to us via legend and oral tradition is often more discursive than the surviving fragmentary chronicles of the times, but the identities of both Macsen and Elen have been inextricably entwined with other peoples having similar names or functions. Macsen or Maximus has been confused with the emperor Maxentius as well as with the Roman senator Maximianus, while Elen has been invariably conflated with St. Helena, mother of Constantine the Great. In order to minimize confusion, I append two genealogies showing the place of Elen and Macsen in the mythological descent of one of the later heroes of the *Mabinogion,* Gereint (figure 4), and the historical descent and relationships of St. Helena (figure 5).

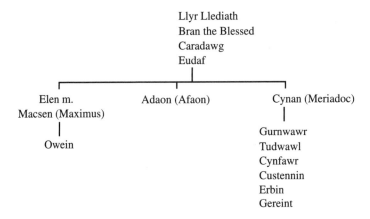

Figure 4. The mythic descent of Gereint from Llyr

Historians are unsure whether St. Helena was a British princess or a barmaid from Bithynia in Turkey, but Britons would be unwilling to relinquish their imperial or saintly connections with her. She lives on in British tradition in the shape of Elen in our story—Elen of the Legions, maker of roads, defender of fortresses, representative of Sovereignty herself—while Magnus Maximus's disastrous career has been glorified into an idealized campaign in which Britain supports his attempt on the imperial city of Rome.

Cole of Colchester		Maxentius
Helena m. Constantius Chlorus		Maximian
Constantine the Great	m.	Faustia
Cole of Colchester		

Figure 5. Helena's imperial connections

Synopsis of "The Dream of Macsen Wledig"

(1) Macsen Wledig is emperor of Rome. (2) One day when he is out hunting, he grows weary and lies down to rest under a canopy, which his men have made of a shield atop their spears. While sleeping, he dreams he sees the highest mountain in the world and then, traveling through the most beautiful country he has seen, he reaches a port where he sets out to sea until he comes to the most (3) lovely island. He crosses this island and arrives at a castle. (4) Entering it, he sees two youths playing chess and, behind them, a man carving chessmen. (5) Nearby sits a beautiful maiden in a golden chair who permits him to embrace her. (6) Just then, the shield canopy collapses, waking Macsen. So smitten with love is he by this dream woman that he is unable to settle into his duties; he wishes only to sleep. Wise men counsel that he send out messengers to find the woman of his dreams, but after a year there is still no sign of her.

(7) Macsen is then advised to go back to the scene of the first dreaming sleep in which he met the lady. Once there, he is able to dispatch messengers in the correct direction. They arrive at Arfon in Wales and recognize their master's dream castle. Entering it, they immediately hail the maiden as (8) empress of Rome. (9) She refuses to come with them, however, saying that if Macsen loves her so much, he should come to her himself. The messengers return to Macsen, guiding him next to Britain, where he (10) conquers the Island of the Mighty and takes it from Beli, son of Manogan. He then travels to Arfon and finds the castle, where he sees brothers Cynan and Afaon playing chess while their father, Eudaf, carves chess pieces. Upon seeing Eudaf's daughter,

_____

Elen, he claims her for his empress. (11) As her morning gift, Elen claims the Island of Britain for her father, Eudaf, the three offshore islands for herself, and three strongholds to be made for her in Britain—at Caer Seint (Segontium), Caerlleon (Caerleon on Usk), and Caerfyrddin (Caermarthen). (12) Elen herself will be responsible for building the roads connecting these strongholds.

Meanwhile, during Macsen's absence from Rome, an ancient Roman custom has been invoked: If an emperor stays outside his land for more than seven years—the period of Macsen's sojourn in Britain—(13) another emperor may be named. Macsen returns to Rome, conquering France and Burgundy on the way, but is unable to raise the siege at Rome's gates. (14) It is not until Cynan and Afaon, with their troops from Britain, come to Macsen's aid that he is able to take Rome. (15) The Britons storm Rome during the noontime break for dinner, and though Macsen fears that they will hold it for themselves, the British relinquish the city to him. (16) Macsen awards his brothers-in-law leadership of the war troop that has successfully besieged Rome so that they might conquer lands of their own. Afaon eventually returns to Britain, while Cynan settles in Brittany, where he and his troops marry with the Breton women but cut out their wives' tongues so that the British speech might not be corrupted.

Commentary

(1) This statement is not strictly accurate. The career of Magnus Maximus can be summarized briefly as follows: He served with Theodosius in Britain, possibly holding the title of Dux Britanniarum (Duke of Britain—originally the title of the military Roman governor based at York), and was proclaimed emperor of the West by his troops. At this point in time there were joint emperors governing the eastern and western halves of the sprawling Roman Empire, for the task of governing such a vast area was beyond any single man. The true emperor of the West, Gratian, engaged Maximus in battle when the latter landed in Europe, but was defeated. Maximus took control of Gaul and

Spain as well as northern Italy, where he was strengthened by British troops. Representations were sent to Theodosius, his old comrade-in-arms, now emperor of the East, that Maximus should be recognized as emperor of the West. Maximus occupied Rome in 388 C.E. but was defeated a few months later when Theodosius's troops cornered him in Aquileia. He was beheaded and his son, Victor, was subsequently killed. Theodosius provided for Maximus's daughters. Of Maximus's unnamed wife we know only that she was very attentive to St. Martin of Tours, who dined with Maximus, but that the saint was unimpressed by Maximus's jumped-up pretensions of imperial glory. The ninth-century inscribed stone called the Pillar of Eliseg in Valle Crucis, Wales, attests to Vortigern's marriage to "Severa, the daughter of Maximus the King who slew the King of the Romans."[145]

The similarity in the names of generals and emperors of this period has not helped the transmission of Maximus's history; Nennius, who knew of the tradition regarding the meeting of Maximus with St. Martin, nevertheless ascribes Maximus's career to Maximianus, who took the British troops to Brittany (see notes 14 and 16, below). Geoffrey of Monmouth likewise calls him Maximianus and makes him a Roman senator and nephew to King Coel (Cole).[10]

(2) Macsen's dream has the quality of an Irish *aisling*—a mystic vision or dream in which a representative of Sovereignty appears to the hero. This genre of story is of great antiquity in Celtic tradition. It has descended through time via the Grail romances, in which Sovereignty is depicted by both the beautiful Grail Maiden and the Loathly Lady, and via medieval romances and native folk stories, to the eighteenth-century poetic vision of a self-governing Ireland, which eventually manifested as W. B. Yeats's Cathleen ni Houlihan, the old hag. Scholars have suggested that the *cyfarwydd* (storyteller) of this story was well acquainted with the Irish genre.[95] Some parallel examples follow in the sections Goddess of the Dream Paths and The Fair Unknown and the Loathly Lady later in this chapter.

In effect Macsen's dream takes him across the western expanse of the Roman Empire wherein the land is laid out as on a map. He crosses the Alps and comes to Britain. At the embarkation point Macsen significantly boards his ship by means of an ivory bridge, an allusion to the emperor's title, Pontifex Maximus, bestowed in token of the emperor's sacral kingship, which, to the Romans' understanding, literally built a bridge between this world and that of the gods. (Interestingly, Gratian, the emperor assassinated by the historical Maximus, was the first to refuse this pagan title, in 373 C.E.; the title is currently held by the pope.)

(3) Macsen sees the land of Britain for the first time in his dream and arrives at the city of Caer Seint (modern Caernarvon). As Segontium, its Roman appellation, it was strongly garrisoned from the time of Agricola (80 C.E.) until about 380 C.E., the time of Maximus's withdrawal from Britain with the better part of Britain's troops. It is also the place where Bran the Blessed was staying when he received Branwen's starling (*Mabon*, chapter 3).

(4) The unfolding dream reveals a wealth of symbolism appropriate to Sovereignty. Macsen sees Elen's two brothers playing *gwyddbwyll*, a form of chess in which the king is defended by a small company of men against the opponent, who has a larger number of more mobile men. The object is for the king to reach the edge of the board. Eudaf, Elen's father, is carving new pieces for the board. As we will see in "The Dream of Rhonabwy" and "Peredur," the gwyddbwyll board, or chessboard, is one of the prime symbols of the land and is usually possessed by a representative of Sovereignty. The pieces upon the board symbolize Britain's men and their opponents, members of a usurping or invading force. Although Eudaf is making new chessmen, he is attired as a nobleman and sits in an ivory chair in which two eagles are carved—symbolic both of Roman imperialism and of the British eagle of Eryri (Snowdon). Eudaf also appears in Chrétien's *Perceval*.[7, 92]

(5) Elen's beauty is compared to that of the sun: She is radiant and queenly—a fitting representative of Sovereignty. It is notable that she is first seen seated, indicative of her establishment in her kingdom. In the section Goddess of the Dream Paths, below, we will discuss the parallels between this episode and the Irish Sovereignty narratives. Macsen sits beside her, and the cyfarwydd remarks that the chair is as comfortable for two as it had been for one—an allusion to Macsen's forthcoming marriage with Elen and the alliance between Rome and Britain.

(6) Just as in the days of modest cinema when love scenes were curtailed immediately prior to the happy couple establishing more intimate contact, so here is Macsen rudely awakened by the makeshift canopy toppling down on him. He is enchanted by love for a woman he has never met, as Culhwch is by his love for Olwen (*Mabon*, chapter 6).

•

(7) He is unable to find his dream woman until he returns to the place of the dream's incubation; from there he is able to determine correctly the path of his dream flight over Europe.

(8) The British princess is hailed as empress of Rome. This story turns upon the fact that the land is represented by the person of Elen. Her inner potency as guardian of the land of Britain is recognized and she is entitled empress of all the known world under Roman occupation. There is also a subtextual connection between pagan goddess and Christian virgin, as David Jones observes in his *Roman Quarry:*

> We'll mix their Bride-lights with the lights of Syriac God-bearers, and gusty flames they coax within the wattle hedge shall call to carried flame lit from Demeter's torch—til, in the woof of time there'll be but one queen of the candles, and by whatever name they call her she'll be in Roman rig.[84]

(9) Elen's reply is not submissive and weak, like that of one conquered. She makes it clear that if she is worth Macsen's impassioned love, then she is worth his personal attendance.

(10) Here the story slips back in time. Beli was the father of Lludd in our previous story, four centuries prior to Maximus's time. The cyfarwydd has telescoped the whole Roman occupation from Julius Caesar's first attempts upon Britain in 55 B.C.E. until nearly the time of Rome's retreat from Britain in 407 C.E.

(11) The custom of the morning gift—a gratuity, usually involving an endowment of land or valuables, which was given by a husband in return for the gift of his new wife's virginity—was a custom common to both the Welsh and the Saxons.[19] Such a gift enabled the wife to retain part of her dowry, which, in the event of divorce or separation, was not liable to distraint. It was also helpful to the widow, who retained her own lands and properties. Both the laws of Hywel Dda (c. 950 C.E.) and the Irish Brehon laws, operative until the sixteenth century, allowed a woman sole rights to her clothing and produce. The morning gift was called the *cowyll* and, in the case of a king's daughter, was always given in land. The extent of the gift was dependent on the status of the husband. Considering Macsen's status as emperor of Rome, Elen does very well and is able to retain the whole of Britain on her father's behalf, as well as the three chief cities of the legions for herself.

(12) In Welsh legend, Elen is known as Elen Lluddog, or Elen of the Hosts. She is also remembered by the network of Roman roads which connected Segontium with the rest of Wales and England, parts of which are still extant. They are locally known as Sarnau Elen, or Elen's Roads. In actuality, the improvements to roads were probably undertaken by Constantine and by Constantius Chlorus, the husband of St. Helena, but in some way their work has been attributed to or placed under the aegis of Elen. The persistence of this legend suggests that

Elen, or St. Helena, has been subsumed into a native cult of some now-vanished tutelary goddess of the ways.

(13) Our story here puts the usurper Maximus in the position of being usurped himself. As stated above, Maximus killed Gratian and ousted his successor apparent, Valentinian, Gratian's half brother. Maximus did indeed rule Gaul and Spain in the brief period before his downfall. His occupancy of Rome is also undisputed.

(14) There is a persistent tradition, and some archaeological evidence, to support the statement that Maximus was partially responsible for emptying Britain of its troops. While the major withdrawal of Rome from Britain is officially dated 410 C.E., successive commanders, each with his own ax to grind, had been drawing on the strength of British levies for some time. Maximus was but one of these. Triad 35 speaks of the "Three Levies that departed from this Island, and not one of them came back."[38] One of those mentioned is "the army that went with Elen of the Hosts and Maxen Wledig to Llychlyn; and they never returned." The three armies are known as "the Three Silver Hosts of the Island of Britain." The understanding running beneath this triad is that the levies are the currency of the island, pouring out of Britain's purse and leaving it beggared. This was not far from the truth, for the next seventy to eighty years were dark times for Britain's defense of her sovereignty. In Welsh or Irish tradition, the Llychlyn or Lochlin of the triad sometimes refers to Scandinavia, although it more often meant any foreign country. The likelihood, however, is that Llydaw (Armorica) is intended (see note 16, below).

(15) Because this is a British tale, it is the British troops who save the day for Macsen. Totally ignoring the courtesies of warfare, they attack the city during the lunch break of the two emperors. This may sound risible, but such were the customary rules of engagement between two opposing powers right up until the nineteenth century. Guerrilla tac-

tics were considered to be dishonorable, although they were employed in many conflicts. The implication of this story is that although Britain had become subject to Rome, she easily could have imposed her sovereignty upon Rome—if she had wanted to. However, Macsen's brothers-in-law are true to their sister's husband.

(16) During the troubled later years of Rome's occupation of Britain, there had already been a steady trickle of emigrants leaving Britain's shores for Brittany. The "official" founder of this colony was Conan Meriadoc, who, as we see from our story, is none other than Cynan, Elen's brother. Afaon or Adaon stays in Britain, while Cynan carves out lands of his own. The episode of cutting out the Breton women's tongues is an onomastic story derived from the Welsh name for Armorica, Llydaw (*lled-taw* = half silent). Nennius's chronicle recalls the ill treatment of the native peoples of Armorica by the British forebears of the present-day Bretons.

> For the Armorican British, who are overseas, went forth there with the tyrant Maximus on his campaign, and, since they were unwilling to return, they destroyed the western parts of Gaul to the ground and did not leave alive those who piss against the wall . . . They are the Armorican British, and they never came back, even to the present day. That is why Britain has been occupied by foreigners and the citizens driven out.[28]

Clearly Maximus's withdrawal with Britain's prime troops rankled deeply. Although their presence in Britain might not have counted for much, Britons could not help wondering what might have been. Interestingly, Cynan and Cadwalladyr, a seventh-century king of Gwynedd, appear in the *Armes Prydein,* or *Prophecies of Britain* (c. 930 C.E.), as two promised deliverers who will liberate Wales from the Saxon yoke. Because Arthur's own ancestors derive from the Breton colonies, it will be seen that Brittany's role as liberator loomed prominently in the British imagination.

Goddess of the Dream Paths

The figure of Elen within this story is a prime example of the Goddess of Sovereignty, a role she shares with many other female characters within the *Mabinogion,* as well as with others from parallel Celtic literature and oral tradition. Elen is primarily a representative of the land of Britain itself, to whom marriage confers regal status. But there is a level of the story which operates in a more mystical sense than simply as a bald parable of Roman occupation.

Elen, like the many famous Elaines of later Arthurian romance, is one of the Daughters of Branwen,[48] those representatives of Britain's sovereignty who carry in their veins the blood of the Grail family. The Daughters of Branwen will be dealt with in more detail in chapter 8, but we may say here that the term is based on a lost triadic tradition, mentioned in "Branwen, Daughter of Llyr," in which Branwen is called one of three ancestresses or three matriarchs of the Island of Britain. This appellation seems incongruous, for Branwen has only one child—a son, Gwern—and he is killed. She therefore has no descendants. However, if we take this title to mean she is one of the three sovereignty-bestowing women—women who represent the sovereignty of Britain in their own person—we might indeed begin to comprehend: The Daughters of Branwen, while rarely queens in their own right, are those women whose royal blood engenders sovereigns, or who confer sovereignty by marriage. These *Mabinogion* stories may be pale reflections of an early British system of matrilinear sovereignty, a system still discernible within the vestigial records of the Pictish royal house of pre-Gaelic Scotland, in which kings were the sons of the royal woman who was the sister of the reigning king.

Elen belongs to the archetype most frequently appearing in Irish aisling tradition as the dream woman: the faery mistress who leads the hero to the Otherworld, the queenly woman who pours the cup for the rightful king. In *Mabon* we encountered many figures of Sovereignty who were goddesses in their own right, but in this volume we meet earthly women who embody Sovereignty in their queenly or heroic lives and who function as priestesses to the Goddess of the Land.

Dreams of Sovereignty or her representatives are necessarily dreams of kingship and spiritual empowerment—dreams that have the power to disenchant the wasteland or the barren soul. So while men dream of the women they love most—their fantasy images—they will always be directed in one of two ways: Men will project the fantasy image either upon every woman they meet, as happens to Peredur at the outset of his quest, or upon that one woman or special symbol representing king-making or spiritually liberating power, such as the woman Elen or the symbol of the Grail.

Let us examine a few of these dreams, bearing them in mind as we read through the rest of the *Mabinogion*. So numerous are the possible examples from Celtic tradition that we must confine ourselves to only a few. The first is the "Aislinge Oenguso," "The Dream of Oengus," from the Irish tradition. Oengus is the son of Dagda and Boann. One night he dreams about a woman, the most beautiful maiden, who vanishes just as he is about to embrace her. The dream recurs every night for a year until Oengus becomes ill from frustration. Doctors are called to attend him, and one divines that the cause is a woman. Bodh, king of the Sidhe of Munster, undertakes to find her. She is eventually discovered among other maidens near a lake, all of whom turn into swans every other year. The maiden is called Caer Ibor-meith. Oengus shares her swan form, mating with her in this shape, and eventually brings her back to his home, Brugh na Boyne.[8]

This story relates the history of two otherworldly beings—Oengus, or Angus mac Og, is one of the Tuatha de Danaan and Caer is the daughter of the king of the Sidhe in Connacht—but the theme of a consuming love engendered by means of a dream is quite clear. In order to be freed from her swan shape, Caer appears to Oengus and draws him to her by means of a dream. This motif, the quest for disenchantment, appears in related stories, as we shall see, and is crucial to an understanding of Sovereignty's shape-changing ability. The aisling, or dream

vision, became an integral part of the later Irish tradition in which the
poet dreams of a beautiful woman—the representative of Ireland—who
draws to her a champion or poet in order to voice her sorrows through
his verse, but this motif is almost absent from British tradition. Elen in
our story does not appear as a sorrowful or distressed woman. Rather,
she is always beautiful, poised, and competent. She appears, in fact, like
"some fair daughter of the Celestial Powers,"[66] a queen of the
Otherworld, like Caer. Indeed, in classical Irish aisling poetry, the
woman who appears to the solitary poet in his vision is called a *speir-
bhean* (literally, "sky woman"). This woman is the true native muse who
takes the dreamer along the ancient dream tracks to deeper knowledge
than the waking consciousness can remember or grasp.

Sometimes the speir-bhean appears as a messenger, as in the Irish
story of Bran mac Febal, who begins his wonder voyage only after being
visited by a faery woman bringing him the silver branch arrayed with
the blossoms from the apple trees of Emain Abhlach, the Irish Avalon.
She sings to him of that wondrous place and specifically tells him
about the Land of Women (Tir na mNa). Bran mac Febal, invited to
make a voyage thither, discovers an otherworldly land offering the
pleasures of the earthly paradise and immortality. He stays in the Land
of Women but finds that return home is impossible, for he has already
entered the timeless realm of the Otherworld and his mortal companions and family are long since dead.[146]

In this story, Bran mac Febal is given a vision of paradise and actually mates with the queen of the Land of Women herself. Here the
woman of his vision is a messenger and foretaste of paradisal bliss; she is
not, as in later tradition, associated with or representative of a heavenly
vessel of power, such as the Grail (see chapter 10). But the empowerment
of the hero with an otherworldly object (usually a vessel or weapon) is a
motif that we find in great profusion in later Celtic and Arthurian tradition. The search for this object is symbolic of the quest for sovereignty—either of a king over his land or of a hero over other strong men.
As we have seen, Elen is representative of Britain's sovereignty, which

Macsen gains, whereas the queen of the Land of Women is a form of otherworldly Sovereignty, granting Bran status as her consort within the Blessed Isles.

Specific instances of Sovereignty appearing in a dream are rare, but there is one such appearance in "Baile in Scail" (The Shadow's Prophecy). Here, Conn of the Hundred Battles steps upon the stone of Fal, brought by the Tuatha de Danaan from the otherworldly island of Falias. The stone shrieks under him, but his druids are unable to tell him anything save that he will be king. Conn is then enveloped in a mist from which a horseman emerges to invite him to his house. Conn rides on and finds himself at a *rath* (hill fort) where the horseman is already seated as host. Before the horseman sits a beautiful woman, dressed richly, and beside her is a silver vat full of red ale, along with a golden ladle and golden cup. The host is none other than the god Lugh, and the woman is the Sovereignty of Ireland. She asks Lugh for whom the cup shall be poured. "For Conn," replies Lugh. Again she asks the question, and Lugh gives the name of Conn's descendant and successor as king. This is repeated until the number of Conn's successors is known. The rath and people then vanish, leaving Conn with the ladle, vat, and cup in his possession.[171]

Although this story tells of a vision rather than a dream, we see that Sovereignty pours out a drink for Conn, who is to be the rightful king. As we discover in chapter 9, this story is closely associated with the Grail legends and shows the connections between Sovereignty and that spiritual vessel of empowerment. Sovereignty appears to Conn in archetypal form, and his spiritual marriage to her is symbolized by his receipt of the vat of ale with its ladle and cup. He gains a land, not an earthly wife, and becomes a king. In the early part of the story, even the land itself, in the shape of the Inis Fal, cries out under his royal foot.

In these three examples we see how the dream or vision reveals the faces of Sovereignty and the ways in which she is won. First, the dream presents an ideal vision: a beautiful land or woman. The dream inspires the quest for the place or woman or the answer to the vision. The

Otherworld has affected the earthly realm, presenting visions of unattainable beauty and longing, and the earthly realm responds by searching until that longing is assuaged. The interconnection of the worlds is finely wrought in Celto-Arthurian tradition. In fact, every land has its inner or archetypal Sovereignty or Goddess of the Land who is represented by an earthly woman or women destined to become queen of that land. The vision woman who appears in the dream of heroes is thus a premonition, forging links between the Goddess and the fantasy woman who is in the mind of the dreamer. He will be satisfied by no woman other than the one who is most like his fantasy.

The description of Elen is very close to that of Sovereignty in "Baile in Scail": Both she and Sovereignty are seated in a chair, clad in the glory of the sun. In Irish tradition there is a definite connection between the inner, archetypal Sovereignty and Lugh, who is the culmination of all heroes and kings. Lugh himself, like the earlier Manannan, appears as a vision to women and fathers many heroes by them. Elen is dressed in red-gold with rubies and pearls as adornments; she is in every respect Britain's answer to the classical Irish Sovereignty figure. In our story Elen reaches out to Macsen on behalf of Britain, sending her image along the dream paths to awaken a virtuous and worthy champion for Britain and a strong, handsome husband for herself. Nevertheless, there remains a certain aloofness in her character, as though she were not acting on her own behalf. Perhaps discernible here are the remnants of an earlier story about her in which she embodies British Sovereignty in a more explicit way.

If that is so, then we have no British originals to draw upon, only successors to the figure that Elen embodies. Looking at these successors, we find some interesting descendants of Britain's Sovereignty and, in so doing, anticipate many of the themes that will recur throughout this book. But the very complexity of Sovereignty demands that we discover many of her themes and aspects or manifestations along the way, in order to gain a full overview of the treasury of stories in the *Mabinogion*.

The Fair Unknown and the Loathly Lady

The Irish aisling tradition, central to the poetic genre, had its main flowering in the seventeenth and eighteenth centuries and was an expression of Ireland's oppression under the invader's yoke. The speir-bhean appeared to the poet who could make an appeal on her behalf to the exiled heroes of Ireland, asking that they come and save her from marriage to an unworthy husband. She appeared as the "Brightest of the Bright . . . the Crystal of all crystals" who was to be married to a ragged churl.[66] She appeared, in fact, as a form of Ireland's Sovereignty who needed to be rescued from oppression and restored to her full loveliness. By the late nineteenth century, W. B. Yeats was writing of the old hag Cathleen ni Houlihan, the ragged representation of Ireland's Sovereignty, whose youth had been squandered and whose land had been laid waste by a foreign power.

A similar pattern can be traced in British tradition. The early Irish models of Sovereignty were modified by British folk traditions and further incorporated into Arthurian tradition throughout the Middle Ages. But within both Irish and British developments of her archetype, Sovereignty demonstrates her age-old facility for shape-changing. (Figure 6 on page 81 outlines some of these transforma-tions.) Like the land she represents, which undergoes seasonal changes, Sovereignty changes from Winter Hag into Spring Maiden (see chapter 9).

The oldest tales of Sovereignty reveal the pattern of an ancient test. One such story is "The Sons of Daire," in which the four sons of King Daire pursue a magical fawn along the river Shannon.

After slaying it, they enter a hut and discover a fearsome hag sitting by the fire. She demands that one of the brothers lie with her that night or she will transform them all into monstrous shapes. Lughaidh Laidhe, the sibling who actually slew the fawn, volunteers. As they lie down he observes that the hag has been replaced by a beautiful maiden. She informs him that she is Sovereignty of Alba and Eire and that he will have a son who will become a great king and likewise cohabit with her.[58]

The true hideousness of the hag is fully stressed in this text:

> *High she was as any mast,*
> *Larger than a sleeping booth her ear,*
> *Blacker her face than any visage,*
> *Heavy on each heart was the Hag.*
>
> *She was one continuous belly.*
> *Without ribs, without separation,*
> *A rugged, hilly, thick, black head*
> *Was upon her like a furzy mountain.*[70]

We recognize the hag aspect of Sovereignty as a representation of the land awaiting a worthy king. This is but one of many texts in Irish tradition in which Sovereignty changes from hag aspect to maiden aspect; the motif will be further discussed in chapter 6. In British tradition the hag aspect recurs as the Loathly Lady, linking the ancient archetype of a Sovereignty-bestowing Goddess with the medieval Grail bearer (see chapter 7).[115] While Sovereignty's ability to shapeshift from hag aspect to maiden aspect in a twinkling is a totally voluntary function in earliest traditions, later storytellers fail to understand the subtleties of this transformation and rationalize it by making Sovereignty's ugliness the effect of a magical enchantment.

In these later stories, where Sovereignty appears as a Loathly Lady, either she is truly an ugly old hag or she is enchanted into a monstrous shape, such as that of a dragon, worm, or serpent. However, the means of disenchantment in later stories remain true to the original tale: A kiss is sufficient. In medieval romance, where the latter versions soon abounded, this kiss is known as the *fier baise,* or daring kiss. In this translation of the narrative, Sovereignty is represented by two women: the maiden messenger who summons the hero in person to his quest and the enchanted maiden who takes a monstrous shape. One story in which these motifs are in transition is "Le Bel Inconnu," or "The Fair Unknown."

The story appears in a variety of versions during the Middle Ages. The main version was written by Renaut de Beaujeu sometime between 1185 and 1190 C.E. R. S. Loomis has discovered what he considers to be connections between this tale and "The Dream of Macsen Wledig."[92] There are connections to be found between "The Fair Unknown" and other stories within the *Mabinogion* as well. For that reason it seems best to tell the story here so that we may refer to it later in our discussion. The version here is from the English metrical *Libeaus Desconus,* written about 1350 C.E.

The hero of the story was brought up by his mother, who kept him secluded, calling him only Beau-Fis (Handsome Son). Once grown, he accoutred himself in a dead knight's armor and went to Arthur's court at Glastonbury. Because the boy could not name himself, Arthur called him Libeaus Desconus (the Fair Unknown). He was knighted and taught arms by Gawain. One day, a maiden called Elene rode into Arthur's hall demanding help to rescue her mistress, who was imprisoned in the castle of Sinadoun. Libeaus Desconus claimed the adventure and Arthur granted it to him, to Elene's disgust, for she expected an experienced knight to ride with her. After many adventures, they came to Sinadoun where Libeaus Desconus learned from the steward that the lady of the castle had been imprisoned by two clerks: Mabon and his brother, Yrain. They were magicians and kept the lady in durance until she granted Mabon her hand in marriage. Libeaus Desconus entered the castle and found only minstrels and beautiful furnishings there. As he proceeded, the music ceased and the castle shook as with thunder. He fought Mabon and Yrain, overcoming them, but their bodies vanished. Dismayed, he prayed to the Virgin and saw a worm with the face of a woman emerge from a wall. Libeaus was transfixed with terror as the worm twined about him and kissed him. As she did so, the wings and tail fell from her and she appeared as a naked woman. She said that she had been enchanted by Mabon and Yrain, and that she would marry him, bestowing upon him her possessions. The lady was dressed and crowned, and then married him.[30]

In the earlier tale, "Le Bel Inconnu," the lady tells the hero his name after he has kissed her: He is the son of Gawain by a water fay and he is called Guinglain. We are immediately struck by certain points in this story. The Fair Unknown, like Peredur, is a son of his mother, raised in ignorance of arms. There is little doubt that *Libeaus Desconus* furnished Malory with the material for shaping Gareth, or Beau-Mains, whose story this one much resembles.[25] The maiden messenger, Elene, is impatient with her mistress's champion, but in all other respects behaves in much the same manner as Lunet in "Owain" ("The Lady of the Fountain"), as we shall see; both women represent the Black Maiden aspect of Sovereignty. Loomis makes much of the fact that the name Elene appears in this story, as well as a visit to a castle in Snowdon (Sinadoun), and indicates that on these points the story converges with "The Dream of Macsen Wledig": Both tales include a woman called Elen and both are set in Snowdonia. That both share these aspects may not be entirely accidental, but the links between them cannot with certainty be identified from literary sources. If we look beneath the surface of the story, at the symbolic shapes that emerge, we may come to another conclusion.

In "The Fair Unknown" the enchanted lady is held prisoner by Mabon and Yrain, brother enchanters. As we have already seen in *Mabon and the Guardians of Celtic Britain*, Mabon is a figure inherited by medieval storytellers, who depict a character very different from what was originally presented: Instead of Mabon, the imprisoned, he is Mabon, the one who imprisons. He also takes on the function of cowardly enchanter, due to the medieval storytellers' misunderstanding of the Celtic symbolism surrounding his mythos. That Mabon should be linked with a character called Yrain is interesting in that Yrain is etymologically linked with both Urien and Owain. As we have already seen (*Mabon*, chapter 9), Mabon is the son of Modron, but then so is Owain, by Urien of Rheged, according to the story from Llanferres (see *Mabon*, page 192). The author of *Libeaus Desconus* knew the tradition that made Mabon and Owain brothers. This may further explain why in *Erec and*

Enid, Chrétien's version of "Gereint and Enid," the Red Knight in the enchanted garden is called Mabonograin, a possible linking of the names Mabon and Owain to create one character who is both prisoner and champion of the Otherworld garden (see chapter 6).

The woman disenchanted by Libeaus Desconus is in the form of a *wyvern,* according to "Le Bel Inconnu," although the English version calls her a worm. This is consistent within British folk tradition, where many ladies are so enchanted by jealous stepmothers (see chapter 5). This kind of enchantment must be seen as an alternative to the Loathly Lady's enchantment in British tradition. According to this storyline, the Loathly Lady—who appears in Chaucer's "Wife of Bath's Tale" as well as in Arthurian tradition as Dame Ragnell—is bespelled into ugliness by Morgan le Fay or a stepmother.[78] In both manifestations she is able to give the answer to a question upon which the life of the hero depends: *What is it women most desire?* She will vouchsafe this lifesaving answer only if the hero agrees to marry her. The answer reveals that the Loathly Lady is indeed a direct descendant of Celtic Sovereignty: *Women desire to have sovereignty,* or, more prosaically, *Women desire to have their own way.* (See chapter 9.)

Here, the kiss demanded by Sovereignty has become marriage and the ritual question has emerged from a tangle of traditions. Instead of Sovereignty representing the land and all that royal rule entails, she has become, still in her shapeshifted form, an enchanted woman who represents all women. It is a fascinating diminution of the original role, but still instructive. The most famous disenchanter of the Loathly Lady is Sir Gawain, whose son (by a faery) rescues the enchanted lady of the castle of Sinadoun.

But what of Elen and her part in this schema? There is perhaps a way in which Elen of Caer Seint, the Lady of Sinadoun, and the Elaine of another Arthurian story are intimately connected to the motifs of both Sovereignty and the Grail quest, in the light of the dream or vision we have discussed.

The connection lies at the far end of the Arthurian tradition, in the work of Malory, who derived the most part of *Le Morte d'Arthur*[25] from the *Vulgate Cycle,* itself a compendium of traditions about the Matter of Britain. The *Vulgate Cycle* represents, in a vast canonical form running to five volumes, the entire Matter of Britain from the coming of Joseph of Arimathea with the Grail to the death of Arthur. Within it are found many stories reworked from ancient sources as well as a boiling-down of many early medieval Arthurian romances so that the transmutation of the Lady of Sovereignty from Goddess of the Land to Grail bearer can be distinguished quite clearly.

The episode of Malory in which this transmutation is most clearly demonstrated lies within Book Eleven of *Le Morte d'Arthur:* A hermit comes to Arthur's Round Table and explains that the Siege (seat) Perilous—which, like the Lia Fail, cries out under the rightful possessor of that seat, at least in *Didot Perceval* [32]—shall be occupied by one who will be conceived that year and who shall win the Holy Grail.

After this incident, Lancelot rides out until he comes upon the tower of Corbin. The people there all acclaim him as the best of knights and beg him to release a maiden from the enchantment of imprisonment in a boiling tub of water. She has been bespelled by Morgan le Fay and the queen of Northgalis. Because only the best knight may do so, Lancelot takes the naked woman by the hand and draws her from her prison. Then the people of Corbin further beg Lancelot to deliver them from a serpent that waits in a nearby tomb. On the lid of the tomb is a prophecy concerning the conception of Galahad ("the which lion shall pass all other knights"). Lancelot then dispatches the serpent, whereupon King Pelles approaches and asks his name, explaining that he himself is cousin to Joseph of Arimathea.

Lancelot accompanies Pelles to his castle, and as they sit at table, there enters a maiden bearing the Grail. Lancelot asks what this means and is told that it is "the richest thing that any man hath living." Then Pelles begins to devise how Lancelot might be made to sleep with his daughter, Elaine, for by their union alone might the Grail winner be conceived. After securing the help of Dame Brisen, who knows of

Lancelot's unfailing love for Guinevere, Pelles commands Elaine to go to the Castle of Case and ready herself. Brisen causes Elaine to assume Guinevere's outer appearance and sends a ring to Lancelot to arrange an assignation between him and his supposed mistress and queen. And so Lancelot sleeps with Elaine, believing her to be Guinevere, and on this night, Galahad is conceived.

In this late Arthurian story, itself the culmination of many story-tellings, we can perceive a significant subtext illuminating Sovereignty's association with the motifs of disenchantment and the woman of dreams and visions. Malory is silent upon the identity of either the enchanted maiden or the Grail Maiden in this extract, but the likelihood is that both are presumed to be Elaine. The land of Corbin, consistent with the enchanting of the land of Sovereignty, is a wasteland awaiting the best knight in the world in order to be released. The maiden under enchantment, representing the land of Corbin, has been associated here with the motif of the maiden transformed into a serpent. Although Malory makes these separate incidents, they follow upon each other too significantly not to be connected. It is possible that Lancelot, in some lost oral tradition, disenchanted the maiden who had been transformed into a serpent and who dwelt among the tombs awaiting release by means of the fier baiser.

Lancelot appears here as the best knight in the world, which exemplifies a theme we shall find again and again in the literature of Sovereignty: Only the best or most worthy hero can be her champion. Lancelot arrives at Corbin for one destiny only, to him unknown—to engender Galahad, who will surpass his father and become the Grail winner. When the Grail Maiden enters—and she may be identical to Elaine, who is the daughter of Pelles, the Grail guardian—Lancelot asks the significance of her appearance and is given a significant answer: "the richest thing that any man hath living." Does Pelles refer to the Grail or to its bearer? Is he being purposely evasive? A similar confusion occurs in von Eschenbach *Parzival*,[40] in which Feirfitz, the parti-colored pagan half brother of Parzival, is brought into the presence of the Grail. Because he is a pagan, he can see only the Grail bearer, not the vessel itself. And in order to win the beautiful maiden, he becomes a Christian.[39] This is consistent with the motif of a more ancient Sovereignty, as we have already noted: the vision woman as both incentive and prize, rather than the vision woman of later stories who serves as merely a messenger or adjunct of the spiritual vessel or Grail.

But what of Elaine herself? Her role in Malory's story seems outrageously passive, condoning her father's dream of spiritual destiny by means of a cheap deception. However, we need to read this episode with the mirror of Sovereignty in our hands, for a deep and archetypal pattern is worked out here. With the agreement of Pelles and the connivance of Brisen, Elaine becomes a simulacrum of Guinevere for the sole reason that Lancelot will respond sexually to no other woman but Arthur's queen. Elaine becomes then a kind of succuba, the embodiment of a dream woman or fantasy. While Lancelot responds physically to his supposed Guinevere, Elaine evokes the psychic image of the Grail winner that is to be born of the Grail guardian's daughter and the best knight in the world. An ancient pattern is reworked to great effect: Instead of the Loathly Lady being disenchanted—transformed into a beautiful woman by the kiss of a hero—Elaine is the means of the disenchantment of the wasteland by conceiving Galahad, the Grail winner, through Lancelot's singular passion for Guinevere.

Elaine is thus an authentic sovereignty-bestowing woman, like Rhiannon (*Mabon*, chapter 4), mother of Gwair. She is a Daughter of Branwen, a vessel of the blood of the Grail family. She is literally a Grail bearer, carrying both cup and child.

So we see the cross-tracked and sometimes tangled line of Sovereignty's influence. Elen, the queenly representative of Britain's blood and Sovereignty, becomes the wife of Macsen Wledig by means of a dream. She exercises her ancient role as goddess of the dream paths, probably inherited from an even more remote figure in British tradition who is now lost to us. The Elene of *Libeaus Desconus* may derived in part from Elen, but more important to us is the link between

Transformed Source	Transformed from	Means of to	Sovereignty's Transformation	Gift
Irish Sovereignty of Sovereignty	hag	Goddess	kiss/cohabitation	gives kingship of Ireland to champions and descendants
Loathly Lady (Dame Ragnell/ Wife of Bath)	enchanted hag	beautiful maiden	marriage/kiss	answer saves the king/hero
British folk tradition (Kempe Owyne/ Libeaus Desconus)	serpent/monster	beautiful maiden	kiss	land/castle
Grail Stories	hideous damsel/ wasteland	Grail Maiden/ fertile land	question answered	spiritual kingship

Figure 6. The pattern of Sovereignty's transformations

the motifs of the enchanted maiden and the Loathly Lady in that story. Last, Malory's Elaine shows us the final permutation in the pattern of Sovereignty: She bears sovereignty-bestowing power, but in the form of the Grail. She accepts only the best hero as her mate. She brings peace and plenty to the land by engendering the hero who will represent her, the one who will find the Grail and heal the wasteland, bringing an end to all enchantments. She assumes a dream form in order to evoke her destined mate's eros, but transmutes that eros to agape, selfish love into selfless love, for the healing of the world.

So is Sovereignty transformed from a king-making goddess to a Grail-bearing maiden. Her transformations may be shown more clearly in figure 6.

4
The Dream of Rhonabwy

The sage has invented a battlefield, in the midst of which the king takes up his station. To left and right of him the army is dispersed, the foot-soldiers occupying the rank in front. At the king's side stands his sagacious counsellor advising him on the strategy to be carried out during the battle.

FIRDAUSI, *SHAHNAMA*

And then he saw around him so many birds that all the air about him was full of them and they were blacker than anything he had ever seen.

DIDOT PERCEVAL

Three Nights in Avalon

"The Dream of Rhonabwy" is one of the most mysterious tales in the *Mabinogion*. It is nearest in nature to "Culhwch and Olwen." In it

Arthur is still the king of the Heroic Age with a mere patina of medieval overlay; his men are the same warriors as those listed in "Culhwch and Olwen" and are not yet medieval knights. Many ancient and curious remnants are littered about in this story, and perhaps some of them would still have been intelligible to a medieval Welshman, though they are certainly not so to us. As with many of the earlier stories of the *Mabinogion,* it is the traditions to which the story alludes that explain it, and these have been left out of the narrative. Fortunately, it is possible to reconstruct from existing parallel sources some of the cultural underpinnings necessary to our understanding.

The central question that the reader will ask is this: Are Owain's ravens real birds or are they a troop of men called ravens? The story leaves us in no doubt that real ravens fight Arthur's squires: "[C]lapping their wings in the wind . . . they seized some by the heads and others by the eyes, and others by the arms and carried them up into the air."[22]

These are not figurative ravens, but real scavengers of the battlefield, the kind of carrion birds commonly seen after any bloody fray. Although the action of the story takes place within a dream, we need not be dismissive of it for that reason. Indeed, hidden within the story and its dream symbolism lies the identity of one of the chief exemplars of Sovereignty in the person of Owain's mother (see chapter 5).

The locations of the story shift from twelfth-century Wales—the world in which Rhonabwy has the unfortunate task of hunting down one of his own countrymen—to the dream location of the ancestral past, in which he meets Arthur and his mighty host. From an all-too-real world of Wales in disarray, Rhonabwy awakes to a dream of the Otherworld, where the strength and glory of Britain is an ever-living reality. Because the Celtic conception of the Otherworld was not one of gloom and decay but of a paradisal present in which it is possible to fulfill all the normal actions of earthly life, Arthur and his men engage Osla Big Knife in a rematch of the Battle of Badon. Once the reader understands the time scale of the dream to be that of a living reality in the Otherworld, the story becomes much clearer. Although men are wounded and even die in the combat of the ravens, they, like the pieces on the gwyddbwyll board, will be set up on the field of battle another day.

Central to the dream is the gwyddbwyll game that Owain plays against Arthur. As we shall see, this game is a combat for Sovereignty, but not in the usual sense, for it takes place within the Otherworld and, like the Battle of Badon, is a match whose outcome has already been decided in linear time.

Owain is Arthur's nephew, the son of Urien of Rheged. We will meet him again in "The Lady of the Fountain," in which he is the chief protagonist. He is not called Arthur's nephew in "The Dream of Rhonabwy," although we know from parallel and later tradition that Urien married Morgan, Arthur's half sister. Owain ap Urien Rheged was a historical character, existing a good two generations after the passing of the Dark Age Arthur at Camlann (c. 530 C.E.). Like many other heroes of roughly the same era, Owain was drawn into the Arthurian corpus. Because of his unique links both with Arthur himself and with Modron, the otherworldly queen in the Llanferres folk tradition story (see *Mabon*, chapter 9), his mythos is of great significance to our discussion of this story.

The Battle of Camlann ended the brief independence of the British—barely 120 years had elapsed since the Romans left the island. Rhonabwy knew, as any well-brought-up youth should, the stories of that fatal battle. That he should meet its survivors in his dream and encounter those who actually died there is wonderful enough; that he should be permitted to witness the game between Arthur and Owain— itself a ritual challenge of Sovereignty's king and champion—is a great privilege. In that combat, more than the fate of the game is at stake.

There are many interesting parallels between "The Dream of Rhonabwy" and the early Irish story "The Destruction of Da Derga's Hostel."[179] As we saw in *Mabon*, Irish themes and motifs are very evident within the *Mabinogion*. This borrowing on the part of British storytellers was not because they lacked their own themes or innate skills, but because Britain and Ireland shared a common tradition of stories and mysteries. Rhonabwy's dream is not of a common order—but then he sleeps on an ox's hide, unconsciously following an ancient druidic practice of inducing prophetic dreams by incubating within the skin of a sacred animal. The original method was to sleep in a bull's hide; perhaps it is the cyfarwydd's unstated and ironic comment on the state of Wales that Rhonabwy sleeps in the skin of a castrated bull—an ox. Whatever his intention, the storyteller certainly allows Rhonabwy a full vision of Arthur and his men within the realms of the Otherworld.

Synopsis of "The Dream of Rhonabwy"

(1) Madawg, ruler of Powys, has a brother, Iorwerth, who is displeased with Madawg's position and his own obscurity. Although Madawg offers his brother the position of commander of his troops, Iorwerth prefers to go raiding in England. Three hundred men are sent to search for him, including Rhonabwy. (2) With a company of his fellows, Rhonabwy seeks shelter at the house of Heilyn the Red. It is a singularly dilapidated household, and the company is offered very poor hospitality. (3) Rhonabwy sleeps on a yellow ox hide on the floor, and there he dreams that he and his companions are crossing the plain in Montgomeryshire.

(4) They are overtaken by Iddawg, who was the cause of the conflict at Camlann: Sent by Arthur to deliver a message of truce to Medrawt, Iddawg framed the message as rudely as he could. (5) Rhonabwy and his companions come to where Arthur is encamped on an island in the middle of a ford. Arthur expresses sorrow for Britain that such morally diminished men now guard it. (6) Iddawg points out to Rhonabwy the stone in Arthur's ring: Whoever looks on it will remember all that he sees thereafter. They watch several troops of differently accoutred men ride by, including those led by (7) Afaon, son of Taliesin, who splashes Arthur and his bishop with water. His horse is struck by Elphin in rebuke for this offence. (8) Caradawg mac Llyr, Arthur's chief coun-

selor, expresses doubts that so many men can be contained in that space, especially because they were scheduled to fight the Battle of Badon against Osla Big Knife by noon. They watch the coming of other troops and then notice a commotion in the middle of the assembly, (9) caused by all the men wishing to see Cai's great prowess at riding.

(10) Arthur is armed with his sword by Cadwr of Cornwall, (11) his mantle is placed on the ground for him to sit upon, and his (12) gwydd-bwyll board and pieces are placed ready for a game with Owain ap Urien. (13) The two play and after a while a man comes to tell Owain that Arthur's squires are harassing Owain's ravens. Although Owain requests that the king call off his men, Arthur plays on. Three times in all, messengers come with reports of the worsening plight of the ravens, until Owain (14) finally tells the messenger to raise his standard in the thick of the fighting. The combat is then reversed. Messengers now come to Arthur to tell how the ravens are overcoming his squires. Although Arthur requests his opponent to call off his ravens, Owain plays on. (15) Three times this happens until Arthur squeezes the gold chess pieces into dust. Owain then asks that his standard be lowered.

(16) Osla Big Knife sends envoys to request a truce of six weeks until the fighting of their battle. (17) Arthur consults his men about the suitability of the truce. (18) Twenty-four donkeys arrive, burdened with gold and silver, the tribute of the islands of Greece, while the bards sing a eulogy in praise of Arthur. The truce is agreed upon and the gold and silver is awarded to the poets. Cai exhorts everyone to be in Cornwall ready to fight Osla at the end of the truce. (19) Such is the sound of their acclamation that Rhonabwy awakes—after a sleep of three days and nights. No one is able to tell this story without a book because of the many colors and various equipment and clothes mentioned.

Commentary

(1) The geographical and historical setting of the story is entirely accurate. The scene takes place in central Wales—Powys—over which region

Madawg ap Maredudd did indeed rule from 1138 to 1160 C.E. There was a good deal of unrest and political strife following his death until his grandson, Llewellyn the Great, took possession of Powys. This preamble, which tells of a renegade Cymro (Welshman), is offset by the loyalty shown by Arthur's host in the main story of "The Dream of Rhonabwy." Indeed, as we will see, the whole story revolves around the dichotomy of medieval Wales, which looked to an ideal Arthurian kingdom but actually lived in a state that was far from ideal, being partially governed by English kings.

(2) Celtic hospitality was universally warm and lavish, according to the circumstances of the host. It was everywhere an honorable thing, indeed a sacred duty, to feed strangers, just as it still is in parts of rural Greece today. The house of Heilyn the Red is not simply poor; it is downright inhospitable: Dung and urine muddy the floor, the food is unwholesome, and the fire is smoky. This episode can be compared with the story of the visit of the Munster king Fedlimid to the house of Guile the satirist. In this Irish story, Guile sends his daughter out to his guests to give an account of the hospitality they could expect: The old food has been eaten, the new food hasn't arrived, the women are pregnant, the cows are dry, mice swarm about the floors, and the benches are rotten.[179] The house of Heilyn represents the state of Wales, impoverished by its overlords, willing enough to offer hospitality, but too poor to provide the best.

(3) Offered a choice of beds, Rhonabwy chooses the yellow ox hide and wraps himself up in it for the night. Little does he know that this action triggers his dream. According to druidic practice, sleeping in an ox hide brought prophetic and precognitive dreams. In "The Destruction of Da Derga's Hostel," a bull feast, or *tarbh-feis,* is prepared on the death of King Eterscel in order to determine who the next king will be. A druid kills a bull, eats a broth of its flesh, wraps himself in its skin, and sleeps as a spell of truth is chanted over him. By such a

method the new king, Conaire, is recognized. This is not the only similarity between these two texts, as we shall see. The setting of a story within a dream is not a common Welsh tradition, although it is often used by Irish storytellers.

(4) Paralleling Rhonabwy's real-life search for a renegade Cymro is his meeting with such a man in his dream. Iddawg, the Churn of Britain, was the chief cause of the last battle fought between Arthur and his son/nephew, Medrawt (Mordred). He, along with six others, escaped the slaughter of Camlann, according to tradition, and it is told that he completed his penance for this act after seven years at the Grey Stone in Scotland. Rhonabwy has certainly gone back in time and no mistake. The survivors of Camlann are variously given as follows:

> Here are the names of the men who escaped from the battle of
> Camlann: Sandde Angel's form because of his beauty, Morfran son of
> Tegid because of his ugliness, St Cynfelyn from the speed of his horse,
> St Cedwyn from the world's blessing, St Pedrog from the strength of
> his spear, Derfel the Strong from his strength, Geneid the Tall from
> his speed. The year of Christ when the battle of Camlann took place
> was 542.[38]

There is an obvious parallel between these six and the seven who returned from Ireland with Bran (see *Mabon*, chapter 3) and from Annwfn with Arthur (*Mabon*, chapter 6). See also note 8, below.

(5) The scene of Arthur's encampment shows the king surrounded by his counselors and retainers. When he sees Rhonabwy and his companions, Arthur laments that Britain should be governed by such little men as these. It is now obvious that Rhonabwy is indeed in the Otherworld by the power of his dreaming. He meets the archetypal warriors and guardians of Britain's former greatness, and doubtless feels about this encounter as a young man about to go to the Crusades was reported, by Giraldus Cambrensis, to have felt: "What man of spirit

can hesitate for a moment to undertake this journey when, among the many hazards involved, none could be more unfortunate, none could cause greater distress, than the prospect of coming back alive?"[12] Doubtless, though, Rhonabwy's distress was more from failure to measure up to the ideal warrior.

(6) As we all know, dreams fade rapidly once we are awake. Iddawg shows Rhonabwy that he may recall all that he sees by looking at Arthur's ring. Despite a list of Arthur's goods, weapons, and possessions, this is the only mention of his ring (see notes 10 and 11). However, in his novel *That Hideous Strength*, C. S. Lewis makes this ring the object of a mystery question which Merlin asks of Ransom, the successor to the long line of Pendragons:

> "Where is the ring of Arthur the King? . . . " "The ring of the King . . . is on Arthur's finger where he sits in the House of Kings in the cup-shaped land of Abhalljin [i.e., Avalon] . . . For Arthur did not die; but our Lord took him to be in the body till the end of time . . . with Enoch and Moses and Melchisedec the King."[89]

(7) The striking of Afaon's horse by Elphin is also significant. Elphin is here described as Arthur's sword bearer. He is the same Elphin who rescued Taliesin from the weir and was in turn rescued by Taliesin from imprisonment by Maelgwn (see *Mabon,* chapter 7). This episode in "Hanes Taliesin" is traditionally meant to correspond with the freeing of the youth Gwair (a manifestation of Mabon) from imprisonment in Annwfn. In the Succession of the Pendragons, the Pendragon always frees his successor from otherworldly detainment, as Arthur frees Gwair in the "Preiddeu Annwfn." The identification of Elphin as a type of Mabon is established in our story when Elphin stands before Arthur as his sword bearer. We will also remember that Taliesin bade Elphin's jockey strike all Maelgwn's horses as he overtook them in the race. Here Afaon, the son of Taliesin, splashes Arthur with water and his horse is

struck by Elphin. Iddawg's comment on this action is strange: He praises Afaon as the wisest and most accomplished youth in the kingdom, while Elphin is called a perverse and overanxious boy.

Triads 7 and 25 describe Afaon as one of three "Bull-chieftains and Battle Leaders" of Britain. He is further described as having avenged his death from his grave—an allusion to an unknown tradition. Elphin is always known as "the unfortunate." That he should be described as overanxious is strangely familiar: The name of Pryderi, another Mabon, means "anxiety" (see *Mabon,* chapter 2). This mysterious passage shows that the cyfarwydd was familiar with related traditions of these characters.

(8) The Battle of Camlann, at which most of those mentioned in this story perished, was fought in about 530 C.E. The Battle of Badon—Arthur's greatest victory—was fought in about 495 C.E. Badon is generally identified as Caer Baddon or Bath. Osla Big Knife—who also appears in "Culhwch and Olwen" as the bearer of a large knife which spans all rivers, enabling Arthur and his men to cross water—is not so easy to identify. His appearance in "Culhwch and Olwen" establishes a distinguished tradition of the sword bridge in Arthurian legend, but although he appears in "Culhwch and Olwen" as Arthur's ally, he is, in fact, his historical enemy. "Only one English king is directly stated to have fought at Baddon and his name was Oesc of Kent,"[123] which is sufficiently like Osla to be acceptable. But it is more likely that Octha is the one intended here. He is the kinsman of Hengist, whom Vortigern allowed to settle in the lands north of the Wall. This area, agreed to be Dumfries, takes its name from the Frisians who settled there.

Caradawg mac Llyr is also called Caradawg Freichfras, or "strong arm." Triads 1 and 18 speak of him as the chief elder of Britain and one of three battle horsemen. In Welsh and Breton tradition he was incorporated into the noble genealogies. In Arthurian literary tradition he was translated into French as Karadues or Carados Briefbras; the

French storytellers did not understand Welsh and many stories abounded concerning his shortened arms.

(9) Cai's reputation as one of Arthur's chief warriors gradually declined over the years. Here, as in "Culhwch and Olwen," Cai is still one of the "Battle Diademed Men" (Triad 21) of the Island of Britain. With Bedwyr he performs great feats of supernatural strength and cunning. It is only later that he becomes the discourteous Kay, as we can see in the later romances of "Peredur" and "Gereint and Enid." His prowess at riding causes the group of men to look as though it is "turning inside out." It seems as though the cyfarwydd is using a poetical allusion common at the time of this story's transcription. The Battle of Camlann became a byword for futility, furious combat, and tumult.[38] The word *cadgamlan,* derived from Camlann, was coined to express "a confused mob or rabble," such as is caused by Cai's expert riding here.

(10) The arming of Arthur is unique among stories concerning his exploits. As stated elsewhere, it is rare that Arthur performs any feats on his own behalf in the later legends. "The Dream of Rhonabwy," apart from supplying a further list of Arthur's men, goes into great detail concerning his possessions. The sword that Elphin bears is brought to Arthur by Cadwr of Cornwall, who holds Arthur's personal domain in trust for his king. The sword has two golden serpents on the hilt: When it is unsheathed, flames of fire issue from the mouths of these serpents, dazzling his foes.

(11) Arthur's mantle, Gwenn (white), is placed on the ground. The rule regarding it is that nothing that is not white can be placed on it, and its special property is that anyone wrapped in it becomes invisible. This mantle is listed as thirteenth of the Thirteen Treasures of Britain (see *Mabon,* chapter 3). The mantle of invisibility is likewise used by Caswallawn in "Branwen, Daughter of Llyr," although he uses it mali-

ciously to usurp Bran's throne and cause death to Britain's faithful troops. It is clearly one of Sovereignty's empowering hallows, like the gwyddbwyll board (see note 12). The fact that only objects of the same color can be placed on it seems puzzling at first, but white is the color whose purity belongs to worthy kings, heroes, maidens, and queens. The implication is that it cannot be used for evil purposes.

(12) This is the second time we've come across the gwyddbwyll board. Wherever serious matters of sovereignty are debated, there we will find this gaming board. The exact method of playing gwyddbwyll is uncertain, but it was likely to be similar to other games of the period, like the Irish *brandubh* or *fidhchell,* which had two sets of men: the king piece and his companions and the opposing king and his men. There is an extant Irish poem from the works of Tadhg Dall O hUiginn, which speaks of the brandubh board as a microcosm of Ireland itself. The center square represents Tara (the sacred center of Ireland), while the surrounding four squares to north, south, east, and west are the royal seats of Ulster, Munster, Leinster, and Connacht, respectively.[13] There is an unwritten tradition, which can be surmised from the folk traditions and oral culture of Celtic (and other) nations, that the king often gains his kingdom (or retains it) by winning a board game between himself and an otherworldly king. This is significant with respect to our story, as we shall see.

(13) The mysterious game begins and, with it, an equally mysterious series of messengers appears. Those who come to Owain do not greet Arthur first, as courtesy demands they should. To Owain's repeated request that Arthur call off his squires from Owain's ravens, the king merely responds, "Your move," in the manner of one who has the game sewn up. The nature of this game and the significance of Owain and the ravens will be discussed in the following sections Modron, Queen of Ravens, and The Game of the Goddess, respectively.

(14) It is only when the raven standard is raised that Owain's side gains the upper hand. This action is talismanic and Owain seems to allow it only as a last resort. If we look at parallel Celtic tradition, we will see exactly why. There is a firm tradition that battle standards were somehow empowered in their own right to wreak vengeance and slaughter.[116] The Fairy Flag of Dunvegan, in the keeping of the MacLeods, was given to the ancestors of the MacLeod clan to be used only in desperate times. It is said to have stopped a cattle plague, extinguished a fire, and aided the clan in battle—but it is removed from its chest only in times of dire need.[121] It is regarded as an otherworldly gift which empowers mortals. Of course, the standard, as with any heraldic device, is but a manifestation of a tribe's totem. Owain's particular right to use this device is discussed in the section Modron, Queen of Ravens, below.

(15) Arthur ends the conflict by crushing the chess pieces. The game of gwyddbwyll has been operational on two levels: as a board game and as an actual combat. At the same time, Owain orders the lowering of the raven standard and there is peace between the kinsmen.

(16) The truce by arrangement may seem farcical to modern understanding, to which the chivalry of war is a thing of the past, yet such truces were frequent and acceptable in the Middle Ages, when hostilities would break off by agreement in honor of a major feast of the Church. The duplicity of the Britons' lunchtime assault on Rome in "The Dream of Macsen Wledig" is a rare event in historical terms. The Battle of Badon to be fought here is technically a repeat match: Because neither side exists in linear time but only in the ever-living reality of the Otherworld, they can refight old battles with impunity.

(17) The extent and power of Arthur's reign is due entirely to his ability to ally with fellow kings and leaders of Britain. This story, like "Culhwch and Olwen," gives us a full list of his allies and chief officers. These lists represent the earliest literary examples of Arthur's court, a

far more authentic numeration than that of the later Round Table knights. Although the casual reader who wishes to read the story and not be delayed by these lists may be tempted to pass over them as full of difficult-to-pronounce Welsh names, it is worth looking closely at them, for they reveal a good deal about the way in which Arthur was understood.

Many characters from other parts of the *Mabinogion* appear in this story. Edern ap Nudd (who is called the king of Denmark here!) we will meet again in "The Lady of the Fountain." Apart from Arthur's usual warriors, Gwalchmai (Gawain), Bedwyr (Bedivere), and Cai (Kay), there are Trystan, Morfran (the son of Ceridwen and Tegid), and Gwrhyr and Menw, who both help to find Mabon in "Culhwch and Olwen." Peredur, whom we will meet later on, is mentioned in the same breath as Goreu and Mabon, a significant juxtaposition. The tradition that Arthur had children other than Mordred is not generally known, but Llacheu is mentioned here as Arthur's son. In later Arthurian romance he becomes Loholt and is said to have been killed by Cai. Present also are some anachronistic kings, including William of France (Gwilym) and Howel of Brittany. The storyteller is at pains to show the extent of Arthur's power. Ironically, Gildas ap Caw is included—the same Gildas the Priest whose chronicle *The Ruin of Britain* was written in the period of the Dark Age Arthur and which singularly fails to mention the king.[13] The silence of Gildas on the subject of Arthur has been variously interpreted as either confirmation of the complete nonexistence of such a king at that time or the purposeful ignoring of a tribal enemy (Gildas's father, Caw, a Pict of the northern Clyde, was probably subdued by Arthur).[123]

(18) So vast is Arthur's power and influence that even the islands of Greece send him tribute. This is intended to contrast with the numerous mentions in oral tradition of Britain having to send tribute to Rome, reference to the ignominious period after Julius Caesar's attempted invasion of Britain, when many minor kings kept their titles

and lands only by dint of paying such tribute. The lands of the extreme east, Greece included, are often cited by storytellers in lieu of the Otherworld, as we will see in chapter 7.

The praise song that the bards sing to Arthur is so obscure that only Cadyryeith understands it, says the text. Because Cadyryeith is called Fair Speech, we must conclude that he himself is skilled in poetic conventions. This obscurity on the part of professional poets was often remarked upon in the Middle Ages and later, attesting to a lore and tradition with its own allusive symbolism the full implications of which only another poet could comprehend.

(19) The death of the oral tradition and the rise of the new, fashionable literary tradition are alluded to here: So complex and various are the colors and armaments that no one is able to tell the story without a book. Such a statement does a disservice to the actual memories of the storytellers of both Ireland and Wales, whose professional repertoire (in Ireland, at least) included some 350 stories, many of which were not only longer than this one but also exceedingly more complex in their descriptions. But with the onset of literacy in the noble and clerical classes—especially the latter, who would have been professional poets or storytellers in a non-Christian society—the skill of memorizing was forgotten.

Just as Macsen was awakened at the climax of his dream, so Rhonabwy is awakened after his prodigious sleep because of the acclamation of Arthur's host.

Modron, Queen of Ravens

Owain's ravens have been universally understood to mean his troops in this story, in much the same way that Achilles' men are called Myrmidons (ants). However, there is a deeper significance to the ravens' presence in "The Dream of Rhonabwy." In order to discover its inner meaning, we will need to look at some parallel texts relating to Owain and his family.

Owain is associated with ravens because of his birth. Here is the story of his conception: There was a ford at Llanferres where people dared not go due to the sounds of dogs howling and barking. Urien of Rheged came to the ford and there met a woman who was washing. He lay with her and she told him that she was the daughter of the king of Avallach and was fated to wait there until she conceived a son by a Christian. Her name was Modron. Returning at the end of the year, Urien found that she had had two children by him: Owain and Morfudd. These twins are also mentioned in Triad 70 as one of three "Fair Womb Burdens": "Owain Son of Urien, and Morfudd his sister, who were carried together in the womb of Modron ferch [daughter of] Afallach."[38]

This late-sixteenth-century story from the oral tradition, combined with the triad, gives us an extraordinary key with which to open the door of a great mystery. Owain is of joint otherworldly and mortal parentage, just as Pryderi is in "Pwyll, Prince of Dyfed." Moreover, he is the son of Modron. As we have learned, Modron is a title rather than a personal name. It means "mother" and is applicable to many women who represent the Goddess as mother of the Mabon, or Son. The identity of the woman whom Urien meets is not difficult to discover. Later tradition speaks of Arthur's sister, Morgan, as being married to Urien and as being mother to Owain. What clinches the identification is Morgan's own parentage: In the *Gesta Regnum Britanniae* (c. 1235 C.E.), her father is given as Rex Avallonis—king of Avalon (see *Mabon*, chapter 9).

The thread of Morgan in Arthurian tradition is a strangely tangled one. She appears as Arthur's sister (or half sister) only in later texts. She first appears in Geoffrey of Monmouth[10] as Morgen, chief of nine sister prophetesses and healers. In Chrétien de Troyes's *Erec and Enid* she is Arthur's sister.[7] Later tradition makes of her an evil enchantress at odds with Arthur. In fact, her enmity is at the root of the decline of the Round Table in all later versions (see chapter 10).

If we look at Morgan in the earlier traditions, we find her likeness to the Irish Morrighan, goddess with triple aspects who appears as the Dark Woman of Knowledge, as the Washer at the Ford and as the battle crow or raven. What is surprising is that the name Morgan is never used as a female name in Welsh tradition, although it is common enough as a male name. Geoffrey of Monmouth calls her Morgen, but we cannot look to Welsh tradition to furnish a prototype of Morgan from any genealogy or chronicle earlier than Geoffrey. Insofar as she can be identified with the name Modron, she is present in earlier tradition only as Owain's mother and the daughter of the king of Avalon or Annwfn. So where did Morgan originate?

Morgan le Fay is a character in her own right in Breton tradition, where she appears as queen of the Otherworld, a giver of gifts and a haunter of wells and springs. Whether she stems from the same tradition that Pomponius Mela spoke of—the nine Korrigans, or prophetic sisters, who lived on a holy island off the coast of Brittany[168]—or from some other source, this tradition is remarkably close to Geoffrey's account of Morgen in the *Vita Merlini*.[11]

The lineage of Morgan in oral tradition has been too thoroughly tangled for complete certainty of reconstruction. It is, however, remarkably consistent—as though a common tradition concerning a prototype Morgan existed and has been parceled out among the Celtic nations. It is only by assembling the evidence from each country that a complete Morgan can be found (see figure 7).

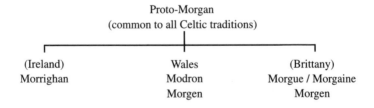

Figure 7. Morgan in Celtic tradition

If we look at the characteristics of each of these seemingly separate women, we will see a family likeness to one archetype—the consort/healer of the dead hero or Pendragon:

Morrighan appears as a battle crow, or raven, scavenging the battlefield. She also appears as the Washer at the Ford, to warn warriors of their impending death—the clothes that she launders are the bloody garments of a man she meets at the ford. She is at enmity with a chosen hero (in particular Cú Chulainn), whom she first loves and then, on being refused, hates, hounding him to his early death.

Modron appears as the Washer at the Ford in order to conceive a child by a Christian man. She is the daughter of the Otherworld king and people fear to frequent the ford because they imagine they will meet the Washer in her aspect of bringer of death. Modron bears a son, a Mabon who will be her champion in battle. Likewise, by right of his maternal descent, Owain bears the raven upon his standard.

Morgue/Morgaine appears as an otherworldly priestess whose island, or *temenos,* is a place of healing and learning. She is the royal virgin of Avalon who heals Arthur's wounds with her own skill; she keeps him with her as her consort after the Battle of Camlann.

The proto-Morgan, the great Celtic goddess who can appear as the battle raven or the hag washing the clothes of those destined to be slain, is also the Dark Woman of Knowledge, whose healing skills restore the wounded king and who is destined to bring forth a new Mabon to replace this king in the outer worlds. The composite of these three women creates the later Morgan le Fay of Arthurian tradition. Meanwhile, we are able to see that the daughter of Afallach, or Modron/Morgan, is fully at liberty to bequeath the aid of her raven totem to her Son/Mabon, Owain. If this is so, what then is the real nature of Owain's gwyddbwyll game with Arthur and of the combat between their respective troops?

We are fortunate that a further strand of this tradition, directly relating to "The Dream of Rhonabwy," is extant in a later twelfth-century text known as the *Didot Perceval*, also called the *Prose Perceval*.[32] This relates a unique narrative concerning the exploits of Perceval and his quest for the Grail. Written in French and closely related to the works of Robert de Boron, it yet retains some ancient features which doubtless strayed in from British oral tradition. One episode in particular concerns us here, that of Perceval's combat at the ford with a character called Urban of the Black Pine.

While on his quest, Perceval comes to a ford near which a pavilion is pitched in a beautiful meadow. A knight emerges from the pavilion and challenges Perceval's crossing. They fight and Perceval overcomes his opponent, though he will not grant him mercy until the knight tells his tale. The knight tells Perceval that he is called Urban, son of the queen of the Black Pine. He had been a knight of King Arthur's and, while on adventure, had followed a maiden seated upon a mule but was unable to overtake her. Eventually, she led him to a castle and there Urban fell in love with her, promising that he would pitch his pavilion at the ford and challenge all comers. He has held the ford for the best part of a year, at the end of which time he expects to win his maiden. Perceval tells Urban that he does not wish to guard the Ford Perilous himself and that Urban need not guard the place any longer. Then a great noise sounds, a shadow overcomes them both, and a voice is heard to say:

"Perceval li Galois, accursed may you be by whatever we women can contrive, for you have caused us the greatest sorrow today that we could ever have." Then it addresses Urban and forbids him to stay and guard the ford: "If you stay there longer, you will lose me."

As Urban makes haste to go, hundreds of black birds fill the sky and start to attack Perceval. Urban helps him beat them off. In this process, Perceval wounds one bird so that it falls to earth, where it becomes a woman. Amazed, Perceval asks the meaning of the transformation. Urban says that "the voice that you heard was she who called to me, and when she saw that I could not escape from you, she changed herself and her damsels into the semblance of birds and they came here to oppress you . . . this one whom you wounded, she is the sister of my lady, but she will suffer no harm, for within the moment she is in Avalon." Urban recognizes Perceval as a worthy man and the best knight in the world, and Perceval continues on his way.[32]

We will be returning to this theme of the raven woman in chapter 7, but it is evident that much of the mystery of "The Dream of Rhonabwy" is solved by this passage. The Ford Perilous is the boundary of the Otherworld where the maiden rules as queen. Like Pwyll in pursuit of Rhiannon, Urban was not able to catch up with his maiden. He is set to guard the borders of the Otherworld after the fashion of a knightly Rex Nemorensis (chapter 5). Perceval, because of his successful challenge, should by rights become the champion of the maiden, although he abrogates this duty in the text. He is cursed by the disembodied voice of the maiden and then is physically attacked by her in her shape of a black bird. Though he is able to bring down one of the birds, it is not killed; instead it becomes a woman and is spirited to Avalon to be healed.

The maiden is evidently a shadow of Modron/Morgan: She appears in raven shape and has the power to heal her sister in Avalon. It has been authoritatively established that Urban is based on Urien. In modern Breton folk tradition, the Forest of Brocéliande is Morgan's domain. Overlooking the Fountain of Barenton in the forest is the famous Pine of Barenton, from which otherworldly birds sing. In the *Didot Perceval,* Urban is the son of the queen of the Black Pine. Taking all this together with the encounter at a ford, we have the complete key to "The Dream of Rhonabwy": Owain is the champion of his mother's kin, the people of Avalon, who have the ability to shapeshift into ravens. As the grandson of Rex Avallonis, he champions the Otherworld in a game against Arthur, who, since his defeat at Camlann, is a newcomer to Avalon. Why should Owain do this?

The long enmity between Morgan and Arthur is persistent throughout later tradition, though the real reason for it is misunderstood. In early tradition Morgan—as we shall continue to call this representative of the Great Mother, Modron—stood for Britain's sovereignty, and it is because of Sovereignty and his union with her that the Pendragon is able to reign. Arthur's career and his relationship to Sovereignty's aspects are as follows. (See chapter 10 for a more detailed discussion of Sovereignty's aspects.)

Initiating Mother: Igerna/Igraine, Arthur's mother

Flower Bride: Gwenhwyfar, Arthur's wife

Otherworldly Consort: Morgan, Arthur's healer and receiver

Sovereignty does not allow her earthly consort, the Pendragon, to reign beyond his rightful time. If we recall the pattern of the succession of the Pendragons, we will see this:

Mabon: the Wondrous Youth, the Pendragon's champion and *tanaiste* (successor)

Pendragon: the king who, with Sovereignty's empowerment, holds the land

Pen Annwfn: the withdrawn Pendragon, who becomes king of the Underworld

In "The Dream of Rhonabwy," Arthur is the withdrawn Pendragon; Owain, born to Modron and therefore a Mabon in his own right, stands ready to challenge his uncle, Arthur, for the Pendragonship. A close look at any of the late Arthurian romances will show that, as in earlier tradition, Morgan acts as Sovereignty, continually presenting her champions at court, where they try to oust Arthur or overcome him by combat or magical skill. In early tradition, Owain becomes the son of Modron, who, as a prototype of Morgan, may be seen as a sister of the Pendragon; her son Owain is thus Arthur's nephew and in a prime position to be his tanaiste.

Within Celtic tradition, the complex webs of familial relationships were guided by an older system of reckoning descent and succession through the female. This meant that the nephew or sister's son of a king had a greater right to the throne than the king's own son (who would have been born to a woman outside the royal blood). This situation is clearly shown in later Arthurian tradition, where the sons of Morgause by Lot—Gawain, Gaheris, Gareth, and Agravain—are at odds with Arthur, aware of their prior claims to the succession. The ultimate example of this tradition is seen, of course, in the birth of Mordred, conceived upon Morgause by her half brother, Arthur. Mordred is thus both his father's son and his nephew, which strengthens his claim to reign after his father. (He also attempts to reinforce this by abducting Guinevere in the later traditions—a curious turnabout to an earlier understanding of Guinevere as the Flower Bride and earthly representative of Sovereignty (see chapters 6 and 10).

That Owain is rightfully a Mabon we need have no doubts. The mythic idea of Mabon as a character in his own right may be manifest only in "Culhwch and Olwen," but traditions about him filtered through into Continental developments of the Arthurian legend, and it is here that we find him again, in Chrétien's *Erec and Enid,* as Mabonograin. Scholars argue over the etymology of this name, but it is possible that the traditions of Mabon and Owain—who are both sons of a woman bearing the title of Modron—have been combined to create Mabonograin: Mabon and Ivain (the French name for Owain). Interestingly, Mabonograin is the nephew of Eurain or Urien (see chapter 6).

Owain is, then, the champion of Morgan. The ravens are his otherworldly kin and the contest between Owain and Arthur is to determine the kingship.

The Game of the Goddess

The gwyddbwyll board appears many times in the *Mabinogion* and is central to the theme of Sovereignty, as we shall further discover in chapter 7. The board appears in the list of the Thirteen Treasures of Britain: "The Chessboard of Gwenddolau ap Ceidio: if the pieces were set, they would play by themselves. The board was of gold and the men of silver."[38]

The identity of the Gwenddolau mentioned here is not hard to find: He is the Gwenddolau who was the patron and protector of Myrddin ap Morfryn or Myrddin Wyllt—Merlin the Mad. He was the leader of one of the factions in the Battle of Arfderydd (573 C.E.), described in the triads as one of the three futile battles of the Island of Britain. It was brought about "by the cause of the lark's nest." Gwenddolau perished in this battle, causing Merlin to lapse into madness at the sight of the fray and the loss of so many of his family and friends.

Gwenddolau's reputation was high among poets, who describe him as generously open-handed. The allusion to the battle in which he met his death being caused by a lark's nest is very obscure, and though the phrase "a lark's nest" may possibly indicate "a trifling matter," knowing the nature of Celto-Arthurian texts, there is likely to be a more specific meaning. Gwenddolau appears in another triad concerning one of the three fortunate assassinations. This triad tells of "Gall son of Dysgyfdawd who slew the Two Birds of Gwenddolau. And they had a yoke of gold on them. Two corpses of the Cymry they ate for their dinner, and two for their supper."[38]

Nothing more is known about these birds, but it is indeed unusual that besides "The Dream of Rhonabwy" there should be another tradition concerning the owner of a magical gwyddbwyll board and a pair of carrion birds.

Owain was a fellow countryman and contemporary of Gwenddolau, for they were both men of the north, though they are clearly separate historical characters. Nikolai Tolstoy argues persuasively for the stubborn pagan adherence of Gwenddolau against his Christian enemy Rhydderch, who is described in the *Black Book of Carmarthen* as "the defender of the faith."[152] Tolstoy instances the fact that Gwenddolau was Merlin's patron and the fact that the chronicles describe Gwenddolau as causing a battle fog—a magical device often employed by druids, according to many Irish texts, to confuse their patron's enemy—as evidence of his pagan belief.

If we look at the career of Owain in the following two stories, "The

Lady of the Fountain" and "Gereint and Enid," we find that Owain himself is a clear proponent of the old pagan ways, for he not only encounters and marries the lady of the fountain—a manifestation of Sovereignty—but also in "Gereint and Enid" later on, becomes the king of the enchanted games, the contest that all visitors to Owain's castle must undergo. The enchanted games, like the game of gwyddbwyll, can have only one of two possible outcomes: success or failure. If successful, the candidate for the games emerges from the enclosed paradisal garden as the champion of Sovereignty; if he is unsuccessful, the candidate is summarily beheaded by the Red Knight who guards the garden, and his head is stuck on the surrounding palisade.

It is difficult to say whether or not the mythos of Owain has overlapped with that of Gwenddolau, but clearly there is some kind of connection. We should recall that the Thirteen Treasures of Britain are traditionally supposed to be guarded by Merlin in his glass house on Bardsey Island, and that Merlin's patron was Gwenddolau, historically speaking.[38]

The gwyddbwyll board in Gwenddolau's possession is one of the prime symbols of Sovereignty herself; it represents the land of Britain, over which so many champions, invaders, and defenders have fought in game after endless game. In "The Dream of Rhonabwy," the board is in Arthur's possession—for all that the time scale of the story indicates that he is in the Otherworld, he is king of Britain. But the pieces on the board, moved by the hands of Arthur and Owain, are represented by their respective troops, who "play by themselves."

The game played by Owain and Arthur is nothing less than the game of the Goddess—the ultimate contest to determine who shall have sovereignty over the land. This theme is echoed on every possible level of the story: Rhonabwy's master, Madawg, seeks to overcome his brother Iorwerth in historical time; Arthur seeks to overcome Osla Big Knife in a replay of Badon Field; and Owain seeks to overcome Arthur, in a more mythological sense, for the position of the master of the Goddess's game.

It would indeed be tempting to draw up the gwyddbwyll board exactly according to the story of "The Dream of Rhonabwy," for the placement of the troops on the field seems to suggest the positioning of men upon a gaming board. Triad 59 speaks of the Battle of Camlann as being caused by one of three unfortunate counsels of the Island of Britain, in which Arthur is advised to divide his troops in thirds with Medrawt. This probably refers to the placement and command of Arthur's household troops, or *teulu*, usually numbering three hundred men.

In "The Dream of Rhonabwy" there are indeed three separate groups of troops: those of Rhufawn Pebyr (who asks if Rhonabwy's company might be divided among the battle disposition), those of March, and those of Edern ap Nudd. In the very visual setting of this story we may envision these three companies assembled on the plain before the island in the ford where Arthur sits: Rhufawn's company are in red liveries, March's are in white with black colors, and Edern's are in darkest black, as befits the son of the Underworld. The three troops wear the three sacred colors of Sovereignty.

Seated centrally in the field are Arthur and his household warriors, counselors, and servants. On either side of Arthur are Bedwini, his bishop, and Gwarthegydd ap Caw. Before him stands his champion Elphin, while his servitor Eirin and Earl Cadwr, who arms the king, stand ready to accoutre and equip Arthur. Behind the king is Caradawg ap Llyr Marini, his chief counselor. Arthur's horseman, Cai, rides among the host, dressed in his white and red colors.

This story makes much of detail—especially of color and equipment—which might be overlooked as a storyteller's convention. We find, however, that these details are very exact as well as visually compelling. The tents and mounts and colors and emblematic beasts of the separate messengers who come to Arthur and Owain all bear investigation.

The messengers who come to Owain and the tents from which they come are as follows.

Selyf: from a white, red-topped tent flying the black serpent

Gwgawn: from a yellow tent flying the red lion

Gwres: from a spotted yellow tent flying the golden eagle

The messengers who come to Arthur and the mounts on which they ride are:

Blathaon: on a dapple-gray horse, helmet crested by a yellow-red leopard

Rhufawn: on a white horse, helmet crested by a yellow-red lion

Hefeidd: on a black horse, helmet crested by a griffin with a stone of power in its head

We note that except for Gwres, who bears a severed head on his spear, Owain's messengers are on foot and carry only swords, while Arthur's messengers are all mounted and carry swords and spears. Arthur's men bear beasts of royalty upon their helms. Gwgawn, Owain's second messenger, comes from a tent flying what will become Owain's emblem in "The Lady of the Fountain"; when he has overcome the lady of the fountain's husband, Luned arms him with a golden lion shield. The eagle is clearly an emblem of royalty, and as for the tent from which Selyf appears, there we find the colors of Sovereignty clearly arrayed: the white, the red, and the black with the serpent over all as a banner. The serpent or dragon is the totemic manifestation of Sovereignty just as much as the other beasts are. We have already noted the connection between the Goddess and the dragon, a theme we will encounter again in chapter 9. These two sets of messengers may represent the different moves that were possible upon the gwyddbwyll board, a game which no one has yet successfully reconstructed.[90, 104] Owain's messengers in their tents may remind us of rooks or castles in modern chess, while Arthur's messengers may seem identical to the knights in that game—but there can be no such identification, for the two games are culturally far removed from each other.

Arthur closes the triple contest, manages not to lose his men, and avoids loss to Owain's ravens only by the expedient of squeezing the golden gwyddbwyll pieces into dust. As the owner of the board, as king of Britain, he calls for the end of the game/battle and sets to planning the comical rematch of Badon with as much deliberation as any football coach faced with a match called off because of bad weather.

The game of the Goddess can be played on many levels. Sometimes she utilizes the formal framework of a gwyddbwyll game, as here, but more often she sets up complex quests, tests, and contests into which her champions blunder without the least knowledge that they are playing her game. This perilous game is a case of winner take all, with the gamble that failure means death. It is a game which Owain is well qualified to play, and to which Gereint after him finds himself inextricably drawn.

5
The Lady of the Fountain

> What will the naiads . . .
>
> *do now, poor things:*
>
> the lady of the ffynnon
> Es Sitt *that moves the* birket, *fays* del lac, *the donnas of the*
> lyn, *the triad-*matres, *the barley-tressed mamau and the*
> *grey-eyed* nymphae *at the dry* ffynhonnau *whose* silvae-*office*
> *is to sing:*
>
> *VNVS HOMO NOBIS*
> *(PER AQVAM)*
> *RESTITVIS REM*
>
> DAVID JONES, *ANATHEMATA*

The Lion and the Unicorn

In "The Lady of the Fountain," or "Owain," as we shall call this story
for convenience, we perceive the evolution of Owain from lord of the
ravens to knight of the lion. In "The Dream of Rhonabwy," Owain
appears as a powerful otherworldly lord, able to call upon his mother's
people for assistance. In "Gereint and Enid" we will see how he resumes

his otherworldly guise as king of the enchanted games. In "Owain," however, he does not stray far from the Celtic earthly paradise; indeed, we see how he is drawn farther into its realms by becoming the champion of the fountain and the husband of Sovereignty's representative.

The lady of the fountain remains unnamed in the *Mabinogion;* she is merely referred to as the countess (although Chrétien calls her Laudine). She is, in fact, not the lady of an earthly domain at all, but the powerful mistress of an otherworldly realm. As we shall see, the real lady of the fountain is Sovereignty herself. Like Diana, the goddess of the grove, the countess is in need of a champion to guard her fountain; the one who overcomes this champion becomes, in turn, the new champion and consort of the countess. We shall speak more of this theme later in this chapter in the section Rex Nemorensis.

Owain and his countess are represented by the lion and the unicorn in a mythic sense—that same pair of beasts about whom the famous rhyme runs:

> *The Lion and Unicorn were fighting for the crown.*
> *The Lion beat the Unicorn all about the town.*[50]

These beasts are today the heraldic supporters of the Royal Coat of Arms; the royal lion of England and Scotland and the mystical unicorn of Scotland were adopted as the supporters of James VI's armorial bearings. The rhyme above referred originally to the manner in which the lion and the unicorn changed sides during their heraldic associations with the crowns of England and Scotland. These heraldic beasts have their roots in the British consciousness in a deeper sense as the totemic beasts of Sovereignty and her champion. In the course of this story, Owain acquires a new set of arms as a result of having slain and succeeded the lady of the fountain's husband; the golden lion is his new crest. The lady of the fountain herself is a representation of Sovereignty, and, as we shall see both in "Gereint and Enid" and in

"Peredur," the Goddess is symbolized by both the white hart and the unicorn.

Throughout the course of our study of the relationship between Sovereignty and her champion, we note that the Goddess is not submissive, mild, and biddable; rather, she is a powerful force armed with subtle skills and deep wisdom. Here in "Owain" we find that the lady of the fountain is no exception to the rule. She opposes Owain until he is championed by Luned (pronounced Lin'net), who acts in this story as a form of the Black Maiden. Luned is a far more sympathetic character than her mistress, whom she in some senses represents. The struggle of the lion and the unicorn is perennial: The lion, Sovereignty's would-be champion, fights the Goddess's proven champion, the unicorn. As we shall see, this is a story in which a number of substitutions take place and chief among them is the exchange of one champion for another.

As we read "Owain," we are aware of certain lacunae in the text. These may be partially supplied from Chrétien's *Yvain*, which can be read for comparison's sake. Also hidden within the text are images of reflection mirroring the otherworldly continuum into which Owain falls. These reflections are apparent among the characters of the story, who continually mirror or double for one another.

There are overlaps between "Owain" and *Libeaus Desconus* (see chapter 3): Both heroes champion a lady at the behest of her handmaiden messenger, both overcome a serpent, and both rescue a lady from imprisonment or death. Furthermore, the maiden messengers in both stories are similarly named. We shall see further parallels between these stories and the folklore version of the tale of the Loathly Lady, in which she is enchanted into the form of a monster.

Most remarkable is the striking number of shared themes between "Owain" and the Gawain cycle of stories, in which host and oppressor are one and the same. Tying all these together is the motif of the damsel representing Sovereignty, who presents a talismanic gift to her chosen champion.

Synopsis of "The Lady of the Fountain"

(1) While Arthur holds court at Caerleon upon Usk one day, Owain ap Urien, Cynon ap Clydno, and Cai ap Cynyr are talking together as Gwenhwyfar sews by the window. There is no gatekeeper, although Glewlwyd Mighty Grasp acts as one. Arthur feels sleepy and begs his companions to tell stories while he sleeps. (2) Cynon tells a story against himself in which he had ridden seeking adventure. He came to a beautiful land wherein stood a shining fortress and there he was royally entertained. The company in that place directed his steps to an adventure, telling him to seek a certain mound (3) on which he would see a great black man having one eye in the center of his forehead and one foot. Cynon did as they told him. The black forest guardian demonstrated his sovereignty over the animals of the forest and directed Cynon to (4) a large tree beneath which was a fountain. On the stone next to it was a silver bowl; Cynon was to fill the bowl with water and throw the water on the stone. At the sound of thunder, a great shower would fall, stripping the tree of leaves. (5) Next, a flock of birds would alight and sing. Then a black rider would come and challenge him. All transpired as Cynon had been told: The black rider taxed him with causing the death of many beasts and men because of the shower that ensued from his action. They fought and Cynon was ignominiously overcome.

(6) After the story, Owain suggests that they ride and find the place again, but Cai casts aspersions upon him and Gwenhwyfar rebukes Cai. Just then Arthur awakes and while the company goes in to eat, Owain slips away. He discovers the place Cynon described in his story and all befalls him as it had Cynon—except that he overcomes the black rider, wounding him severely. Giving chase to the departing rider, Owain follows him to a castle. The portcullis is lowered so that Owain and the front half of his horse are within the castle while the back of the horse remains outside. (7) A girl arrives and offers her friendship to him. (8) She gives Owain a ring which, while it is concealed within his fist, will render him invisible. She then leads him to a chamber and waits on him. While in the chamber, they hear a cry followed by an outbreak of

---

lamentation. The girl tells Owain that the lord of the castle, whom Owain had fought, has died and is to be buried.[9] Owain watches from a window as the lord's widow follows her husband to the church. Although her appearance has been marred by mourning, Owain falls in love with her. The girl explains that her mistress is the countess of the fountain, and though she believes the lady must loathe Owain, she nevertheless agrees to court the countess on his behalf.

(10) The girl, Luned, pleads with the countess to accept a new husband. Luned reminds her that her lands could be held only by strength of arms; they must find a defender quickly to hold the fountain. Luned tells the countess she will go to Arthur's court and procure a warrior. The countess gives her reluctant permission. Pretending to begin her journey, Luned instead returns to her chamber and eventually returns to her mistress to announce the arrival of a Round Table knight. Luned has arrayed Owain (11) in yellow garments bearing the device of a golden lion, but the countess is not convinced by this ruse and calls together her retainers to decide what she should do: Either one of them should marry her or she should be married to a man from outside their realm. They decide on the latter course and, amid splendid preparations, (12) she is married to Owain. All the retainers of the countess swear him fealty.

Three years later Gwalchmai is walking with Arthur, who expresses great sorrow at Owain's absence. Taking a small company with him, Arthur sets out to find Owain. They follow the route of Cynon's story and (13) Cai throws water on the stone. Many of Arthur's servants are slain in the ensuing shower. A black rider appears, pitches his tent, and on the morrow he and Arthur's men joust. First Cai is overcome and then Gwalchmai fights the rider. The Black Knight recognizes Gwalchmai and identifies himself as Owain. Both men attempt to relinquish their arms into each other's custody, but neither will accept mastery of the joust. (14) Arthur then bids them give their swords to him. Owain leads them back to the castle, where for three years he has been preparing a feast in honor of Arthur's foreseen coming. Arthur sends messengers to beg the countess's leave for Owain to accompany Arthur back to his court, which she reluctantly grants.

While Owain is feasting with Arthur, a woman rides into the hall and pulls the ring from Owain's finger, charging him with treachery. (15) As she turns to go, Owain recognizes Luned and recovers memory of his life in the Land of the Fountain, which has faded from his mind. Grief-stricken, he sets out to wander the four corners of the earth, (16) growing unkempt and becoming accustomed to the company of animals. In his wild state he comes to the park of a second countess, where she finds him asleep in a weakened condition.

The countess gives orders that he be tended to. Her damsel anoints him and leaves a horse and clothing nearby, which Owain takes. She then greets him and tells him about the land he is in. Because the countess has been widowed, she has only one house remaining after the depredations of a neighboring earl. The damsel takes Owain back to the countess's house and heals him with her mistress's ointment, despite that lady's annoyance at her handmaiden having used so much.

After three months, Owain is well enough to overcome the neighboring earl and offers him as hostage to the countess in payment for having used up so much ointment. The earl returns the countess's lands and property, after which, although the countess bids him stay, Owain leaves to continue his wanderings.

(17) He encounters a lion trapped in the cleft of a rock by a serpent which leaps up at each of the lion's attempts to get away. Owain slays the serpent and finds himself followed by the lion as by a greyhound. The lion brings Owain a buck to eat and while they are eating it, Owain hears a cry. (18) It is the voice of Luned. She has been imprisoned in a stone chamber because of a quarrel she has had with two of her mistress's chamberlains concerning Owain, whom they had reviled in her hearing. She rebuked them and is awaiting Owain to defend her, but has had no one to search for him. Owain shares his food with her and then leaves after getting directions from her to the nearest castle, where he might find shelter.

(19) Owain is served well at the castle, but the company there is the saddest he has ever seen. The earl explains to Owain that the reason for their sadness is that his two sons have been seized by a marauder who will kill them before their father's eyes unless the earl renders up his only daughter to him. The giant marauder approaches the castle the next morning; Owain fights him and, with the lion's help, kills the giant. Restoring the earl's sons to their father, Owain rides off to rescue Luned. He arrives just in time to see two men seizing her to put her on a pyre. In order that the fight will be fair, Owain locks the lion in Luned's prison, but it escapes and kills both of Owain's assailants.

Luned and Owain then return to the Land of the Fountain, where he finds his countess and takes her to live with him at Arthur's court.

(20) Owain next goes to the court of the Black Oppressor, where twenty-four maidens are kept in their sadness. The oppressor has killed each of their men. Owain fights him, and the Black Oppressor begs for mercy, for it has been prophesied that Owain would overcome him. He offers to give up his evil ways, cease to be a robber, and turn his court into a hostel for both weak and strong. These terms Owain accepts, then takes the twenty-four maidens to Arthur's court, where he is welcomed. Afterwards, he returns to his ancestral lands with the three hundred swords of Cynferchin, his grandfather, and his flight of ravens, who are victorious wherever they go.

Commentary

(1) In many early Arthurian tales, Arthur's court is held not at Camelot but at Caerleon upon Usk, one of the great legionary cities, as we have already seen in "The Dream of Macsen Wledig," in which it is called by the Romans Castra Legionum. The insistence upon there being no gatekeeper for so great a court may seem strange. According to "Culhwch and Olwen," Glewlwyd Gafaelfawr is the gatekeeper only on the first of January; the rest of the year his post is filled by Huandaw, Gogigwr, Llaesgymyn, and Penpingyon. In "Culhwch and Olwen" it is obvious that Glewlwyd is an ancient figure whose exploits are shared

by Arthur. An ancient Welsh poem, "Pa Gur," preserves a dialogue between Arthur and Glewlwyd in which Arthur is obviously the man seeking entrance and Glewlwyd is the porter at the gate, possibly at the fortress of Wrnach the Giant. He is but one of several gatekeepers who appear in Owain.[87]

It is significant that Arthur sleeps during the relating of Cynon's tale. As we have already seen in "The Dream of Macsen Wledig" and "The Dream of Rhonabwy," in which part of the action occurs in a dream, Cynon's tale can be seen as a dream of Arthur's. Within this sleep many mysteries are revealed under the aegis of the Sleeping Lord,[84] just as in the myth of the Golden Age, in which the things Zeus premeditates Kronos dreams (see *Mabon*, chapter 3). Cai here fulfills his traditional role as Arthur's butler by going to fetch Cynon food and drink to sustain him during his telling.

(2) Cynon unfolds a tale of an otherworldly journey he has undertaken in the supreme hope that he will meet someone who can overcome him or whom he can best in order to prove himself invincible. At the shining fortress he is served by a man dressed in yellow, who is possibly a figure inherited from an Irish story (see the section The Hospitable Host, later in this chapter, for a discussion of this theme). Cynon inadvertently insults Gwenhwyfar in his story, saying that the least beautiful of the women attendant upon him at this fortress was more beautiful than Gwenhwyfar arrayed in her best, but the queen does not make any remark, nor do his listeners spring to her defense. This is explainable only if the women in question are faery women or fays and therefore not to be compared in the same breath to mortals.[58] The purposeful insulting of Gwenhwyfar, however, is a recurrent theme in the romances, as we shall see in chapters 6 and 7.

(3) The monstrous black guardian, or Wild Herdsman, whom Cynon encounters springs whole and entire from Celtic mythology. He is a *bachlach* carrying a club, a herder of animals, and, as we shall see, is cru-

cial to our understanding of this story. We are reminded of the figure of Cernunnos from the Gundestrup cauldron (see *Mabon,* chapter 8), except the Wild Herdsman here is a one-legged and one-eyed man. Certainly he seems reminiscent of Custennin, the father of Goreu in "Culhwch and Olwen," the mighty shepherd who never allows his flock to stray and whose breath could blast a tree. The Wild Herdsman is an interpreter and guardian, one of great perspicacity, who shows the way. He shares his role with Merlin in Celto-Arthurian mythology, where Merlin becomes a lord of the forest during his madness and seclusion.[52] (See the section The Hospitable Host later in this chapter.)

(4) The great tree near which the Wild Herdsman sits is the axial tree of tradition, the tree of knowledge, the *axis mundi* around which are grouped times, dimensions, and objects of power within Celtic tradition. Such trees appear within many mythologies. They connect the earthly world with both Underworld and Overworld and, in some cultures, have been physically represented as the shaman's ladder. The fountain under this axial tree is a direct descendant of the Celtic Fountain of Knowledge, whose waters enlighten the ignorance of the earth and fructify the gardens of the Otherworld. As we will see in the following section, Rex Nemorensis, Chrétien and others associated this fountain with the famous Fountain of Barenton in Brittany. We recall also that Rhiannon and Pryderi vanish in a thunderstorm and mist (see *Mabon,* chapter 4). The appearance of thunder and rain within the Otherworld represents a reversal of normality and an enchantment which is being worked out.

(5) The birds in the flock that alights on the tree are otherworldly, akin to both the birds of Rhiannon, which conduct souls to blissful existence in the paradisal realms of peace, and the birds encountered by both Bran mac Febal and Maelduin in their wondrous voyages,[146] which sing of the wonders of paradise. The Black Knight is nameless in "Owain," but Chrétien calls him Esclados. He is the champion of the

lady of the fountain, defending her lands against all comers. At his hands Cynon learns that, despite what he has thought, he is not, after all, the most puissant knight. It is interesting that the Black Knight taxes Cynon with the destruction of both men and beasts who have been caught in the hailstorm. As we shall see, the Wild Herdsman and the Yellow Man have much in common.

(6) Cai lives up to his reputation of being an unmannerly churl by insulting Owain's avowal to seek the place of Cynon's story. We note that Arthur does not awake until the story is complete. Owain's successful encounter with the Black Knight leaves him in a sad predicament, caught, with his horse, between two gates. It is possible that this incident at the gate is a medieval retelling of an Irish story in which Cú Roi mac Daire has a revolving fortress (see the section Rex Nemorensis, below). There are notable overlaps between "Owain" and the cycle of Irish stories that gave rise to the Green Knight's challenge in Arthurian legend, as we shall see.

(7) Owain is befriended by Luned. The role of Luned in "Owain" is hard to accept: She acts as messenger and confidante throughout and is self-effacing with regard to her personal love for Owain. We need to look again at the lady in *Libeaus Desconus,* Elen (see chapter 3), who comes to fetch a champion to free her mistress. Luned is a variant of the Welsh Eluned, a name very much like Elen. The similarity between both women is close enough to warrant further attention.

In later Arthurian literature Luned becomes Linnet. With her sister Lionors, or Lyones, she has more to do with the Orkney clan than with Owain—she, in fact, becomes the wife of Gaheris, while Lionors marries Gareth. Linnet rides to Camelot to fetch a knight to rescue her sister, who is besieged by the Red Knight of the Red Laundes, in much the same way as Elen comes to fetch Libeaus Desconus. Like Elen, Linnet is fobbed off to a young knight, Beaumains, which is Kay's cruel name for Gareth, who has come to court incognito. The overlaps are easy to find between the early story and the later one.[25, 92]

In Chrétien's stories, which predate the literary existence of Gawain's brothers, Gareth and Gaheris, it is Gawain who loves Lunet. Chrétien makes a play on Lunet's name and on Gawain's reputation as a knight whose strength waxes as the sun rises to midday by referring to them poetically as the moon and the sun.[7]

(8) The ring that Luned gives Owain is mentioned in a supplement to the Thirteen Treasures of Britain as a ring of invisibility. In this property it is similar in function to the thirteenth treasure, "the Mantle of Invisibility, which belongs to Arthur and which is also used by Caswallawn to usurp Bran's kingdom."[22] In Malory, Lyones gives Beaumains a ring which saves him from loss of blood.[25]

In the chamber with Luned, Owain hears three cries of lamentation, the great triple *ochone* (mourning cry) at the death of the champion and husband of the lady of the fountain.

(9) Significantly, Owain falls in love with the countess while she is wretched, grieving, and unkempt, being covered with self-inflicted wounds. In effect he has fallen in love with a Loathly Lady under whose veneer of unloveliness he yet discerns a beautiful woman. As we have seen from the tales concerning the hag aspect of Sovereignty, Owain's avowal of love immediately makes him worthy to replace the lady's husband.

(10) In Chrétien we learn that Lunet is known for her outspokenness[7]; she apparently is sent by Laudine, her mistress, on an errand to Arthur's court and is so rude in her behavior that no knight will deign to speak with her save Owain. This archetype, clearly related to the Black Maiden, became known as the Damoiselle Maldisante. This incident is absent from "Owain," but Luned is certainly still very forthright in her speech. We learn in her harangue of courtship on Owain's behalf that only a knight of Arthur's court can defend the fountain.

(11). Owain is armed by Luned in the fashion of a Celtic hero who is destined to win the arms of his mother or lady, who represents Sovereignty. He also gains a fresh livery: the golden lion. This device is foreign to Owain's native totem of the raven, and it would be interesting to know for certain whether Chrétien's Ivain, the knight of the lion, suggested it. In the context of our story it is a prophetic arming, for Owain later wins a lion as his companion.

(12) This is the only mention of canonical marriage in the whole of the *Mabinogion*. Even "Gereint and Enid" contains no mention of it—Gereint and Enid are laid in Arthur and Gwenhwyfar's chamber and there they sleep together—while in "Peredur," Peredur seems to form several casual liaisons of varying degrees of intimacy. Owain's marriage lasts three years without interruption.

(13) This incident, in which Cai purposely provokes the hero of our story and is then justly overcome in combat, appears in all three romances ("Owain," "Gereint and Enid," and "Peredur"). Similarly, in all three, Gwalchmai (Gawain) appears to make peace and tactfully to approach the hero. Gwalchmai's role seems to be that of intermediary between the harsh reality of Cai's bluster and the fay, often distracted air adopted by the hero acting under otherworldly influence. Significantly, Gwalchmai intervenes in order to help the hero express himself, whether the hero is Owain, Geraint, or Peredur. This usually occurs at a crucial point when the hero is defending Sovereignty in some manner, as Owain is here by acting as the countess's champion.

Here Owain has adopted a third set of colors; he has become the new Black Knight of the fountain. Perhaps because they start fighting at the stroke of noon (the time of Gwalchmai's greatest strength; it diminishes after noon), neither Gwalchmai nor Owain can beat the other.

Gwalchmai is described in Triad 75 as one of three men of the Island of Britain who were most courteous to guests and strangers.[59]

He is perhaps helped in this regard by his status as one of those Triad 91 names as the three fearless men of the Island of Britain.

(14) Owain virtually relinquishes his championship of the fountain to the hands of Arthur: "Give me your swords," says Arthur, "then neither of you will have overcome the other." There seems to be something of a lacuna in the text here, for the implication is that Owain is granted leave to remain with Arthur for three months, but stays for three years instead. In Chrétien, Laudine lets Owain go for a year and gives him a ring, which acts as a shield against wounds.[2] In both stories, Owain stays away longer than the time agreed—a slip in time is common to otherworldly locations.

There is here an echo of a theme common in medieval romances: the temporary absence of the hero from his faery mistress. This theme is central to many medieval stories and *lais,* including "Désiré"[134] and "Lanval,"[59] in which an earthly knight has an assignation with a faery woman at a spring. They cohabit for a while, but once away, the hero fails to return or vouchsafes the name of his mistress to others, a thing he has sworn never to do, for doing so also reveals her nature.

At this point in Chrétien's story, Gwalchmai launches into a long speech about the inadvisability of remaining so closely yoked to a woman to the detriment of manly deeds.[7] Of course, this theme accords closely with the role of Sovereignty, who has here become a faery woman. Medieval romancers failed to handle this theme according to its original lights and, in many tales, recast the hero as a henpecked man tied to a woman's apron strings, as in *Erec and Enid,* Chrétien's version of "Geraint and Enid." We will take this up again in the section Rex Nemorensis, below.

(15) It is clear that Owain's has been an otherworldly sojourn, for as soon as he returns to court, he forgets his adventure and that its outcome has resulted in his marriage! It is not until Luned strips the ring from his finger that Owain remembers all that has passed. It

would appear there is a gap in the text here, for the ring in question has not proved to be a ring of invisibility. It is likely that, as in Chrétien,[7] the countess has given her husband a ring on their parting to serve as a remembrance and magical communication between them, in much the same manner as the Beast gives Beauty a ring in the French faery story. But Owain wears the token unworthily, failing to honor the bestower of the ring until Luned takes it from his hand. Like Arthur's ring in "The Dream of Rhonabwy," Owain's is a ring of remembrance. However, the ring of invisibility, like the otherworldly silver branch given to Bran mac Febal,[46] may function as a token of Sovereignty's faith in her champion: While he possesses it, he is in communion with her.

(16) With full memory restored to him, Owain suffers the pangs of remorse and self-reproach. The madness into which he now falls is a classical reaction to shock in Celto-Arthurian legend. Owain, like Lancelot and Merlin, who also go insane temporarily, is stripped of every normal faculty, resigning his position as knight and champion of the fountain in order to live among wild beasts.[107, 149] This period of insanity has its healing properties, however. The curative effect of living close to nature is adopted by Celto-Arthurian madmen as a form of therapy in which they regard the wonders of creation and understand their own relationship with both plant and animal life. Owain becomes, in effect, a wild man, familiar to the medieval mind as a woodwose, a hairy, animal-like mythical being thought to haunt the great forests which still covered Europe at that time.

The subsequent incident in which Owain is discovered by a countess and her damsel is likely to confuse the reader. Does the storyteller, who leaves both ladies unnamed, intend us to understand that the woman who finds Owain is the same as the lady of the fountain and that her damsel is Luned? If we refer to Chrétien, it would appear not, for the lady who finds him is called the Lady of Noroison.[7] Whatever the common source for both "Owain" and *Yvain*, there is a point of confusion here.

Owain receives exactly the same treatment as in the former episode when he arrives at the countess's castle: He is tended by the maiden, given arms, and made well without the countess's knowledge. The incident of the healing ointment is interesting. In Chrétien, the Lady of Noroison gets her lotion from Morgan le Fay, who, as we will see, is perhaps also responsible for healing Gereint in a later story. The duplication of incidents attests to a lost original story in which Owain's finding of the fountain and his championship of the lady are paralleled by his restoration to sanity and championship of Sovereignty in a more direct sense. At this remove it is impossible to piece together the evidence. Perhaps both countesses and their maidens are intended to be the same women in alternate forms. The important point is that the women effect Owain's partial restoration to sanity.

(17) Having accepted the second countess's championship and then relinquished her hand in marriage, Owain rides on to champion a lion. Scholars have written endless commentaries on how Owain's lion is derived from all kinds of medieval and classical originals, including Androcles' lion or St. Jerome's.[46, 127] Certainly the lion enjoyed the status of king of the beasts from medieval times onwards, and the epithet *lion* has been applied to many kings and heroes, both historically and in literature. But perhaps we can approach the appearance of the lion from another viewpoint.

Owain, at this point, is hardly reconciled to human company. He has only recently emerged from an animal-like state and is in the process of winning back self-respect and regaining the high status he once enjoyed through force of arms. Luned once armed him with the heraldic device of the lion, which he forsook to wear the black livery of the lady of the fountain. Within this story an extraordinary transformation is under way: Owain, having once succeeded to the place of the Black Knight, now succeeds to the role of the Wild Herdsman, the master of beasts. Only Owain fulfills the roles of both knight of the fountain and Wild Herdsman, lifting them out of their former alignment and ennobling them with all his personal qualities. In so doing, Owain has assimilated the roles of his challengers and, by means of his madness, now emerges as a new man.

(18) The imprisonment of Luned and her fortuitous discovery by Owain are very sketchily dealt with in our story. In Chrétien, Yvain inadvertently hears of Lunet's love for him from her own lips. But, as both stories tell, despite Lunet/Luned's impending execution, Yvain/Owain rides off to find shelter for the night. It is possible that in the proto-story Owain was totally disenchanted from his madness by the sound of Luned's voice, for so is Lanzelet released from his enchantment in Ulrich von Zatzikhoven's story.[42]

(19) The next incident is drawn from a common Celtic theme, the Ridere gan Gaire (knight without laughter), in which the impending demise or accomplished death of a knight's offspring causes him such sorrow that he is unable to make merry.[68] A similar incident occurs in "Peredur" (see chapter 7). Luned's plight is thus considerably heightened during this intervening episode. In Chrétien, Yvain similarly rescues the knight's children, who are discovered to be Gawain's nephews and niece. Chrétien also tells a long story about a pair of sisters, the elder of whom succeeds to their father's estates, disinheriting her younger sister, who then goes in search of a champion. This incident is paralleled by the story of the two sisters Lyones and Linnet in Malory.[25] Lyones and Linnet seem to be later identities for Laudine and Lunet in Chrétien and for the lady of the fountain and Luned in "Owain."

(20) The last episode of our story is paralleled in Chrétien by Yvain's experiences at the Castle of Evil Adventure, where the king of the Isle des Puceles (Castle of Maidens), in order to save his own life, has promised a tribute of maidens every year to a pair of diabolic brothers. Until Yvain rescues them, these maidens are retained at the Castle of Evil

Adventure and there are made to embroider in a kind of otherworldly sweatshop for the devils' profit. This episode is reminiscent of *Libeaus Desconus,* in which Mabon and Yrain keep the Lady of Sinadoun captive. In Chrétien's *Perceval* we find a similar Castle of Maidens, which Gawain visits (see chapter 7).

In our story Owain defeats the Black Oppressor, whose identity, as we shall see, is not hard to discover. If we turn back to the beginning of Owain and read about the shining fortress where the Yellow Man plays the hospitable host and where embroidering maidens surround the hero, we will experience a sense of déjà vu, for the Black Oppressor is none other than the Yellow Man in another guise. This duplication of characters is all part of the mirror image set up between the earthly realms and the Otherworld, which is perhaps most clearly seen in "Peredur."

Rex Nemorensis

It has been pointed out by numerous scholars that "Owain" bears traces of the famous Roman myth of Rex Nemorensis, the king of the sacred grove. The sanctuary of Arician Diana, near Lake Nemi, is protected by a priest who remains in office only as long as he can fend off contenders. In the sanctuary grows a tree whose branches may never be broken save by a slave who, in order to become a worthy contender for the office of Diana's priest, must tear off a bough.[73] While we might conveniently call this myth by its Roman title, we must remember that this story is not confined to one culture alone, but does indeed occur frequently within Celtic and Arthurian sources. That there may have been a marriage made between Latin and Celtic myths during medieval times is very probable. The cult of Diana, the huntress and protectress of women, spread speedily throughout Europe with the expansion of the Roman Empire. Native cults of goddesses of the sacred grove were long established in all lands of Celtic occupancy. The most famous sacred grove, or wood, complete with its own spring, was that of the Brocéliande in Brittany, where the Fountain of Barenton was celebrated in local tradition and medieval romance. Here Morgan, Nimue, Niniane, and Diana had their meeting in one archetype.[134]

Chrétien, if he was indeed working from a British original, made his spring conform to the verbatim reports of Barenton, even making his whole story of Yvain cross the Channel at one point, without explanation, in order to encompass this phenomenon. The fountain or spring was well known to medieval writers such as Alexander Neckam, the twelfth-century scholar, who wrote: "It is said that there is a fountain such that if water is drawn from it and thrown upon a stone which is near that fountain, a storm arises from the stone . . . much rain suddenly falls, with hail and vehement wind."[96]

The Norman chronicler Wace actually visited the spring in order to see faeries and, while ruefully disappointed in his wish, reported: "Thither hunters are used to repair in sultry weather; and drawing up some water with their horns, they sprinkle the stone for the purpose of having rain."[96]

That the fountain in "Owain" or the Fountain of Barenton has little to do with the historical cult of Arician Diana is obvious, for our spring and stone generate rain, whereas Diana was worshiped on August 13 in order to invoke her help to avert storms injurious to the harvest.[73] The similarities are gratuitous, though they were certainly enhanced by classically minded medieval writers. But what of the lady of the fountain herself?

What becomes apparent from our reading of the story is that the countess and Luned correspond to two faces of Sovereignty: the mistress of the Otherworld, or inner Sovereignty, and her representative messenger, or outer Sovereignty. We will see that this dual identity occurs within the Grail stories as well: The Grail messenger corresponds to the dark face of Sovereignty, the wasted land; the Grail bearer corresponds to the beautiful face of Sovereignty, the fertile land. The countess is not able to leave her land except through the person of Luned, her messenger. But her land cannot be governed except by a worthy champion, whom she must find in the earthly realm and bring to the Otherworld. This situation is the theme of countless Celtic and medieval tales wherein the otherworldly woman must draw to her realm an earthly man to play the part of her champion or consort.

We have already seen how, in the Irish voyage tradition, Bran mac Febal is coaxed to visit the Land of Women by the maiden messenger of the otherworldly queen, who bears a branch from the paradisal tree of bliss. Her form and her song are sufficient to incite Bran to set sail. When he arrives, the queen begs him to stay with her, but Bran's men are homesick. She tries to bind him to her by magical threads, but he departs, only to find that time, which in the Land of Women passes pleasantly and easefully, has sped past and all his generation in Ireland is long dead.[146]

From the tradition exemplified above arise the many tales of men who wander into the land of Faery, become the consort of the queen, and there remain with her. Thomas the Rhymer is one such, but his service is concluded after seven years, during which time he has gained otherworldly knowledge.[64] The length of time the hero spends with inner Sovereignty varies greatly, and although he sometimes becomes her champion, unable to leave her until he is bested by another man who becomes her consort, this is not always the case.

The question arises—an important one, for it is relevant to "Owain," "Gereint and Enid," and "Peredur": Why does the Goddess of Sovereignty retain certain men in her domain? Owain becomes the countess's champion; Gereint fights such a champion in the enchanted games; and Peredur is retained in the service of many mistresses. What strange pattern is being enacted in this retention, and what is its purpose?

The classical pattern of Diana and the priests of Nemi is only a partial explanation, and it cannot be totally accommodated within the Celto-Arthurian mode. We are left with the evidence of parallel texts. On the face of it there seem to arise four kinds of retention:

1. The fostering in Faery of such characters as Lancelot and Mabon as children. Both babies are removed from earthly danger and are raised in the Otherworld.

2. The teaching of the hero by otherworldly women or goddesses, as occurs in the stories of Gwion/Taliesin and Peredur.

3. The retention of a champion who serves a term but is replaced by another, as with Mabonograin (in Chrétien's *Erec and Enid*), Lancelot, and Owain.

4. The retention of an earthly knight or king as the consort of an otherworldly queen, as is the case with Arthur and Bran mac Febal. This consort does not return from Faery, at least not within the same life cycle.

It will be seen that this pattern corresponds, with variations, to the succession of the Pendragons discussed in *Mabon*. The roles that Sovereignty takes in each of the four imprisonments above are as follows.

1. Mother: The Lady of the Lake and Modron function as mothers to Lancelot and Mabon, respectively.

2. Teacher: The Dark Woman of Knowledge appears in her role as teacher to Gwion/Taliesin and Peredur as Ceridwen and the hag of Gloucester, respectively.

3. Consort: Sovereignty appears in her beautiful aspect of otherworldly queen and consort to Mabonograin, Bran, Lancelot, and Arthur and to Owain in the shapes of the orchard woman and Morgan. Though Morgan is not successful in retaining Lancelot as her consort, she does succeed in retaining other non-Arthurian heroes of medieval story, including Ogier, Renoart, and Alisander l'Orphelin.[79]

Each of these partnerships between Sovereignty and the hero demands an exchange of power by which both earthly and otherworldly realms are energized. The mother nourishes her fosterling or her own child in order that he may become the champion of her rights, just as the Dark Woman of Knowledge or the Loathly Lady teaches her secrets to her initiates so that her pupils may be empowered to act on her behalf,

Knights and heroes who experience this kind of fostering generally prove worthy to be Sovereignty's champion or consort. Those who enter Sovereignty's service are rarely released from it. Theirs is a bargain which goes beyond personal concerns or earthly lifetimes. Her champions may be temporarily released in order to visit the earth once more, as Owain is, or they may be allowed to live their whole lives in the earthly realm as kings in the service of the land itself, as Arthur does, only to be drawn back into the paradisal realms once again at the end of their reign.

The seemingly malicious enmity with which Morgan pursues her half brother, Arthur, in the later Arthurian stories can be properly understood in this light, as can the mysterious imprisonment of Merlin by Nimue/Viviane. The partnership that both Arthur and Merlin enjoy with the otherworldly powers is not broken by death. Their whole lives are shot through with miraculous happenings, difficult tests, the averting of dangers, and the bestowal of blessings. Neither Arthur nor Merlin is born or dies in the usual way: Their conceptions are planned by the otherworldly powers; their deaths are really passings back into the paradisal realms. Both men follow the cycles discussed in *Mabon:* Arthur follows the Succession of the Pendragons, while Merlin follows the Poet's Wheel (*Mabon,* chapter 9).

The pattern is less easy to discern in Owain's career from the evidence of this story alone, but it will be seen that he fits into the Succession of the Pendragons (see figure 8 below).

Owain's Role	Sovereignty's Appearances	Sovereignty's Role
as Mabon	Modron/Morgan	mother
Pendragon/champion worthy to be king	lady of the fountain	consort
Pen Annwfn/withdrawn Pendragon	the orchard woman in "Gereint and Enid"	otherworldly queen

Figure 8. Owain and the succession of the Pendragons

In his last role, Owain becomes the master of the enchanted games in "Gereint and Enid" (see chapter 6), while his role as champion knight is told in "Owain." We deduce his role as Mabon from the sixteenth-century oral story of Urien at the Ford of Llanferres, which speaks of his conception by Modron as Morgan. We note, too, that Owain follows in his father's footsteps as guardian of the otherworldly borders of the Goddess's realm, for Urien becomes a guardian of a ford, the knight of the Black Pine, in the *Didot Perceval*, while Owain likewise guards the fountain. Both men are defenders of the wells, bound in the service of the primal Goddess of Sovereignty, who can change from woman to raven, from beautiful maiden into ravaged hag, in a twinkling.

The man who has once dreamed of her or received her token is never again free to be his own man, living an ordinary existence. He is in service both in and out of time. He is bound to come at the call of his otherworldly mistress, whatever shape she may assume. It is in such faith that Owain appears as Kemp Owyne in a late ballad.

In this remarkable song, Owyne's lady (or sister, in some versions), Isabel, is transformed into a worm or serpent by her stepmother and is doomed to remain thus until Owyne returns from overseas and gives her three kisses. He comes and she bids him kiss her, but he is warned to beware touching her, either tail or fin. She gives him three tokens in exchange for three kisses: a belt, a ring, and a sword that will prevent his blood from being spilled.

> *He stepped in, gave her a kiss,*
> *The royal brand he brought him wi';*
> *Her breath was sweet, her hair grew short,*
> *And twisted nane about the tree,*
> *And smilingly she came about,*
> *As fair a woman as fair could be.*[64]

We immediately notice the likeness of this story to the original transformation of Sovereignty by means of a kiss and pledge. As in *Libeaus Desconus*, Owyne is able to free his mistress from enchantment only by means of the fier baiser. Her gift of talismanic tokens brings us immediately back to "Owain," in which Luned gives Owain a ring when he is in danger. We remember also that Owain defeats a serpent which is attacking the chained lion, and that immediately after that incident, he hears Luned's voice asking for rescue. Does "Kemp Owyne"preserve a lost part of the original story in which Sovereignty's role was more clearly defined? Around the area of Bamborough (where the ballad and its legend were supposed to have been enacted), schoolgirls used to call boys to champion them against bullies—the Childe o' Wane—remembering Owain and his role. That was in the nineteenth century, a not inconceivable time for Sovereignty's champion to be remembered, if the traditions are as persistent as we have seen them to be.

This ballad marks the strange manner in which both Owain and Gawain are connected, for hidden within "Owain" is a series of themes and motifs which draw upon the long-standing cycle of Gawain stories and an even more ancient tradition of pre-Celtic origin.

The Hospitable Host

During the course of both *Mabon and the Guardains of Celtic Britain* and *King Arthur and the Soveriegnty of the Land,* we have had cause to mention the English medieval romance of "Sir Gawain and the Green Knight" more than once. It certainly holds more than a few clues to help us unravel the mystery at the heart of "Owain." Briefly, the story goes as follows.

While Arthur is holding court at Christmastime, a gigantic green knight enters the hall and challenges the court to a Christmas game: He who accepts his challenge is to behead the Green Knight, providing that in a twelvemonth and a day hence the Green Knight might return the blow. Arthur first offers himself in the dumbstruck silence of his court, but then Gawain comes forward and agrees to the challenge. No sooner has he beheaded the Green Knight than the knight stands, gathers up his head, and bids Gawain meet him at the Green Chapel in a year and a day.

Gawain starts out in search of the place late in the year and arrives at a castle on Christmas Eve, where the lord, Sir Bertilak, and his lady make him welcome. In attendance on the lady and held in great honor is an aged crone, her ugliness richly adorned with fine clothes and jewels. Gawain agrees to stay until New Year's Eve, after which his host will lead him to the nearby Green Chapel. In the interim, he and Bertilak make an arrangement: For three days Gawain will rest at home with Bertilak's beautiful wife while Bertilak goes hunting, and each evening, each man will exchange what he has won during the day.

Lady Bertilak visits Gawain's bedchamber three times while her husband is hunting. The two exchange courtesies, pretending that Gawain is a prisoner and she his captor. Gawain offers her his knightly service and assures her that she is his sovereign lady. She kisses him on each occasion, which kiss Gawain dutifully gives to Sir Bertilak on his return in exchange for the game his host has won in his hunting. As for Sir Bertilak's end of the bargain, from each beast slaughtered he offers Gawain the raven's fee—the piece of gristle adhering to the breastbone, which huntsmen threw to the carrion. On the third day the lady offers Gawain a ring, which he refuses, but she persuades him to accept her girdle made of green silk, which protects its wearer from death. Although Gawain renders Bertilak that day's kiss, he hides the gift of the green girdle.

On the day appointed for his meeting with the Green Knight, Gawain is directed by Bertilak to the Green Chapel. Beside a roaring stream he sees a mound with an entrance at one end and a hole in either side and this he takes to be the place. The Green Knight emerges from the chapel and Gawain bends to receive the blow. After making two feints with his ax and nicking Gawain's neck with the third stroke, the Green Knight reveals himself as Sir Bertilak. Gawain's whole visit had been a test of fidelity, and the third "blow" was for concealing the green girdle. Bertilak likewise reveals that the old crone's identity is Morgan the goddess, and that her purpose in sending Bertilak to the court of Arthur as the Green Knight was to drive the knights mad and

to terrify Guinevere to death. He commends Gawain as the most courageous and truest of knights and invites him to return to his castle.
Gawain refuses and returns to Camelot, where he tells the shameful
account of his doings to much laughter. He vows henceforth to wear
the girdle to remind him of this event and keep himself humble.
Arthur announces that all knights of the Round Table should likewise
wear a green baldric as a special honor.[31]

There are, of course, many similarities between the two stories: The
point of the challenge is that only the bravest and most worthy knight
can be successful. The Green Knight is here the messenger and agent of
Morgan. The two women, Lady Bertilak and Morgan, represent the two
aspects of Sovereignty. Lady Bertilak behaves in an intimate fashion
with Gawain much as Luned does in her attendance upon Owain.
Gawain also accepts a talismanic token, though here he refuses the
ring. The Green Knight's appearance at the Green Chapel is over-
whelmingly reminiscent of the Wild Herdsman at the mound.

Interestingly, there are two champions present in the story of
Gawain and the Green Knight, for Bertilak is working on behalf of
Morgan. The text tells us he is an elderly man, implying that he is a
champion of long standing in Morgan's service. This is further hinted
at in Bertilak's gift of the raven's fee when he returns from hunting—
we have already seen in the previous chapter that Morgan/Modron's
totemic beast is the raven and that this bird is a frequent symbol for
the Dark Woman of Knowledge. Gawain, although he makes a courtly
game of it, champions Lady Bertilak, whom we may see as an aspect of
the Goddess of Sovereignty in her beautiful form.

Despite the medieval and Christian overlay of the story, "Sir
Gawain and the Green Knight" reveals hidden depths. The Sovereignty
motif, which follows Gawain's whole career, is somewhat constrained
here by the format of enchantment and courtly honor, but it is clear
enough: Instead of one figure assuming two different guises, as in the
case of Bertilak, Sovereignty's former champion, we have Lady Bertilak
and Morgan appearing together as polarized aspects of Sovereignty.

What to Gawain is a shameful incident in his life (paralleling the shame of the assertive Cynon in "Owain") is made into a great honor of chivalry by Arthur, who turns the green girdle into something approaching the Order of the Garter. This last incident brings us squarely back into alignment with the original Sovereignty theme: Only worthy champions can serve her or are fit to mate with her. As king, Arthur himself has already wed Sovereignty in both her mystical incarnation as the land and her earthly guise as Guinevere, who acts as Sovereignty's representative (which would partially explain why Morgan, as the inner Sovereignty, is often cast as an antagonist to Guinevere). The Round Table knights, by extension of Arthur's mystical marriage, are all entitled to wear Sovereignty's green girdle as a badge of their king's allegiance and honor.

Gawain's own special duty in the service of the Goddess is dealt with more fully by John Matthews in his *Sir Gawain: Knight of the Goddess*,[175] but the poet of "Sir Gawain and the Green Knight" has this to say about Gawain's future armorial bearing—the pentacle or endless knot, which is the device he wears after the game of the Green Knight:

> *First he was found faultless in his five wits,*
> *Then the fellow failed not in his five fingers.*
> *All his faith on earth was in the five wounds*
> *Of Christ on the cross, as the creed doth tell.*
> *Where'er this Man in melee was placed*
> *His thoughts were upon them above other things;*
> *So that all his force he found in the five joys*
> *That the Fair Queen of Heaven had felt in her child.*
> *For this cause had the Knight in comely fashion*
> *On the inside of his shield her image depicted,*
> *That when he viewed it his valour never failed.*[31]

And after the game:

> *On his shining shield shaped was that knot,*
> *All with red gold upon red gules*
> *Called the pure pentangle among the people of*
>   *lore.*[31]

It will be seen that Gawain does not alter his allegiance in any way. He serves the Blessed Virgin and, like Arthur in the earliest texts, carries her image on his shield, which gives him courage. He merely exchanges the Christian for the pagan image of the fivefold pentacle, which is here the badge of Sovereignty herself.

Although certain passages of "Owain" are doubtless lost, a very clear pattern emerges from the remaining text. There are distinct similarities between "Owain" and an Irish story from the Ulster cycle, "Bricriu's Feast,"[179] the lineal forerunner of "Sir Gawain and the Green Knight." (See figure 9, on page 138, for the similarities among all three stories.)

In "Bricriu's Feast," the heroes of Ulster are set against each other to contend for the sovereignty of the hero's portion, a cut of meat awarded only to the best warrior. Bricriu incites their jealousy and contention, being a satirist and a twisted man, and is justly avoided by most of Ulster society. So troublesome and uncontrollable do the heroes Conall, Laegaire, and Cú Chulainn become that Conchobar sends them to his neighbors, Medbh and Ailill, to decide between them. Although the heroes are each awarded a beautifully ornamented cup, none is satisfied and their king sends them on to meet Buide mac mBan (Yellow, son of Fair), who also greets them hospitably but sends them on to Uath mac Imomain (Terror, son of Great Fear), a terrible giant. Again, none is satisfied with the verdict, and they go on to Cú Roi mac Daire, whose wife, Blanaid, warmly welcomes them all.

Cú Roi's *rath,* or fortress, is magically protected: It revolves like a millstone so that each night the entrance cannot be found. Each hero protects the rath from a giant who comes every night to attack it. Cú

Chulainn bests the giant and makes him promise Cú Chulainn the victory, which is agreed. However, there is still dissension among the heroes when they return to Conchobar. As they argue, a great *bachlach* (club-carrying herdsman) comes into the hall and challenges the warriors to a beheading game. One warrior accepts the challenge but is dashed to discover that the bachlach's head returns to his shoulders and that he will come the next night to claim the return blow. In turn, the bachlach offers the challenge to Conall and Laegaire, who fail to meet their return appointments. Only Cú Chulainn, in the full sight of his people and king, bends his head for the return stroke. The bachlach proclaims Cú Chulainn the champion worthy to have sovereignty over all other warriors. Then the bachlach vanishes—he is Cú Roi mac Daire, who, in the herdsman's guise, had come to fulfill the promise he had given to Cú Chulainn.[8]

Again we see the immediate similarities that link "Bricriu's Feast" with "Sir Gawain and the Green Knight," but more interesting are the parallels between "Bricriu's Feast" and "Owain." The part of Bricriu in "Owain" is played by Cai, who similarly tries to cause dissension among knights. The figure of Sovereignty in "Bricriu's Feast" is present both in Medbh, the queen of Connacht, and in Blanaid, Cú Roi's wife, who, as we saw in *Mabon* (chapter 3), rejects Cú Roi in favor of Cú Chulainn in a later story (see chapter 9 in this text).

The Irish heroes are hospitably entertained by a Yellow Man, just as Owain and Cynon are when they enter the otherworldly realms for the first time, and, like the Ulster heroes, encounter a terrible figure immediately afterwards. In the Irish tale, terrible giants are duplicated at every angle of the story, but are similarly described as the bachlach, whom they all mirror. While Cú Roi's wife entertains the Ulstermen, Cú Roi himself returns as the giant threatening the rath, taking the role of both host and aggressor, like Bertilak. In fact, Rachel Bromwich has noted that Bertilak is derived from the Irish *bachlach*.[38] The turning rath with the gate that can never be found after sunset is possibly the origin of the portcullis detail in "Owain." The beheading game, which occurs in the Green Chapel in "Sir Gawain and the Green Knight" and in "Owain" is restricted to a combat at the fountain, happens in "Bricriu's Feast" in full view of the court, no member of which can dispute the outcome that Cú Chulainn alone has the sovereignty of warrior-kind.

This Irish text further explicates the mysterious appearance of Glewlwyd at the beginning of "Owain," who seems to be present in such a gratuitous way. When the bachlach comes into the hall he utters these words: "Neither in Erin nor in Alba nor in Europe nor in Africa nor in Asia, including Greece, Scythia, the Isles of Gades, the Pillars of Hercules, and Bregon's Tower, have I accomplished the quest on which I have come."[8]

These words are familiar to us from "Culhwch and Olwen," in which Glewlwyd asks Arthur's permission for Culhwch to enter the hall:

> I have been also in Europe, and in Africa, and in the islands of Corsica, and in Caer Brythwch, and Brythach, and Verthach; and I was present when formerly thou didst conquer Greece in the East. And I have been in Caer Oeth and Anoeth, and Caer Nefenhyr; nine supreme sovereigns, handsome men, saw we there, but never did I behold a man of equal dignity with him who is now at the door of the portal.[23]

Another lost piece of the riddle of the *Mabinogion* falls into place as we compare the words of these two men, for as Cú Roi defends Conchobar's kingship by testing the sovereignty of his warriors, so Glewlwyd defends Arthur's kingship from the incursion of unworthy men into his hall. Both Cú Roi and Glewlwyd are gatekeepers of an ancient kind and have a direct bearing on the role of Owain as champion of the fountain.

It will be seen that Owain passes through a number of encounters and assimilations of three roles: Champion, Host, and Wild Man. He first meets the Yellow Man, who is the hospitable host welcoming him to the borders of the otherworldly realms of adventure; and next the

	"Owain"	"Bricriu's Feast"	"Sir Gawain and the Green Knight"
Adventure's Purpose	a quest only the best knight can fulfill	ascendancy of the best knight	bravest knight must defend Arthur's life and rule
Sovereignty's Game	enchanted games (in "Gereint and Enid")	beheading game	beheading game
Hospitable Host	the Yellow Man	Cú Roi and Buide mac mBan	Sir Bertilak
Talismanic Token	ring of invisibility or ring which guards wearer from bloodshed	cups given to each hero	green girdle which guards wearer against death
Guardian of Sovereignty's Realms	Wild Herdsman	Bachlach and Uath	Green Knight
Goddess of Sovereignty	lady of the fountain	Medbh	Morgan
Her Messenger or Representative	Luned	Blanaid	Lady Bertilak

Figure 9. The games of Sovereignty

Wild Herdsman, who shows him the way to the combat of the fountain; and finally, at the fountain, he meets the Black Knight, the current champion of the countess. Thereafter, Owain succeeds to each of these three roles. He himself becomes a hospitable host to Arthur and his men, even acknowledging that he has been preparing a feast for this occasion for three years. He goes mad on leaving the realms of the countess, befriending the wild beasts and growing hair all over his body to match their condition. Like the Wild Herdsman, he discovers an ability to master animals, especially the lion, traditionally believed to be the king of the beasts. He takes over the role of the Black Knight as defender of the fountain and becomes the husband of the countess. But before the story ends, he is instrumental in establishing the model of the Black Oppressor as a hospitable host who will aid wayfarers, rather than attack them.

There is a pleasing circularity and reflection of images throughout "Owain." Although the aspect of the beheading game is absent from the tale, the enchanted games of "Gereint and Enid" are a reflection of this theme, for, as we will see, the champion of the orchard beheads his opponents. And it is consistent that Owain, like Bertilak in "Sir Gawain and the Green Knight," should be portrayed as the reluctant and aging games master in that story.

Just when the Black Oppressor becomes the hospitable host, an exchange takes place between Owain and the Black Knight. Is it possible that the Yellow Man of Owain's first encounter is, like Sir Bertilak, a host who is also an aggressor? From the evidence of our parallel stories, it seems likely.

We perceive yet another pattern arising from this story which provides a clue to the Sovereignty tradition. Just as Sovereignty assumes two forms, so does her champion. He is both hospitable host and champion, presenting both an ordinary countenance and a darker, threatening face when he is keeper of the games by which Sovereignty tests those who seek her favor. Owain is not exempt from a threefold cycle of transformations, for, though he tries to resume his former life at Arthur's court, he plunges into madness rather than maintain his guise as the Black Knight, who must attack and kill all comers to the fountain or be killed himself. By a circuitous route he is able to overcome his destiny for a short while, but in the end he must appoint a proxy champion. Owain avoids his destiny by handing over the sovereignty of the fountain to Arthur, supreme overlord and king, for Arthur is also Sovereignty's man. But, as we shall see in the next chapter, Owain returns to his post as king of the enchanted games—no longer fighting himself, but still operative through his proxy champion. This is a pattern repeated throughout the Arthurian legends by Arthur himself, who ceases to ride out or hazard his own person in single combat, appointing instead several knights (usually his nephews) to act on his behalf.

Beneath the many layers of this tradition is an otherworldly polarity of roles: The Wild Herdsman, or bachlach, and the Dark Woman of Knowledge in her many guises rule in the Otherworld as king and queen of the realms of knowledge. In *Mabon* (chapter 8) we have already spoken of their roles. Their persistence—in various guises—throughout the *Mabinogion* is sufficient to point to an earlier level of tradition. They are the same couple who left the deep lake in Ireland, bearing with them the Cauldron of Rebirth. They are the primal parents of Britain's native mystery tradition, the inner guardians of knowledge and wisdom (see this text, chapter 8). Within "Owain" we see them still in their developed guises as the Lady Sovereignty and her consort who takes on many disguises in her service. Both are shapeshifters and can appear in bright or dark forms, according to need. It is they who are the Lion and the Unicorn of our inner vision, guardians of the land and its sovereignty for all time.

6

Gereint and Enid

Morgan:	Daughter, dear daughter oh what are you looking for?
Gwenhwyvar:	An apple tree in an orchard oh that is what I am looking for.
Morgan:	What will you do when you find it, dear daughter?
Gwenhwyvar:	I will call out the white stag that runs wild beneath the branches.

JOHN ARDEN AND MARGERETTA D'ARCY,
THE ISLAND OF THE MIGHTY

The Rites of Summer

The closest resemblance between Welsh and French traditions can be found in the *Mabinogion*'s "Gereint and Enid" and Chrétien's *Erec and Enid*, which is often called the first Arthurian romance because it was the first work from Chrétien's pen—though he cannot be credited with being the story's "onlie true begetter."

141

Despite the sophisticated courtliness of the story, "Gereint and Enid" reveals a number of more archaic aspects. We discover, for example, that the love of Gereint and Enid is set within a wider context of the games of Sovereignty, wherein the hunt of the white hart, the sparrowhawk contest, and the enchanted games are separate tests at which the hero must succeed. Lying somewhere beneath the surface of the early part of the story are traces of the abduction of Gwenhwyfar—a variant of a once popular theme for spring and summer revels. Gwenhwyfar's position as the Flower Bride or Spring Maiden is consistent throughout Arthurian tradition and is often hinted at, as here.

Without an understanding of the mythic archetypes and patterns underlying "Gereint and Enid" (see figure 10) it is impossible to form a fair judgment of the story. Indeed, without them, Gereint himself is merely a bully on the make and Enid is but a wilting violet. Certainly Gereint undergoes radical changes in attitude throughout the story, especially with regard to Enid, whom he eventually comes to value in a more mature light, but we cannot read this story as social realism, employing modern psychological insight, for such a reading is not true to either its context or the storyteller's intention.

Enid goes from rags to riches in quick succession, but her transformation has less to do with her marketable value as a wife than with her role within the story as Sovereignty's representative. Although Chrétien rationalized the original story to eradicate its coarser elements, it is obvious that the adventures of Gereint, or Erec, take place against an otherworldly backdrop where faery women, dwarfs, and black knights exert their influence on the world of humankind.

"Gereint and Enid" is undoubtedly the most transparent of the three romances because Chrétien's *Erec and Enid* is virtually a counterpart to the Welsh text—what is missing in one is supplied in the other. Chrétien's boast that *Erec and Enid*—the tale that most professional storytellers fragment and corrupt—shall be remembered as long as Christendom endures may well be warranted. It gives us pieces of the

	Innerworld Roles and Designations	Represented by
Mythic Level	supreme champion and Sovereignty	Mabonograin and orchard woman
Archetypal Level	Summer King and Summer Queen	Arthur and Gwenhwyfar
Mundane Level	untried champion and Spring Maiden	Gereint and Enid

Figure 10. The mythic structure of "Gereint and Enid"

pattern surrounding Sovereignty's empowerment of men and women more clearly than many texts within the *Mabinogion*.

It is perhaps the most human story, because it deals, on all levels, with the mutual love and trust that should exist between partners, whether those partners are man and woman, king and queen, or the king and his land. The prime symbol of this love is the white hart, which appears at the beginning of the story and which acts as the Goddess's messenger, summoning Arthur and his men to the chase. Its appearance in both Irish and Breton texts helps us locate mythic details which are common to *Erec and Enid* and "Gereint and Enid."

The appearance of the otherworldly orchard at the end of the story gives us a rare view of Sovereignty surrounded by her regalia, holding court, as it were, and sitting in judgment on her champions. The orchard woman appears in many texts; she will be further discussed in chapter 9 along with the mysterious incident of the enchanted game, which Chrétien terms the Joy of the Court. Owain appears again—a much more mature figure than in "Owain"—as the master of the enchanted games, which Gereint undergoes in a great Celtic tour de force that restores him to his senses, to his sovereignty over his lands, and to the fair and long-suffering Enid.

Synopsis of "Gereint and Enid"

(1) Arthur is holding court at Caerleon upon Usk on Whitsun. Whenever his court assembles for a major feast, thirteen churches are set aside for their use: one each for Arthur, Gwenhwyfar, the steward Odiar the Frank, and their companions; and one each for Arthur's nine captains, especially Gwalchmai. Glewlwyd Mighty Grasp is gatekeeper at only one festival, sharing his duties with seven others. (2) On Whit Tuesday a forester of Arthur's, Madawg from the Forest of Dean, brings news that a pure white stag has been seen, and Arthur gives orders to hunt it. (3) Gwenhwyfar begs to watch the hunt. Gwalchmai suggests that whoever is successful in cutting off the stag's head should present it to his lover. Arthur rides forth early, but Gwenhwyfar sleeps late so that (4) she rides out with only her maid accompanying her. The two meet Gereint out riding and he agrees to accompany the queen. Together the three come upon a dwarf bearing a whip and a richly dressed woman in the company of a mud-spattered knight of great size. Gwenhwyfar's maid asks the dwarf who his companions are, but he refuses to speak with one so low born and strikes her across the face with his whip.

(5) Gereint rides to the maid's defense and is also struck by the dwarf. Because the dwarf is unarmed, Gereint will not punish him and secures Gwenhwyfar's permission to ride instead after the knight. He pursues the knight's party and sees them enter a castle in a walled town, (6) after which he finds lodging for himself in a rundown hall outside the town. The household consists of an old man and woman dressed in ragged, once fine clothing and a beautiful maiden, who tends to the needs of Gereint and his horse. After they have sent out for good food for their guest, (7) the old man tells Gereint that he was once earl of the castle in the town, but that he lost the title and lands to his nephew. Gereint asks about the preparations of armored men he has seen in the town (8) and is told that there is to be a game the next day, which the young earl will play. Two forked sticks will be placed in the ground with a silver rod resting between them. On the rod a spar-

rowhawk will be set and every man is to bring his lady and joust for the bird. The knight Gereint pursues, whose name is Edern, has won the game for two years running. If he wins a third time he will be known as the knight of the sparrowhawk. The old man offers Gereint his own armor and horse for the joust, but warns him that he cannot enter the tournament without a lady. (9) Gereint asks if he might joust in honor of the old man's daughter, promising to love and serve her loyally if he survives, and the girl's father consents.

They all rise early to make the challenge to the presumptive knight of the sparrowhawk, and Gereint jousts with him. The old man acts as Gereint's squire, and he and his family cheer on Gereint. He offers Gereint the spear which he had been given when he was knighted, and with this Gereint is able to unhorse his opponent so that he and the knight must continue their fight on foot. (10) Seeing him wounded and flagging, the old man urges Gereint to remember the insult to Gwenhwyfar. Gereint is thus able to disable his opponent, who begs for mercy, but Gereint will grant it only if the knight makes amends to the queen in person for having insulted her. (11) Gereint asks his opponent's identity, which is revealed as Edern ap Nudd.

The young earl then invites Gereint to his castle, but Gereint declines and returns with the old man, whose name is Ynwyl. The young earl sends his servants to furnish Ynwyl's court with food and clothing. (12) Gereint forbids the maiden to wear anything but her shift and mantle until they return to Arthur's court, where Gwenhwyfar will dress her. Gereint is able to reinstate Ynwyl to his lands and titles, and with Ynwyl's daughter he rides off to Arthur's court.

(13) Meanwhile, Arthur has been hunting the white hart. His own hound, Cafall, corners the beast and Arthur himself beheads it. Cadyrfieth had noticed that Gwenhwyfar was unaccompanied and Arthur gives order for her to be accompanied home by Gildas ap Caw and the clerics of the court. (14) There is dispute over who should have the head of the hart and Gwenhwyfar makes everyone wait until Gereint comes home before this is decided. Edern, his lady, and the

dwarf arrive, submit themselves to the queen, and tell the whole story of events so far. (15) Gwenhwyfar forgives him his insult and Arthur takes sureties for Edern, along with Caradawg ap Llyr, Gwallawg ap Llenawg, Owein ap Nudd, Gwalchmai, and others. (16) Arthur also bids Morgan Tud, his physician, attend Edern. Gwenhwyfar's watchmen warn of Gereint's approach and Gwenhwyfar thanks him for avenging her. (17) Gereint introduces her to the maiden in whose person the queen has been avenged. The maiden goes with Gwenhwyfar to her chamber and is there attired according to her rank. The king and queen themselves give up their bedroom for Gereint and his maiden and (18) the queen proposes that Enid be given the hart's head. The couple remain at court, engaged in tournaments and companionship, for three years.

(19) After this time, word comes from Gereint's father, Erbin, in Cornwall, that Arthur should send Gereint home to defend his lands because Erbin himself is aging. (20) Arthur allows Gereint to go, accompanied by a host from the court. (21) Erbin relinquishes the rule of his lands to his son's hands. Cadyrieth listens to the suppliants at Gereint's wedding and Gereint receives the homage of the Cornishmen. Gereint's companions advise him on the best method of ruling.

(22) Eventually, Gereint's reputation spreads so far that he no longer exerts himself, preferring to stay at his court with Enid. His retainers grow discontented and Erbin challenges Enid as to whether or not she is the cause of Gereint's lethargy, but she denies this. One morning, while Gereint and Enid are in bed, Enid awakes and laments her husband's lapse from deeds of greatness. Gereint then awakes and, seeing her tears, assumes that she is in love with another. (23) He orders that horses be brought for them and that Enid wear her worst riding habit, swearing that she should not return until she sees that he has not lost his strength. He leaves the realm in Erbin's hands and mounts his horse, telling Enid to ride out ahead (24) and admonishing her that whatever she sees or hears about him, she is to remain silent until he speaks first.

Enid overhears robbers planning to attack them and warns Gereint. He rebukes her and fights off the robbers, taking their armor and horses. This happens twice more, until he has twelve horses laden with armor. Enid and Gereint then meet a boy taking food to the mowers in the fields and are fed by him. The boy then goes to the town and tells the Brown Earl about the couple. The earl later persuades Gereint to lodge with him. Seeing how badly Enid is treated by Gereint, the Brown Earl encourages her to love him instead and forsake Gereint. Enid asks the earl to carry her off, as though she is agreeable to his offer. While Gereint sleeps, she readies his armor and wakes him to warn him. Although angry, he prepares himself and they depart from their hostel, leaving eleven horses and armor as payment. The Brown Earl and eighty men follow the couple and Enid, seeing the dust of the men's pursuit, warns Gereint—but he ignores her. Soon Gereint defeats all eighty knights and the Brown Earl and he and Enid set off on their way.

(25) They approach a walled city set in a lovely valley, which, they are told, belongs to Gwiffert Petit or Y Brenhin Bychan. Gereint is warned not to cross the bridge and continue in that direction because the little king allows no knight on his lands without challenging him. Shortly, a little armored man encounters them, challenging Gereint. The little man is overcome by Gereint and begs mercy, bidding Gereint rescue him if ever he meets with trouble. Refusing the little king's invitation to come to his court, Gereint rides on with Enid, although sorely wounded. (26) While they rest in a forest, they hear hunting horns and the approach of Arthur's court. They are spotted by a servant and Cai follows to investigate. Although Gereint recognizes Cai, Cai does not recognize him; Gereint refuses his name to Cai and fights him. After Cai retreats, Gwalchmai comes to see the unknown aggressor for himself. Although more courteous than Cai, Gwalchmai is soon fighting Gereint as well and recognizes him.

(27) Gereint refuses to see Arthur, so the king's pavilion is set nearer Gereint and Gereint is persuaded to see his cousin. Arthur begs Enid to leave off following her husband, but she is determined to follow him

still. Gwenhwyfar tends to her while Morgan Tud sees to Gereint's wounds. The next day, the two continue on their way. Hearing a scream, Gereint investigates and finds a young woman lamenting her dead knight, the result of an attack by three giants. While Enid tends the woman, Gereint sets out to find the giants, but as he is killing the third, his wounds burst open. He staggers back to Enid and collapses. Hearing her screams, Earl Limwris rides up. He buries the dead knight and sees that Gereint is borne back to his hall. Although the earl believes Gereint dead, Enid believes otherwise. Earl Limwris offers himself as a protector and lover to Enid, but she refuses him. She will neither eat nor drink as long as Gereint lives. The earl boxes her ears and it is her subsequent shrieks which awaken Gereint from his coma. Appearing to rise from the dead, from the hollow of the shield in which he had been laid, Gereint starts up and slays the earl. (28) When he looks on Enid, Gereint feels two sorrows: for the loss of her looks and for the realization that she has been in the right. They ride on and are met by the little king, who rescues the wounded Gereint and tends him.

When Gereint is well, the couple continue their journey and find the domain of Earl Owain. (29) A man has warned them against going there because of a hedge of mist in that place and, within the hedge, enchanted games from which no one returns. None is permitted to lodge in the town except those who are to go to Owain's court. Gereint and Enid are sent on to the court where they are received with honor: Gereint is seated at one side of Owain and Enid at the other, with the little king next to Enid and Owain's countess next to Gereint. Owain considers Gereint and is grieved that he had ever instituted the enchanted games if a good man like Gereint is to be lost. He tells his guest to stop worrying about the prospect, for Gereint is not obliged to go to the games and, if his guest would grant it, the games would be abolished. Gereint, however, tells Owain that he is eager to go.

(30) Gereint approaches the hedge, noticing that men's heads are posted there on every stake but two. The little king asks to accompany Gereint, but Owain forbids it. (31) Gereint enters the mist and emerges

in a fair orchard wherein is set a red tent next to an apple tree from which hangs a horn. Inside the tent there is a maiden sitting in a golden chair, with a vacant seat beside her. She warns Gereint against sitting in the empty seat because its owner never permits this. (32) A well-armored knight then challenges Gereint and the two men joust. As Gereint moves to behead him, the knight begs mercy, granting whatever Gereint should desire. Gereint wishes for nothing else but the abolition of the games, and orders that the mist be dispersed. (33) The knight tells Gereint to blow on the horn, for not until he has been overcome and his successful assailant has blown the horn will the mist depart. (34) The company (Gereint, Owain, Enid, and the little king) meet again and peace is established among them. Then Gereint returns with Enid to his own realms, which he rules wisely with her henceforth.

Commentary

(1) We hear further about our old friend Glewlwyd, the porter or gatekeeper. The storyteller of "Gereint and Enid" relates details cross-referencing "Culhwch and Olwen," in which Arthur's court is composed of wondrous warriors, each with his own magical power. But we are no longer in Dark Age mode; Arthur's court here shifts to medieval times. The importance of Arthur's company and their different needs are acknowledged by the provision of thirteen churches wherein they might hear mass honorably. The assembly is particularly large because it is Whitsuntide, one of the major feasts of the church's year.

(2) The appearance of the white hart is the signal of otherworldly penetration of the earthly realm. We saw how Pwyll was inveigled into Annwfn's domains by the hunting of a similar beast in chapter 2 of *Mabon*. The white hart, like the unicorn, bore a mystical significance which wove together the strands of pagan and Christian Europe. An otherworldly beast representing the high powers of the gods, it is sometimes an emblem of the wild hunt and its lord, and is sometimes the emblem of the Goddess, as we shall see. In Christian tradition, the

white hart became a symbol of Christ or of the Christian soul yearning for the waters of salvation.[144] Its appearance here is the signal for an ancient, ritual enactment by Arthur and his court, for the hart is to be hunted after the custom of Arthur's father, Uther (see note 14).

(3) Both in Chrétien's *Erec and Enid* and in *Lanzelet*,[42] the awarding of the stag's head to the fairest lady is well established, though here it is Gwalchmai who suggests it. While Gwenhwyfar sleeps late, Arthur departs with his squires, among whom is Amr, or Amhar, his son—a rare reference to any child of Arthur beyond Mordred. According to Nennius, one of the wonders of Britain was a spring called Llygard Amr, near which was buried "a son of the warrior Arthur, and he killed him there and buried him."[28] The grave is supposed to be unmeasurable because its dimensions seem to change. Of Arthur's killing of Amr there is no extant story. One of Amr's squires is Goreu, who, we will remember, is Arthur's cousin and, according to the triads, the one who releases Arthur from imprisonment (*Mabon,* chapter 6). Certainly the juxtaposition of these two young men is significant. Perhaps their stories, lost to tradition, suggest parallels in the mind of the storyteller?

(4) Gereint champions Gwenhwyfar, becoming both her escort and her avenger. The insult to her maid is really an insult to Gwenhwyfar herself. We have already noted that the insulting of the queen occurs in some form in each of the romances, and here she is particularly vulnerable. Gereint himself has no lady and so behaves as the queen's knight when Edern's dwarf strikes the queen's damsel. As we shall see, Arthur is unable to champion Gwenhwyfar because of his absence at the hunt and because he is cast in the archetypal role of the master of the custom of Uther Pendragon (see note 14, below).

(5) It is possible that in the original sources of this story there was some faint reference to Gwenhwyfar's abduction by Melwas, a story which appears in the *Vita Gildae*.[21] Melwas was king of the Summer

Country, clearly an otherworldly domain. Here Gwenhwyfar is insulted by Edern ap Nudd, the Eternal Son of Night—a medieval variant of the Underworld lord jealous of the Flower Bride.[95]

(6) As in "The Dream of Rhonabwy," in which the hero finds himself in a ramshackle hall, so Gereint takes lodgings in a decrepit court. His first vision of Enid is hardly propitious to their love. But unlike Pryderi, who finds manual work repugnant to his upbringing (*Mabon*, chapter 4), Enid willingly stables Gereint's horse and performs tasks more suitable for a page than for a gentlewoman. There are distinct elements of Enid's character that correspond with Rhiannon and the many women in British folk story who are enchanted into the form of a broken-down mare. In this story, the enchanted mare speaks sound horse sense, which the mare's owner has good reason to heed. In this medieval story, Gereint is not so astute until forced to listen to Enid.

(7) The dispossession of Ynwyl, Enid's father, is very like that of Custennin, Goreu's father (*Mabon*, chapter 6).

(8) The joust of the sparrowhawk was a very popular motif in medieval romance and can be found in many related texts, including *Libeaus Desconus*. Like the hunting of the white hart and the enchanted games, the sparrowhawk contest is one of the games that Sovereignty sets in order to establish both her champion and her representative.

(9) The sparrowhawk contest is not open to a man without a mistress to champion, so Gereint selects Enid in what seems to us an arbitrary gesture. But this is Gereint's only way of legitimately attacking Edern, the knight who has insulted Gwenhwyfar.

(10) Ynwyl spurs Gereint's flagging efforts with a reminder of the queen's insult, exemplifying a time-honored theme in Celtic literature: Only by being incited to great rage can the hero exert his fullest

powers. Laegaire, Cú Chulainn's charioteer, urges on his master to perform his greatest feat in the Ulster cycle—the salmon leap against Ferdiad.[8] In the *Vulgate Cycle* Gawain is similarly encouraged by a hermit in his attempt to rescue Guinevere.[33]

(11) Gereint avenges Gwenhwyfar and sends Edern back to Caerlion for judgment. Edern ap Nudd survives into later Arthurian romance as Yder fiz Nut. On the famous archivault in Modena Cathedral, Edern turns up as Isdernus, with a certain Winlogie, whom commentators have identified as Guinevere.[87] This may indeed offer a faint connection between "Gereint and Enid" and the abduction of Guinevere, which the Modena archivault supposedly illustrates.

(12) This is the first time that Gereint forbids Enid the wearing of suitably noble clothing. His insistence on her wearing her old dress is not from any desire to humiliate his intended bride, but rather from his wish to submit all his affairs to the judgment of Arthur and Gwenhwyfar, so that he may receive his bride, suitably attired by the queen, as his prize.

(13) The suggestion, mentioned in note 11, that Gwenhwyfar's abduction might have once played a part in this story is strengthened here through Arthur telling Gildas to take the queen home. Gildas ap Caw was a historical chronicler and monk writing in the sixth century. His life, the *Vita Gildae*, written by Caradoc of Llancarfan, relates how Gildas personally reconciled Arthur with Melwas, who was retaining Gwenhwyfar.[21] Although Gwenhwyfar suffers no rape in "Gereint and Enid," she is unaccompanied by armed men and thus prey to abduction.

(14) The bestowal of the white hart's head is, in *Erec and Enid*, a cause of turmoil, for the killer of the hart is allowed to kiss the fairest maiden, which right all good knights will defend. This is called the custom of Uther Pendragon, after the man who instituted it. The same

custom is mentioned in *Lanzelet*,[142] in which Arthur hunts the white stag, but just as he is about to practice the custom of Uther, Guinevere is abducted by King Valerin, a neighboring vassal king. All this is clearly significant to the strange roles adopted by both Gwenhwyfar and Arthur in "Gereint and Enid." Arthur, when he is engaged in the hunt for the white hart, is no longer an earthly king and husband, but rather a sovereign lord with *droit de seigneur*—a sovereign lord's right—as once practiced by both European and Irish kingships. Gwenhwyfar reverts to her guise of Flower Bride, the Spring Maiden over whose possession the bright and dark lords fight. While exercising the custom of Uther Pendragon, Arthur cannot champion the queen in this battle. Gereint substitutes for Arthur and fights Edern, who in some early version played the part of Melwas.

(15) At the conclusion of these otherworldly challenges and with the return to normality, Gwenhwyfar—at Arthur's bidding—exercises her queenly rights of forgiveness and charity. The Celtic custom of taking sureties, or making promises, for the good behavior of an offender—a kind of bail—is upheld by Arthur's court.

(16) Edern's wounds are tended by a person called Morgan Tud. Lucy Paton[134] has written extensively about this healer and proposes that Morgan le Fay cannot be intended here. However, Morgan's salve heals Erec in Chrétien. Paton establishes that Morgan is a common enough male Welsh name but is not applied to women. In Geoffrey, she is called Morgen (derived from "seaborne," *mor gen*).[10] As we shall see later, Morgan is not absent from traditions relating to "Gereint and Enid," and it is perhaps possible that she is remembered here.

(17) Gereint's words to Gwenhwyfar, "Here is the girl for whose sake you were avenged," immediately help us to place Enid's role in this story. She is a substitute Gwenhwyfar in terms of the insult, a focus to help Gereint avenge the queen. But Enid herself is far more than this.

She is a representative of Sovereignty, a bride fetched from another world. The fact that Enid is dressed in the queen's own clothes and is honorably received at Arthur's court points to this, as does a later episode in *Erec and Enid* (see the section In the Apple Orchard later in this chapter.)

(18) The bestowal of the white hart's head upon Enid is the queen's suggestion. In Chrétien's *Erec and Enid*, it is at this point that Arthur upholds the custom of Uther Pendragon and gives Enid a kiss. This may once have replaced a feature in the story which might have disturbed courtly listeners—the *droit du seigneur*, or the sovereign lord's right to the first night with the bride. While there is little to suggest that this custom was widely observed in Britain, it was certainly common enough in Ireland. Irish legal tracts of the earliest period and certain stories still speak of the king's circuit of the land, during which he slept with the wives of notable lords. It is while making one such circuit, for example, that Conchobar mac Nessa is present at the birth of Cú Chulainn.[8] Arthur himself is destined to win the white hart after a hunt which might be dangerous to an ordinary man, if we are to judge from similar romances, such as "Graelent"[26] and "The Lay of Guigamor,"[134] in which the hero departs into Faery in pursuit of a magical beast and is thereafter lost to humankind. The risk that Arthur takes in absorbing the otherworldly dangers of the hunt in his own royal person is compensated by his pairing with the most beautiful maiden. In effect, he is the hunter king so familiar from traditional spring rites in which a man takes the place of a proto–Robin Hood character and a woman assumes the role of the Spring Maiden, or Maid Marian. But instead of taking Enid to his own bed, Arthur bestows her upon Gereint, who, as the queen's champion, is the hero of the hour.

(19) Gereint's duties now become mundane. He has won a fair bride and goes to "beat the boundaries" of his land, but he has many trials to endure before he is worthy of either bride or land.

(20) It is worthwhile to compare the list of Arthur's court that is given in "Gereint and Enid" with those appearing in both "Culhwch and Olwen" and "The Dream of Rhonabwy." Apart from the established kings and lords whose experience will help him, Gereint takes with him many of the younger men, notably Goreu, Gwair (the prisoner of Annwfn), and Peredur.

(21) Gereint makes a circuit of his land in the manner of Celtic rulers, exchanging gifts and taking promises of service. Thus he establishes his sovereignty over his inherited domain, though things soon change.

(22) The theme of the hero who appears to be so caught in the grip of a woman that he fails in his manly duties is one common to "Gereint and Enid" and "Owain," for both Gereint and Owain stand so accused by their *meinie* (company). Medieval texts abound concerning this dichotomy between love of one's mistress and duty to one's lord, but earlier texts reveal an older motif, that of the inner mistress or Sovereignty being projected onto an earthly woman so that the hero who seems in thrall to his wife is truly serving the Goddess herself. Enid's unfortunate remarks put her in much the same position as Psyche, who loses her husband, Cupid. Like Psyche, Enid is forced to undergo a series of trials in order to win back her spouse.

(23) Until Gereint comes to his senses and is reconciled with her again, Enid must assume a ragged appearance. She becomes, in effect, a dolorous lady, akin to the Dark Woman of Knowledge or the Black Maiden, who assumes a woeful appearance but still faithfully accompanies the hero in his wasteland search, like Luned and the Grail messenger. The ensuing episodes are to show Enid that Gereint has not lost his manly strength.

(24) The encounter with robbers is paralleled by Gareth's ride with Linnet in Malory.[25] Enid's enforced silence, like that of Rhiannon or of

Chaucer's faithful Griselda,[6] seems a stock medieval harassment for wilting damsels—and while she is unable to maintain this silence because of her love for Gereint, it serves to hide her real power and self-possession. It also forces Gereint into more and more ludicrous tests of his strength, all of which we can see as part of the games of Sovereignty.

(25) Gwiffert Petit, the little king, has aroused a good deal of scholarly speculation. It has been suggested that he derives from Auberon, king of Faery, or indeed from Gwiddolwyn Gorr, who appears in "Culhwch and Olwen" as the dwarf whose magic bottles keep drinks warm from the east to the farthest west.[92] Gwiffert is a friendly opponent and one who, once bested, gives hospitality to his vanquisher. There is a good deal of the *gruagach*, or friendly brownie, about him. In many Gaelic stories, the gruagach, himself king over his own domain, agrees to serve as companion to the hero and help him in his quest.[61]

(26) In one of the most amusing episodes of the story, Gereint exchanges a very literal conversation with Cai. This is the ubiquitous "taunting by Cai" and "appeasement of Gwalchmai" episode that occurs in all three romances.

(27) Gereint's childish behavior is balanced by Enid's patient insistence on following him. In Chrétien, Earl Limwris is the lord of Li Mors, "death." But Enid refuses him as she has refused the Brown Earl. It is her shrieks that revive Gereint in a macabre scene which causes the castle's occupants to flee in terror.

(28) Enid's love has brought Gereint back from the dead, and now he acknowledges her in a moment of sorrowful revelation. He at last deigns to protect her at the approach of his old ally, Gwiffert Petit.

(29) Here we reach the heart of the story, where Gereint and Enid meet with Owain, who is now master of the enchanted games. This is Gereint's

supreme test. Later Arthurian tradition parallels this incident with the Val sans Retour, into which knights go but never return.[33] In *Erec and Enid* Owain becomes Evrain and his castle is called Brandigan—the raven's castle. We note that it is Owain who institutes the games.

(30) There is no disparity between the garden or orchard as described by Chrétien and that described in "Gereint and Enid"; the descriptions in both tales have much to complement and illuminate each other. Present in both is the hedge of stakes with men's heads upon them. This is a common feature of Celtic folk stories, and the hero invariably arrives to find one stake vacant, ready for his head, as does Art mac Conn when he goes to win his bride, Delbhchaem.[171] Gereint's garden is derived from native sources, while Chrétien's is closer to the Breton land of the fays. Both are types of terrestrial paradise.

(31) Chrétien describes the garden as an orchard bearing fruit in summer and winter alike, though it is impossible for those who pluck any fruit to leave the orchard—a description consistent with that of the faery realms, where mortals must not eat if they wish ever to leave. In Chrétien, the enchanted games are called the Joy of the Court, an expression which has given a good deal of confusion, since the Joie de Cort can mean the joy of the "court," "horn," or "body," depending on slight variations in spelling. There is a way in which all three can be seen as valid, which we shall discuss in chapter 9. The mystery of the joy, as it is called, is dependent on the subtle exchange that passes between the mistress of the orchard and her champion, for the woman in the golden chair is none other than Sovereignty herself, complete with the emblems of her cult: the horn, the apple tree, and the golden seat. The vacant seat reminds us forcibly of the Siege Perilous in which Perceval sits in the *Didot Perceval* (*Mabon,* chapter 4).

(32) Gereint's unnamed opponent is called Mabonograin in Chrétien, and is yet another guise of Mabon himself as eternal prisoner. We

note that he is a prisoner of the orchard insofar as he has sworn never to leave it undefended or leave his lady alone.[7] In this way he has become what Gereint's meinie accused their lord of being: in the thrall of a woman. We may ponder the significance of Mabonograin's appearance in collusion with Evrain or Owain in *Erec and Enid*. This is not the first time we have noted the joint appearance of these men in one story. In *Libeaus Desconus*, Mabon and Yrain are brother magicians, while Mabon and Owain share a conception story (see *Mabon*, chapter 9). Their close association is further borne out in "Gereint and Enid," for although the Welsh story omits the name of the champion in the orchard, his name of Mabonograin in *Erec and Enid* is seen by one commentator as a combining of Mabon and Owain.[132] (See also chapters 3 and 4.)

If we consider Owain's career, the connection between him and Mabonograin will become clearer. In the previous chapter we saw how Owain relinquishes his guardianship of the fountain and returns to Arthur's court. Now Owain, having been a champion who has beaten his challengers, becomes a challenger himself and one who sets tests as master of the enchanted games. Instead of defending the orchard himself, Owain appoints a proxy champion—his doublet, Mabonograin.

(33) The blowing of the horn dispels the mists of enchantment that surround the orchard, for the games of Sovereignty are ended. The significance of this episode will be discussed in chapter 9.

(34) Gereint is rightful lord not only of his own lands, but also of the inner realms belonging to Sovereignty. The seal of this association is set by Enid, Gereint's wife and Sovereignty's representative.

The Hunting of the White Hart

One of the central features of "Gereint and Enid" is the hunting of the white hart. All hunts in early literature are laden with symbols of mystery and power, though none more so than this one. But what is the real significance of the white hart? We have already noted its affiliation with Christian symbolism as an emblem of spiritual yearning. Both the white hart and the unicorn have been applied to Christ himself as emblems of unique power. In addition, both animals were believed to be able to find medicinal herbs, and both were considered impossible to catch without the help of a virgin. While there are aspects of the later Christian understanding of these beasts, particularly within Chrétien, it is to an earlier set of symbols that we now turn.

As the forester tells Arthur, the hart is pure white, and out of arrogance and pride in its lordliness it will travel with no other animal.[22] As such, it is clearly marked as the proper quarry for a king. Its appearance heralds Arthur's assumption of a ritual role, that of the huntsman consort of Sovereignty, whose beast the white hart is. Similar to the unicorn, which lays its head without protest in a virgin's lap while the huntsman slays it, the white hart "offers" its head to the most beautiful maiden. And from this maiden Arthur is expected to exact a kiss—a token of a more explicit surrender which the Spring Maiden once rendered to the huntsman king.

There are three tasks or tests that are to be achieved in this story: Arthur hunts and kills the white hart, while Gereint wins the sparrowhawk contest and the enchanted games. Taken together, these contests can be seen as part of a once widely observed set of ritual games, which we might term here the games of Sovereignty.

The finding and fetching of the hallows is the task of the king, and the winning of the games of Sovereignty is the task of the best of the king's companions and warriors. The fact that Gereint does not achieve the three contests himself but shares the rostrum with Arthur, who gives his prize—Enid—to Gereint, is very significant, and emphasizes that Gereint is acting as a champion of Arthur and thus, by extension, of Sovereignty as well.

But how may we establish the mythical occurrence of such a set of ritual games and with what warranty? Of the many Celtic stories that relate to both Sovereignty and the hunting of a wondrous beast, let us look at one of the most relevant parallel texts in Irish tradition: "The Sons of Daire."

It tells how Daire reverently celebrates the games at the fair of Tailltiu, the foster mother of the mighty god Lugh, who inaugurates games in her honor every year, on August 1, at Lughnasad. It was Tailltiu, earth mother and progenitor of agricultural skills, who cleared the plains of trees in order to help Ireland become cultivated. Such was her labor that she died:

> Long her sorrow, long her weariness,
> In sickness was Tailltiu after heavy toil.
> To her came the men of Ireland,
> To whom she was in bondage.[146]

Daire has five sons, and because of a prophecy that one of them named Lughaidh would succeed to the Sovereignty of Ireland, Daire calls each of them Lughaidh and inquires of a druid which of his sons should be king. "The one who succeeds in overtaking the golden doe, which shall appear at this fair," says the druid. Shortly after, a golden doe does appear and is chased by Daire's sons as far as Beann Eadair, where a magical mist descends. One of the sons overtakes the doe and another kills her, and in this way each has a part in hunting the magical creature.

A great snow falls as they hunt and the brothers each go in turn to find a house where he might sleep. One by one they encounter a hideous hag who promises each shelter in exchange for sleeping with her. Each refuses and is told by the hag that his refusal is refusal of the kingship and sovereignty of Ireland. Then the hag names each of the Lughaidhs by their part in the hunting; for example, the one who had flayed the carcass is called Lughaidh Corb forever afterwards.

At last the final brother comes to the house. It is he who had overtaken the doe, and he sleeps with the hag. In turn, she names him Lughaidh Laidhe (the strong) and is transformed herself so that "the light of her countenance was as the sun rising in the month of May."

And she identifies herself thus:

> *"I say unto thee, O mild youth,*
> *With me the arch-kings cohabit,*
> *I am the majestic, slender damsel,*
> *The Sovereignty of Alba and Eire."*

She promises that his son should win her and combine the skills of druid, prophet, poet, and king.[129]

So we see that at the ritual games of an earth goddess the kingship of Ireland is decided by the outcome of the hunt. Lughaidh Laidhe overtakes the doe in order to win Sovereignty, which echoes Pwyll's attempt to overtake Rhiannon, whose pace is always just faster than his own (*Mabon*, chapter 2). As to the games of Tailltiu (Teltown, in modern Irish), Maire MacNeill has collected all known traditions surrounding this festival in her colossal study *The Festival of Lughnasadh*.[103] Most modern animal fairs in the British Isles are held in a season or on a date that was at one time dedicated to a local deity. On such a date sacred games were held, animals bartered, and marriages arranged. The fair of Teltown was particularly associated with matchmaking. There are legends extant concerning the abduction of a woman to a nearby faery hill to become a *beansidi* (woman of the *sidi*, the faery hills); traditions relating to a duel between two giants or a giant and a hero, caused by their competition for a woman; and tales of a brawl which results from insulting a woman. The chief protagonists in most folk traditions relating to this festival are Lugh, the mighty God of Light; Crom Dubh, literally, "the black bent one" (a harvest deity, symbolic of summer's end); and Tailltiu herself, Lugh's foster mother, who occupied in early tradition a position similar to that now enjoyed by St. Brigit, foster mother of Christ in native Gaelic tradition. If we also remember the story "Baile in Scail" (chapter 3), in which Lugh enjoys a particularly powerful partnership with Sovereignty, with whom he prophesies lines of kings, we have a fascinating series of overlays with "Gereint and Enid."

The festival of Lughnasad represents the mythic tradition of a God of Light and a God of Summer's End in combat for a Goddess of the Land. This pattern lies behind the archetypal roles played by Arthur in "Gereint and Enid," where he appears as the hunter of the white hart; by Edern ap Nudd, who attempts to abduct or at least insult Gwenhwyfar, and who represents the darkness of winter; and by Gwenhwyfar, who is representative of the Goddess of the Land, no longer the Spring Maiden but the Summer Queen. At another level of the story these roles are enacted by Gereint, as Arthur's champion, defender of the queen, and contestant in Sovereignty's games; by the Brown Earl, Earl Limwris, and Mabonograin, as the representatives of the failing otherworldly powers; and by Enid, who, as an unwed maiden, represents the Spring Maiden, or Sovereignty's messenger.

If we turn to chapter 8, we will find a list of other such triplicates interacting in a similar fashion within the *Mabinogion*. We note that each of the levels on which "Gereint and Enid" may be understood in its Celtic context revolves around the theme of loving partnership. This is the real meaning at the heart of "Gereint and Enid," for the white hart betokens true love and exchange of powers, whether between the king and Sovereignty, the king and his queen, or the hero and the heroine. There is a reciprocal love and duty between each of the protagonists which goes beyond courtly love and chivalric honor. This is the "love strong as death" that poets speak of, love that is need and desire, sacrifice and patient acceptance. It is within this context that Enid must be understood, for her role is least easy to comprehend.

Perhaps it will be easier to come to terms with Enid's unsympathetic role if we look at "The Lay of Guigamor," one of the Breton lais recorded by Marie de France,[26] for here the tradition of the white hart and the patient lover is combined.

Guigamor is trained as a knight at Arthur's court, where he soon excels beyond all others at chivalric feats. But his knightly prowess is not matched by any enthusiasm for courtly love. In fact, he gives no thought to women at all, for which everyone believes him strangely incomplete. One day he goes hunting and chances to pursue and wound a white doe bearing antlers on her head. But the arrow with which he wounds her rebounds and strikes him in the thigh. As he lies on the ground, the doe speaks her dying words to him, saying, "Vassal, you have done me wrong and will never avoid your destiny, which is this: No medicine will heal your wound. The only way you may be healed is by a woman who will suffer such pain and sorrow as no woman in the world has endured before. And to dolorous lady, dolorous knight. For your part you shall do and suffer so great things for her, that not a lover beneath the sun . . . but shall marvel at the tale." So saying, she died.

Guigamor makes his way to a harbor in which is anchored a miraculous ship. Lying upon a bed fashioned by workmen in King Solomon's time, he is transported, without agency of man, to the opposite shore. The king of that country, an old jealous man, has married a beautiful young maiden whom he has immured within a tower in an orchard, with her niece as attendant. Only a priest holds the key, in order to administer the sacraments to her.

Walking in the garden, the two women see the ship miraculously arrive and, seeking to give honorable burial to the knight on board, they bring him into the orchard. The young queen falls in love with him and, hearing his tale, offers to hide him until he is well again. During this period of healing, Guigamor likewise falls in love with the queen. After a year and a half the queen has a foreboding that she will soon lose him, and she asks him to give her a shirt that she might set in it a knot as their covenant to each other, which is that he will never love another woman except the one who unties the knot. Guigamor likewise fastens a belt about the queen, which is secured so secretly that none but he might undo it.

The king's chamberlain sees Guigamor with the queen and tells his master. Hearing Guigamor's story, the king judges that he might go free but only by returning to the ship in which he had arrived and leaving the fates to guide it. Guigamor arrives safely home and is welcomed by his squire and taken to his castle, where he refuses to make merry or take a wife save the one who is able to unloose the knot in his shirt. Soon all the women in Brittany hear about the shirt and come to make the attempt, but all fail.

Meanwhile, for the space of two years the queen has been imprisoned in the gray tower, bound and joyless. One day, while she laments her lost love and wishes she could either go to him or cast herself into the sea, she discovers the tower door is miraculously open. She escapes and, finding Guigamor's ship awaiting her, is borne across the sea to Brittany, to the castle of a lord named Meriadus.

Meriadus finds the queen within the ship and believes her to be a faery, so fair is she. He shelters her and bids her love him, but she refuses him, saying that only he who can loose her belt might have her. Meriadus then exclaims that there is a knight who will likewise yield to no other save she who can unknot his shirt. Meriadus arranges a tournament which Guigamor attends and there recognizes the queen. Meriadus bids her loose the knight's shirt, and she is able to do so. Then Guigamor, seeing that it is truly his mistress and hearing her story, begs Meriadus to release her to him. Meriadus refuses him and, after a long campaign, is successfully besieged by Guigamor, who slays him and carries off the queen to his own lands.[16]

In "The Lay of Guigamor" we see the interwoven motifs of the white hart and the power of love to overcome. The destiny that the doe lays on Guigamor is in the nature of a geis or proscription which, as will become increasingly obvious in this study, is a feature of many stories dealing with Sovereignty and her successors in medieval literature. In these tales, the geis is the command of the Goddess shaping the hero's destiny, a challenge to overcome, fail, or balance in some way. Guigamor's initial problem is his lack of love for any woman. In this he is a perfect candidate for Sovereignty's contest. Marie de France points out a very obvious classical archetype in this story: The moment of the wounding of Guigamor by his own arrow is the moment when the possibility of love enters his heart, as if he has been pierced by one of Cupid's darts. But the wounding of the hero by his own weapon or hounds is also a feature of myths concerning the goddess of venery, Artemis or Diana. Here, however, the chase for quarry becomes the quest for love.

Guigamor's queen is imprisoned in a tower within an orchard, which becomes a temenos where love can develop. Both she and Guigamor undergo sorrow and suffering for their love. The miraculous ship that transports them is a descendant of the faery *curragh*, or crystal boat, which bears heroes to Tir na mBan, the Land of Women; as a barque shaped by Solomon's craftsmen, it will appear again in the *Quest del San Graal*, becoming the ship that carries the Grail finders to the city of Sarras.[29] The many correspondences between Guigamor's story and "Gereint and Enid" suggest a tradition of related stories. Even the abduction and enforced captivity of the queen by Meriadus is paralleled by the abduction of Gwenhwyfar by Melwas underlying "Gereint and Enid."

In "The Lay of Guigamor" the importance of the white hart is fully revealed: It comes as a messenger from the Otherworld to lead the hero into a contest which goes beyond human strength and knightly prowess. It is by love, trust, and enduring patience in times of sorrow that the lovers are reunited. And although Gereint and Enid are not separated physically, they are separated with regard to communication. The white hart leads Gereint to find Enid and marry her, and the games of Sovereignty enable him to fully love her.

In the Apple Orchard

It is in the apple orchard that all is revealed in "Gereint and Enid," although we are forced to turn to *Erec and Enid* in order to corroborate our findings. Let us focus on this episode in the orchard and its antecedents.

Throughout Celtic and Arthurian literature the orchard is a paradigm for the terrestrial paradise. It is Insula Avallonis, according to Geoffrey of Monmouth, the Isle of Apples.[11] Gaelic tradition locates it as Emain Abhlach (island of apples) on Arran in the Firth of Clyde, which is for us a significant identification: Mabon's own stomping ground in the Firth of Solway is not far distant, and Chrétien calls the guardian of his orchard Mabonograin.

In *Erec and Enid,* the knight who successfully sounds the horn will have greater renown than any other man living, for so will the Joy of the Court be announced. This mysterious Joy of the Court is, as we know, Chrétien's name for the enchanted games of "Gereint and Enid." Erec approaches the lady of the orchard only to be challenged by a Red Knight, whom he overcomes. He then demands to be told why the Red Knight is in the garden, after which the knight relates his story: He had once been at the court of Erec's father, King Lac. His mistress, the lady of the orchard, had asked him a favor without specifying its nature, to which he agreed. Immediately after he had been knighted by Evrain (Owain), whose nephew he was, the Red Knight's mistress demanded he obey her favor: He must never leave that place until some knight should overcome him. And so he has been forced to defend the garden, unwillingly killing many knights, because of his promise. But now that Erec has overcome him, he is free to leave and return to his uncle's court, which will bring joy to all assembled there. For this reason is the Joy of the Court so named. The Red Knight bids Erec blow the horn to signify the coming joy and reveals himself to be none other than Mabonograin, a knight no longer remembered in his country. The ladies of the court immediately compose and sing a lay of joy and acclaim Erec.

And so Erec becomes one who frees Mabon and, if we follow the convention of the Rex Nemorensis combat, the new guardian of the orchard—except, of course, the games are now abolished because the enchantment has been lifted.

Chrétien's orchard woman is very much an earthly lady, peeved at the frustration of her plan to keep Mabonograin imprisoned. This retention of the hero by an otherworldly woman is a theme we have already encountered in "Owain" and occurs again and again in Celto-Arthurian literature. In the romances "Graelent," "Désiré," and "The Lay of Guigamor" all three knights are similarly held captive by a faery woman who retains power of life and death over them. Chrétien's rationalization of a faery woman is at odds with the rest of his story, but something interesting is revealed at this point: When Enid goes to comfort the lady, she finds that they are in fact cousins, just as Erec and Mabonograin discover that they were raised in the same court, almost as foster brothers. It is noteworthy that, following the last section, Mabonograin is laid under a geis and is forced to accept or deny his destiny, while Erec swears his love to Enid but does not fulfill it in a mature way.

Erec and Enid are thus shown to be the earthly counterparts of Mabonograin and the orchard woman. Both men are challenged on their honor by women, but while Mabonograin defers to his mistress's demands, Erec is foresworn to his. Eventually, both come to a point of perfect relationship: Mabonograin is released from his arduous service to prove himself freely, and Erec recovers his honor by fully respecting Enid. As for Enid, she rejects the abject obedience that her counterpart, the tyrannical orchard woman, extorts from her lover in favor of her own loving obedience and watchfulness.

If we return to "Gereint and Enid," we will find that the mysteries of the story are unraveling before us. It becomes clear that we have here a story in which three distinct levels are in operation, but without reference to one another, they render our understanding void. These levels can be seen as centering upon the three female protagonists of "Gereint and Enid": Enid, Gwenhwyfar, and the orchard woman.

The orchard woman is the Sovereignty figure within "Gereint and Enid," and though she has a seemingly negligible role in the action, she is nonetheless the prime mover of events. It is her white hart that the court hunts and that acts as her messenger to summon Arthur and his men to otherworldly adventures at her games. Her appearance in a type of earthly paradise at the conclusion of the story marks Gereint's restoration to his real self, for up until this point he has been seeking to become whole.

His championship of Gwenhwyfar is a courteous response to his lord's lady and his entrance in the sparrowhawk contest rests upon his having his own lady, for which role he picks Enid almost arbitrarily. The reader is half aware that, like Guigamor, he is not a man accustomed to the love of women. In fact, his temporary infatuation with the joys of married love is soon replaced by a reversal of behavior. Instead of cherishing Enid, he puts her through much mental torment and physical danger in order to prove his manly prowess, succeeding only in appearing foolish to his peers and almost killing himself in the process. It is this brush with death that brings him to his senses and impels him to aid Enid, who is struggling in Earl Limwris's arms.

The final seal of his adventures is his meeting with Sovereignty, the ultimate mistress of mistresses, whose garden is death to any knight who cannot fight her champion. As Gereint has never shown any modesty about what is due him, so here he sits in the vacant chair by Sovereignty's side. He has learned, through the trials of combat and much unnecessary trouble, that true love is his friend and requires a balanced response. It is in this way that he truly earns the right to his lands, for, as we have already noted, a man cannot use his people unjustly—as Gereint has done in ill-treating Enid—or waste his lands and be worthy of his sovereignty. Only a man who can submit to love, whatever its appearance, in sickness and in health, can rule justly.

The orchard woman offers Gereint the final challenge to submit to Sovereignty's rules: Only a man who is just and honest, truthful and loving may hold the land or partner Sovereignty's representative.

Gwenhwyfar's part in the story is not the mythic role of the orchard woman, but that of archetypal queen. As Gereint strives to find himself and be reconciled with Enid, so Arthur once strove to win his wife and hold her against abduction. The newly made king has many trials ahead of him. He must be empowered in his kingship by the hallows, the mystic symbols of his reign. These he obtains by undertaking a hazardous Underworld foray, as in the "Preiddeu Annwfn" (*Mabon*, chapter 6), and holds them balanced in his kingdom until his reign is concluded, at which time they are returned to their bearers, as Excalibur is returned to the Lady of the Lake or the Grail to Sarras.

The other main test for Arthur, the new king, is the finding of a suitable wife. This woman has to be, in mythic terms, Sovereignty's representative, the young Flower Bride or Spring Maiden in whom all the qualities of the fruitful land are immanent. Gwenhwyfar embodies all these qualifications, and it is not surprising that every stratum of the Arthurian legend has some story in which she is abducted or propositioned by rival kings. We may view in this very light Lancelot's love and his abduction of Guinevere from the stake, two circumstances from late Arthurian tradition. From this point onwards the institution of the Round Table ceases to be effective, civil war breaks out, and Arthur is forced to fight the last battle of his reign and pass back into Avalon. Some versions tell of Mordred imprisoning Guinevere in the Tower of London in order to force her into marriage with him: a clear signal that the queen, who was once a Flower Bride, remains important to claimant kings.

Gwenhwyfar represents the Goddess of Sovereignty: Through marriage to her, Arthur becomes a landed king. It is easy to forget that at the beginning of the Arthurian story, Arthur, like Gereint at the beginning of "Gereint and Enid," is a landless warrior who, even after he has been inaugurated as king, must put down numerous revolts until he wins the right to marry his bride. In the later stories, it is Guinevere who brings the dowry of the Round Table. She can be seen, then, as the matron who endows Arthur's reign with the dowry of chivalric honor. Gereint, by his championship of Gwenhwyfar, shows his desire to serve Sovereignty's representative in the person of his queen. The fact that Gwenhwyfar's insult is canceled by Gereint's championship of Enid at the sparrowhawk contest is a sign that the mantle of Flower Bride or Spring Maiden falls upon Enid. We remember that Gereint refuses to let Enid wear fine clothes until he brings her to the queen, who dresses her from her own wardrobe.

Enid then represents the final level of the story, the earthly woman who becomes Sovereignty's representative. We may be sure that if Gereint's choice had fallen upon some other woman, he might never have won the sparrowhawk contest, nor would his chosen lady have been presented with the white hart's head. But when Arthur assumes the guise of the Goddess's huntsman, taking upon himself the otherworldly dangers inherent in such a chase, he gives Gereint an unparalleled prize. At this point in the mythic structure, Arthur might well have chosen to take Enid for himself and repudiate Gwenhwyfar as a faded flower, perhaps increasing the length of his reign as a result of marrying the Flower Bride aspect of Sovereignty. But such a thing does not come to pass. Enid is accorded the highest place at court next to the king and queen. Her role is queen for the feast, just as Gereint's is honored champion of Sovereignty for his defense of the queen. Such roles must be earned, and both Enid and Gereint have had trouble in good measure. Like Guigamor and his queen: "and to dolorous knight, dolorous lady."[26]

If Enid's claim as Sovereignty's representative seems negligible, let us look at the evidence. Rachel Bromwich has suggested some possible meanings for the names Erec and Enid, as these appear in Chrétien. She concludes that Erec derives from the Breton Bro Weroc, "the land of Guerec," and suggests that Enid derives from a territorial Breton district of the once powerful tribe of the Veneti: Bro Wened. While this is ingenious, she in no way urges our acceptance of such derivations, although she, too, recognizes aspects of Sovereignty in Enid.[56]

We have already seen in chapter 3 how the legends of the transformed hag attach to Sovereignty's mythos. Might not Gereint's insistence on Enid assuming her worst dress and covering her beauty have a relevance to this hag motif? As a tattered lady, Enid can hardly be a Loathly Lady, though Gereint certainly treats her as such. However, we have seen how the Irish story "The Sons of Daire" combines the themes of the white hart and the transformed hag who bestows sovereignty upon the hero. Here Gereint can be said to cause his Spring Maiden to suffer an unseasonal frost, for once equipped with the loveliest wife and kingly domains, he abandons his duty, becoming a morose husband and absentee landlord, until, in traveling with Enid, he realizes his true self. This is more in keeping with the folk theme of the enchanted mare: The hero is encouraged to choose the worst mare in the stable, which turns out to be the most helpful beast as well as the enchanted woman who will become his mate.

The end of *Erec and Enid* is substantially different from that of "Gereint and Enid" in that the story concludes with the crowning of Erec and Enid. They are received by Arthur and Guinevere in a scene which echoes their former arrival and acclaim. At the sight of the pair, the queen is "so above herself with joy that you might have used her for hawking."[7] Their joy is somewhat blunted at hearing of the death of Erec's father, King Lac. Then Arthur says, "We have to go from here to Nantes in Brittany. There you shall bear the tokens of kingship, a crown on your head and a sceptre in your hand: this favour and this honour I bestow upon you."[7]

Arthur endows Erec and Enid with many riches, including ivory thrones and a rich robe woven by four faeries and depicting four of the liberal arts: geometry, arithmetic, music, and astronomy. Guinevere clothes Enid herself, while Arthur provides crowns for them both. And so they are crowned in the presence of all.

It is indeed a pity that no part of this episode is retained in "Gereint and Enid," for it is of supreme importance. Erec is confirmed in his lordship as king at Arthur's behest. It is obvious that, having made Gereint his champion in so blatant a manner, Arthur could not relinquish the kingship of Britain to his knight. Gereint's lands are in Cornwall and not Brittany, as they are in Chrétien, but he is nonetheless their true lord at the end of the story, with his own Flower Bride at his side. And in the land where the white hart once ran, the magic mist lifts from the otherworldly orchard. The orchard woman and her champion depart, leaving only Gereint and Enid to flourish in their turn.

7

Peredur

Who caught the blood?
I, said the Fish,
In my little dish:
I caught the blood.

"THE DEATH OF COCK ROBIN"
(TRADITIONAL RHYME)

Of no account was he held at first, yet afterwards was his accoutrement right noble, and so thoroughly did he search out amidst the land . . . that he found the Court . . . Perceval li Galois was he.

THE ELUCIDATION

In the Wasteland

With "Peredur" we reach the last of our commentaries on the *Mabinogion* and find perhaps the most complex and pied of the stories. "Peredur" has excited more interest and more study than any of the other texts that comprise the *Mabinogion* because of its Grail associa-

172

tions. But, as a quick reading will inform anyone, this story is quite unlike later and more sophisticated texts which relate the Grail quest.

Although many talismanic gifts feature in "Peredur"—rings, cups, spears and swords—there is no classic Grail. The vessel that is borne during the procession of the hallows at Peredur's uncle's castle is described as a *dysgyl,* a wide, shallow dish, and it contains a severed and bloody head.

Everything in "Peredur" leads us to look to earlier texts for clarification, for although the storyteller was aware of Chrétien's *Perceval,* he did not draw on it extensively. That there was a proto-story in circulation can be proved from cross-reference to other texts in which Perceval appears.[74] "Peredur" proves to be in the same tradition as the Amadan Mor stories about the Great Fool who accomplishes wonders, wins a wife and lands, and vindicates his wronged family. There is also a distinct overlay with the *macgnimartha* (youthful exploits) stories of Celtic tradition, especially with those of Fionn mac Cumhail.

The motivation for Peredur is not a quest for the Grail, but rather a threefold purpose: to avenge his family, to find his intended wife, and to alleviate the enchantments *(gormesiad)* which are upon the land. This last purpose accounts for the only appearance in "Peredur" of the wasteland motif now so familiar from other texts. The quest for the Grail, that object which we can see here to be one of the hallows, is ultimately derived from Peredur's search for lost sovereignty—the avenging his father's loss of lands. In one later romance, through a French rationalization of his name, Peredur becomes Perd-les-vaus, or "he who has lost the valleys." But though Peredur's quest starts as one of vengeance, like that of Maelduin the voyager, who begins his *imram* (voyage) for a similar reason,[162] his journey proves more fruitful.

There is also a secondary quest interwoven through "Peredur": the search for a name or a truer understanding of his name. Throughout the story, three otherworldly beings acclaim Peredur by name: the dwarfs, the witches of Gloucester, and the Black Maiden. He is also called the dumb knight, the knight with the spear, or the knight of the mill. In Chrétien his mother calls him nothing but dear son. This is consistent with the Celtic tradition of the hero having to earn his name, for though he may have a childhood appellation, it is by his deeds that he acquires his adult name.

There are many inconsistencies within the text of "Peredur" and the reader is advised to refer to more than one translation, for each varies slightly depending on which manuscripts were used. The Gwyn and Thomas Jones text is particularly helpful. In this version, however, the way the narrative falls over itself to get to the next incident and the duplication and triplication of characters and events are striking.

Some questions emerge from any reading of "Peredur": Why does Peredur not marry the disinherited maiden? How can Peredur's career be reconciled with his role in the other Perceval texts? The answer to the first question will be revealed as we study the many female figures within this text. Whereas Gereint encounters knights, outlaws, and other combatants, Peredur seems fated to fall in with unmarried women and a great many guises of Sovereignty. This will form the discussion of the section The Royal Blood in the Holy Snow, later in this chapter.

The answer to the second question will perhaps disappoint avid Grail seekers. Because of the nature of "Peredur" and the many crosscurrents of earlier tradition that run through the tale, I have chosen to concentrate on the story in its proto-Celtic context. A full comparison between this and the many other associated texts, including the *Didot Perceval*,[32] Chrétien's *Perceval*,[7] and von Eschenbach's *Parzival*,[40] not to mention the later texts, would render this chapter book length. I shall not attempt such a comparison here other than to make reference to specific points which elucidate "Peredur." A complete listing of these related texts as well as Glenys Goetinck's study of "Peredur"[74] can be found in the bibliography.

I offer no apology for choosing an unusual framework for comparison—drawing parallels between "Peredur" and its Irish cousins, the oral folk stories collected in the nineteenth century, in order to illuminate many of the more obscure and primitive aspects of the story. The

Grail corpus has suffered comparisons to the cult of Adonis,[73] the Orthodox liturgy,[157] Middle Eastern astrology,[40] tales of templar relics, and the theology of Cathars from outer space.[159] Such analogues may prove diverting to the scholar, but they are hardly helpful in illuminating Peredur's British mythological context.

"Peredur" reveals a wealth of Otherworld characters and archetypes which are readily identifiable from a pan-Celtic understanding of native mythology. Most striking are the many female characters who throng this story. Their functions and natures are discussed at length in the third section of this chapter, The Royal Blood in the Holy Snow.

Synopsis of "Peredur"

(1) Earl Efrawg had seven sons. He and the first six were killed in wars and tournaments, leaving the last, Peredur, to be raised by his mother, who has determined that her remaining son grow up in ignorance of warfare. (2) They live in seclusion in the forest. Peredur, however, soon shows his strength and prowess, despite ignorance of arms, as well as his amiable stupidity. (3) On seeing three knights ride by, Peredur asks what they are. His mother tells him they are angels, but the riders soon enlighten him and he resolves to follow them. (4) His mother, shocked, nevertheless gives him advice about courtesy in such an unworldly and confused way that he is subsequently led into danger and discourtesy as a result of following her words: She tells him he is to recite a paternoster when he sees a church; take food and drink if he has need and they are not offered; attend immediately if he hears a woman cry out; take any jewel he sees and offer it to another; and pay court to beautiful women.

(5) Providing himself with makeshift weapons and a mount, Peredur rides into the forest and comes upon an unattended tent with a maiden inside. He snatches up food unasked and then takes the maiden's ring and kisses her. Meanwhile, the proud knight of the clearing returns, accuses his lady of being unchaste, and swears that she should not remain in the same place for two nights together.

(6) Peredur arrives at Arthur's court and there witnesses a knight throwing wine at Gwenhwyfar and striking her. Soon after, Cai mocks Peredur and is angered when a male and female dwarf, hitherto dumb, greet Peredur by name and acclaim him best of knights. Cai strikes both dwarfs and bids Peredur follow the knight who has insulted the queen. Peredur pursues the knight and overcomes him, though he is unable to drag the corpse out of the armor until Owain unfastens it for him. Peredur bids Owain tell Arthur that he has served him faithfully but that he will not come to court until he has avenged himself on Cai.

Peredur then goes forth, and after the first week he overcomes sixteen knights and sends them to Arthur to submit to the king's justice, with the same message—that he will avenge Cai's insult to the dwarfs before he returns. (7) In his travels he comes to a lake where a richly dressed old man sits among youths who are fishing from a boat. Peredur stays at this man's court and is instructed in arms. The old man reveals himself as Peredur's maternal uncle and gives his nephew additional advice on manners: Do not ask about strange sights unless you are told about them. (8) Peredur then leaves his uncle and continues on to another court ruled by an old man. Here he is challenged to break an iron column with a sword. With each attempt both the sword and column break in two and then reunite, but Peredur's third attempt is unsuccessful, for the column and sword break but do not reunite again. The old man of the court reveals himself to Peredur as his second maternal uncle and reports that his nephew has reached only two thirds of his strength—but when he is fully grown, he will be invincible.

(9) As they talk at dinner, a spear is borne into the hall and drips three drops of blood. This is followed by a dish on which a man's head floats in blood. Peredur does not ask about either event, true to his first uncle's advice. (10) The next morning he rides off and hears a woman cry. It is a maiden lamenting a dead knight. She addresses Peredur as accursed because he has been the cause of his mother's death. She explains that the two dwarfs at Arthur's court were once servants of his parents and that she herself is his foster sister. The knight who slew her

husband appears suddenly. Peredur overcomes him and bids him marry his foster sister and submit to Arthur. He sends a message to Cai that he will yet avenge the dwarfs. Arthur is impressed by Peredur's deeds and vows to set out in search of him, for Peredur will not come to court and Cai will not leave it in search of him.

In the meantime, Peredur arrives at a castle, where he is welcomed by (11) a poorly dressed but beautiful maiden. Her household has been kept alive by the nearby convent of nuns, for its goods have been seized by a young earl who has courted her, to her displeasure. Her foster brothers bid her sleep with Peredur that he might champion their cause. Peredur sends her from his chamber to sleep and fights the young earl, overcoming him and restoring the tattered maiden's lands. He also returns to the forest to overcome the proud knight of the clearing and bids him forgive his lady, who is innocent.

(12) He next reaches a mountain castle where a tall woman rules. She bids him sleep elsewhere if he values his life, for nine hags live nearby with their parents and are laying waste the country. Peredur stays, however, and hears screams at dawn. A hag is attacking the watchman, but Peredur strikes her and after this she acknowledges him by name and speaks of a prophecy in which she is to train him in arms. He stays with the hag for three weeks, learning battle skills, after which he chooses a horse and arms and sets out again.

While staying with a hermit he sees (13) a sight which transfixes him: the blood of a wild duck upon the snow as a raven feeds on the dead bird. The redness of the blood, the whiteness of the snow, and the blackness of the raven put him in mind of his ideal woman, the woman he loves most. While his vision holds him rapt, Arthur's men approach. Cai tries to rouse him but Peredur absently strikes him down. (14) Then Gwalchmai approaches him with more tact and leads him to Arthur. Peredur realizes that he had avenged the dwarfs on Cai, albeit absentmindedly, and he returns to Caerleon with Arthur. (15) While there, following his mother's instruction to court women even if they are unwilling, he asks a woman called Angharad Golden Hair to marry him, but she rejects his suit. He is insistent that he loves her so much that he will speak to no Christian until she confesses her love for him. For this he is afterwards called the dumb knight.

Peredur resumes his now silent wandering and slays a lion guarding a giant's castle. A maiden bids him beware the Round Valley, the name of their land, or all the giants will kill him. He then fights and kills many of these giants, but in overcoming the chief giant, Peredur grants him mercy on condition that he be baptized and submit to Arthur. The giant admits that no Christian has previously remained alive in the Round Valley, and Peredur is glad he has not broken his oath of silence, for he has spoken only to unbaptized people on this adventure. (16) He next slays a serpent which has been devastating the land and wins the golden ring it guards. Growing weary of solitude, Peredur turns and rides back towards Arthur's court. On the way, he meets Cai, who, not recognizing him, asks Peredur his identity three times. He then strikes Peredur in the thigh with his spear, but Peredur does not respond. Peredur goes on to defeat an unknown knight who has challenged Arthur's men, and then he returns to court on foot.

Angharad now professes her love for Peredur, who is able to speak again, and everyone who has not recognized him does so now.

(17) While out hunting a stag with Arthur, Peredur comes to a hall in the wilderness where the Black Oppressor lives with his daughters, the eldest of whom begs Peredur to leave and convinces her father to refrain from killing him. After Peredur has asked a taboo question warranting death, the Black Oppressor tells him that he has lost his eye while fighting the black serpent of the Dolorous Mound. This serpent guards a stone which when it is clasped in one hand gives to the other hand as much gold as the possessor wishes.

In the ensuing combat, Peredur overcomes the Black Oppressor, who (18) gives Peredur directions to find this serpent: He will come first to the court of the sons of the king of suffering, so called because an *addanc* (underwater monster) kills one of the king's sons each day.

After this he will come to the court of the countess of the feats, who has a retinue of three hundred men. Every stranger who goes there hears the tales of her war band. After that he will reach the Dolorous Mound. On receiving these directions, Peredur then kills the Black Oppressor.

(19) At the court of the sons of the king of suffering, Peredur witnesses the revival of the dead sons in a bath of water, after which they are anointed. Every day the addanc comes and kills one son, after which he is revived, only to be killed again another day. (20) The next day he follows the men to their assignation with the addanc and he encounters a beautiful woman seated on top of a mound. She warns him that the addanc hides behind a pillar in its cave and from there kills its foes. If he promises to love her beyond all women, she offers, she will grant him the stone of plenty. She gives him a ring bestowing invisibility, and when asked by Peredur where he can find her again, she bids him look towards India.

(21) Peredur then comes to a valley divided by a river. On one bank a flock of black sheep graze, on the other, a flock of white sheep. As they switch sides, they exchange colors. On the bank there is a divided tree, one half burning and the other half green. (22) Beyond this tree, on a mound, sits a royal youth with a brace of greyhounds. Peredur hears hounds across the valley flushing out a stag. The royal youth tells him that the three roads ahead lead to his own court where his wife may be found and where Peredur is welcome to stay; or to a fortress, where Peredur can pay lodging; or to the addanc's cave. Peredur finds the cave and slays the addanc. The three sons of the king of suffering then beg him to choose one of their sisters as a wife, but Peredur refuses. (23) He takes along Etlym Red Sword, a young earl, as his companion and together they arrive at the court of the countess of the feats. Peredur overthrows the three hundred knights of the countess's war band in order to sit next to her, then offers her Etlym as her lover, whom she accepts. The many men surrounding the Dolorous Mound refuse to pay homage to Peredur, who has killed two hundred

of their retainers; the three hundred knights submit to him. He then kills the serpent and gives its stone to Etlym.

Peredur next lodges at a miller's house in a valley full of mills. Because the empress of Constantinople is visiting, there is great need for grain to be milled. (24) Peredur gazes on her daily and is overcome with love for her. The miller lends Peredur money so that he may purchase arms for the coming tournament, which angers the miller's wife. On the third day the miller rouses Peredur from his reverie of love by striking him with his ax handle and bids him attend the tournament. Peredur obliges and, known as the knight of the mill, he overcomes all comers, sending all the knights to the empress and the horses and arms to the miller's wife. He eventually meets the empress and is talking with her when a black man enters, with a gold cup, asking the empress not to give the cup to anyone except to the knight who will fight for her. (25) Peredur asks for the cup and after being given it sends it on to the miller's wife. Another black man arrives, bearing a cup in the shape of a monster's claw, which Peredur likewise asks for and sends on. Third, a red-haired man arrives bearing a crystal cup, which is likewise given to Peredur, who then kills the three cup bearers. The empress bids him remember the promise he made her when she warned him about the addanc. He remains with her for fourteen years.

(26) Later on, when Arthur, Peredur, and others are at Caerleon, a hideous damsel rides into court, greeting the whole assembly but berating Peredur for not having asked about the spear and the dish at his uncle's court. Apparently this oversight has been the cause of great suffering. She then tells of a besieged castle near her home, Castle Syberw (the proud castle); whoever lifts the siege will gain the greatest honor in the world. Inside there is a maiden to be rescued. Gwalchmai resolves to rescue her, while Peredur swears he will not rest until he discovers the meaning of the spear and dish. Each man goes his separate way. Gwalchmai first slays a knight[27] and then proceeds to a castle, where he is met by a maiden. An old man taxes the girl with welcoming her father's murderer. When her brother returns, Gwalchmai nei-

ther admits nor denies planning the deed, but he asks for a year's respite, during which time he is to be going about Arthur's business.

(28) Peredur sets out to find the hideous damsel who appeared at Caerleon and meets with a priest who tells him it is Good Friday, a day on which he should not bear arms. Peredur spends Easter there in a towerless fortress and asks the priest to tell him of the Castle of Wonders, for which he then embarks. En route he meets a king who is out hunting, and he is subsequently imprisoned because of the familiarity he has shown to the king's daughter. (29) While in prison, Peredur learns that the king is threatened by a neighboring earl. The king's daughter provides Peredur with arms and releases him to help her father. Peredur overcomes the earl and returns to prison, from whence the king releases him and offers him his daughter as wife. Peredur refuses and asks the way to the Castle of Wonders.

(30) Soon he finds the castle and inside it a gwyddbwyll board playing against itself. The side he supports loses and Peredur throws the pieces and board into the nearby lake, whereupon the hideous damsel appears, telling him it is the empress's board. If he wants to retrieve it, he must go to the Castle of Ysbidinongyl, where the Black Man lives who has ravaged the empress's lands. Upon meeting him, Peredur grants the Black Man mercy on condition that the man return the board. The hideous damsel then appears and berates him for not killing the Black Man. He is forbidden to see the empress until he has killed a further oppressor. (31) A stag with a single sharp horn on its forehead has laid waste the forest and has drunk all the fish pools, leaving the fish exposed. Peredur uses the empress's lapdog to help flush out the stag, which he then beheads. A horsewoman then appears and berates him for killing the best jewel of her realm. She bids him seek a stone slab beneath a bush and fight three times with a man he will find there. Peredur finds the bush and a black man rises up from under the slab and fights him, but disappears before Peredur can slay him.

At last, Peredur arrives at a hall where a lame old man sits next to Gwalchmai. (32) A golden-haired youth comes in, salutes Peredur, and reveals that he has been the hideous damsel, the horsewoman, and the Black Man. He has also carried the dish and the spear. The head belonged to Peredur's first cousin, who had been beheaded by the hags of Gloucester, those responsible for laming his uncle as well.

The youth is Peredur's first cousin and it is destined that Peredur should avenge him. Peredur and Gwalchmai send for Arthur and his men and then fight the hags. Peredur strikes one, who proclaims to the others that Peredur has come, the one who has learned battle skills from them, the one who is destined to destroy them. Arthur and his men then kill the hags of Gloucester. So runs the story of the Castle of Wonders.

Commentary

(1) Two triads speak of Peredur: Triad 86 calls him one of three knights who win the Grail, while Triad 91 calls him one of three fearless men. The name of his father, Efrawg, is derived from Eboracum (York). There was a historical Peredur, possibly he who is mentioned in the *Gododdin,* that epic by the sixth-century poet Aneurin, which tells of the battle of Catraeth fought between the Britons of the north and the men of Bernecia and Deira.[14, 74] In the long arguments that have raged about the existence of this story before Chrétien, it must be remembered that while Peredur was a common British name, Perceval was not—prior to the written evidence of the Grail romances. It would seem, then, that Perceval was derived from Peredur, not the other way around.

(2) The upbringing of Peredur is archetypal: He is raised in seclusion, brought up in ignorance of arms, and, according to Chrétien, has no name. It is tempting to compare his youth with that of Llew, who similarly has no name and is fated never to be given the arms of manhood or a human wife. This all seems to be a part of the hard destiny that the hero must overcome, but whereas Llew's relationships with Sovereignty via Arianrhod and Blodeuwedd are abrasive, Peredur is considerably assisted by the many women he encounters. His exploits with the deer

are paralleled exactly in the *macgnimartha* (boyhood deeds) of Fionn:
Two women warriors who are fostering the young Fionn find themselves unable to catch two deer, so Fionn drives them back with his
hands alone.[8]

(3) The three knights whom Peredur mistakes for angels are three of
the most prominent of Arthur's court: Gwalchmai (Gawain), Gwair,
and Owain. They are searching for "the knight who had distributed
apples in Arthur's court," a curious detail which is explained no further. Peredur claims to have seen the man. It is not stated whether the
knights are seeking to harm him or detain him, and no other details of
this lost story appear elsewhere. We may only speculate, drawing upon
traditional lore for the answer. It is usual, before the appearance of a
great wonder or before the institution of a quest, for an otherworldly
being to make an appearance, bearing some token of the wonder or
quest. Often the bearer carries a branch from the otherworldly tree,
which boasts fruit, blossom, and bud all on one bough. The fruits of
the Otherworld sustain life and enhance awareness, as Maelduin finds
on his voyages.[162] It is possible, then, considering the importance of
these knights, that the man who distributed apples at Arthur's court
was the messenger of the coming adventures and that Gwalchmai,
Gwair, and Owain (all seasoned otherworldly visitors) have set out on
the quest already. Gawain's part of the Grail quest figures largely in
Chrétien, and while in later romances he proves to be an unworthy
Grail winner, in a lost original he may have played a larger part than he
does in "Peredur."

(4) Peredur's mother's advice to him is a sweeping précis of courtly
behavior and the storyteller makes him implement this advice in the
very next incident. Up until the point when he reaches his uncles' castles, Peredur behaves totally as the Amadan Mor, the Great Fool, in his
headlong career to become a trained knight.[61]

(5) A careful analysis of this incident shows us that the maiden in the tent is not synonymous with the frightened girl in Chrétien's version. The maiden in "Peredur" shows no fear and is described in much the same way as the orchard woman of "Gereint and Enid," for she wears a golden diadem and sits in a golden chair. She offers food to Peredur, which is one of Sovereignty's first actions, and allows him to take her ring. The text indicates that rather than rising in alarm, she remains seated because Peredur must kneel to kiss her. We may take this to be Peredur's first encounter with a representative of Sovereignty, but because he is immature, no empowering exchange yet takes place between them (see note 20). Her encouragement of Peredur shows that she recognizes in him a future champion. All the tests and encounters that he subsequently endures only serve to develop him as a man and as a knight. The proud knight of the clearing is, like the Black Knight in "Owain" and Mabonograin in "Gereint and Enid," Sovereignty's champion.

(6) This insult to Gwenhwyfar is the most grave such instance appearing in the three romances, for it is a gross insult to Sovereignty herself. As Arthur's queen, Gwenhwyfar represents the land and the Goddess. Triad 53 intriguingly speaks of three harmful blows struck in Britain. The first is that which Branwen receives at the hands of Matholwch and the second is the blow which "Gwenhwyfach struck upon Gwenhwyfar, and for that cause there took place afterwards the Action of the Battle of Camlann." This is further borne out in Triad 84, where Camlann is described as one of three futile battles brought about because of a quarrel between these two protagonists. Gwenhwyfach was Gwenhwyfar's sister, according to "Culhwch and Olwen."[23] Triad 54 further confuses matters by telling us that Medrawt (Mordred), who is seen in early tradition not as Arthur's son but as an independent and worthy young man, left neither food nor drink in Arthur's court, who drags the queen from her royal chair and strikes her.[38] This account gives notice of a tradition much concerned with this very incident of

the queen's insult. The theft of the queen's cup is a loss of sovereignty to Arthur, for the Goddess bestows kingship by means of her cup. In the section The Maidens of the Wells in chapter 9, we will see that an entire text is devoted to telling this archetypal story.

The curious incident of the dumb dwarf couple is paralleled in Chrétien by a maiden who has not laughed for six years and who, the fool says, will laugh to acclaim the best knight.[7] In Chrétien, Kay strikes both dwarfs, as he does here. Goetinck is of the opinion that Chrétien's version was drawn from the original or proto-story, and I am inclined to agree. Dwarfs appear frequently in Breton stories but seldom in British ones. The prophetic laugh is also a feature of Celtic tradition, especially in the *Vita Merlini*,[11, 149] in which Merlin exhibits it. The function of both maiden and dwarfs is to name the hero and prophesy his future merit. This is the first time anyone speaks Peredur's name, which may not, in the proto-story, have been known to him.

Peredur defends Arthur's sovereignty by vanquishing the insulting knight and by returning Gwenhwyfar's cup after avenging her affront. His refusal to come to court until he is avenged on Cai shows another part of the unfolding vengeance motif of this story. Cai is reproached by the arrival of the sixteen knights overthrown by Peredur, each of whom bears the same message. Cai's renown is somewhat tarnished, for Peredur is not a knight, nor does he have any training in arms but instead relies on his strength alone.

(7) Much ink has been spilled concerning the number, function, and designation of Peredur's uncles. The first uncle does not fish himself but his squires do while he watches. Is he the Fisher King? He is also said to be lame. Is he also, then, the Wounded King? It is revealed at the conclusion (see note 32) that the witches of Gloucester lamed him, though Peredur is not told this until the end of the tale. But what of the second uncle? Within the context of "Peredur" we can find no clear answer to these questions, nor, perhaps, should we attempt to squeeze this story into the mold of the later Grail romances, which give us

either clear or even more confused archetypal roles to draw on. It is sufficient to remark that the roles of these figures of Wounded King and
Fisher King became hopelessly confused during the transcription and
reweaving of these stories. The first uncle tests Peredur and prophesies
that he will be the best swordsman of Britain. He gives the advice that
obviates the asking of the Grail question, as later texts call it. He also
makes Peredur a knight.

(8) While Peredur fights with a stick at the court of the first uncle, his
second uncle bids him fight with a sword in a test of strength which is
otherworldly in its magical reuniting of pillar and sword torn asunder.
The implication of Peredur's entire career to this point is that if he can
perform tasks which outdo other men when he is not yet an experienced knight, what will he be able to do when he is fully experienced
and possessed of his whole strength? The broken sword becomes an
emblem of the Grail quest in later texts.

(9) This second uncle is neither lame nor wounded, according to the
text, nor do we know the name of the castle where Peredur is at this
point. These details are inconsistent within the text. The Grail procession, if it can truly be called such, consists of very different hallows from
those of later sources. The spear appears to be that very weapon which
causes the Dolorous Blow, the weapon that wounds the Wounded King
and causes the devastation of the land—hence the blood that flows
from it continually, indicating the unhealing nature of the Blow on
both flesh and earth. The head on the dish is later revealed to have
been Peredur's first cousin—doubtless the son of the second uncle at
whose table he sits. A fuller discussion of this incident follows in the
section The Royal Blood in the Holy Snow later in this chapter.

(10) For the first time Peredur obeys his mother's dictum about
answering a woman's cry. This incident seems strangely astray and in
other texts is usually the signal for the Black Maiden to appear to

reproach Peredur for not asking the Grail question. The sum of Peredur's thoughtless deeds is increased at this point by the accusation that he killed his mother by leaving her. It is possible that the foster sister, of whom no previous mention has been made, was originally the Black Maiden.

As in both "Owain" and "Gereint and Enid," Arthur is eventually forced to seek out his new knight, for Peredur will not visit him. The removal of Arthur from court enables each of the three heroes of the romances to acquire some of Arthur's authority, as he becomes the king's champion in the retention of sovereignty.

(11) The tattered maiden goes unnamed here, though Chrétien names her Blanchflor. Her description fits the later blood in the snow episode (see note 13), but while it may be puzzling at first that Peredur does not take up her offer to sleep with him, he is chaste, like Pwyll with Arawn's wife (*Mabon,* chapter 2), both from honor and because he has a combat to face. After he has restored her lands, she thanks him by name and offers her help if he should ever stand in need. It has been suggested that this episode owes something to "The Tragic Death of Cú Roi mac Daire" (*Mabon,* chapter 3), and that the tattered maiden's original name may indeed have been a British variant of the Flower Bride, if Chrétien's Blanchflor is any proof. The acquittal of the maiden in the tent seems extraneous and is but one instance of the doubling and sometimes tripling of incidents in the text.

(12) The mountain castle seems analogous to the ubiquitous Castle of Maidens or Island of Women. Its gatekeeper is a prodigious child who bears arms, and its lady a seated countess. She is yet another appearance of Sovereignty who suffers under the affliction of a *gormes* (plague) of witches. This is the first mention of a prevailing theme throughout Peredur: the hero ridding the land of a host of plagues. Dressed only in his shirt and trousers, Peredur pursues and captures one of the witches, who acquiesces to a prophecy which says she shall

train him in arms. She and her sisters follow in the Celtic tradition of women warriors who train unskilled youths in battle.[120] The most famous instance of this is, of course, Cú Chulainn's training at the rath of Scathach, faint traces of which can be found within "Peredur." It is also possible that Peredur has had transferred to him a story once told of Cai, for the poem "Pa Gur"[44] speaks of Cai's destruction of the nine witches of Gloucester. The similar incident of the pitch-black witch in "Culhwch and Olwen" may be part of this fragmentary tale. In that instance, the *anoeth* (impossible task) is fulfilled by Arthur himself, we will recall (see *Mabon*, chapter 6).

(13) The hermit does not, as in other texts, explain the events of the quest to Peredur—this task is left to others. The blood in the snow episode forms one of the central tableaux of the story. The colors of white, red, and black in proximity form an archetypal kaleidoscope into which the hero or heroine of a folktale looks to see his or her lover revealed. The simplicity of this motif should not be dismissed; these very colors also signify the symbolic processes of alchemy. Here a kind of soul alchemy is effected in Peredur, who at last responds fully to the dream image within his heart. He has met Sovereignty in many guises and has been propositioned by one earthly woman, Blanchflor, whose coloring this image represents. The Blanchflor of Chrétien's story is blond—romantic convention made all beautiful women fair rather than dark. But in British and Irish tradition, the desired one is dark, not fair. This episode is very like that in "Culhwch and Olwen" when King Doged's wife swears the destiny of marrying only Olwen to Culhwch. Peredur, like Culhwch, has never lain with a woman. This episode, therefore, represents his sexual maturity, when the dream image of his heart matches the one woman who has offered him her love. (See the section The Royal Blood in the Holy Snow later in this chapter.)

(14) For the last time Cai insults and is bested by the hero in these romances. Again, Gwalchmai is the intermediary. In this case he is the

most suitable of Arthur's knights for this task. His own experience in matters of love and otherworldly quests makes him a sensitive choice. The triads speak of Gwalchmai as one who is most courteous to strangers and guests, and this makes him, with Peredur, one of the most fearless men in Britain.[38]

(15) Peredur exhibits his newfound facility in courting women, as advised by his mother. In an excessive expression of courtly love, he lays a geis on himself not to speak to a Christian soul. This is but one of many tasks which, as a newly recognized knight, Peredur undertakes as a way of increasing his powers. He then enters an otherworldly place, the Round Valley, where his encounter and that of note 17 are very similar in kind. They remind the reader of Culhwch's meeting with Custennin at Yspaddaden's court (see *Mabon*, chapter 6). The old giant is a shapeshifter who, like Yspaddaden, is close-lipped in his agreements and has an obliging daughter who is willing to help the hero.

(16) The serpent lying on the gold ring is the first of three such monsters slain by Peredur. Cai's "wounding" of Peredur, in the terminology of the Grail corpus, makes our hero a wounded knight, but the wound is healed by Gwenhwyfar—a fair exchange for the healing he brought to her. Peredur is seen here as the dumb knight, one of his many aliases. When Angharad proclaims her love for Peredur, thus releasing him from his self-imposed geis, he does nothing about it, according to the text. Similarly, in other texts the hero who has reached sexual maturity thinks little of sleeping with many court ladies before he marries. This is especially true of Lancelot and Guigamor, Gawain's son.[42]

(17) The Black Oppressor, with his single eye, is similar to Balor, the grandfather of Lugh (see *Mabon*, chapter 5). Like Balor, the Black Oppressor is a gormes, or plague, who lays waste the surrounding countryside. The encounter between Peredur and the giant is very

much like that between Culhwch and Yspaddaden, for Culhwch asks a question which breaks the custom of the giant—namely, whether or not he can marry the giant's daughter—and here Peredur asks about the loss of the Black Oppressor's eye. He receives information only after he has bested the oppressor.

(18) Like both Yspaddaden, who lays anoethu upon Culhwch, and the Wild Herdsman, who acts as a guide to Owain, the Black Oppressor gives directions to the Mournful Mound. The tripling of serpents is very confusing for the reader, who may feel that he or she is reading in circles. Before Peredur finds the black serpent, he kills an addanc, a water monster, sometimes described as a giant beaver. The episode of the court of the sons of the king of suffering that follows is a familiar theme in Celtic literature, associated with the story of Ridere san Gaire—the laughless knight. In this the hero's task is to find the cause of the knight's sorrow and to make him laugh once again. Always involved in this feat is the restoration of the knight's dead sons, who have been slain by giants, after which the giants are made to share their victims' fate—which causes the knight to laugh. In some measure, Custennin's role is that of the laughless knight in "Culhwch and Olwen" (see *Mabon,* chapter 6). This episode is also a parallel of the sorrow at the Castle of Wonders, where Peredur sees the Grail procession. The king of suffering is wounded by grief, not by the Dolorous Blow. It is as though Peredur, having failed the earlier test, fulfills his role as liberator on the human level by restoring the sons.

(19) This episode of reviving the sons is, of course, analogous to that of the Cauldron of Rebirth in "Branwen, Daughter of Llyr," into which dead man are placed, to be pulled out alive but dumb. The properties of the Grail include the gift of immortality or regeneration, but here the vessel of rebirth is a bath of warm water. In Celtic folk tradition such a vessel is often employed by an old woman, or cailleach, who aids the hero. She is able to revive the dead, and sometimes has two vessels, a

cauldron of poison and a cauldron of cure, into which she plunges the hero to harden him in his combats and to heal his wounds. The cailleach, like Ceridwen or the goddess depicted on the Gundestrup cauldron, is plunging warriors into a vat of immortality, a prime figure in the regenerative mythos of the cauldron. In later tradition, which inherits all the earlier analogues, the Grail is represented by two figures: the Grail Maiden and the Loathly Lady. These representatives of Sovereignty have the joint task of healing and hardening the hero.

(20) Peredur finally meets Sovereignty in her undisguised form, seated atop a mound, symbolic of the land she guards. While before he took a ring from the maiden in the tent, now he is given one in return for his undisputed love. This is one of the clearest sovereignty-bestowing episodes in the whole *Mabinogion,* for Peredur receives a ring from the very hand of Sovereignty. The juxtaposition of this incident with his slaying or overcoming of so many serpents may lead us to conclude that in the proto-story, Peredur may have disenchanted the Black Maiden from her dark aspect into its beautiful counterpart. In all other key Sovereignty stories, the hero has to perform the fier baiser: kissing the hag or lying with her to change her into her beautiful queenly aspect. The fact that Sovereignty disappears at this point, to reemerge as the supreme royal woman, the empress of the Eastern World, is significant.

In Celtic folk story the woman destined to become the hero's wife is invariably the daughter of the king of Spain or Greece or is simply called the daughter of the king of the Eastern World. In these stories the otherworldly location is subsumed in an exotic Eastern province, though the East is described in exactly the same terms as one of the Blessed Isles. In *Parzival*[40] von Eschenbach attempts to replace the proto-story's Otherworld location with a more contemporary Middle Eastern one. Parzival's half brother, Feirfitz (who is "piebald," being the son of a white father and a black mother), marries the Grail Maiden, Repanse de Schoy, and returns with her to India, where their son, Prester John, is born.

(21) From here on it is impossible to doubt that Peredur does indeed enter the Otherworld on his quest. The sheep that change color also appear in the *imram* of Maelduin: His ship comes upon an island bounded and divided by a brass fence, with black sheep on one side and white on the other. They are guarded by a giant shepherd who transfers white sheep into the black sheep's pen, where they become black instantaneously.[162] We have, of course, already come upon the other-worldly shepherd in "Owain," where the Wild Herdsman guards the animals. Custennin in "Culhwch and Olwen" occupies this same role. It is possible that the noble youth whom Peredur meets was intended in the proto-story to occupy the same place in this story.

The green and burning tree having both flames and leaves is the tree guarding the perimeter of the Otherworld. It reminds the traveler that the Otherworld is a mirror image of the earthly realms, that here things become or meet their opposites.

(22) The meeting of Peredur and the noble youth is very like that of Pwyll and Arawn, even to the invitation to visit the youth's wife (see *Mabon*, chapter 2). As in "Pwyll, Prince of Dyfed," there is more than a suggestion that Peredur and the youth exchange places, for, as the text states, this border of the Otherworld is where opposites meet and each then becomes the other. The youth acts as the guardian who shows the way for Peredur, offering him a choice of paths.

(23) The sudden appearance of Etlym may lead us to suppose that he and the noble youth are one and the same, for Peredur is instrumental in obtaining his bride for him. We will recall that Pwyll and Arawn changed places in order that Arawn's enemy, Hafgan, might be over-thrown. Though he has the opportunity to sleep with Arawn's wife, Pwyll abstains. Moreover, Pwyll occupies the place of the king of Annwfn while Arawn becomes merely a prince of Dyfed, just as Etlym agrees to be Peredur's man. Although the noble youth already has a wife, it is possible that he is unable to come to her save through

Peredur's offices, for the countess of the feats already knows and loves Etlym. The countess herself is an aspect of Sovereignty in her guise as mistress of the games. We also note that Peredur gives up his right to the countess, just as Cú Chulainn forgoes sleeping with Aoife during his weapons training and gives her up to his brother-in-arms, Laegaire.[8]

(24) The storyteller rationalizes the Valley of Mills by remarking that the reason so many mills exist there is that the empress's army requires much grain to make bread. The components of the Otherworld are consistent among texts of great variance, and it is clear that this valley is analogous to the island encountered by Maelduin and Ua Corra, where the miller of hell grinds to dust all possessions hoarded in the world. This valley, together with the green and burning tree and the sheep, all indicate that we are indeed in the Otherworld (see chapter 8).

The empress of the Eastern World is Amherodres of Constantinople, the seat of the great Byzantine empire, which, by the time this tale was transcribed, had become a place of fabulous reputation. She and the woman of the mound are identical, for when she gives Peredur the ring in order to help him slay the addanc, she tells him to look to India to find her again. Her beauty corresponds so closely with his mystic vision of blood in the snow that Peredur falls into a trance of contemplation until roused by a blow from the miller, who acts here in the role of the beheading knight, much like the Green Knight in "Sir Gawain and the Green Knight." The blow makes him come to his senses.

(25) The three cups that Peredur drinks from are crucial to the Sovereignty theme, for, in Irish tradition, she offers three cups to the hero: the milk of fostering, the red wine of lordship, and the dark drink of oblivion—the white, red, and black of Peredur's vision. Here all the cups contain wine, but he drains them all (see chapter 9). And because one of the cups is a monster's claw, there is also a suggestion that the three black men and three cups are symbolic of the three serpents that Peredur has overcome.

Peredur reaches the conclusion of one of his quests—to find a
wife—for he lives with the empress for fourteen years. As in "Owain"
and "Gereint and Enid," whose pattern "Peredur" is almost bent to fit,
the hero lives content with his wife for a time but reemerges to continue his adventures and conclude his other task, which is invariably to
fulfill his knightly duty.

(26) The appearance of the Black Maiden here seems misplaced, if
indeed she has come to complain about Peredur's failure to ask the
Grail question. There is also an inconsistency in the text, because she
accuses him of failing to ask about the spear and the dish at the court
of the lame king, but it is at the court of his second uncle that Peredur
sees the spear dripping blood. Other Grail texts place this incident
directly after the Grail procession. The Black Maiden's appearance here
seems more in keeping with the parallel incident in "Owain" in which
Lunet rides into Arthur's court to accuse Owain of failing to return to
his wife, the countess, for Peredur has indeed just left his wife. Either
the incident is misplaced or the storyteller has changed the Black
Maiden's speech.

The Black Maiden is the Goddess in her guise as the Dark Woman
of Knowledge. Because Peredur is no longer united with his empress,
she takes on the form of the hag to reproach him. Her appearance is
very like that of Eriu (lreland): "One time she was a broadfaced, beautiful queen and another time a horrible, fiercefaced sorceress, a sharp-
nosed, whitey-grey, bloated, thicklipped, pale-eyed battlefiend."[70]
Besides reproaching Peredur, she brings news of a quest which
Gwalchmai immediately sets out upon.

The adventures of Gawain occupy a great part of Chrétien's
Perceval, in which he is seen to be on a quest parallel to that of Perceval.
The one who lifts the siege of the maiden will earn the greatest honor,
says the Black Maiden. In Chrétien the prize is the sword of the Strange
Baldric. The knight whom Gwalchmai kills in the *Mabinogion* is the
knight in Chrétien who accuses Gawain of killing his lord.

(27) The storyteller has little time to relate Gwalchmai's exploits in his enthusiasm for Peredur's adventures and so they are much reduced here. Although Chrétien left *Perceval* unfinished, it rather looks as though he intended to tell the story of the finding and wielding of all the hallows, for Gawain's concern is with the sword and the chessboard, and Perceval's with the Grail and the spear. In Chrétien, Gawain defends himself with the chessboard in this incident, while the maiden of the tower throws the pieces as weapons against their assailants. The incident as it exists in "Peredur" makes very little sense and one needs to supplement the story with reading Chrétien from line 4,684 to 6,216 and from line 6,519 to the end, where it will be seen that Gawain's quest takes him into some deep, otherworldly adventures.

(28) Peredur's quest has spanned a year and he arrives at a priest's house on Good Friday. We will remember that part of his quest is to discover the story and meaning of the spear that drips blood, but there follows no disquisition on the Christian analogues to the spear, which a priest might well have given. In Celtic tradition, the spear of the Dolorous Blow, that which lames Bran and is the rightful weapon of the young hero (as typified by Lugh/Llew), was later associated with the lance of Longinus, the centurion who pierced Christ's side while he was on the cross, causing blood and water to flow from his body. This biblical story (John 19:34) enters apocryphal Grail tradition as the origin of the two cruets borne to Europe by Joseph of Arimathea (see chapter 9).

There is another inconsistency in the text where Peredur asks for instructions on how to find the Castle of Wonders—for this is the first mention of the place. The storyteller clearly intends us to understand this to be the court of the second uncle, where the Grail procession appeared.

The king's daughter seems to be yet another aspect of Sovereignty—she upholds Peredur's cause and arms him herself. This incident, in which the hero is unjustly imprisoned and then released to help win a tournament, is almost obligatory in medieval literature.

(29) She clothes him in traditional fool's colors, but Peredur triumphs, refusing yet another bride and winning yet another combat against an encroaching earl.

(30) The following two incidents are part of Sovereignty's games. The gwyddbwyll board is one of the hallows of Sovereignty and appears in the list of the Thirteen Treasures of Britain (see *Mabon,* chapter 3), where the board is of gold and the pieces of silver, and the pieces play by themselves. The board, a prime symbol of Sovereignty, represents the land and belongs to the empress, Peredur's wife—so his action of casting it into the lake is doubly unfortunate. The games that Sovereignty imposes upon him like tests entail in this instance the ridding of the land of yet another plague—Ysbidinongyl, whom Peredur kills, but only after first unwisely sparing him. It has been suggested that Ysbidinongyl may derive from Yspaddaden Pen Cawr in "Culhwch and Olwen" or from the knight called Espinogre, who appears in Malory.[25]

(31) The stag with one horn appears as a malefic unicorn. With only the empress's dog for a guide, Peredur overcomes it. The unicorn seems to fulfill much the same role as the two dragons in "Lludd and Llefelys." No mere otherworldly messenger intended to lure the hero, as in "Pwyll, Prince of Dyfed" and "Gereint and Enid," it is instead the emblem of an otherworldly power loosed chaotically upon the earth. All green things are dead and the waters are dried up, creating the wasteland so familiar from the other Grail texts. Like the two dragons, the unicorn is Sovereignty's beast, and it is Peredur's task to overcome it or bring it under control. The fact that the huntswoman takes up the dog suggests that she is none other than the empress and that she and the Black Maiden aspect of herself are playing off each other in order to guide Peredur to the heart of his quest, rather like a pair of sheep-

dogs with a sheep. It is this killing of the unicorn that engenders Peredur's later guise of the Freer of the Waters, which in turn becomes the honored title of the Grail winner.

The combat with the Black Man under the stone who disappears before Peredur can strike him dead is the last of the tests that keep him from reaching his destination.

(32) The golden-haired youth who admits to having been the many characters within Peredur's adventures is somewhat of a puzzle, for these guises have all been the otherworldly masks of Sovereignty and her representatives, both male and female. The shape of the story almost demands that the empress appear here as the Black Maiden and drop her last disguise to be restored to Peredur as his rightful wife and royal Sovereignty. Goetinck suggests that the storyteller has misheard or misread *damoisel* (youth or page) for *damoiselle* (maiden).

It is at last revealed that the spear that drips blood is the weapon with which the witches of Gloucester lamed Peredur's uncle and that the head in the dish is none other than that of his cousin. Gwalchmai and Peredur join forces once more to do battle with the witches. Peredur is responsible for killing their leader, while Arthur and his men destroy the rest. Thus the witches are no longer a gormes, free to waste the land.

Grail Family and Hallows Quest

Throughout the *Mabinogion* we have noted the way certain heroes succeed to otherworldly roles, becoming Sovereignty's champions or partaking in the Succession of the Pendragons (see *Mabon*, chapter 1). There is also, as we find in "Peredur," a hereditary guardianship with which Peredur's family is deeply concerned. In this pattern the Grail and other hallows are virtually heirlooms which successive members of the Grail family both guard and wield.

Within Peredur's family the guardianship is still upheld, but the active wielding of the hallows awaits the Freer of the Waters, as the Grail winner is traditionally known. How the hallows come to be within the guardianship of a particular family is often the missing part of the story.

We have seen in "Branwen, Daughter of Llyr" that the cauldron—that earliest analogue of the Grail—comes from a lake in Ireland. Matholwch of Ireland has proved unworthy of it, and Llassar and his wife, Cymeidei, titanic Underworld figures (see *Mabon*, chapter 3), bring it to Britain where it is given into Bran's keeping. Its ill use and subsequent destruction at the hand of Efnissien render it inoperative in the earthly realms. Bran then becomes its otherworldly guardian. He has been wounded by a spear in his heel and has thus become a manifestation of the Lame or Wounded King who has been struck by the Dolorous Blow, which afflicts his land as well. His hall at Gwales and Harlech, then, is caught in time, both an otherworldly overlay where heroes rejoice and sing in unending bliss and a place where the laws of life and death are suspended, for though beheaded, Bran still speaks with his faithful companions.

The suspension of time in Bran's hall is a direct precursor to the otherworldly time frame in the hall of the Grail Castle, where the Wounded King, smitten but not killed by the Dolorous Blow, holds court in expectation of the Freer of the Waters. Bran himself has long been understood as the prototype of the Wounded King of later Grail romances.[124] But Bran's guardianship is not a hereditary one, for his sister, Branwen, dies childless and his own son is slain by Caswallawn. The guardianship of both the hallows and Sovereignty is, therefore, mystical; later characters appear to fulfill the roles of Bran and Branwen. As we have seen in *Mabon*, it is Arthur who succeeds to the guardianship of the cauldron in the succession of the Pendragons. The female role in this cycle is that of a Daughter of Branwen, one in a long succession of women who exemplify Sovereignty but who seldom wield her power themselves. Peredur's mother and Rhiannon are other representatives of this line.

When a hereditary guardianship is established, the hallows are normally bestowed upon a worthy ancestor or are won by him or her from a god. Because not all descendants of the ancestor are worthy, the hallow may be lost or it may be stolen by an enemy. In such scenarios, the empowering sovereignty is thus robbed from that family and it falls to a young champion to win it back. Such is the pattern within "Peredur." For further verification of this, however, we must consult the parallel career of Fionn mac Cumhail, whose youthful exploits closely follow those of Peredur.

The Fionn cycle is amorphous and almost as sprawling an epic as the Matter of Britain itself. It is not generally thought of in terms of a hallows quest, though that is indeed the theme of the *Macgnimartha Fionn*, which focuses on the recovery of the crane bag, the receptacle for the Treasures of Ireland.

The crane bag originally belonged to Manannan, otherworldly king of the Blessed Isles, and was made from the skin of a woman, Aoife, who, for love of Manannan's son, had incurred the jealousy of Iuchra, an enchantress. Iuchra bespelled Aoife into the shape of a crane and so she lived for two hundred years. When Aoife died, Manannan placed all the Treasures of Ireland into the bag made of her skin: the shirt and knife of Manannan, Goibhne's belt and smith's hook, the king of Scotland's shears, the king of Lochlann's helmet, and the bones of Asail's swine. "When the sea was full, its treasures were visible in its middle; when the fierce sea was in ebb, the crane-bag in turn was empty."[76]

The crane bag was then given to Lugh, the many-gifted champion of the Tuatha de Danaan. After his withdrawal from the affairs of men, it descended to many other kings and heroes, among whom was Cumhail, brother-in-law of Lugh.

Cumhail is the chief of Ireland's *fianna* (war band), and the primacy of his clan is due to his possession of the crane bag. During the battle of Cnucha, the man who guards Cumhail's treasure bag treacherously strikes a blow at his master and thereafter runs away with the bag, leaving Cumhail to be slain by the sons of Morna, his enemies. In order to fight, Cumhail has left his wife pregnant and in time Muirne, the half sister of Lugh, bears a boy called Demne. She is so fearful of Cumhail's enemies that she gives her son into the fostering of a druidess, Bodmall, and a woman warrior, Liath Luachra. Demne's youthful exploits are prodigious during his secret upbringing. He beats all the youths at hurling and when they complain to the king, the king asks for a description of the boy who has bested them "He is fair," they say. "Then let him be called Fionn," says the king.

Later, Fionn is on his way to seek the remnant of his father's fianna when he comes upon a wailing woman with a bloody mouth, weeping tears of blood and lamenting for her dead son who has been slain by a mighty champion. Fionn pursues the warrior, slays him, and discovers that in the man's possession is the crane bag, for it was this man who had struck Cumhail, Fionn's father. Fionn then finds his father's old companions-in-arms and shows them the bag. One of them, Crimnall, opens the bag

> ... and laid bare its priceless treasures one by one, and as his old comrades watched him, their eyes grew bright, their weapon-hands tightened on their spears and swords, and age seemed to drop from them instantly.[76]

Then Fionn left them and apprenticed himself to the poet Finneces, who was awaiting the day when he might eat the salmon of knowledge. Fionn caught it and while preparing it to be eaten, licked the drops that had fallen upon his thumb. Forever afterwards he bore the thumb of knowledge, which he only need put under his tongue in order to predict the future.[171]

We note that Fionn's upbringing follows the classical pattern of the hero: Raised in obscurity and given a boyhood name, he succeeds in besting his enemies and in winning back the hallows of which his father was guardian. His subsequent career shows the empowerment the crane bag gives, for Fionn becomes chief of the fianna and a great hero, though his career comes to its close when he attempts to prevent the representative of Sovereignty—whom he seeks to marry—from eloping with a younger man.

In a similar manner, Peredur, though raised in ignorance of arms and without knowledge of his family's heritage, finds himself led along the path to vengeance and the restitution of the hallows, which, though inoperative, are not lost in this story. The family tree of Peredur may be tentatively reconstructed as shown in figure 11.

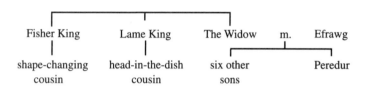

Figure 11. Peredur's family tree

The responsibility of wielding the hallows is at any time an awesome burden and, looking at the characters in Peredur's family tree, one that has taken its toll. Efrawg and his six other sons do not seem to have ever entered into the guardianship, for their main occupation has been war and tournaments, in which they have all died. Peredur's mother, the widow, seems to have kept from him the knowledge of both his father's heritage and his matrilinear family's guardianship. Her brother, whom we will call the Fisher King, though he does not actually fish in the text, may be the father of the shape-changing cousin who attempts to wield the hallows and is enchanted by the witches of Gloucester for his pains, and who appears at the end of the story to explain matters. The Lame King, at whose court the hallows appear, may be the father of the cousin whose head is paraded in the dish, causing such lamentation. It is possible that this cousin is also a failed Grail winner. Certainly his father, the Lame King, bears the unhealing wound of the Dolorous Blow.

The attempt to match "Peredur" with later Grail symbolism becomes a struggle. The title of Fisher King is a case in point, for it is an amalgam of two ideas from the French romances, *pécheur* (sinner) and *pêcheur* (fisher)—the one who has lost the empowerment of the hallows has lost it through sin, according to this scenario, which, as we have seen, is but a Christianized interpretation of the king's failure to ratify his bond with Sovereignty. But behind the title Fisher King we may discern a faint trace of the proto-story in which Peredur's uncle was Ri faoi Thonn (king under the wave). We may establish such a connection via a body of Celtic folk stories which, though collected in the nineteenth century, were found in oral tradition, that most persistent preserver of stories lost from literary sources. These stories are: "Coldfeet and the Queen of the Lonesome Isle"; "Wishing Gold and the Queen of the Turning Wheel"; "Baranoir and the Daughter of the King Under the Wave"; "Gold Apple"[68, 69]; and "The Well at World's End."[83] I shall not attempt to retell these tales in full here, but merely will establish archetypal patterns from their contents, which are remarkably similar and corroborative. All five are from traditional Irish storytellers and it is indeed doubtful whether any folklorist could prove cross-fertilization with later literary sources. They all magnificently represent the Otherworld archetypes of a shared Celtic culture—which show a marked resemblance to those images and characters appearing in "Peredur."

Coldfeet's name derives from his size, which is so titanic that his feet stick out from his mother's house. His titanic strength is advantageous, however, when it comes to running down cattle and bringing them home in one hand for dinner. His mother, unable to feed or clothe him adequately, sends him away so that he can make good. He meets three giants, whom he overcomes. The giants' mother, a cailleach, then lays on him a geis to bring to her from the Lonesome Isle the sword of light which never fails, a loaf of bread which is never entirely eaten, and a bottle of water which is never drained. Coldfeet is the Amadan Mor (great fool) but he sets off on his quest. He encounters three old men, one seven hundred years old, one fourteen hundred years old, and the last twenty-one hundred years old, who direct him on his journey. The Lonesome Isle is ruled by a queen who sleeps as her castle revolves, and round her bed the hallows are to be found. Coldfeet takes them all, with the old men's advice, but also lies with the queen while she sleeps. He then brings the hallows to the cailleach but refuses to yield them to her because doing so is not part of the bargain. Instead he beheads her with the sword of light.

On his return to his mother's house, Coldfeet is tricked into parting with each of his treasures, which the cunning owner of his lodgings replaces with mundane counterfeits. Coldfeet and his mother are thus as poor as before. Nine months later the queen of the Lonesome Isle awakes and finds at her side a child who grows unusually fast. She vows to seek out the one who has taken the hallows and made her pregnant. In her search she stops at each of the three lodgings visited by Coldfeet and observes the inexhaustible loaf and bottle of water and the supernatural light of the sword, each of which she appropriates until she finds Coldfeet's house, where he admits to taking them and fathering the child. Together they return to the Lonesome Isle with the hallows.

This humorous folktale might stand beside "Peredur" only as a faint parallel if not for the wealth of corroborative material to be found in the other stories. "The Well at World's End" is a near variant of "Coldfeet." In this, the king of Connacht has a wounded foot and sends out his three sons to fetch the curative bottle of water from the well at world's end. The two eldest brothers are cunning, but though the youngest, Ceart, is simple, he is the destined finder of the well.

He is hosted by a cailleach, who sends him on to her sister hag. On his way Ceart meets a queenly figure dressed in red silk, who encourages him on his quest. The second cailleach sends him on to her brother, an old man, who bears Ceart on his shoulders across the waters that guard the Island of the Well. As it is in "Coldfeet," the castle where the queen of the island sleeps is guarded by beasts and monsters, which Ceart overcomes. A wheel throws the water of the well and Ceart fills two bottles—one for his father and the other for the old man. He is told to touch nothing else, but takes a bottle marked WATER FOR

THE WORLD, the loaf marked BREAD FOR THE WORLD, and the sword of light. He also lies with the queen and each of her eleven waiting women, who are asleep. The old man pours the water over himself and his sisters and becomes young, as do they. They then trick Ceart into giving up his hallows, though he keeps the bottle intended for his father. His brothers steal it in order to get the credit and cure their father. The queen of world's end and her ladies all bear children, and she leaves the island in search of Ceart, bringing with her the three hallows. She rejects the false brothers and she and Ceart marry.

In "Wishing Gold" the hero is the offspring of the queen of the Lonesome Isle and the king of Erin. Wishing Gold's father marries a false queen who wishes the boy dead. She causes the king to send Wishing Gold to fetch the curative water from the well of the Queen of the Turning Wheel. On his way, Wishing Gold is hosted by three women, each of whom tends one of three senile, sick old men who turn out to be his uncles, brothers to his mother. They give him advice on entering the Castle of the Turning Wheel, where the queen is asleep. The castle is in the sky and it can be brought to earth only by Wishing Gold picking three apples from the tree and throwing them into the air. He gains his prize and sleeps with the queen, and the castle returns to the sky when he again casts up the three apples. Wishing Gold makes all his uncles young again through application of the water. But when he continues his journey, his stepbrothers, sons of the false queen, waylay him, steal the water, and pretend he is dead.

Meanwhile, Wishing Gold returns to the Lonesome Isle. His mother commands him to go to Erin and defend his father's kingdom, now under threat by the Queen of the Turning Wheel, who is demanding the head of the man who visited her while she slept. Wishing Gold and the Queen of the Turning Wheel fight and are reconciled, while the false queen is punished.

In "Baranoir," the quest is for a destined wife and the cure of the seven kings of Gleann Glas (the gray glen). Baranoir is aided by Fear Gansaol (the lifeless man) and Bromach Caol Donn (the slender dun filly), which bears him through the great Wheel of the World to the Well of Fortune, the location of the curative waters. Baranoir also gains the sword of light from three battle hags and engages in a riddle game with the daughter of the king under the wave, who turns out to be his destined wife, though Baranoir must succeed at many tests to gain her. The dun filly is revealed to be a woman under enchantment, the sister of the seven kings, whom Baranoir disenchants. The Fear Gansaol is revealed as a dead man whose debts Baranoir has lifted, thus enabling the man to rest in peace.

In "Gold Apple" the king of Erin marries a hag who turns into a beautiful queen. She plots, however, to destroy Gold Apple, the king's son by a former wife, and to this end lays a geis on him to bring her the eight-legged dog's head. Gold Apple stays with each of three giant uncles, who separately give him an apple to use in finding the next uncle's house. Last, he arrives at his grandfather's house. From here he follows his family's directions to the place where the eight-legged dog is kept—the realm of the king under the wave, and he promptly falls in love with the king's daughter. He refuses his stepmother the head of the eight-legged dog, for the agreement was only that he should bring it home, not that he should bring it home and give it to her. She subsequently falls dead at his touch. He returns to his grandfather's house, where he learns that the queen of the Lonesome Glen has stolen his grandfather's ring of youth, pot of health, and rod of enchantment, the lack of which renders him old and ill. Gold Apple regains these hallows and marries the queen of the Lonesome Glen,[69] having disenchanted his uncle, who has in the meantime been bespelled into the eight-legged dog.

It is clear that a pattern is emerging in the common themes that arise in these Irish folk stories—one which may allow us to deduce the outline of Peredur's quest (see figure 12).

The many common elements that can be derived from these stories lead to some startling discoveries: (a) The hallows quest is usually prompted by the hag's geis; (b) the hallows themselves are in the keeping of an otherworldly queen; (c) while the hallows vary in kind, there is a consistent emphasis on their restorative properties, among which the healing quality of the otherworldly waters is paramount; (d) the hero is aided and directed by three siblings who are usually male; they are, moreover, related to the hero. In "Coldfeet" these uncles are increasingly elderly, representing a tradition which we perceived in the "oldest animals" story in Mabon (see chapter 8). It is possible that this was a feature of the proto-story of "Peredur," for the tradition of increasing ages among hallows guardians is found in the German Grail cycles *Parzival* and *Diu Cröne,* in which three generations of Grail guardians are represented by Parzival, Anfortas, and Titurel, as in a series of nesting boxes. These helpers aid the hero by training him in certain magical skills or in feats of arms, as in "Peredur," and act as staging posts along the path of his quest.

In three of the stories, the hero begets his successor upon the sleeping hallows queen, and here we may perceive the mythic foundation for the conception of Galahad by Lancelot and Elaine, who is disguised as Guinevere. The hero's act is not a rape, but rather an otherworldly engendering of his successor in the hallows guardianship. The hallows queen is magical and deadly to any but the bravest champion, as we find in "Baranoir," who has a magical riddle contest with his bride, and in "Gold Apple," who physically fights with his.

The restoration of the hallows to the earth must be effected by the hero's penetration of the otherworldly gates, represented by the revolving castle or wheel. This image is paramount in the initiation of the seer-poet, as we learned from Taliesin's experience. He physically enters the womb of Ceridwen and speaks figuratively of his initiation: "I have been three periods in the prison of Arianrhod.[23] Arianrhod, the Silver Wheel, has for her castle Caer Sidi, the turning castle, which is a place of death or wonder, depending on the abilities of the one who approaches it. As we saw in "Math, Son of Mathonwy" (*Mabon,* chapter 5), Arianrhod's mythos is paralleled by that of Ethniu, Balor's daughter, who is similarly marooned upon a solitary island because her son

Text	Origin of Quest	Object of Quest	Hero Aided by	Keeper of Hallows	Hallows Guarded by	Nature of Enchantments Lifted
"Coldfeet and the Queen of the Lonesome Isle"	hag's geis	to fetch hallows for the hag	three ancient men	queen of the Lonesome Isle	revolving castle	not specified, though hero overcomes giants
"The Well at World's End"	king's wound	to fetch curative water	to cailleachs and their elderly brother	queen of the well at world's end	water wheel and monsters	helpers regain youth; father is healed
"Wishing Gold"	false queen's geis	to fetch curative water	three sick uncles	queen of the Turning Wheel	Castle of the Turning Wheel	uncles are healed and made young; false queen is punished
"Baranoir"	Fear Gansaol's geis	to fetch curative water	Fear Gansaol and woman enchanted into a filly	three battle hags and daughter of the king under the wave	wheel of the world	Fear Gansaol is able to rest; enchanted filly becomes a woman
"Gold Apple"	false queen's geis	to fetch eight-legged dog and hallows	three giant uncles and grandfather	queen of the Lonesome Glen and grandfather	not specified	implied healing of grandfather
"Peredur"	Black Maiden's geis	to discover meaning of dish and spear that drips blood	two uncles	empress of Constantinople	Valley of the Mills	implied healing of lame uncle; implied disenchantment of cousin; ridding land of plagues

Figure 12. The Grail quest in Irish folk story

will oust her father. Only the daring hero can impregnate her because of the dangers of the island. Because Ethniu's son is the great god Lugh and Arianrhod's child is Llew, we do not have to stretch the parallel at all. Both gods wield the spear or the sword of light, wrenching it from their grandfather's evil use, under which it had become the weapon of the Dolorous Blow, and restoring the land to its regenerative function by ridding it of plagues and invasion and bringing healing. Thus the sword of light in our stories is really an analogue of the spear that heals and wounds and here drips blood.

Consistent throughout the stories is the motif of the turning wheel or turning castle. It is an otherworldly barrier, as we have seen, but it also represents the Wheel of Life and Death. In "Peredur" this symbolism is not totally lost, but rather is rationalized, providing us with a Valley of Mills. The juxtaposition of this episode with Peredur's final encounter with the empress should leave us in no doubt that the mills are a relic of this powerful Celtic symbol.

Despite the variety of the heroes' adventures, the outcome of the quests is the same: The land is put to rights; the false queen, who in these tales takes the place of the Black Maiden and perhaps of the false Sovereignty, is punished or killed; the helpers are disenchanted or healed; and the hero wins his queen and goes with her to live in the Otherworld, where the two will start a new line of hallows guardians.

This hereditary guardianship of the hallows becomes a prime feature of later Grail stories and represents the passing of one mythic pattern to another. In the succession of the Pendragons, successive heroes win and wield the hallows in order to become king. In the hereditary guardianship of the hallows, specifically of the Grail, this royal role becomes a holy one. This process reveals a deeper association with the roots of kingship, which is holy as well as royal, a combination not lost even today in Britain's constitutional monarchy: The political right of government is relegated to Parliament, while the sacral bond of monarch and land is retained.

It is this linking of holy and royal roles which lies at the heart of

"Peredur," for it is the hero's encounter with Sovereignty, the hallows queen herself, that establishes the shape of the Grail corpus for all time.

The Royal Blood in the Holy Snow

Much has been made of the etymological pun arising from the medieval San Greal (Holy Grail): By rearranging one letter it becomes Sang Real (Royal Blood). It is a pleasing and mythically veracious play on words which is appropriate for "Peredur," for there is a way in which the Grail is holy and the blood royal without referring to Christian paradigms, though these paradigms are likewise appropriate and mythically bonded with both Christianity's own mystical tradition and the earlier pagan glyphs discussed below.

"Peredur" is not a Grail-quest story in the later sense of the term, for at no point does the Grail appear in the story, either in a vision or to physical sight, as it does in other texts. The only direct quest that Peredur undertakes is voiced by the Black Maiden as follows:

> When you went in to the court of the lame king and saw the squire carrying a sharpened spear, with a drop of blood running from the point to the lad's fist like a waterfall, and other marvels as well, you asked neither their cause nor their meaning. Had you asked, the king would have been made well and the kingdom made peaceful, but now there will be battles and killing, knights lost and women widowed and children orphaned, all because of you.[22]

This admonition is made only in the last quarter of the story. It is possible that this episode is misplaced, as suggested earlier, but even so it still follows that part of Peredur's charge is to discover the meaning of the Dolorous Blow struck by the very spear which he sees paraded about the hall.

It will be seen, then, that Peredur's quest is to undo the damage wrought by the spear and by his own silence and thereby to lift the enchantments upon the land. This theme, as we have already seen, is pervasive throughout the *Mabinogion;* it is also the motivation for

Manawyddan, Branwen, Culhwch (in the hunt for Twrch Trwyth), and Lludd.

Let us briefly examine the motif of the Dolorous Blow in "Peredur." The first dolorous stroke occurs before the beginning of the story, in the wounding of Peredur's second uncle, the Lame King. We are told by Peredur's shapeshifting cousin that this blow has been struck by the nine witches of Gloucester. From this we must conclude that the witches had in their possession the hallow of the spear which heals and wounds.

This brings us to a consideration of the witches themselves. What is their function in "Peredur"? We have already seen in "The Well at World's End," as well as in the story "Balor on Tory Island" (*Mabon*, chapter 5), that the hallows queen is accompanied by a number of women in waiting—usually eleven or twelve—whom the hero impregnates as they sleep. In "Balor" they are set to protect and guard Ethniu, by whom Sovereignty may be won, together with monsters and other barriers to the hero's success. The witches may be seen from this viewpoint or, alternatively, we can look to a feature of Celtic mythology in which nine sisters or priestesses guard an otherworldly island.[168]

For instance, Morgen and her eight sisters from the *Vita Merlini* guard the island of Avalon to which Arthur is ferried by Barinthus for the healing of his wounds.[11] These sisters are otherworldly women possessed of specific arts; each is the genius of a quality or otherworldly gift. The Celtic and Greek mythologies overlap on this feature: The Celtic ninefold sisterhood is analogous to the Greek Muses, who are the daughters of Memory, Mnemosyne. However, the function of these two groups, though similar, is not identical, for the Celtic sisterhood has two modes of manifestation: In the Otherworld they are beauteous women to whose island heroes sail in order to enjoy unending bliss, but in the realm of the earth they frequently assume the guise of hags. They are aligned with the archetype of the Dark Woman of Knowledge.

We have already noted how aspects of the Goddess of Sovereignty are similarly polarized. She appears both as a beautiful maiden bearing kingship and as a fearsome hag bearing a loathly challenge. The transformative nature of Sovereignty, like the land or the seasons which change the land, is a major feature of the hero's quest. She is beautiful and may bestow kingship on the hero, but she is likewise deadly and dangerous to the unworthy.

The witches of Gloucester are a sisterhood of nine who represent the hag aspect of the Goddess of Sovereignty in her guise as hallows queen. They function as a group of female warriors who guard the hallows and who are able to bestow battle skills upon Peredur, whom they train so that he can overcome them, as is prophesied. The hero who seeks the hallows and their empowerment is always met by a hag—in Peredur's case, the nine hags of Gloucester. They are the three times three—ninefold—emanation of the triple goddesses of Celtic tradition and, more specifically, of the Goddess Sovereignty herself.

In "Baranoir" and "Gold Apple" we see how these two aspects are combined in the hallows queen, who actually engages in personal combat with the hero. In "Peredur," this identification is obscured by the polarization of aspects in different characters. The extreme danger of the unworthy approaching the hallows is instanced in all Grail texts: Lancelot is unable to enter the Grail Chapel in Malory's text because of his sin with Guinevere; attempting to help the priest who is raising the Grail, he rushes forward and is blinded for his temerity.[25] The Grail's action is like that of the spear: It may heal or it may wound.

All the hallows are otherworldly tokens of high powers; their ability to regenerate does not impede their ability to devastate. This polarity of function is demonstrated in all the texts involving a hallows quest and it is the moral integrity of the bearer of the hallows that determines whether their effect is destructive or regenerative. Unworthy bearers or heroes become protagonists of cosmic evil, while worthy ones become protagonists of cosmic good.

There is no such dichotomy, however, in the Celtic proto-story. The hallows are neither good nor evil while they abide in the Otherworld;

they are merely powerful. But it is the intention with which they are wielded in the earthly realms that causes them to be either regenerative or destructive. Thus, an unworthy hero seeking the empowerment of the hallows (an action which symbolically entitles him to be a consort of Sovereignty and a ruler in his own land) suffers an encounter with a hag and receives the Dolorous Blow, which results in him bearing an unhealing wound and his land becoming waste.

The implications of this understanding provide us with a conundrum: The hag aspect of Sovereignty is responsible for the wasteland and the Wounded King, administering a Dolorous Blow which causes the hallows queen to be without a consort and the land to assume its dark or wasted appearance. Yet simultaneously, the hag aspect of Sovereignty encourages the hero, even to the extent of providing him with the skills that will enable him to overcome both ills she has wrought.

Thus Peredur's lame uncle doubtless quested once for the hallows and failed. The Dolorous Blow may even be seen as extending to the cousin who has been beheaded. It is then left to the lame uncle's nephew to succeed, armed with the misleading advice of his family and the battle skills that the witches of Gloucester provide.

Further "dolorous blows" may be discerned in "Peredur." Parallel to the wounding and healing of the Lame King, Peredur is himself wounded by Cai, though he is healed by Gwenhwyfar. Likewise, the insult to Gwenhwyfar is a notable blow. The absence of a Grail proper has worried some commentators, who have discarded "Peredur" as a corrupt text tangential to the mainstream tradition. If we focus once more upon the insult to Gwenhwyfar, however, it will become obvious that Gwenhwyfar's cup is the prototype of the Grail, for it is Sovereignty's own cup which she offers to kings. Its possession by Gwenhwyfar is apposite—she is Arthur's manifest Sovereignty.

At the opening of Peredur's active career, the imbalances wrought by the unwielded hallows are already at work. The warrior who insults Gwenhwyfar by casting wine upon her, snatching her cup, and boxing her ears is an agent of that hallow's otherworldly guardian. The power of the Grail, which is properly the empowering hallow wielded by a queen, is almost withdrawn. Only the action of Peredur prevents this from happening, although he is powerless to prevent the cup's regenerative powers from being reversed prior to his arrival. His immediate handling of the situation and his championship of Arthur's queen show his eager yet immature ability to champion Sovereignty.

Another "dolorous blow" is effected by the unicorn, which dries up the fish pools, devastates green and growing things, and kills other beasts. The description of the unicorn reveals that its function is like that of the spear: "[The] single horn on its forehead [is] as long as a spear shaft and as sharp as the sharpest thing."[22] As the spear wounds the Lame King, so the unicorn devastates the land. The horsewoman who appears to remonstrate with Peredur for killing this beast is shown to be none other than the empress whose lands the unicorn devastates.

It would perhaps be valuable to look at the list of objects that are possible hallows either won by or given to Peredur.

Ring: taken from the maiden in the tent

Cup: stolen by an otherworldly knight; restored to Gwenhwyfar

Sword: given by his second uncle, the Lame King, to test Peredur's strength

Ring of invisibility: given to Peredur by the woman of the mound (the empress)

Three cups: won in combat with three otherworldly champions; given to the miller's wife

Chessboard: cast away by Peredur and won from Ysbidinongyl

Unicorn's head: taken by the empress

To this list we must add the spear that drips blood and the head in the dish, which Peredur sees but does not win. The archetypal list of hallows is reduced in later Grail literature from the Thirteen Treasures of Britain to four items: sword, spear, Grail, and dish.

As can be seen in chapter 3 of *Mabon,* the list of Thirteen Treasures is as repetitive as the above list from "Peredur." The ring, which appears in the list of Thirteen Treasures as Luned's ring of invisibility, appears twice in "Peredur." The maiden in the tent and the woman of the mound are one and the same character and both can be identified with the empress. Gwenhwyfar's cup and the three cups of Sovereignty overlap, for Peredur restores the first cup to the queen and sends the three other cups to the miller's wife, who is analogous to the witches of Gloucester and to the Black Maiden in her admonitory role. The sword plays a minimal part in "Peredur," although it is greatly developed in later texts[119] and is analogous to the sword of light, which the hero requires to enact his role as Sovereignty's champion. The spear, which inflicts the Dolorous Blow and is thus responsible for the Lame King's wound, remains a mystery, but the unicorn's head, which, as we have seen, serves the same function, is won by Peredur. We can discern, however, that the spear opens the hallows quest and it is the winning of the unicorn's head that ends it. In addition, we know that the spear is wielded by the witches of Gloucester, while the unicorn's head is given into the hands of the empress, who is the hallows queen in "Peredur." A complex polarity thereby brackets the protagonist's quest.

Finally, there remains the chessboard, which belongs to the empress and has always been one of the Thirteen Treasures. It represents the land itself and its relationship with the Otherworld; its black and white squares are a concretization of the mystic image of the sheep. The chess pieces represent the earthly and otherworldly characters that appear in Sovereignty's games—for such is the hallows quest.

A further discussion of the hallows that relate to Sovereignty will follow in chapter 9, but within "Peredur" the central hallows, culled from the list of possibilities above, appear to be:

- The ring of invisibility, which is also the token of Peredur's union with Sovereignty

- The sword of light
- The cup of Sovereignty, from which Peredur drinks three times
- The horn of the unicorn, analogous to the spear
- The chessboard, representing the lands in which Sovereignty will empower Peredur

As well as winning these hallows, Peredur accomplishes many great feats, overcoming these triple gormesiad:

- Three serpents (the ring-bearing serpent, the addanc, and the black serpent)
- Three "black" men (the Black Oppressor, Ysbidinongyl, and the Black Man)
- Nine witches (three times three)

The time has come to encapsulate these wondrous feats and apply them to a study of the figures of Sovereignty in "Peredur." That is, how is the blood royal and the snow holy? In our discussion of the hallows of Sovereignty, we have noted that apart from her polar aspects of hag and maiden is Sovereignty's aspect as hallows queen. Each of these three aspects is symbolically denoted in Celtic tradition by the colors black, white, and red. This is why the blood in the snow vision is so crucial to an understanding of "Peredur," for these colors are not just representative of his fantasy mistress but are also the mystic emblems of Sovereignty in her three aspects. This is borne out in Irish tradition, where the hero is offered the white milk of fostering, the red wine of lordship, and the dark drink of forgetfulness at various points in his career (see chapter 9).

To understand the complex relationship that Peredur has with Sovereignty, it will be useful to enumerate the female characters in the story in the order in which they appear.

1. Peredur's mother
2. the maiden in the tent

3. Gwenhwyfar
4. female dwarf
5. dish-bearing maiden
6. Peredur's foster sister
7. tattered maiden (called Blanchflor in Chrétien)
8. countess of the mountain castle
9. nine witches of Gloucester
10. Angharad Golden-Hair
11. maiden of the Round Valley (the Black Oppressor's daughter)
12. woman of the mound
13. countess of the feats
14. miller's wife
15. empress of Constantinople
16. Black Maiden
17. chess-playing maiden (in Gwalchmai's adventures)
18. king's daughter
19. horsewoman of the forest

To find so many female characters in a text is by no means remarkable, but their effect upon Peredur's life is more than usually important. Peredur's mother, although determined to shield him from danger, actually endangers him more seriously, for he is unprepared for his quest. We have already remarked upon the misfortune wrought in Peredur's family by its members' failure to wield the hallows. This misfortune also falls upon other members of the household—both the female dwarf and her husband suffer under an enchantment of silence at Arthur's court, while Peredur's foster sister loses her husband to the otherworldly forces that cause chaotic violence. Finally, Peredur is himself the cause of his mother's death.

Peredur's encounters with the other women in this tale may be seen as a cumulative set of meetings with Sovereignty's three aspects. Blanchflor (the tattered maiden), Angharad Golden-Hair, and the king's daughter may be seen as types of the beautiful maiden, whom he desires but does not marry. The maiden in the tent, Gwenhwyfar, the mountain castle countess, the woman of the mound, the countess of the feats, the empress of Constantinople, and the horsewoman of the forest are all types of the royal or queenly aspect of Sovereignty. The hag aspect is represented in this text by the nine witches; the maiden of the Round Valley, whom the text implies is less than lovely; the miller's wife; and the Black Maiden. The two exceptions to this division of aspects are the dish-bearing maiden, who partakes of all three aspects as the sorrowful woman who is bound to carry the lamented cousin's head, the maiden who will potentially take the role of queen of the hallows of Sovereignty; and the chess-playing maiden, who appears only in Gwalchmai's part of the quest and never meets Peredur, though her chessboard makes her a hallows-bearing guardian of queenly stature.

Peredur is offered in marriage to numbers 7, 11, 13, and 18 in the list above; he professes love to 10 and 12 (who is the same as 15); he defends or avenges 2, 3, 4, 6, 7, 8, and 18; he compensates 3, 6, 14, 15, and 19; and he marries 15. There is little space here to consider each of these relationships, though contemplating their interaction with our hero is certainly an illuminating pursuit. To reflect the possibility that Sovereignty may operate under four aspects, rather than three, we can assign the Black Maiden here to the aspect of cailleach.

Although the Grail as a manifest hallow seems absent from "Peredur," it is, in fact, present within the text. The clue to this resides in Peredur's vision of blood in the snow—the combination of white, black, and red puts him in mind of the woman he loves most. His unfocused yearning after Sovereignty takes on the shape and coloring of the tattered maiden, whom we shall call Blanchflor, after Chrétien. The unattainable longing in Peredur is wrought not of spiritual desire but of physical attraction. He is virgin, unmated, incomplete. He does not seek union with the divine, which is the gift of the Grail in later texts, but instead seeks physical union with the object of his desire. Peredur's Grail is a woman, whether the earthly representative or the otherworldly hallows queen herself—the empress in this text.

Such an understanding can be verified through reference to *Parzival*. At the end of the Grail quest, when the chaos of wasteland, war, and wounded king has been resolved, Parzival's half brother, Feirfitz, sits at the table as the Grail bearer, Repanse de Schoy (fullness of joy), enters and serves the company from the holy vessel. Feirfitz is entranced by her beauty and charmed by the mysterious way all the cups seem to be filled: "Then [said] the fair Anfortas, who sat by the heathen's side, 'Seest thou not the Grail before thee?' But Feirfitz replied, 'Naught I see but a green Achmardi [emerald] that my Lady but now did bear.'"[140]

Feirfitz is stricken with love for the Grail Maiden, but he is unable to see the Grail itself. He asks what he has to do to win her love. The old Grail guardian, Titurel, judges that Feirfitz's inability to see the holy vessel is due to his being a pagan, and that baptism will rectify matters. The font, when it is turned towards the Grail, miraculously fills with water and Feirfitz is baptized. Shortly afterwards, he marries Repanse de Schoy and returns to India, where they have a son, Prester John, who becomes the great Christian king of the East.

It would be simplistic to overstate von Eschenbach's case that pagans perceive the Grail bearer while Christians perceive the Grail itself, but there is a manner in which this is valid: Although Peredur is nominally Christian, his Christianity is shown to be minimal—he mistakes a pavilion for a church and is uncertain about the rites of Holy Week. His helpers are mainly otherworldly, not angelic beings. He is inspired by the representatives of Sovereignty, who lead him to marry the hallows queen herself, the empress of the East. (Constantinople was the Christian center of Eastern Europe, though the empress's retainers seem strangely otherworldly.)

In Peredur there is no dual vision: He perceives the spiritual benefits of the hallows through the mediation of Sovereignty. Her gifts and her love are one and the same. It is this kind of vision that is obscured in later Grail texts, for though she is still present, Sovereignty becomes fragmented into many distressed damsels, disinherited maidens, and lamenting widows. The pattern of Sovereignty within the Grail texts

can still be perceived by the presence of the Loathly Lady, the Black
Maiden, or Cundrie in *Parzival,* for where the hag aspect of Sovereignty
is present, Sovereignty herself as the gift-bearing hallows queen cannot
be far away. (See chapters 9 and 10 for a further discussion of
Sovereignty as Grail queen.)

Peredur's quest for a wife has been amply explained in this chapter—he seeks none other than Sovereignty, whose final appearance is in
the person of the empress herself. Following the mythic pattern of the
transformative Goddess, which we explored in figure 6 (page 81), we
would normally expect Peredur to have to face and embrace the
Loathly Lady before being allowed to possess the empress. Though
obscured by the storyteller, this episode does indeed occur at the
mountain castle where Peredur first confronts the witches.

Clad only in shirt and trousers, he brains one of the witches with
his sword—a feat which no one else has been able to perform, for, as the
countess says, "they have overrun and laid waste the entire realm except
for this one house."[22] This is no embrace, save one of combat perhaps,
which reminds the reader of the grappling of Scathach, Cú Chulainn's
female battle teacher.[8] The storyteller shows that the witch is at
Peredur's mercy, and though he does not say so, she is firmly gripped
by her prophesied bringer of doom. In folk song, one of the disenchanting skills is this very ability "to hold me fast and fear me not,"[164]
which Tamlin's mistress employs in "The Ballad of Tamlin" as the faery
queen changes Tamlin into fearsome shapes. Likewise, Peredur may, in
the earlier proto-story, have transformed Sovereignty.

In Peredur's vision of blood in the snow he is aware of these same
three aspects of Sovereignty, which rearrange themselves into the configuration of the woman he loves most. Such alchemy works upon his
senses until he passes from boyhood to manhood during his contemplation. Even the three birds that bring about the vision correspond to
the three aspects of the Goddess: the wild hawk representing the dangerous hallows queen, the duck representing the innocent maiden
aspect, and the raven representing the hag aspect. Peredur's career is

encompassed by this vision, for he defies the challenges of the hallows queen, liberates the innocent from danger and enchantment, and is admonished by both the witches and the Black Maiden, who serve as his teachers and guides.

Implicit within the vision is the wounding of both land and people, from the king down to the youngest child orphaned by the gormesiad, which devastate the country. The enchantments upon the land can be overcome only if Peredur succeeds in his quest and becomes the consort of Sovereignty, for only then can the royal blood of the Grail family become one with the holy earth of the land. The order of events in "Peredur" makes it very difficult to perceive the shape of the hallows quest and the Sovereignty challenge, for in our story Peredur lives with the empress for fourteen years before he is challenged to find the meaning of the spear. However, his severance from the empress brings him greater maturity, with which he completes his quest and passes further tests: those of the chessboard, the unicorn, and the man under the stone.

The meeting and mingling of two levels of existence—the earthly and the otherworldly—bring honor and an awesome responsibility upon the worthy hero, for he is representative of his race. He does not, like Gereint, marry an earthly woman who is Sovereignty's representative, but marries Sovereignty herself. He may no longer live a personal life, but rather must live a redemptive one, standing between the worlds as the reflective and kindling burning glass of the Otherworld and a channel between mortal and immortal realms. Empowered by the hallows, he is responsible for wielding them and holding the land in balance until the next cycle, when he will no longer be able to maintain his role and it will pass to another.

Once more the land will become waste; Sovereignty will assume her guise of hag and wander the land in search of a new champion; the hallows will be lost to the earthly realms; and a new Grail quest will begin. This cycle of barrenness and fertility, failure and success, is repeatedly found within the Grail legends. The empowerment of the hallows is never permanent. Even great kings like Arthur fail, diminish, and pass back into the otherworldly realms, like the hallows they once wielded. Sovereignty, like the face of nature itself, changes aspects, from hag to maiden to queen, returning to hag as her consort's power wanes.

How such a vision and such a quest may be relevant to us in our own time is the Grail question we have yet to answer. The very existence of humanity and the earth may yet depend upon it, for all mortals share the holy blood of Grail winners, and the Grail family's responsibility of finding and wielding the hallows to balance the wasted land is now the work of all people.

8
The Green and Burning Tree

Even at the confines
　　Where this is that, that, perhaps was this,
even there, where is the moving wall of mist where
was the pillared hall . . .
Yet, even here,
　　Where the mixed-men most mix their magic, where the
exchanges are . . .

DAVID JONES, *THE ROMAN QUARRY*

In the Lands of the Living

The *Mabinogion* presents the reader with a unique vision of the Otherworld. While the Otherworld narratives of Irish tradition are perhaps better known through the stories of *immrama*, the voyages to the Blessed Isles, the British tradition reveals its own view of the paradisal realms inhabited by gods and other beings.[146]

While the texts comprising the *Mabinogion* were transcribed very late in terms of the survival of pre-Christian tradition—in the twelfth and thirteenth centuries—the stories nevertheless stem from early oral tradition, where the gateways and methods of entry to the Otherworld were yet remembered and where the old gods could be found shimmering on the borderlands between the worlds.

The stories reveal certain characteristic patterns from which a map of the Otherworld may be drawn. They show how, time and again, certain characters constellate in mythic configurations which together are recognizable as a distinct tradition. In *Mabon* we explored the earlier stories of the *Mabinogion,* those that stem from the mythical past in which the protagonists are clearly godlike beings conforming to the unrecorded mysteries of Britain. In this book we have seen how the mantles of these earlier mythic personae fall upon Arthur and his court. The protagonists have become analogous to earthly heroes and heroines, but they still meet otherworldly personages who challenge, help, and grant gifts.

Certain features that appear consistently in the *Mabinogion* combine to give us a fairly developed view of the British Otherworld tradition. The presence of the Otherworld and its operators can usually be discerned by characters and events originating in the Otherworld but affecting the earthly realms. The way in which the two worlds interlock is quite subtle. Rarely do characters visit a distinct Otherworld location, as Pwyll does in his visit to Annwfn. Even Arthur, who, as we know from the "Preiddeu Annwfn" (*Mabon,* chapter 6), voyages to the Underworld, is said to sail to Ireland in his ship *Prydwen.* The Otherworld borders the earthly world so subtly, almost as a supra-reality superimposed upon the landscape, that the reader is often unaware when a story becomes operational on another level.

In figure 13 (page 225) we see a table of brief clues to otherworldly activity within the stories. One of the most obvious ways to travel into the Otherworld is to follow an unearthly or totemic beast. Such animals are harmonics of both the Otherworld and the earthly character's destiny, as we have discussed in *Mabon* (chapter 8). The hunting of such beasts draws the character from one world into another without his knowledge. As Pwyll is drawn into an encounter with Arawn, so his son, Pryderi, in pursuing a white stag, falls prey to the otherworldly trap set by Llwyd. In "Culhwch and Olwen," the chase is somewhat different: The search for Mabon is in the nature of a conscious quest, but the oldest totemic animals draw the seekers into deeper levels of time, to the roots of time itself, in order to find the Son of Destiny. There are other examples of this: The hunting of the white hart in "Gereint and Enid" likewise draws the hunters into participation in an otherworldly game. It is Peredur's vision of blood in the snow, involving the hawk, duck, and raven, that initiates him into manhood and into the realm of the empress, who represents Sovereignty. The one-horned stag or unicorn of "Peredur," however, has a malefic effect upon the land and is more in the nature of a gormes than an otherworldly messenger, except insofar as it denotes the imbalance that exists between the worlds.

The borderlands of the Otherworld are always guarded by an awesome figure who challenges all comers. There are distinct archetypes apparent here. In "Pwyll, Prince of Dyfed," Arawn acts as both king of Annwfn and otherworldly guardian. His majesty and nobility are reflected in "Peredur" by the noble huntsman whom Peredur meets near the green and burning tree. Both characters invite the hero into their world and offer a choice of roads or possibilities. Related to these guardians is Lord Bertilak of "Sir Gawain and the Green Knight," who similarly acts for Gawain as the hospitable host and one who shows the way to the Green Chapel. Just as Bertilak appears as a genial and obliging mortal man but as an awesome otherworldly figure as the Green Knight, so too does the threshold guardian assume a more fearsome guise in the figures of Custennin and the Wild Herdsman. The semi-giant, semi-bestial figures who appear in both "Culhwch and Olwen" and "Owain" represent challenge at the gateway between the worlds. Those who pass muster may travel onwards into the Otherworld; those

	"Pwyll"	"Branwen"	"Manawyddan"	"Math"	"Culhwch"	"Lludd"	"Rhonabwy"	"Macsen"	"Owain"	"Gereint"	"Peredur"	"Taliesin"
Animal Leading to the Otherworld	stag		white boar		the oldest animals					white hart	hawk, duck, raven, unicorn	salmon
Threshold Guardians	Arawn				Custennin, Glewlwyd		Iddawg		Wild Herdsman		noble huntsman	
Hallows Guardian and Hallow	Rhiannon's bag	Llassar and Cymeidei's cauldron, Caswallawn's mantle			Twrch Trwyth's treasures	Gwyddno's hamper	Arthur's sword, ring, mantle, chessboard	Eudaf's chessboard	Luned's ring	orchard woman's horn	hag's spear, empress's cup, ring, chessboard	Ceridwen's cauldron
Characters Who Shapeshift	Rhiannon (mare), Pryderi (foal)		Rhiannon (mare), Pryderi (foal), Llwyd's wife (mouse)	Gilfaethwy and Gwydion (deer, pigs, wolves); Llew (eagle); Blodeuwedd (owl)	King Tared (boar), Gwrhyr (bird)	dragons become pigs	Owain's family (ravens)					Taliesin (hare, fish, bird, wheat grain); Ceridwen (greyhound, otter, hawk, hen)
Otherworldly Plagues (Gormesiad)		cauldron folk, magic mist	magic mist, mice	Trwyth,	Twrch dragon's Yspaddaden	Corannyeid, shout, theft of provisions		Oppressor	Black games	enchanted serpents,	witches, Black Oppressor, unicorn	
Otherworldly Combatants	Hafgan	revived cauldron warriors	Llwyd	Pryderi, Gwydion		Twrch Trwyth, Yspaddaden	Gwyddno	Owain, Arthur		Black Knight, Black Oppressor	Edern, Mabonograin	witches, insulting knight, Black Oppressor, Ysbidinongyl, various Black Men

Figure 13. Otherworldly features in the *Mabinogion*. Titles of all stories have been abbreviated.

who fail or fear too much are already barred by their own inadequacies.

The ability to command speech, set riddles, and ask questions is also a feature of the threshold guardians, both male and female, as we discern from the figure of Iddawg in "The Dream of Rhonabwy." It was his misleading words that caused the Battle of Camlann and it was he who first conducted Rhonabwy into the interior of his dream to confront the historical Arthur. Prime among such guardians is, of course, Glewlwyd Mighty Grasp himself, Arthur's porter, whose importance in "Culhwch and Olwen" and in the romances has been mentioned in some detail. Instead of guarding some lonesome ford in the forest, he stands forthrightly at the doors of Arthur's court, forbidding entry to the unworthy. As we have noted, Arthur's court, especially in "Culhwch and Olwen," takes on an otherworldly dimension as the feasting and assembly hall of all the mighty dead of Britain. Culhwch's ride thither is really an otherworldly journey.

The presence of the Otherworld within earthly realms is usually signified by the appearance of the hallows and their guardians. Such otherworldly treasures are most often wielded by people of power who, if not immortal themselves, are empowered by close association with the Otherworld. Both Rhiannon's bag and Ceridwen's cauldron are treasures wielded only in the Otherworld. But Gwyddno's hamper is brought from the Otherworld in order to take the provisions from Lludd's court. The reviving cauldron of Llassar is used to terrible effect in "Branwen, Daughter of Llyr," in which the dead Irish warriors fight on, to Britain's loss. This incident is closely related to Arthur's voyage to Annwfn for the hallows and to the quest for the treasures of Twrch Trwyth—these sets of regalia or otherworldly treasures are primarily the objects of sovereignty quests. As the Cauldron of Rebirth is responsible for the devastation of Britain's troops in Ireland in "Branwen," so the hag's spear wreaks havoc in "Peredur," in which both king and land are laid waste.

The land itself is represented in the *Mabinogion* by the chessboard or gwyddbwyll board. Peredur quests to recover the empress's chessboard, which he has so carelessly thrown away, while in "The Dream of Macsen Wledig," Elen's father, Eudaf, is shown creating the pieces for the board—in a symbolic manner, he empowers Britain's war bands, who then accompany Macsen to Rome, for chessmen and warriors are identical in the mythic schema of the Otherworld.

These hallows or otherworldly treasures appear again and again. The ring of invisibility is closely related to the mantle of invisibility, which both Caswallawn and Arthur assume. In "Owain" Luned's ring denotes an otherworldly talisman which Owain wears while in the earthly realm. Arthur has both ring and mantle in "The Dream of Rhonabwy" as well as his sword of light and chessboard, for Rhonabwy travels to the Otherworld in his dream and sees Arthur in his full regalia as king of Avalon. The horn of the orchard woman in "Gereint and Enid" is the horn of disenchantment by which other-worldly afflictions are lifted. It is paralleled in folk tradition by the horn that awakens the sleeping Arthur in the Sewingshields legend (*Mabon,* chapter 9).

Much like the possession of the hallows, the ability to shapeshift denotes an affinity for the otherworld for certain characters in the *Mabinogion.* Such shape-changing is noticeably present mostly in the earlier stories of the Four Branches and in "Taliesin" and "Culhwch and Olwen," though, as we have seen, Owain's ravens are likely to be of the same shapeshifting otherworldly kin as his mother, Modron/Morgan.

Beyond the threshold guardians, the presence of the hallows and their guardians, and instances of shapeshifting, the most telling evidence for otherworldly interference in human affairs is the gormesiad, the enchantments or plagues that afflict the land of Britain. As we have noted, the Otherworld, its archetypal characters, and its empowering hallows are not in themselves either good or bad, but when the balance between the worlds is shifted—as by an unworthy king's greed or weakness—then this imbalance results in a series of enchantments which affect the whole kingdom.

The magic mist that shrouds Arberth in "Manawyddan, Son of Llyr" and "Branwen, Daughter of Llyr" and that pervades in the garden in "Gereint and Enid" shows a localized infringement of the borderlands that separate the worlds. The gormes of invading peoples afflicts the land in both "Branwen, Daughter of Llyr" and "Lludd and Llefelys" in the form of the cauldron folk and the Corannyeid, respectively. Similarly, in "Peredur" it is the witches who afflict the country. Serpents and dragons that emerge from the earth in "Peredur" and "Lludd and Llefelys" do so as a result of unbalanced forces loose in the land. These creatures are related to the tradition of Merlin Emrys and the dragons who sleep under Vortigern's tower.[10] When the unworthy Vortigern attempts to erect his tower, his masons disturb the slumbering dragons, which causes the edifice to collapse, just as Vortigern's kingship, without foundation, is vulnerable to ruin.

Sometimes the afflictions and enchantments are caused by a giant, such as Yspaddaden, who, Balor-like, attempts to sustain his kingdom by forbidding his daughter to marry a husband who will replace him. The Black Oppressor of both "Owain" and "Peredur" is akin to him. Yspaddaden is also responsible for setting the anoethu (impossible tasks) that Culhwch must fulfill, feats that are akin to the enchanted games of Owain's otherworldly court. In each instance the hero, Culhwch or Gereint, accepts the challenge and wins the prize: sovereignty over lands and control over his destiny.

Sometimes the affliction is in the shape of an otherworldly beast, like Twrch Trwyth or the unicorn of "Peredur," which, like other serpents and dragons, exhibits a devastating ability to scar the land as it dries up waters and renders the fields infertile. Likewise, the otherworldly folk of Llwyd, in the shape of mice, actually help to devastate Manawyddan's crops.

These gormesiad are invariably overcome by the combat between the hero, who represents the afflicted land and its peoples, and an otherworldly champion. Many of these combats take place at a ford (see figure 14), the borderland between the worlds which is neither water nor dry land. Of the combatants from the Otherworld, only Manawyddan does not engage in a hand-to-hand fight with Llwyd; as a great otherworldly archetype, Manawyddan needs only to outwit his opponent through the use of superior skill. Such is not the case for Pryderi and Gwydion, for both are semi-mortal; Gwydion must use magic to overcome Pryderi's human fairness in combat, though only one encounter is required. The overcoming of Twrch Trwyth occurs when the boar vanishes after the scissors, comb, and razor have been filched from behind his ears—and it is with these items that Yspaddaden is ignominiously overcome when his hair and beard are shaved. The combat between Owain and Arthur in "The Dream of Rhonabwy" is a sportsmanlike contest over the gwyddbwyll board. But in other instances, Owain, Gereint, and Peredur overcome their opponents in a more warrior-like fashion.

British tradition as represented in the *Mabinogion* lacks the sumptuous description of the Otherworld that abounds in Irish tradition, yet we are still able to discern its general configuration from the consistent images that arise in the stories (see figure 14, page 231).

Certain natural features of the landscape have always acted as otherworldly doorways. These places are normally considered sacred, are surrounded by traditional lore, and are numinous and well avoided by ordinary mortals. One such place is the Mound of Arberth, which can inflict blows or wonders depending upon the nature of the lord of Dyfed standing upon it. Pwyll sights Rhiannon from its top, but his son, Pryderi, and Pryderi's family fall under otherworldly enchantment there. The tradition among the lords of Dyfed is to sit upon the mound during or after a feast, which may give us another important clue to how otherworldly entry is gained. Otherworldly gateways open more easily at the sacred overlays of linear time and otherworldly timelessness: during the major Celtic agricultural feasts of Samhain (which marks both the New Year and the beginning of winter, and is the time when the dead are abroad); Imbolc (which marks the coming of Brighid, spring lambing, and the combat between the Winter Cailleach and her rival the Spring Maiden); Beltane (May Eve, the time of enchantments and the beginning of summer); and Lughnasad (harvest-time, marked by the autumn games of sovereignty, when the Summer and Winter Kings often fight).

The custom of the lords of Dyfed is translated to the custom of Arthur, who, in later texts, refuses to eat the feast set before him until a marvel happens. This geis, for such it appears to be, prevents the king from eating before an adventure has begun. The most famous example of this can be found in "Sir Gawain and the Green Knight," which begins on the solar festival of the Winter Solstice. In many of the later versions of the romances, Arthur's court meets at Whitsun (Pentecost) to compare adventures, and it is at one such gathering that the Grail appears.[29] Time also plays an important part in the stories "Lludd and Llefelys" and "Taliesin," for the dragon's shout goes up at Beltane in the first tale, and in the latter Taliesin manifests in the waters of the weir on May Eve.

Another means of crossing into the Otherworld is by water, as both Bran's and Arthur's voyages to Ireland testify. Rhonabwy, though he comes to the ford and meets Arthur, does not cross the river; rather than becoming a participant, he remains an observer. The dreams of Macsen and Rhonabwy gain them access to the Otherworld, but Macsen's dream journey is soon followed by an actual voyage to Britain, whose otherworldly loveliness is much extolled in the text. Interestingly, in these stories the "lands to the west" act as the Otherworld in relation to earthly realms: Ireland is Britain's Otherworld, Britain is Rome's.

The earthly paradise of British tradition is a rugged place of hills, valleys, forests, and running rivers—as much like British topography as it could be. Here is no pretty paradise garden, no *hortus conclusus* for the meeting of medieval lovers, but rather an awesome landscape in which mighty archetypes are met.

Central to the landscape of the Otherworld is the tree of tradition, the axial world tree around which the symbols and archetypes

	"Pwyll"	"Branwen"	"Manawydan"	"Math"	"Culhwch"	"Lludd"	"Rhonabwy"	"Macsen"	"Owain"	"Gereint"	"Peredur"	"Taliesin"
Otherworldly Gateway	Arberth		Arberth				dream	dream	forest	magic mist	water	
Otherworldly Castles	Arawn's fortress	Harlech, Gwales	fort of the golden bowl	Caer Arianrhod	forts of Yspaddaden Wrnach; Caer Loyw; seven caers of Annwfn, Oeth, and Anoeth			Caer Seint	shining fortress, countess of fountain's castle	Court of Joy (orchard), Limwris's castle of death	Castle of Wonders, chessboard castle	Caer Arianrhod
Otherworldly Trees				Tree of Nantllew					fir tree	apple tree	green and burning tree	
Otherworldly Birds		birds of Rhiannon							birds in fir tree			
Water Crossing as Otherworld Entryway		voyage to Ireland			voyage to Ireland	voyage to France		voyage to Britain	river		lake crossing, river valley of green and burning tree and of Castle of Wonders	
Ford Combats	Hafgan and Pwyll at ford in Annwfn			Pryderi and Gwydion at yellow ford			chess game between Owain and Arthur at ford		Black Knight and Owain at fountain			
Mounds and Their Guardians	Arberth (Lords of Dyfed)		Arberth		Custennin				Wild Herdsman		woman of the mound	

Figure 14. The configuration of the Otherworld in the *Mabinogion*. Titles of all stories have been abbreviated.

constellate. This is nowhere more apparent than in "Owain," which affords us one of the most detailed accounts of the Otherworld in the *Mabinogion*, along with a complete itinerary for us to follow. The tree in "Owain" is a fir or pine tree and under it is the very fountain of otherworldly life, the well of knowledge, sometimes called the Well of Segais, akin to the Irish well of nine hazels. In "Gereint and Enid" the magic garden, surrounded by the hedge of stakes with severed heads, encloses an apple tree, the emblematic token of the orchard woman or Sovereignty herself. Her fruits, like those of the Avalonian apple trees or those which Thomas the Rhymer offers to pick for the queen of Faery, bring otherworldly knowledge but death to mortal-kind. In "Peredur" we see the green and burning tree, wrought of leaf and flame and emblematic of the mortal and immortal lives of humans and faery-kind, respectively. The tree of Nantllew in "Math, Son of Mathonwy" follows this tradition: In its branches the wounded Llew, bereft of human shape, sits as an eagle, awaiting the restorative magic of Math and Gwydion to transform him again.

The birds of Rhiannon alone represent the British tradition of otherworldly birds that is so prevalent in Irish mythic lore. Their singing brings the suspension of linear time, as in "Branwen, Daughter of Llyr," in which Bran's company sits feasting in an otherworldly time frame. The birds of the fir in "Owain," which descend only when the tree is defoliated by the force of a storm, seem related to the birds of Rhiannon because of their sweet singing, and to the birds in the combat-at-the-ford episode in the *Didot Perceval*, in which Perceval fights Urban of the Black Pine. The birds are really otherworldly women who fight on Urban's side.[32]

Ford combats, fought at the borders between the worlds, occur in "Pwyll, Prince of Dyfed," "Manawyddan, Son of Llyr," "The Dream of Rhonabwy," and "Owain," although Owain's combat with Arthur is fought on the gwyddbwyll board, rather than with arms and warriors.

Last, we note that the otherworldly gateways are frequently depicted as mounds and that these mounds have guardians. The monstrous totemic shepherds like Custennin and the Wild Herdsman are typical threshold guardians, but in "Peredur" we meet the woman of the mound, herself a type of Sovereignty and an aspect of the empress whom Peredur vows to marry. The Green Chapel of "Sir Gawain and the Green Knight" is obviously intended to be a hollow mound like the examples above. It is fortress, stronghold, and gateway all in one. The superstitious dread in which such mounds were held was due to the correct belief that they were burial mounds wherein lay the ancient dead.

Late Celtic and early medieval tradition invested the Otherworld with castles, or caers, from which the otherworldly archetypes operated. Caer Arianrhod appears twice: once as the abode of Gwydion's sister and again as the initiatory caer of Taliesin's poetic vision. Even earthly castles take on supernatural roles in "Branwen, Daughter of Llyr" and "The Dream of Macsen Wledig," in which real places come under otherworldly rules. Gloucester, Caer Loyw, has its place in legend as the site of Mabon's imprisonment, and a similar shining fortress reappears in "Owain," where in place of Peredur's nine witch tutors, an array of beautiful maidens and youths wait on the hero. These otherworldly castles are also treasure houses, like the fort of the golden bowl, whose powerful magic lures Rhiannon and Pryderi into enchanted servitude, and like the Castle of Wonders, where Peredur sees the undying splendors of the hallows. But the treasures are often housed within the dark caers of Annwfn, to which both Pwyll and Arthur descend. Pwyll's experience of Annwfn is of a magnificent palace of entertainment and joy, while Arthur is said to wear a face scarred with anxiety after having raided Annwfn for the cauldron and other empowering hallows.

Sometimes the castles are places of testing, as in the forts of Yspaddaden and Wrnach or the Court of Joy, where the enchanted games are played. The Castle of Wonders is part of this tradition as well, for it is there where Peredur should have asked the Grail question. Owain is able to gain entry to the castle of the countess of the fountain only with Luned's help, and in Earl Limwris's castle, Gereint is saved from oblivion and death by the force of Enid's impassioned shrieks.

In the lands of the living that are the Celtic Otherworld, the ways are clearly marked so that no chance traveler might stray in unaware. For those who know the customs of the country, the path is clear to see—earthly beings may yet enter the Otherworld. If they do, there are many challenges and dangers to be faced before they emerge in the earthly realm once again. Like Arthur, Rhiannon, and Pryderi, they may return haggard though vindicated from their sojourn in those lands. Like Culhwch and Gereint, they may return victorious to their lands and loved ones. Or, like Bran, Arthur, and Owain, they may never truly return to affairs of earthly estate, remaining in the Otherworld to resume guardianship over the inner sovereignty which lies under and around us even today, until they in turn succeed to the role of Mabon in the long succession of the Pendragons.

The Bright and the Dark

It is apparent in the stories of the Mabinogion that otherworldly characters often bear names associated with brightness and appear to be fair when they are in the Otherworld, yet have names and appearances that reflect blackness and ugliness when they show up in earthly realms. Like the sheep that change color from black to white or white to black in "Peredur," so are otherworldly characters altered when they cross the way between the worlds. Noticeable too are those characters whose names and natures do not match; some bear bright names and dark natures.

It is not possible to give definitive etymological meanings to the names of all such characters in the *Mabinogion*, but following are some examples of this bright/dark dichotomy.

In "Pwyll, Prince of Dyfed": Hafgan is "summer song"; Gwawl ap Clud is "radiance." Hafgan bears a marked resemblance to Gromer Somer Jour of "Gawain and Ragnell,"[78] that otherworldly challenger called Lord of Summer's Day.

In "Branwen, Daughter of Llyr": Llassar Llaes Gyfnewid gives his name to the blue enamel that Manawyddan uses in the next branch. The root of the name is *glas* or "blue-green," indicating the transparent color of sea and sky. The same root is incorporated into the name of the Glass Caer of Glastonbury, under whose tor another bright/dark figure, Gwyn ap Nudd, is said to have made his abode.[80]

In "Manawyddan, Son of Llyr": Llwyd ap Cil Coed is "the gray one." We have already noted his similarity to both Caswallawn (in his ability to spread the magic mist) and to Cú Roi mac Daire of Irish tradition (*Mabon*, chapters 3 and 4), who might well be called "the man in the grey mantle."

In "Culhwch and Olwen": This story contains many such characters. Apart from the shining fortress (Caer Loyw), there are Goleuddydd (bright day), Gwyn ap Nudd (white son of night), the bright-white witch, the pitch-black witch, and Gwenhwyfar (white phantom), among many more.

In "Owain": The Yellow Man, host of the shining fortress, is mirrored in reverse by the Black Oppressor. The Wild Herdsman is black and one-eyed.

In "Gereint and Enid": Edern ap Nudd means "eternal son of night."

In "Peredur": Many black men, including the Black Oppressor, become opponents to Peredur in this story. It has been suggested that Ysbidinongyl is Lord of the Black Pine,[92] which may associate him with Urban of the Black Pine, whom Perceval fights in the *Didot Perceval*.[32]

In "Taliesin": Ceridwen's son is Aflagddu (utter darkness) and is also called Morfran (great crow) in accordance with his appearance. He is contrasted with Taliesin himself, "the radiant brow."

These are but a few such characters who appear in the stories of the *Mabinogion*. These polarities show not only the transformative nature of the borderlands between the worlds, where the green and burning tree represents mortality and immortality, but also the nature of the combatants who fight for the hand of Sovereignty. The motifs that arise from the stories are telling evidence of a mythic pattern subsumed in British tradition, that of the combat for the Flower Bride, in which a mortal (a hero, a bright king of summer) and an immortal being (an Otherworld king or the dark king of winter) fight over the maiden aspect of the Goddess of Sovereignty.

This fascinating discovery shows how it is that Gwenhwyfar succeeds to all the panoply of the Flower Bride of proto-Celtic tradition (see figure 15). However, before we look at the final development of this tradition, let us attend to the mythic pattern of this combat in the *Mabinogion* and related Celtic texts.

Seven of the twelve stories comprising the *Mabinogion* reveal distinct combats for the possession of a woman. The woman in question always holds some gift, either sovereignty or one of the hallows, and is always beautiful. The prime template for this pattern is established in "Culhwch and Olwen," where we read of Creiddylad, daughter of Lludd Llaw Eraint (Geoffrey of Monmouth's Cordelia and Lear), who, before she can sleep with Gwythyr ap Greidawl, is abducted by Gwyn ap Nudd. The judgment upon them is given by Arthur, who orders: "Creiddylad was left in the house of her father undisturbed by either side, and every May Day the two men would fight, and the one who conquered on the Judgment Day would keep the girl."[22]

Such are the mythic circumstances preserved in the capacious bag of the storyteller, where they huddle with other fragments of great mysteries. But this is no lone scrap of tradition, for these circumstances are found again in related British tradition in the early Welsh text of *Drustan ac Essyllt (Tristan and Isolt)*. The lovers, pursued by March (King Mark), submit their case to Arthur, who rules that Essyllt shall be with Drustan while leaves are on the trees and with March when the

Text	Flower Bride	Bright Combatant	Abductor/ Otherworldly Dark Combatant
"Pwyll, Prince of Dyfed"	Arawn's wife and Rhiannon	Arawn Pwyll	Hafgan Gwawl
"Branwen, Daughter of Llyr"	Branwen	Bran	Matholwch
"Math, Son of Mathonwy"	Goewin, Arianrhod, Blodeuwedd	Math, Gwydion, Llew	Gilfaethwy, Math, Gronw
"Culhwch and Olwen"	Olwen, Creiddylad	Culhwch, Gwythyr ap Greidawl	Yspaddaden Gwyn ap Nudd
"Owain"	countess of the fountain	Owain	Black Knight
"Gereint and Enid"	Enid, Gwenhwyfar, orchard woman	Gereint	Brown Earl and Earl Limwris, Edern, Mabonograin
"Peredur"	Blanchflor	Peredur	the earl
"Tochmarc Etain"	Etain	Eochaid Airem	Midir
"Toruigheacht Dhiarmada Agus Ghrainne"	Grainne	Diarmuid	Fionn
"Aided Cú Roi mac Daire"	Blathnait	Cú Chulainn	Cú Roi mac Daire
Triad 67 and "Cynddelw"	Fflur	Caswallawn	Julius Caesar
Drustan ac Essyllt	Essyllt	Drustan	March

Figure 15. The combat for the Flower Bride in Celtic tradition as shown in the *Mabinogion* and related texts. The bright and dark combatants are to some extent interchangeable, for in most instances the Flower Bride determines with whom she will live.

trees are bare. Essyllt acclaims this Solomonic pronouncement with glee: "Blessed be the judgement and he who gave it! There are three trees that are good of their kind, holly and ivy and yew, which keep their leaves as long as they live!"[81]

Both Creiddylad, and Essyllt are in the role of Flower Bride, the otherworldly woman of unearthly beauty who will succeed to the Goddess of Sovereignty and for whose hand many men fight. The prime example of the Flower Bride in the *Mabinogion* is, of course, Blodeuwedd, wrought of flowers by Math and Gwydion to be given to Llew. The text of "Math, Son of Mathonwy" reveals a succession of Flower Brides, as the reason for Blodeuwedd's creation is the geis that Arianrhod lays upon her son: He shall never have a wife of earthly kind. Arianrhod is herself in the role of Flower Bride at the beginning of the story, a role which she strongly wishes to have. But Math's wand reveals the true state of his disposition, and she gives birth to twin sons. Gilfaethwy, meanwhile, has raped Goewin, the footholder of Math. Goewin's virginity is symbolic of the inviolability of the land: While Math's feet are in her lap, there is no war. The war magically provoked by Gwydion gives Gilfaethwy the opportunity to rape Goewin and steal the sovereignty.

A similar succession of women to the role of Flower Bride appears in "Gereint and Enid," and Gereint champions them all in the manner we have discussed (see chapter 6). Owain's Flower Bride, the countess of the fountain, is really a fully developed representative of Sovereignty. Her maiden aspect is exemplified by Luned, who loves Owain and helps him to achieve her mistress's band. Enid and Gwenhwyfar similarly share a role in "Gereint and Enid."

Rhiannon represents the most otherworldly of Flower Brides, for she is stolen directly from Annwfn. The prior combat that Pwyll has fought with Hafgan on behalf of Arawn may well be fought on behalf of her as well, for as we have discussed in chapter 1 of *Mabon*, Rhiannon and Arawn's wife may be one and the same. In the later combat, Pwyll wins her from Gwawl, in the manner of King Orpheo.[64]

Branwen's undoubted claim to the role of Britain's Sovereignty is championed by Efnissien, her brother, in another kind of combat involving the dishonoring of the Irish king Matholwch.

The Flower Bride is usually easily identified by her flowery name. Olwen's name, "white track," refers to the white flowers that spring up as she passes. Peredur's first love is unnamed in the story, but Chrétien calls her Blanchflor, and it is she whose image kindles Peredur's devotion to Sovereignty.

This mythic pattern of combat for the Flower Bride is discernible in many other stories within Celtic tradition, a few of which are noted here. "Tochmarc Etain" ("The Wooing of Etain") tells of the abduction of Etain, a woman of the *sidi* (faery hills), by Eochaid Airem. But Etain has forgotten that she was once the wife of Midir, a lord of the sidi, for she has been through a number of reincarnations. Midir comes to take her back and fights Eochaid in a series of chess matches to win one kiss from Etain's mouth. He embraces her and, flying through the opening in the roof, they hasten back to the sidi, where they are besieged by Eochaid. The prior relationship between the Flower Bride and her dark combatant is likewise a feature of "Pwyll, Prince of Dyfed" and, as we shall see, is perhaps part of the submerged cycle attached to Gwenhwyfar.

Related to *Drustan ac Essyllt* is the proto-story of "The Toruigheacht (pursuit) of Diarmuid and Grainne." The triangular relationship in this tale is the basis for the later stories of Tristan and Isolt. It tells how the beautiful Grainne is to be given in marriage to the elderly Fionn. She remarks on her intended husband's gray hair and then casts her eyes upon Dairmuid, his handsome young follower. By laying a geis upon Diarmuid and causing the company to be drugged into sleep, she escapes her fate with Fionn and flees with Diarmuid. Their long flight, during which they are forbidden to lie more than one night in the same bed, is attested to in Irish topography, where numerous prehistoric monuments and standing stones are still termed the beds of Diarmuid and Grainne.[142]

We have already noted the lost story, alluded to in the triads and in

Welsh poetic tradition, of Fflur and Caswallawn. In this lost Sovereignty story Fflur is carried off to Rome by Julius Caesar, but Caswallawn follows her, dressed as a shoemaker, in order to win her back.[38] Fflur (flower) may well have represented the sovereignty of Britain over whom the invading Julius Caesar and the native King Caswallawn fought.

"The Tragic Death of Cú Roi mac Daire" (Aided Cú Roi mac Daire) is yet another story concerning the proto-Irish Flower Bride, in this case, Blathnait. Like Blodeuwedd, Blathnair overcomes her husband by guile in order to escape with her lover.

The combatants who fight over the Flower Bride may be earthly or otherworldly, and though they may bear bright names, like Gwawl and Gwyn, they are nonetheless dark combatants. The earthly combatants usually appear in the role of Summer King, while the otherworldly combatants, who, like Math, are often versed in magic, usually take the role of Winter King. This schema may seem arbitrary, but there is much evidence to support it, notably from the stories of Creiddylad and Essyllt, in which the Flower Bride is fought over by a young lover and an elderly or otherworldly husband or abductor. Matholwch, king of Ireland, appears as an otherworldly king because Ireland is opposite Britain, as the Otherworld is opposite the earthly realm. Yspaddaden is a Winter King who is almost paralyzed by his Cronos-like grip upon both his kingly powers and his daughter, Olwen. It was once the fashion of scholars, following in the footsteps of Fraser's *The Golden Bough*, to sort all deities into two heaps, the Solar and the Lunar, in a simplification which we might do best to avoid. The combatants for the Flower Bride, however, do fall into the pattern of Summer and Winter antagonists, after the mythic schema established above.

These antagonists and the role of the Flower Bride appear again and again within the progressive unfolding of the Arthurian legends, but though the combatants or abductors vary, the Flower Bride is always present in one woman—Gwenhwyfar, the Guinevere of early tradition, as we shall see in chapter 10.

The Mythic Company

Certain characters within the *Mabinogion* betray traces of ancient mythic archetypes which have been almost forgotten. The gentle erosion of powerful gods into the status of heroes, queens, and mighty adversaries was greatly aided by the Arthurian legends, which have acted as a kind of clearinghouse for this transformation. Usually, the later the text, the less we are able to perceive the resemblance of a character to a mythic archetype, but nevertheless there are some surprises and exciting confirmations of older patterns to be found.

It would be simplistic merely to associate each character with a mainstream god form, after the fashion of certain classical mythographers. Such a process would be totally inappropriate for archetypes of a proto-Celtic provenance. The problem with the pigeonholing of Celtic gods is perhaps associated with the dearth of native statuary depicting them. The custom of depicting deities representationally was not a British or Irish practice, though it was a Roman habit which spilled over into local custom.

Celtic tradition reveals that deities and spirits, as well as mythic heroes, were associated with places. Land features—natural outcrops of rock, springs, wells, and trees—not temples built by men, are the loci of these deities. The Irish *dindschencas* (stories of place-names) relate the topography of Ireland through association with deities and mythic peoples whose great deeds are remembered at particular spots and who gave their names to those locations. British chroniclers such as Nennius reveal a very similar tradition: History is the land beneath our feet. The earth is sacred because it is deeply infused with mythic activity invisible to mortal sight but perceptible to seers and storytellers, who, in Celtic tradition, are the priests of the gods.

Imperceptibly, the mantles of gods fall onto the shoulders of earthly men and women who, due to the Celtic storyteller's total disregard for proper definitions, merge with mythic archetypes, becoming their exemplars. This process is very clearly visible in Hindu tradition, where men and women are seen to embody characteristics of the gods, becoming their avatars through whom the gods are active in human affairs. The Otherworld tradition of the Celtic countries is at once similar and very different from this, for it replaces a formal religious tradition. Although there are constants among the characters who appear and the locations that are described as existing within the Otherworld, the variations of detail within the Otherworld boundaries are immense. The borders between the worlds are but a thought away within the Celtic imagination.

The sacred points of the Celtic year mark the overlapping of the earth and the Otherworld. Temples existed only after Roman occupation; before that *nemetons* (sacred groves) and springs were visited by those seeking communication with the otherworldly entities whom we call gods.

When gods of the wild places were subsumed into Christian saints, a further interesting variation crept into the mythic consciousness of Britain. But if we look for permanent shrines for the ancient god forms, we need look no further than the *Mabinogion,* whose stories enshrine these old archetypes, mixing history, myth, and tribal belief in one rich draft. Like the Cauldron of Rebirth, which made the dead alive again, these stories ensure the immortality of the mythic archetypes. The roll call of Arthur's court in "Culhwch and Olwen" shows us the feasting hall of the Otherworld, where heroes, gods, and kings assemble in one throng under the aegis of Arthur as Pen Annwfn, Lord of the Underworld.

Figure 16 shows the main mythic archetypes arising from the theme of the kingly or heroic relationship with Sovereignty in the *Mabinogion.* It will be noted that some characters appear in more than one role. This is consistent with the mythic progressions that occur in the stories, wherein a woman who is the Flower Bride in one part of the story may become Sovereignty or even the Dark Woman of Knowledge in another.

The Sovereignty figures are those women who represent the full-blown qualities of the Goddess—they are queens, like Gwenhwyfar and

Title	Function	Typified by
Flower Bride	sovereignty-bestowing maiden	Blodeuwedd, Goleuddydd, Olwen, Creiddylad, Enid, Gwenhwyfar, Blanchflor, [Fflur]
Sovereignty	the Goddess of the Land	Rhiannon, Gwenhwyfar, Elen, countess of the fountain, orchard woman, woman of the mound, empress of Constantinople, [Morgan, Brigantia]
Dark Woman of Knowledge/ Lady of the Wheel	initiator and guide; Lady of Death/Rebirth	Ceridwen, Arianrhod, nine witches, Black Maiden, Custennin's wife, Luned, countess of the fountain, Modron as raven queen, miller's wife, [Morríghan]
Daughter of Branwen	heiress of Britain's sovereignty	Branwen, Goewin, Custennin's wife, Luned, Peredur's mother, [Eigr/Igraine, Morgause, Elaine]
Black Maiden	messenger of Sovereignty; guide and admonitory voice of the land	Luned, Black Maiden, Peredur's sister, [Scathach, Morríghan, Elene]
Mabon	Sovereignty's son; restorer of innocence	Pryderi, Gwern, Llew, Goreu, Peredur, Gwion, [Segda]
Pendragon	sovereign lord of the land	Pwyll, Manawyddan, Pryderi, Math, Macsen, Lludd, Arthur
Pen Annwfn	sacrificial king; guardian of the land	Bran, Math, Arthur, Yspaddaden, Lame King, [Vortimer]
Thief of Sovereignty	dispossessor and despoiler of the land	Gwawl, Caswallawn, Llwyd, Gwydion, Black Oppressor, Edern, knight of the apples, Gwyddno, earl who dispossesses Blanchflor, [Medrawt]
Guardian of the Totems/Lord of the Wheel	lord of wild things; instructor and guide; Lord of Death/Rebirth	Custennin, Wild Herdsman, Noble Youth (in "Peredur"), Black Oppressor (in "Peredur"), miller, [Green Knight, Cú Roi, Mog Ruith]
Provoker of Strife	guardian of Sovereignty	Iddawg, Efnissien, Cai, [Bricriu, Medrawt]
Seer-poet	inspired prophet of Sovereignty	Llefelys, Taliesin, [Merlin, Segda]

Figure 16. Myths and archetypes in the *Mabinogion*. The characters in brackets are from parallel Celtic tradition.

Rhiannon, or otherworldly women who, like Elen, appear wearing the diadem of royal rule, seated in the golden chair that represents the earth.

The Dark Woman of Knowledge shows the dark aspect of Sovereignty, which may take the form of an admonitory hag such as the Black Maiden in "Peredur" or one, such as Luned, who has retained her maiden beauty. As Lady of the Wheel she shares with the Guardian of the Totems the role of adjuster and restorer of balance. As we saw in chapter 7, from her revolving castle she guards the portals of the Otherworld. Arianrhod's Caer Sidi is a prime example of this gateway.

The Daughters of Branwen are those women who are rightful heiresses of Britain's sovereignty, but seldom, if ever, embody this for long. They are those from whom the land is repossessed. Custennin's wife is important in this role, for she is one of the daughters of Amlawdd Wledig who become the Cornwall sisters of later Arthurian tradition (see *Mabon*, chapter 6). If we look at her sisters' roles, we find that Igerna (Igraine) becomes Uther's queen and that Goleuddydd becomes the queen of Cilydd. Custennin's wife is nameless but it is possible that her rightful name should be Anna, a suggestion that arises from a study of the Welsh genealogies (see figure 19, page 283).

The Daughters of Branwen often suffer an obscure fate or are the bearers of great burdens. The archetype is difficult to establish in many cases, but the prevailing guidelines may be that the woman in question is rarely queen in her own right but is married and that her blood confers the sovereignty of the land upon her children. One of the old medieval names for Britain was the Nest of the Pelican and this seems a very apposite title when applied to the Daughter of Branwen archetype. The pelican, according to medieval bestiaries, was supposed to peck open its own breast in order to feed its young upon its own blood. This erroneous belief became attached to the symbolism of Christ's sacrifice upon the cross, the redemption of the world by his blood. Britain as the Nest of the Pelican, then, symbolizes the fostering place of Christ and especially of his mother, after whom England was called Mary's Dowry. The Daughter of Branwen is accustomed to sacrifice, suffering, and sorrow, but she is also tenacious of her children's rights.

The role of king, corresponding to Sovereignty, falls to many characters in the earlier stories of the *Mabinogion* but is exemplified primarily by Arthur, whose mythical influence extends beyond the Heroic Age into medieval times. Kings may come and kings may go, but Arthur is king forever, it seems.

When the king is withdrawn to the Otherworld, he sometimes becomes a special guardian of the land, as does Bran, whose head is buried under White Mount, and as does Arthur, who, though undying, is said to sleep beneath the land of Britain in very many places, awaiting a time of need when he will come again. To these two we might add Vortimer, Vortigern's worthy son, who is buried on the shores of Britain as a palladium against invaders. The Lame King of "Peredur" extends his role as guardian of the hallows, just as Bran does for the cauldron. Yspaddaden is no longer operative within this archetype: Like Cronos, who devours his own children, he keeps a viselike grip on Olwen's life, never allowing her to progress. Math, however, passes from his kingly role into that of withdrawn king as Llew grows up.

A character who emerges from our study in a startling way is the Thief of Sovereignty, who is often one and the same as the Flower Bride's abductor, such as Caswallawn or Edern. He may be an otherworldly warrior who comes to steal the goods and possessions of the kingdom, like Llwyd in "Manawyddan, Son of Llyr," or Gwyddno, the mysterious figure in "Lludd and Llefelys." Medrawt appears to follow this role in Triad 54, where he is said to have raided Arthur's court, stealing all food and drink. Further, he is said to have compounded this assault by dragging Gwenhwyfar from her throne and striking her. Gwydion empties Pryderi's kingdom of pigs. Gwawl, in "Pwyll, Prince of Dyfed," is closely associated with Rhiannon's bag of plenty, and, considering his attempt to abduct her, he consistently exemplifies this role of thief.

The Guardian of the Totems is also Lord of the Wheel, an adjuster like the Dark Woman of Knowledge or Lady of the Wheel. Together they exemplify the ancient parents of all the gods. The guardian is often also the threshold guardian of the Otherworld who presents tests and challenges to the hero. He directs the way into the Otherworld and may appear as a lordly man, like the Noble Youth whom Peredur meets near the green and burning tree, or else as a forestman, uncouth and of giant stature, like the Black Oppressor or Wild Herdsman. Celtic tradition supplies further characters in this role: Lord Bertilak as the Green Knight[78] and Cú Roi mac Daire, who both play the beheading game and challenge the heroes Gawain and Cú Chulainn, respectively, to become the best warriors. Mog Ruith, whose name means literally "servant of the wheel," appears in Irish mythology as one who flies through the air by means of his rowing wheel—a kind of air boat. He is said to have been a disciple of Simon Magus (who, we will remember, also tried to fly). Mog Ruith's dwelling place in the southwest of Ireland is very near Cú Roi mac Daire's revolving castle, and it is possible that there are mythological parallels between the two men.[171] The Lord of the Wheel is concerned with the progress and initiatory testing of the hero and it is thus not surprising that he makes an unusual appearance in "Peredur" as the miller who patronizes Peredur.

A subtle archetype in the tales which might be overlooked is that of the Provoker of Strife, who acts as a contradictory guardian of his land's sovereignty. It is possible that originally this role was an extension of the Lord of the Wheel. Iddawg, Churn of Britain, provokes the Battle of Camlann with his rash words. Similarly Efnissien provokes war between Ireland and Britain after Branwen's marriage to Matholwch. And though Cai does not instigate wars in any of our stories, he certainly follows in these characters' footsteps by provoking arguments and dissension among Arthur's knights in each of the romances. Furthermore, in *Perlesvaus* it is Cai who kills Arthur's son

Loholt (Llacheu).[29] It is interesting to recall that in "Culhwch and Olwen," Cai reminds Arthur that the king is breaking custom by allowing Culhwch into the hall after the feasting has begun. It is possible that Cai's original role was as a preserver of the traditions or mysteries of Britain. The satirist Bricriu, in the Ulster Cycle, is the Irish incarnation of this role. We have already seen how the role of Provoker of Strife is often portrayed by a satirist whose stinging rejoinders and wicked wit cause cracks to appear in the king's realm.

The character opposite the Provoker of Strife is the Black Maiden, whom we have identified as a fourth aspect of Sovereignty. Her role has been considerably obscured in the texts but is clearly very important to our study. She often appears as the sister or helper of the hero and as such appears to play no great part, but the Black Maiden archetype acts as the representative of Sovereignty in a definite way. In "Peredur" she is shown to be the admonitory voice of the land, urging Peredur to rectify his mistakes and face up to his responsibilities, while in "Owain," as Luned, she gently encourages Owain to win Sovereignty's games with skill and flair. This role is related to that of foster mother or woman warrior in Celtic tradition, for it is the responsibility of each of these characters to arm, name, and give a destiny to her fosterling or student. Cú Chulainn's boyhood, for instance, is spent on the Isle of Skye, where Scathach teaches him battle skills.[8] Later on in his career he encounters the goddess Morrighan, who, disguised as a female satirist, conducts a heated debate with him.[88]

The Black Maiden aspect of Sovereignty may also be seen as the voice of the land, the one who bears the messages of Sovereignty. At times her voice, like the nagging of conscience, swells to indignation and fury, like the shriek of the dragon of Britain in "Lludd and Llefelys," which denotes the suffering of the land and causes devastation, acting like a vocal Dolorous Blow. The shriek of the lady of the fountain at the death of her champion heralds a possible interregnum during which her lands are laid waste, but Owain hears her cries and answers them by marrying her, thus becoming the land's champion. The cries of Enid, struggling in the embrace of Earl Limwris, brings Gereint to his senses to save her, his representative of Sovereignty. As we shall see, the land is served by the damsels of the wells, whose rape causes a terrible silence to fall on the land; no one is able to hear the voices of the wells, that indwelling voice of the land, of Sovereignty herself. And finally, in one other example of the Black Maiden aspect of Sovereignty, Arthur hears the voice of the Goddess and is restored to his former glory and courage (see chapter 9).

The Black Maiden became the *damoiselle maldisante* in medieval romances—the maiden whose nagging tongue spurs on the hero to magnificent deeds by dint of her encouragement. We have seen her in the person of Elene in *Libeaus Desconus;* she also appears in Malory as Linnet, the sister of Lionors.

The heroic role of the Black Maiden, so prevalent in Celtic tradition, did not surface again until its revival by Shakespeare, whose heroines Imogen and Viola combine the roles of Black Maiden and Daughter of Branwen in their guise as young men. This combination is also present in two medieval romances: "The Story of Grisandole," in which a young woman dressed as a man is enabled by Merlin to wed the emperor of Rome; and in "Le Roman du Silence," in which Silence dresses as a young man in order to obtain her inheritance.

Last on our list of archetypes is the seer-poet, of whom we have only two examples: Taliesin, the prophet of the race of Troy, and Llefelys, Lludd's brother. Both uphold the role of the king and prophesy or advise the ruler about the nature of his reign. Sometimes, as does Merlin Emrys and Segda, he stands in for the king when the reign is an unworthy one, acting as a judge or standard of justice for the realm in the absence of true judgment. In such instances, the seer-poet is a harmonic of Mabon, Sovereignty's son.

It can be seen that some of these archetypes fall into pairs of opposites between whom the energy of Sovereignty is exchanged. The male and female versions of each archetype function similarly (see figure 17).

Female Roles	Male Roles
Flower Bride	Mabon
Sovereignty	Pendragon
Dark Woman of Knowledge	Pen Annwfn
Daughter of Branwen	Thief of Sovereignty
Black Maiden	Provoker of Strife
Lady of the Wheel	Lord of the Wheel/ Guardian of the Totems

Reconciler: Seer-Poet

Figure 17. Male and female archetypal roles

The relationships between these mythic archetypes are as various as the turnings of a story. Some of the main points of these relationship have been dealt with in chapters 7 and 9 of *Mabon,* where the male and female archetypes are exemplified by the roles on the Poet's Wheel and in the succession of the Pendragons. Each of the female and male roles above represents a level or pitch of otherworldly energy. They are reconciled by the seer-poet, a neutral role which can be wielded by either a male or a female character embodying the archetype of Mabon and skillfully tuning and playing upon the strings of otherworldly harmony. The purity of the seer-poet's role is the result of a perfect balancing of earthly and otherworldly modes of operation. He or she reconciles each primal pair of archetypes to a state of perfect neutrality. In the case of both Merlin Emrys and Segda, for example, the king is in an unbalanced relationship with the land's sovereignty and the wise men of the land require the sacrifice of an innocent child. This sacrifice does not, in fact, happen, although in the case of Gwern, who in "Branwen, Daughter of Llyr" is thrown upon the fire by Efnissien, the sacrifice is enacted. Likewise, Taliesin is cast upon the waters by Ceridwen.

The ancient punishment among Celtic peoples for certain offences, including incest, was to put the offender in a boat without rudder or oars so that he or she drowned or survived at the mercy of the waters. It is possible that the plunging of Dylan into the waves at birth may be a remembrance of this theme, for, as we have noted (see *Mabon*, chapter 5), his death is remembered in the triads as an unfortunate accident or possibly a sacrifice. There is also a submerged tradition concerning Arthur's slaughter of the innocents, which comes about because Mordred, the child conceived by Arthur and his half sister, is born on May Day; Arthur commands that each child born on that day be set adrift in an open boat and in this way hopes to purge his own child, who is of incestuous origin. It is interesting to remember that Taliesin also suffers the ordeal of the waters on May Eve.

The earliest harmonic motif of the seer-poet, then, may well be tied to a primitive cult of child sacrifice in which chieftains established their sovereignty by "giving" a child to the Otherworld. Although this tradition clearly does not appear in the later Arthurian cycle, there remains the mystery of the deaths of Arthur's various children—Llacheu, Amr, and Gwydre—who are not the sons of Gwenhwyfar in early Welsh tradition. They are said to have died in Arthur's lifetime: Gwydre is slain by Twrch Trwyth in "Culhwch and Olwen"; Llacheu dies in battle in the early sources but is killed by Kay in *Perlesvaus*[29]; and Amr is said to have been killed by Arthur himself.[78] Of course, in early tradition Mordred was considered to be not a son of Arthur, but rather a nephew.

If we look at the list of the Pendragons in figure 16 (page 243), we will see that there are few kings in whose reign a child is not killed or abducted to the Otherworld. Pryderi suffers a dual abduction—in "Pwyll, Prince of Dyfed" and in "Manawyddan, Son of Llyr." Dylan is lost in "Math, Son of Mathonwy," and Arthur's reign, laid alongside the evidence of the *Mabinogion* stories, shows a similar pattern.

The later harmonic motif of the seer-poet shows it to be firmly lodged in its modes of prophet, giver of justice, and revealer of inner wisdom. This is the threefold role of Merlin in later Arthurian tradition—it is he who establishes Arthur in his sovereignty and afterwards retires from the world's affairs to his observatory of seventy doors and windows from which he can view the heavens and earthly realms. It is due to this myth that Welsh tradition, perceiving the overlay of our world with the Otherworld, called Britain Clas Merddin, or Merlin's Enclosure. To anyone aware of the depths of Britain's mythological heritage, this guardianship is still active, perceptible through meditation and ritual insight.

We can see how the seer-poet is a figure who steps into and out of the Otherworld at will, for he is a son of Sovereignty who never aspires to the kingship yet functions as its guardian on a mystical level. Within Clas Merddin lies Llys Arthur, the mystical center of the land—the Hollow Hills, the subterranean chamber of Arthur's return. It is perhaps of this concept that William Blake, one of Britain's great mythographers, wrote in the voice of Enitharmon, the Great Mother of his poem "Jerusalem":

> *I will Create secret places,*
> *And the masculine names of the places, Merlin and Arthur.*
> *A triple Female Tabernacle for Moral Law I weave . . .*[51]

Whether we see Sovereignty in her three aspects or four, she is the land itself, surrounded by the palladium of Merlin's Enclosure, and at her heart is Llys Arthur, the Court of Arthur, where the mythic company still throng her hills, valleys, and secret places.

9

The Joy of the Court

Now tell me the name of that wondrous queen,
With her couch of crystal and robe of green.

"Bruiden Caerthainn"

And Peredur stood, and compared the blackness
of the raven and the whiteness of the snow, and the
redness of the blood, to the hair of the lady that best
he loved, which was blacker than jet, and to her
skin, which was whiter than the snow, and to the
two red spots upon her cheeks, which were redder
than the blood upon the snow.

"Peredur"

The Symbols of Sovereignty

Every British sovereign, at his or her coronation, is invested at the solemn moment of *saining*, or consecration, with numerous objects called regalia. This hallowing of an earthly being with what are, in effect, otherworldly empowerments is an awesome enactment, causing frissons of atavistic remembrance among many of its witnesses. The importance of the sovereign's regalia is not based upon the extrinsic value of each object, though many are indeed beyond price, or on each piece's association with the former sovereign who caused it to be made, though, again, such association invests the object with commemorative importance. To understand its true value, we have to look beyond these considerations to the function of the regalia, for each piece, whether it be worn, carried, or used, is symbolic of the qualities of Sovereignty herself.

There is a mysterious symbolism attached to the present British coronation regalia, with its swords, scepters, bracelets, spurs, crown, ring, and mantle, all of which derive from earlier models.[50] Some of these we can see plainly from the traditions embodied in the *Mabinogion*. Celtic kings were not crowned and so had no coronation; they were, however, inaugurated upon the sacred earth of their kingdom. The present queen of England was crowned while seated over an ancient inauguration stone, the Stone of Scone, which now resides in Edinburgh Castle as part of the Honors of Scotland. So an ancient tradition continues.

Figure 18 (page 259) lists the hallows of Sovereignty found throughout the *Mabinogion* and the form each may take in certain stories. The land is symbolized by the gwyddbwyll board, and possession of it denotes sovereignty. The list of the Thirteen Treasures of Britain (see *Mabon*, chapter 3) awards the board to Gwenddolau ap Ceidio, who was the patron and protector of Myrddin and one of the leaders of the factions who died at the Battle of Arderydd. But in our stories we see the board in the possession of three different individuals and used in three different ways. In "The Dream of Macsen Wledig," Eudaf, Elen's father, seems to be its possessor, for he also makes the chess pieces for the board. The appearance of the gwyddbwyll board in this tale denotes his future sovereignty over Britain. It is Arthur who owns the board in "The Dream of Rhonabwy," in which he fights Owain in a

game, perhaps for the sovereignty of the Otherworld, while in
"Peredur" the board is owned by a Sovereignty figure, the empress of
Constantinople. Peredur is unable to achieve his quest until he
retrieves the board he has so rashly thrown away.

The royal chair or throne of the king may once have been a sover-
eignty-investing seat in Celtic tradition. In the *Mabinogion* this seat is
represented by the golden chair in which sits a representative of
Sovereignty: Elen, the orchard woman, or the maiden in the tent. But
in "Gereint and Enid," Gereint also seats himself in the vacant golden
chair in the orchard. And later tradition speaks of the rash way in
which Perceval sits in the Siege Perilous, the seat at the Round Table
which only the destined or worthy champion may take. This role is
later filled by Galahad.[32, 106]

The ring with which the British sovereign is invested is called the
wedding ring of England. When Elizabeth I was urged by her counselors to marry and beget heirs, she held up the hand on which she
wore her coronation ring and said, "England is my husband and all
Englishmen my children."[50] Likewise, the ring that most often appears
in the *Mabinogion* is sovereignty-bestowing—or is invested with another
otherworldly property. Arthur's ring in "The Dream of Rhonabwy"
confers the power of remembrance upon all who see it, which is how
Rhonabwy is able to relate his dream afterwards. In "Peredur" the
woman of the mound gives Peredur a ring, which is a token of devotion
and also empowers him to become invisible to the dreadful addanc he
must slay. Luned's ring in "Owain" has two properties similar to
Peredur's: It confers invisibility and there is also the suggestion that it
serves as a token of Owain's union with both the land and the countess of the fountain.

The mantle of invisibility is mentioned in the list of the Thirteen
Treasures of Britain as the possession of Arthur, as indeed it is in "The
Dream of Rhonabwy," although Caswallawn and Llwyd both create, in
their stories, a magic mist which becomes very like a mantle. Later in
Arthurian tradition, the mantle is transformed into a chastity-proving

garment which covers chaste women and shortens upon those who are unfaithful. The mantle of Tegau Gold Breast is one such garment, mentioned in an appendix to the Thirteen Treasures. The transformation of this hallow represents the diminution of the sovereignty tradition: The Goddess of the Land and her relationship with the king is portrayed in a more mundane way—as a quest for what women most desire, which is found in the stories of both Gawain and Ragnell[73] and in the Wife of Bath's Tale.[6]

But the mantle also represents the land, if we read closely the description from Nennius of the incident of Vortigern's tower. Emrys interprets the meaning of the dragons but says the cloth that covers them "represents your kingdom."[28] We have seen how the story of Merlin Emrys and the dragons is associated with the story of Lludd (see chapter 2); therefore, the dragon's covering may be seen as a type of mantle.

The sword of light borne by the hero is represented in "Culhwch and Olwen" by the flashing sword of Lluch Llenlleawg, which, says the "Preiddeu Annwfn," flashes and possibly distracts the cauldron watchers. Goreu accomplishes singular feats at Wrnach's castle, where the sword is the object of one of Culhwch's anoethu: It is also Goreu who beheads Yspaddaden at the conclusion of the story. Traditionally, only a weapon of light can defeat the giant of darkness. Arthur's sword depicts the twin dragons of Vortigern's tower upon its blade, and when it is unsheathed, they breathe fire. Although Peredur's sword, which breaks in two, is an unlikely candidate for the sword of light, we have seen how his prototypes always find and wield the sword (chapter 7).

The various cauldrons and vessels in the *Mabinogion* represent the wisdom of the Otherworld as well as the bounty of the land. The Cauldron of Rebirth amply demonstrates this in "Branwen, Daughter of Llyr," in which the sovereignties of Britain and Ireland eventually contend. In Celtic daily life, the cauldron was the only means of stewing food—all nourishment came from it. The otherworldly cauldrons often supply food as well as bestowing wisdom or life. Just as the Irish regain life in the Cauldron of Rebirth, the sons of the king of suffering are revived in two baths in "Peredur." In the list of the Thirteen Treasures of Britain in "Culhwch and Olwen," we learn that Diwrnach's cauldron will not boil a coward's food. This cauldron is analogous to the cauldron of Annwfn in the "Preiddeu Annwfn," in which Arthur and his men make the voyage to Annwfn rather than a journey to Ireland. The prime cauldron of knowledge is Ceridwen's, prepared over a year and a day, whose outpouring wisdom is imbibed by Taliesin, not Afagddu. Rhiannon's bag, which is never full, and Gwyddno's bottomless hamper seem part of the same tradition of bounty. The abundance given by the land depends, in Celtic lore, on the integrity of the king. His quest for or interaction with the otherworldly cauldrons—which bestow their own wisdom—creates a living contract of plenty which flows from one world through another.

The spear that heals and wounds represents the way in which sovereignty can be promptly removed from a ruler or restored if he proves worthy. Bran is wounded mortally by such a spear but he does not die; neither does the Lame King, Peredur's uncle, who has been wounded by the nine witches of Gloucester. But Peredur is able to gain control of the spear when he slays the unicorn and, with its spearlike horn, turns aside the wasting curse. Gronw's magically forged spear defeats Llew by making Llew break the geasa that surround his death. But Llew does not die either; his career is checked temporarily and he is forced to consider his relationship with the Flower Bride, Blodeuwedd. His sovereignty is taken, but may be restored. Yspaddaden's rule has been an onerous one by the time Culhwch and his company come to the giant's castle: The spears that the giant sends after the men of Arthur are all returned with devastating effect upon Yspaddaden, wounded in knee, breast, and eye. These blows are but forerunners of the shears that will sever the power of his regime with the loss of his life.

Sovereignty's cup, appearing three time in our stories, is perhaps the earliest prototype of the Grail, though the cauldron shares its properties. Like the cup that Sovereignty pours for Irish heroes, it is offered only to the worthy candidate. The Grail-like and cuplike golden bowl to which Rhiannon and Pryderi become stuck is an otherworldly hallow used by Llwyd to ensnare them and avenge the insult to Gwawl. The bowl on chains appears also in "Owain" and in *Perlesvaus*, in which it reveals the sufferings of those trapped in the Underworld. The cup cannot be achieved by the unworthy, thus the reason why Rhiannon and Pryderi suffer is possibly because Pryderi has relinquished his father's sovereignty into the hands of Manawyddan instead of taking it up himself. The empress's cups echo the cup that is stolen from Gwenhwyfar in "Peredur." When an earthly mistake has been made, the emblem of the hallow's power is removed into the Otherworld, where it is encountered by the hero on quest. Restoring to the world the sacred power of the hallows is the challenge.

The horn appears in the list of the Thirteen Treasures of Britain as the horn of Bran the Niggard, which supplies whatever drink is desired. There exists the story that when Myrddin was trying to gather the Thirteen Treasures, all their possessors swore to relinquish them if Myrddin was able to gain the horn of Bran. He did accomplish this and afterwards took the treasures with him to his glass house on Bardsey Island, where, according to legend, he still resides.[85] Obtaining the horn of Gwlgawd Gododin is specified by Yspaddaden as one of Culhwch's anoethu, and this seems to be a vessel similar to the horn of Bran. But we note two further horns in the stories: that won by Peredur when he cuts off the unicorn's head and the horn that sounds in the orchard when Gereint has achieved the test of the enchanted games. The latter horn is for blowing, not drinking, and signifies the end of the hero's tests and his worthy joining with Sovereignty. We will have more to say about this object in the section The Court of Joy later in this chapter.

These, then, are Sovereignty's regalia, the hallows of the Goddess, which she gives into the keeping of her worthy champion. While he remains faithful to her, he is empowered by these gifts; when he fails to uphold the rights of the land, he is bereft of their empowering help. It is in such a way that the Grail is withdrawn from the earth in later tradition, as we shall see in the section The Maidens of the Wells (see page 267), which provides a summary of these hallows along with the king, Sovereignty figure, or representative associated with each.

It remains only to consider how later storytellers portrayed Arthur's sovereignty with the symbol that is known by every child: the sword in the stone. The sword, which has been set in an anvil by Merlin, may not be drawn by any save the rightful king—and because the stone represents the land, it cannot be drawn by any save Arthur. The mythic relationship of king and the Goddess of the Land becomes ever clearer: When Arthur receives Excalibur, his sword of manhood (as opposed to his inauguration or coronation sword), from the Lady of the Lake, he receives an empowerment even more distinct. At the conclusion of his reign he commands Sir Bedivere to cast Excalibur back into the lake, for the sword must return to Sovereignty; it may not be either kept as an heirloom or bequeathed to some future king. Each monarch makes his own agreement with Sovereignty, who will not give her gifts to the unworthy.

Queen Dragon

The gaining of the hallows of Sovereignty depends upon the hero's successful encounter with the Loathly Lady or cailleach aspect of the Goddess. The transformation of the hag into a beautiful maiden is effected by the hero's kiss or by his willingness to sleep with her. A Scots Gaelic version of "The Daughter of the King Under the Wave" retains this motif.[61] The fianna are encamped on a wild rainy night when an ugly woman with hair down to her heels approaches them. She asks at the tent of Fionn and Oisian to be let in, but it is only Diarmuid who receives her. After drying herself at the fire, she begs to be allowed to come under Diarmuid's blanket. The storyteller says, with a phrase which might have been drawn straight from "Peredur": "She was not long thus, when he gave a start, and he gazed at her, and he saw the finest drop of blood that ever was, from the beginning of the universe till the end of the world, at his side."

Symbol	King, Form Symbol May Take, and Sovereignty Figure or Representative
Golden Chair	Elen ("Macsen Wledig"), orchard woman ("Gereint"), maiden in the tent ("Peredur")
Ring	Arthur ("Rhonabwy"), Luned ("Owain"), woman of the mound ("Peredur")
Mantle ("Manawyddan");	Caswallawn ("Branwen"), Llwyd (Manawyddan), the dragon's covering ("Lludd"), Arthur ("Rhonabwy")
Gwyddbwyll Board (Chess Board)	Eudaf ("Macsen Wledig"), Arthur ("Rhonabwy"), empress of Constantinople ("Peredur")
Sword of Light	Lluch Llenlleawg ("Culhwch"), Arthur ("Rhonabwy"), Goreu ("Culhwch"), Peredur ("Peredur")
Spear	Irish spear ("Branwen"), Gronw ("Math"), Yspaddaden ("Culhwch"), Peredur and the nine witches ("Peredur")
Cauldron of Rebirth	Llassar ("Branwen"), the king of suffering ("Peredur"), Diwrnach ("Culhwch")
Cauldron of Knowledge	Ceridwen ("Taliesin")
Vessel of Plenty	Rhiannon's bag ("Peredur"), hamper of Gwyddno ("Culhwch" and "Lludd"), Diwrnach ("Culhwch")
Sovereignty's Cup	golden bowl ("Manawyddan"), empress of Constantinople ("Peredur"), Gwenhwyfar ("Peredur")
Horn	orchard woman ("Gereint"), Gwlgawd Gododin ("Culhwch"), Peredur ("Peredur")

Figure 18. The hallows associated with Sovereignty in the *Mabinogion*. In most cases, names of stories have been abbreviated.

It is this willingness to accept the most unpromising appearance of Sovereignty that lies at the heart of the hero's success. Like a man promising to marry a woman "for richer, for poorer, in sickness and in health," out of love for the land the kingly candidate takes on the government of the land and all that the task entails. The land that is loved and respected gives its best, as do its people, and the reign of that king is bountiful and wise, strong and loving. But it is all too easy, under the rule of a worthless king, for the land to turn sour: Its crops wither, its people turn to violent crime, and the whole body politic is racked with strife.

It is at such times that the sovereignty-bestowing maiden and queen of the hallows transforms into her cailleach aspect. As we have seen in folk stories, this transformation is often accomplished by an evil stepmother or magician who enchants the maiden into a monstrous shape such as a worm or dragon (see chapters 3 and 5). But we also note that Sovereignty has the ability to transform herself at will, as we have seen in "Peredur," and that this voluntary transformation is, in fact, the earlier of the two models.

Each of the three romances reveals the transforming Goddess of Sovereignty in the persons of her representatives. In "Owain," the countess of the fountain appears first as a mourning woman, ugly with grief, yet Owain still perceives her inner beauty. In "Gereint and Enid," Enid is both the most beautiful maiden and the most poorly dressed; she receives the highest honors and then the lowest degradation. In "Peredur," Sovereignty shows all her aspects, from the empress to the Black Maiden and the nine witches of Gloucester. Underlying both "Owain" and "Peredur" are the layers that connect the figure of Sovereignty as a transforming hag with the enchanted damsel who is doomed to take the shape of a monster. While most Irish Sovereignty figures appear as hags, British folklore variants show that the enchanted damsel can be released by means of the *fier baiser* (the daring kiss of medieval romance) given her by the worthy knight. In the case of "Owain," we have seen how the overlay of *Libeaus Desconus* (chapter 3) and the folk ballad "Kemp Owyne" (chapter 5) can be perceived. In "Peredur," the disenchantment scene is missing, but it may be vestigially present in the incident when Peredur slays the addanc, though only after he has been given a ring of invisibility by the woman of the mound.

Each aspect of Sovereignty helps or relates to the others. As we have observed, the action of the cailleach aspect of Sovereignty is not evil. Hers is a scouring, catabolic function by which the disintegration of order and fertility within the land is hastened. The cailleach clears the way with the harsh broom of purgation, bringing a spiritual winter whereby the land can be renewed and hearts made ready to receive the spring.

The action of the cailleach and her transformation into the sovereignty-bestowing maiden are clearly seen in the following story, which relates to the seasons the joint functions of these transformative aspects. This story appears in both the *Leabhar Breac* and the *Book of Lismore* and is remarkable in that it shows the enduring nature—even into the Christian era—of the seeming combat between the hag and maiden aspects of Sovereignty.

The story is called "Don T-Samain Beos," and it relates the meaning of the pagan feast of Samhain (October 31) and how it is connected to the Christian feast of All Saints (November 1). It is probably the work of a clerical commentator who wished to explain, in Irish terms, how such a pagan festival could stand side by side with one of the greatest Christian holy days. Certainly customs pertaining to ancient pagan seasonal rites were practiced on the occasion of the Christian feasts, and are still practiced today.

> This is the reason why the feast of Samhain is called the Feast of All Saints. It came about as Boniface, the successor of St. Peter, was contemplating the Pantheon, the pagan house of the gods in Rome. He remarked to the Emperor that the Pantheon, despite the coming of Christianity, had grown in influence. At this, the Emperor caused the Pantheon to be consecrated to Mary and all the saints of the world, those who stand in the first nine ranks of the blessed. This is why

Samhain is called All Saints, because the pagan house of the gods has now been consecrated to all saints. There is another reason also, namely a game which was played by the boys of Rome every year on the same day: it was a board game with the figure of a hag at one end and the figure of a virgin at the other. The hag set a dragon on the virgin, calling all the demons, while at the other end the virgin let loose a lamb so that the lamb overpowered the dragon. At that the hag set a lion upon the virgin, but the virgin let loose a rain, and the rain was victorious over the lion. Boniface, who watched this, told the boys that this farcical game was unseemly and asked them how they came to know it. The boys replied: "Sibyl, the brilliant prophetess, has taught us this game, through the grace of a prophecy in which she prophesied Christ's combat with the devil." "Thank God," answered the pope. "He who was prophesied has come and the devil is defeated." He added, "Give thanks to God and do not play this game any more." At that this game was not played any more upon Samhain eve.[35]

The game, supposedly Roman in this story, is exactly the kind of game that the Irish played themselves. The storyteller gives the game away by telling us they played it on October 31, Halloween or Samhain, the night when the Celtic New Year began, when winter truly started, when the cailleach reigned. Both Irish and Scottish Gaels (Scottish Celts) personified winter as the Cailleach Bheare or Bheur. She held sway until Imbolc (spring), when, on St. Brigit's day, February 1, the maiden goddess challenged the hag and began battling for the rule of spring. The hag and the maiden of this game are clearly identifiable with the cailleach and the goddess Brighid. The cailleach held folk in the grip of winter with her icy winds and clouds of snow, whereas the goddess Brighid was the fosterer of lambs born at this time of year. She was honored with great celebrations on both sides of the Irish Sea up until recently. On Bride's Morn, in Scots Gaelic tradition, the serpent is supposed to come forth from the ground, signifying the attack of the cailleach, who normally chooses to increase her winter chill at this time:

The serpent will come from the hole
On the brown day of Bride,
Though there should be three feet of snow
On the flat surface of the ground.
On the day of Bride of the white hills
The noble queen will come from the knoll
I will not molest the noble queen.[61]

We note that, even here, the serpent is referred to respectfully as queen. Thus, the beasts that hag and maiden set against each other in the Roman game, the dragon and the lamb, are clearly drawn from Celtic association. It is conceivable that we have here a lost game in which Sovereignty's transformations were played as a form of *fidhchell* during the long winter months when stories and indoor games were the only entertainment. Certainly we know that some fidhchell boards were decorated or formed in the shape of a human body, with arms and legs protruding from their corners.[104] The second move in the game, when the lion is overcome by a shower of rain, is similar to the behavior of the characters of Owain and the lady of the fountain; but this similarity must be considered coincidental.

Certainly the story above is derived from a genuine mythical understanding of the seasonal rituals concerning the transformation of winter into spring, although the change that is brought about here is that from paganism to Christianity. The models that the storyteller has chosen to express his views are from existent Irish pagan customs and have been carefully selected to have the most profound effect upon his hearers, who would have known very well about the struggle between the hag and the maiden. We note that the beast which the hag first sends against the maiden is the dragon, and that this tradition is reflected in the Scots Gaelic belief that the serpent that comes out of the ground to signify the ending of winter is the noble queen herself, the cailleach. If we set side by side this identification of the cailleach as dragon and the tradition of the maiden enchanted into a serpent shape, we discover that Sovereignty may choose to take the shape of the dragon.

Dragons, then, have a curiously contradictory symbolism: They appear in some stories as ravagers of lands and devourers of maidens and youths, and are fit only to be destroyed by great knights like St. George. In other stories, while they are awesomely powerful and are to be approached respectfully, they are also guardians of treasure, some of which they may give up to the one who is brave enough to engage in a contest of wits with them. Both sets of symbols may seem familiar to the reader, and this is not surprising, for both are analogues of the symbolism surrounding Sovereignty herself, who, depending upon the aspect she is manifesting, guards great treasures, devastates the land, gives advice, and indulges in games by which she may be overcome or for which she is the victor's reward.

The most striking aspect of the Samhain Eve story is that the game describes the chessboard of the land over which hag and maiden battle for sovereignty. The sacred games of Sovereignty appear throughout Celtic tradition, and in the *Mabinogion* we have seen some prime examples, notably in "Gereint and Enid," where the games concern the hunting of the white hart, the sparrowhawk contest, and the enchanted games. The chess games in "The Dream of Macsen Wledig," "Peredur," and "The Dream of Rhonabwy" are also rooted in the question of who shall gain the sovereignty of the land. Even the horse race that Elphin stakes against King Maelgwn in "Taliesin" may be seen as part of this tradition, for Taliesin ensures that Elphin, his patron, gains the sovereignty of honor and even compensates for Elphin's persistent misfortune by enabling his master's winning horse to stumble over the place where a great golden treasure lies hidden.

It is not incidental that the sovereignty of the land is guarded by a cailleach or a woman in dragon's shape who has to be either overcome in a game or disenchanted. It is not incidental that the treasures guarded by the dragon are those very hallows that empower the rightful king. Such considerations may lead us into deeper waters.

The mysteries of Sovereignty are expressed by means of many symbols besides the emblems of the hallows. The union of the land with the king is represented by the two symbols of the Grail that are intimately related. The red and white dragons that appear in both Nennius and Geoffrey of Monmouth as well as in "Lludd and Llefelys" have their symbolic analogues in the two cruets brought to Europe by Joseph of Arimathea, for these contain blood and sweat from the world's Redeemer. As R. J. Stewart has remarked in his essay "The Grail as Bodily Vessel,"[115] "the interaction of male and female characteristics . . . [has] long been expressed as The Seed and The Blood."

The basis of the Grail's existence in British tradition is, as we see, founded on the union of the king with Sovereignty, and the emblems of this union are the hallows, which include the Grail in its earliest form—the empowering cup or cauldron. Beneath this understanding is the ancient, tribal concept of the mingling of the royal seed with the holy blood of the land; the magical image is of king and Sovereignty's representative or priestess joined in sexual union, which is that disenchanting kiss or ritual bedding with the cailleach that results in the transformation of the hag into the sovereignty-bestowing maiden and of the wasteland into a fruitful garden. The archetypal symbols representing this union are the two dragons, the red and the white.

All texts speak of the dragons in a political rather than mystical light, but the deeper symbolism emerges. The sleeping dragons, locked safely away, represent the dormant state of Britain's sovereignty. They are chained during Lludd's reign because their uncontrolled manifestation renders the kingdom chaotic. It is during the reign of Vortigern that they are uncovered at the prophetic behest of Merlin Emrys, who comes to rid Britain of a worthless ruler and reestablish the true union of the land with a new dynasty—the Pendragons.

The later reign of Arthur, according to all traditions, ends because the union of the king with his land is ruptured through, perhaps, Arthur and his sister's incestuous begetting of Mordred or the loss of Guinevere to Lancelot. Either way, the energies of the dragons run uncontrolled towards the conclusion of Arthur's reign, bringing in the Saxon invaders, devastating the land, and bringing the Fellowship of the Round Table to an end. It is also possible to see the end of Arthur's reign from the point of view of the Queen Dragon herself—the transforming Goddess, who, having been Flower Bride and representative of Sovereignty, chooses a new consort to rule her land. Such is the career of Gwenhwyfar in the earliest traditions, as we shall see in the next chapter. It is significant that the Battle of Camlann is provoked by an adder, whose appearance—a serpent coming out of the ground, just as the cailleach of winter does—causes one of Arthur's men to strike out, thus breaking the truce between Arthur and Mordred in Malory.[25]

The maintenance and wielding of the hallows is the duty of the king, and if he once wavers, the kingdom soon tilts out of balance. The popular belief in the Sleeping Lord, who lies buried at certain sacred sites throughout Britain and who guards a golden cup or other treasure, is a deeply rooted remembrance of an ancestral mystery. There is a sense in which the hallows are hidden within the land itself at the four quarters of the realm of Logres, the "inner" Britain. These do not constitute buried treasure, which can be found with a metal detector and then unearthed, but rather the guardianship by Sovereignty's champion of the elemental, power-bestowing energies that hold the realm in balance.

It is this tradition that underlies the importance of the Grail in British consciousness. An apocryphal gnostic tradition speaks of the two cruets of Joseph of Arimathea, which are thought to be buried in France and Britain, where they are guarded by Joseph and Mary Magdalene. This constitutes a Christianizing of the native hallows. In British tradition these figures can be viewed as the guardian of the hallows and the Dark Woman of Knowledge, or the Lord and Lady of the Wheel, for they are jointly responsible for the relics of the dead Redeemer and the dissemination of his tradition. The cruets, containing the blood and sweat of the Redeemer, are the Christian analogues for the blood and seed.

Such is the power of this mystery that its symbolism has accordingly been made dense and obscure to human understanding lest it be reduced to atavistic levels involving ritual sacrifice or into modern perversions of genetic manipulation. The mysteries of sovereignty are those of life itself, of the exchange of energies between man and woman, king and Sovereignty, god and goddess.

Within the framework of the Celto-Arthurian world, the blood and the seed and the red and white dragons are symbols which may be applied to the Goddess and the king, or to the Queen Dragon and her consort, the Pendragon. They are the maintainers of Logres, the inner Britain; they are the dragons who are loose once more, scouring the land with their strong breath, rekindling the dreaming fires of creation in each heart.

The Maidens of the Wells

As we are beginning to appreciate, the Grail legends lie at the heart of the Sovereignty story. There is little space here in which to track the course of the Grail's transformation from Sovereignty's cup to vessel of redemption, but we can see how the figure of Sovereignty persists throughout the legend's unfolding.

The purest example of Sovereignty is drawn from "Baile in Scail," in which Conn is abducted into the Otherworld in order to have a vision of his kingly destiny. In it we see the earliest pagan analogues of the Grail tradition, but here the vessel confers kingship, not spiritual redemption.

> They went into the house and saw a girl seated in a chair of crystal, wearing a golden crown. In front of her was a silver vat with corners of gold. A vessel of gold stood beside her and before her was a golden cup. They saw the Phantom himself on his throne . . . "My name is Lug . . . and I have come to tell you the span of your sovranty" . . . The girl was the Sovranty of Ireland and she gave food to Conn . . . When she went to serve the ale, she asked to whom the cup of red ale

[*dergflaith,* or "red lordship"] should be given, and the Phantom
answered her, "For Conn."[170]

When Sovereignty appears as herself, rather than in changed form,
she invariably offers food or drink. We have already seen how this happens in "Peredur" with the maiden in the tent. The giving of nourishment was, of course, a prime requisite of Celtic hospitality.

The giving of cups to the worthiest hero occurs in "Bricriu's Feast,"
in which the great Queen Medbh (Maeve) gives cups to all the heroes
whom Conchobar sends to her for judgment. Her own name means
"intoxication," referring to her reputation as a sovereignty-bestowing
woman; this is further borne out by her many lovers and husbands to
whom she grants, briefly, the right of kingship beside her.[142]

Different kinds of sovereignty deserve different kinds of drink,
which is shown in an Irish genealogical tract concerning the succession
of the Munster kings, the Eoghanacht, the founder of which was Corc.
According to legend, his wife, Aimend, has a dream in which she gives
birth to wolf cubs. She bathes one in wine (the royal drink), one in ale
(the noble drink), one in new milk (the drink of the fosterling), and one
in water (the drink of slaves). A fifth cub comes to bed and she bathes
him in blood (the drink of the warrior) and he gnaws at her breasts.[60]
This dream is prophetic of the sons she actually bears, all of whom settle in various parts of Munster with better or worse success. The fifth
wolf cub refers to her stepson, who proves treacherous. Here the candidates for kingship are bathed rather than given something to drink,
but the classic pattern is shown quite clearly.

Sovereignty offers three cups in all to her candidates; these correspond to the three symbolic colors of her transformations:

- The milk of fostering is white, corresponding to the maiden aspect.
- The wine of lordship is red, corresponding to the hallows queen
  aspect.
- The drink of forgetfulness is black, corresponding to the Dark
  Woman of Knowledge or cailleach aspect.

It is possible that the three cups offered to the empress in "Peredur" are based upon this understanding, representing Peredur's complex relationship with Sovereignty in that text.

The cup of Sovereignty, which later becomes the Grail, cannot be robbed of its original symbolism to which the Grail texts attest in showing the Grail bearer as a beautiful maiden and the Grail messenger—she who summons and prompts the seeker—as an ugly hag.[119] Each of the romances, as we have noted, presents this polarization of two of Sovereignty's aspects. The later Grail texts show a further diminution of the tradition by incorporating into the Grail quest numerous dispossessed or raped maidens, widowed wives, and enticing enchantresses. The Grail seekers go to great lengths to rescue the first and escape the last two, even though their quest is thereby lengthened. We perceive a glimpse of the hero's championship of Sovereignty in such episodes.

A. C. L. Brown, in his book *The Origins of the Grail Legend*,[58] has shown how the quest for the Grail sprang out of a long Celtic tradition of Otherworld journeys in which kings and heroes achieve wonders and bring back various hallows. The women who guard these treasures are clearly otherworldly or faery women, and it is not until the mainstream Arthurian romances that we find Sovereignty being represented by earthly women, although she is often present as a faery mistress in the Breton lais and related stories.[134]

From this fusion of traditions arises a story showing how the usurpation of Sovereignty's function by an unworthy king brings about the wasteland and the ensuing Grail quest. *The Elucidation*, as it is hopefully called, is of unknown authorship, though it was possibly written around 1230 C.E. It serves as an introduction to Chrétien's *Perceval*, or *Conte du Graal*, and is supposed to illuminate the hidden meanings of that story. Because Chrétien left his story unfinished, numerous writers attempted to continue and conclude it; these episodes are called "the continuations," and serve to explain Chrétien's intentions for his heroes, Gawain and Perceval. *The Elucidation* was probably written during this period and is doubtless an attempt at a

prequel to the Grail quest. It is a peculiar kind of introduction, however, for it refers to stories which happen nowhere in either Chrétien or
the continuations, and moreover seems bent on mystifying rather than
enlightening the reader, despite what the title might suggest.

For our purposes it is a key story, for it shows an understanding of
Sovereignty's association with the hallow of the Grail more clearly than
any other text. The following is my direct retelling from the difficult-
to-follow original text:

In ancient times Logres was a rich country but was turned into
wasteland so that it was worth scarcely a couple of hazelnuts, for the
kingdom lost the voices of the wells and the damsels that were in them.
These damsels would offer food and drink to wayfarers. A traveler had
only to wish for food and seek out one of the wells and a damsel would
appear from out of the well with the food he liked best, a cup of gold
in her hand. No wayfarers were excluded from this service.

But King Amangons broke this custom. Although it was his duty
to guard the damsels and keep them within his peace, he raped one of
them and took away her golden cup for his own service. After that time
no damsel was seen issuing from the well and the only service which
wayfarers received was done invisibly. The king's vassals followed their
king's actions and raped the other damsels also, carrying off the
golden cups. And so the service of the wells ceased and the land was
laid waste. Trees lost their leaves, meadows and plants withered, and
the waters dried up so that no man might find the court of the Rich
Fisherman, he who once made the land bright with his treasures.

After this time, King Arthur instituted the Knights of the Round
Table, who, when they heard this story, were determined to recover the
wells and protect the damsels. They swore they would destroy the kindred of Amangons and his men. But though they made vows to God,
they could never hear a voice from the well nor could they find any
damsel, for these had been pierced by the swords of Amangons's followers or else hanged.

The Round Table knights found damsels in the forest accompanied by well-armed knights. One of these knights was captured and brought back to Arthur's court, where he told the following tale. "All of us are the children born of the damsels whom Amangons and his men raped. These great wrongs shall never be redeemed in worldly time. We are bound to travel in common, knights and damsels, through this land until God wills that the Court of Joy be found, for that will make the land bright again. Whoever seeks that Court shall find greater adventures than were ever in this land before."

The Round Table knights decided to seek the court of the Rich Fisherman, who was a shapeshifter. Although many knights sought it and a few found it, none asked the right questions when the hallows were processed around the hall of the Rich Fisherman who appeared in such splendor that none recognized the fisherman he had seen earlier that day. At that table the Grail appeared by itself and served all who sat there, providing food in great variety.

[At this point the writer tells us about the stories we will hear and says that each branch of the story has a guardian appointed to it.]

On the day that the court of the Rich Fisherman was found and the correct answers were received by the seeker, the waters flowed again and fountains which had been dried up ran into the meadows. Fields were green and fruitful and the forests clothed in green leaf on the day that the Court of Joy was found.

Then there came up out of the wells a pitiable kind of people who made for themselves castles, cities, and strongholds. They created for the damsels the rich Castle of the Maidens, but they knew not the service of the wells. They built the Perilous Bridge and the Orguellous Castle. They founded an order called the Knights of the Rich Company in opposition to the Round Table knights. They made war on Arthur and such were their numbers that it was hard to overcome them. For four years they fought against him, and they were at last overcome on the day when the Court of Joy was found.[36]

This mysterious story has many surprising elements, considering it was written as a prequel to the cycle of the Christian Grail quest. The reign of Amangons obviously predates Arthur's reign by more than one generation and in some measure represents an earlier, pagan tradition. Amangons is a mythical, not a historical king, and indeed the whole story reads very like a gnostic parable of the fall of humanity from innocence. Just how much the author or transcriber of this tale was drawing upon imagination or oral tradition is hard to say. Certainly there is something about the damsels of the wells which ranks them with Sovereignty's representatives.

The rape of the damsels and the stealing of their cups is, of course, a parallel to the theft of Gwenhwyfar's cup and her abduction in Arthurian tradition, which, as we shall see, is crucial to an understanding of the mythic patterns within the *Mabinogion*. The fertility of the land is bound up with the fate of the damsels of the wells, and when they are raped and their golden cups taken from them, the harmony that should exist between king and land is ruptured. We note that these prototypes of the Grail are symbolic of the damsels' service in Logres; it is not until the more developed Grail legends that we see Sovereignty's role devolve to that of Grail bearer. Interestingly, the Grail question that so many knights fail to ask when the hallows are paraded about the Grail castle is "Whom does the Grail serve?"—strikingly reminiscent of Sovereignty's question to Lugh in the story "Baile in Scail": "For whom should the cup be poured?"

The relationship of the damsels of the wells with the court of the Rich Fisherman is not explicitly dealt with by the author, but we can hazard that the damsels are otherworldly women who offer food and drink to travelers along a network of holy sites and springs, which are the meeting places between the worlds. The court of the Rich Fisherman, which is also called the Court of Joy in the text, is analogous to the Otherworld paradise, wherein the treasures or hallows are guarded by the Rich Fisherman himself, who is possibly a type of Manannan or Manawyddan. (Manannan traditionally represents the king of the Otherworld and is, like the Rich Fisherman, a shape-changer who can take on humble personae as well as appear in his guise as king of the Blessed Isles.)

It would appear that access to otherworldly communion was effected at the wells by means of travelers drinking from the damsels' cups. By the time that Arthur and his knights appear and swear to destroy Amangons's kind, they have a substantial problem: They cannot destroy the descendants of Amangons without also destroying the descendants of the damsels. Earthly and otherworldly stocks are now commingled and, like the parable of the tares and the wheat in the Gospel, these people must be left alone to effect their own destiny. But among them there are storytellers, like Master Bleheris, who tell Arthur about the Court of Joy, the blessed Otherworld, and how access to it has been withdrawn from mankind but may yet be found.

The one who finds the Court of Joy is, of course, the Grail winner, who is Perceval in the earliest legends and Galahad in the later versions. In the fully developed Arthurian stories we may see that while Arthur himself encounters Sovereignty and becomes king after the early Celtic pattern, it is his knights Perceval, Galahad, and Bors who achieve the Grail quest. Thus a twofold association unfolds: Arthur establishes his championship of Logres, his communion with the land, and becomes its king, while the Grail winner establishes a communion with the otherworldly/heavenly realms by crossing the barrier between the worlds.

The Grail winner is always a scion of a royal line, having in him a share of the mixed parentage that we all inherit—but in him the blood of Sovereignty's representative is paramount. His opponents upon the Grail quest are drawn from a similar mixture of earthly and otherworldly races; they are the Order of the Rich Company in whom the blood of Amangons is paramount. What they do not have, they steal; whoever obstructs them, they destroy. And so the powers of light and darkness oppose each other in a conflict. Sovereignty's cup becomes not only a power-bestowing vessel but also a chalice of spiritual redemption in the late Grail romances.

The text tells us that the land of Logres "lost the voices of the wells," which descriptively evokes not only the loss of otherworldly communion but also the withdrawal of the Grail from earthly realms. In order to obtain this wonder-working hallow by which the land will be restored to its former fertility, the Grail seeker must find the gate and enter the Otherworld, where he will be subjected to tests and challenges to establish whether he is the rightful champion, "he who frees the waters," the destined Grail winner. He must be attuned to the needs of the land so that he may hear the voice of Sovereignty in his heart and answer her urgent questioning.

The Court of Joy

The Elucidation, then, may be considered to be a parable of the loss of the Otherworld by the earthly realm of Logres. It is also, though we should be cautious about using traditional Celtic texts in other cultural contexts, about the loss of communion with the Divine Feminine, with the Goddess of the Land. The later incorporation of Christian motifs of redemption is in no way at variance with the native model of Sovereignty, for both are about the loss of the creative, otherworldly realm that we all stand in need of, whether we see this as a loss of innocence, a loss of paradise, or a loss of creative imagination. For both models the symbol is the same: the redemptive vessel or hallow that may be Grail, cauldron, or cup.

We immediately notice a strong connection between the *The Elucidation,* with its inherent prophecy that the Court of Joy will be found by the most worthy knight, and "Gereint and Enid" or Chrétien's *Erec and Enid,* in which it is foretold that someone will achieve the Joy of the Court. How these two texts correspond is vital to an understanding of the nature of the Grail quest and the restoration of the land's fertility. As we have already seen, there is some confusion arising from the meaning of the word *cor,* which may be interpreted in one of many ways. The two meanings that most concern us here are *li cors,* which can mean "horn" or "body," and *la cors,* which means "court."

We will remember from "Gereint and Enid" that the horn was to be blown by the victor of the enchanted games, and that it is also the horn by which the Joy of the Court is announced in *Erec and Enid,* the French variant of "Gereint." This feat is called the Joy of the Court in that text and signifies the court's happiness at the release of Mabonograin from bondage and the cessation of his enforced combat with the host of challenging knights. In *Erec and Enid* the court at which this joy is announced is at the castle of Brandigan, where Evrain (Owain) presides. The horn *(li cors)* announces a great joy to the court *(la cors),* according to this tradition. But there is yet another meaning which underlies this shapeshifting word *cors:* "body."

We are already familiar with the archetypal figure who is a key to the mystery—Bran the Blessed himself—for he likewise possesses a horn, which gives whatever drink is desired.

It is impossible to stray far from the Grail legends without encountering Bran in some form or other. We have already seen that his sister, Branwen, is intimately associated with the archetype of Sovereignty. Bran himself is a prototype for the Fisher King, as many commentators have pointed out.[93, 125] We have seen that in "Branwen, Daughter of Llyr" he is wounded in the foot with a poisoned spear, yet he threatens the Irishman thus: "Dogs of Gwern, beware of Pierced Thighs."[122] Of course, the Wounded King of Chrétien's *Perceval,* who is called the Fisher King, is likewise wounded in the thigh by a spear.[7] The *Didot Perceval* gives the Fisher King the name Bron, while de Boron's *Joseph* gives Bron the apellation the Rich Fisher.[92] The numerous parallels between the pagan demigod of the *Mabinogion* and the Christian semimortal of the later Grail romances have been admirably dealt with by Helaine Newstead in her book *Bran the Blessed in Arthurian Romance.*[124]

We have noted that the castle where the Joy of the Court takes place is called Brandigan, which, although Evrain (Owain) lives there, is closely associated with Bran. Chrétien describes the castle as a strong one, secure from attack, with rich orchards and meadows all about. Its hospitality is famed, but it is also known as a place of great danger, for all are awaiting the Joy of the Court. Evrain's castle obviously exists in another, otherworldly dimension. It is like the hall at Harlech and

Gwales where the surviving warriors feast with Bran in perpetual joy. It is also like the court of the Rich Fisherman in *The Elucidation,* where great hospitality can be had but where great sorrow is experienced, as those at the Assembly of the Noble Head in "Branwen, Daughter of Llyr" discover when they open the forbidden door that brings them to reality again.

The manner in which Bran represents the Rich Fisherman is overlaid with symbolism. It is possible that Robert de Boron, the first to call the Fisher King by that title, was hearkening to classical antecedents. One of the titles of the lord of the Underworld—Hades—was Plutos, which means "wealth"; it was one of the labors of Heracles to take the Amaltheian horn filled with Hesperidian fruit to Tartarus for Plutos, after which it became known as the cornucopia. We have already seen in chapter 3 of *Mabon* that Bran is associated with Cronos, who is likewise depicted in classical tradition as sleeping on rocks of gold. Bran is also described in the list of the Thirteen Treasures as the owner of a horn. The richness of the Fisherman's court is due to its being an abode of the Otherworld—not a gloomy place of the dead, but instead an earthly paradise in which the mighty ancestors live on, feasting and fighting, as they do in "The Dream of Rhonabwy." It is worth noting that Bran has a connection with Owain, who, in "Gereint and Enid" and *Erec and Enid,* is the guardian of Brandigan castle. Owain's guardianship of the castle is quite natural, for he is likewise a guardian of the inner realms to which his mother's blood entitles him. Both Owain and Bran share the raven as their totem bird.

One of the chief features of Owain's castle is the hedge of stakes with heads upon them that surrounds the enchanted orchard where the Joy is to take place. This image is echoed in "Branwen, Daughter of Llyr" when Bran's head is cut off and brought to Harlech, where it continues to entertain and converse with his followers. Bran's head is in no way horrific to them, but rather conveys the comforting presence of their lord. His sacrificial decapitation occurs to keep the land of Britain safe from invasion, although the immediate result of his foray to Ireland is devastation and the usurpation of his throne by Caswallawn. Bran remains alive, though beheaded, like the Fisher King in the Grail legends who is wounded but cannot die until a successor comes to guard the hallows in his place. The land lies wasted but will be restored by a suitable successor.

The means by which the horn of Bran derives from the Cauldron of Rebirth to become the Christian Grail is one of the great mysteries of folklore. As we have seen above, the storytellers shift their ground by using a method akin to removing a single letter from a word and replacing it with another letter in order to create an entirely different word whose meaning remains a harmonic of the meaning of the original. We are reminded of the medieval word game played with San Greal (holy grail), which becomes Sang Real (holy blood). Such a game has been played with that innocent word *cors* to similar effect.

One of the later Grail romances in the *Vulgate Cycle*[33] calls the castle of the Fisher King Corbenic. The text tells us that the castle was called this "after the holy vessel." Certainly at no point in the Grail legends has the Grail ever been called anything like Corbenic. This would make sense only if the vessel had ever been referred to as the *cor beneit*, or "blessed horn." In the later Grail romances, the horn of Bran, which gives the liquid most desired as drink, becomes the chalice of the Mass by which the wine of earthly realms is transubstantiated into the blood of the heavenly Lord. Bran's cauldron has the property of restoring the dead to life; Christ's covenant with humanity likewise brings new life to the soul and the body, which will be raised up on the Day of Judgment. It is very doubtful that any Grail storyteller was consciously aware of these connections, but the line of tradition is remarkably consistent.

Of course the word *corbenic* has another equally valid interpretation: *cors beneiz* or "blessed body." The blessed body is, of course, Corpus Christi; earthly bread becomes the transubstantiated body of the Savior by which the faithful are nourished. The resonances between mystical Christian symbolism and the legends of both the Grail and

Blessed Bran are overwhelming. In many texts, notably *The Elucidation,* the Grail gives to people the food they most crave or need. In the de Boron text the Grail is the vessel used by the Rich Fisher in his role of provider to the remnants of Joseph of Arimathea's family. It is the vessel which, like the transformed bread and wine, sustains the life of the Grail guardian so that, though wounded, he does not die. In the First Continuation,[93] the Grail procession includes a bier upon which is a sword. The king of the Grail Castle leads Gawain to it and says: "Ah, noble body, lying here, for whose sake this kingdom is desolate, may God grant that you may be avenged so that the people may be glad thereof, and that the land which has long been desolate may be restored."

Such words might well have been spoken by Branwen over her brother Bran's body, for he sacrifices himself to become the Pen Annwfn, the Sleeping Lord, whose physical presence in the land will safeguard it from invasion and keep it harmonized with Sovereignty.

It has been suggested by Frances Rolt-Wheeler that Corbenic is derived from the Welsh *cor-arbennig,* or Sovereign Chair[141]; though this is persuasive, it must be rejected as unlikely, for the *cor y Fendigeid Fran,* the "horn of Bran the Blessed," must take prominence in this argument. The suggestion is hard to square with accepted Welsh etymology, which makes *cor-arbennig* mean "the privileged (choir) stall," rather than kingly throne, although there are places in the locality of Llangollen that might well endorse this speculation: *cadair Fronwen* (Branwen's seat) and *gorsedd Fran* (Bran's throne).

There is no purpose in advancing one meaning of *cors* to the detriment of all other definitions, for they are all valid in this knot of related symbols. The body *(cors)* of the imprisoned guardian is liberated by the sound of the horn *(cors)* to the joy of the whole court *(cors).* The finding of the Court of Joy is a task best handled by the worthiest champion, who, in the person of Gereint, wins Sovereignty or who, as Grail winner, like Perceval or Galahad, wins the Grail. Both sets of heroes break through the barriers that separate the earthly realm from the paradisal, making their riches and wisdom available to common humanity. They are those who unite kingdoms rent apart. The hero thus wins his appointed portion and the king his empowering hallows.

Sovereignty as Grail Maiden, hallows queen, and Loathly Lady comes to invest the world in fresh garments, for the stain of devastation and the marks of wasting are cleansed as the new guardian takes up his appointed task. Bran is succeeded as Sleeping Lord (Pen Annwfn) by Arthur just as Mabonograin and the Fisher King are succeeded by heroes like Gereint, Perceval, and Galahad. The hallows are brought forth as the king is solemnly invested with their symbolic power: the dragon sword of light upon his thigh, symbolic of the dynamic dragons' union of blood and seed; the mantle of the land about his shoulders by which he may pass in many shapes to all regions; a ring upon his finger; the golden chair for his seat; the vessels of healing, plenty, and rebirth before him; the spear of justice in his hands; and, at his feet, the chessboard with its pieces ready to fight for the rights of the land. So is the king invested by Sovereignty with all the powers of earth and of the Otherworld.

10
The Sovereignty
of Britain

*It is believed that when her time has come, this lady
will declare herself. She will choose for herself a
man, and he will be the secret king of the Island of
the Mighty, he will be Bran, reincarnate!*

JOHN ARDEN AND MARGERETTA D'ARCY, THE
ISLAND OF THE MIGHTY

*Consider how to honour her and to perform so well
that she will remain with you and may God aid me,
but I wish in faith that all the women of the realm
of Logres might be of her beauty.*

DIDOT PERCEVAL

The Foster Mother

Throughout this book we have examined many aspects of Sovereignty
as she appears in Celtic tradition. The time has come to see if we can
truly discover Sovereignty, the Goddess of Britain. There are many

contenders for this title, and in order to narrow the field, we shall confine this last chapter to a consideration of Sovereignty in Arthurian tradition.

We have seen throughout the *Mabinogion* countless examples of Sovereignty's representatives, but there are four distinct archetypes in relationship to Arthur himself: the foster mother, the queen of the north, the Flower Bride, and the otherworldly consort. These aspects of Sovereignty arise from a study of the Celto-Arthurian tradition and its fusion with the later romantic tradition, for in order to encompass this study it is necessary to throw our net wide and catch the mythological drift of our elusive quarry.

Some may argue that nowhere does Arthur have a direct encounter with Sovereignty, but this proves not to be the case. He encounters her representatives in the persons of his mother, his sister, and his wife, as well as in more indirect relationships.

We have seen how Arthur's knights champion their sovereign lord and, by virtue of their quests and adventures, actively maintain his passive relationship with Sovereignty. When we look again for Arthur's own encounters with the Goddess, it is necessary to collate evidence from the various strata of his development from oral to literary tradition.

This partially lost mythos of Arthur contains tantalizing clues and fragments giving us only a suggested reconstruction. Early tradition— in the "Preiddeu Annwfn"—hints at his premier role as the first Grail winner, which probably figured largely in his boyhood deeds.[105] All levels of Arthurian tradition speak of his efforts to restore Britain to a state of order and harmony. He is supposed to be ubiquitously available to his country in time of need. Yet there is no extant story that tells of his marriage with the land. At no point does he meet a figure who bears the name of the land, nor does he embrace an ugly hag by a well, as in the Irish traditional Sovereignty encounter.

Almost the whole of Arthur's story, in whatever tradition we approach it, bears such weighty testimony to the underlying presence of Sovereignty, her support and help within his reign, and such otherworldly intervention in his affairs and those of the kingdom that it is hard not to construe her influence in his career. From birth to death, the mythic witness sets its seal upon the life of Arthur, as well as upon his family, his court, and his kingdom. Let us first look at the evidence of genealogy, which has a mythic structure all its own.

The birth, conception, and childhood deeds of Arthur are derived straight from the proto-Celtic storytelling tradition, specifically those archetypal tales of the young hero. As we noted from the story of Mabon (see *Mabon*, chapter 8), the young hero is conceived by the union of a worldly and an otherworldly parent. He is then fostered secretly because his very existence endangers the order of things. During his fosterage he is taught deep wisdom and is prepared for the task to come. His youth and strength, combined with his other advantages of birth into the royal house and his foster mother's empowerment, bring him quickly to prominence and he is soon recognized as a prime candidate for kingship.[112]

This pattern is not confined solely to Arthur's story but is clearly discerned in the stories of such heroes as Peredur, Pryderi, Galahad, and others. Because Arthur's legend has been assembled cumulatively over generations of storytellers and has been embroidered and reworked, we might well expect to find something that departs from this pattern, but instead we find that the later storytellers inherited and enhanced the patterns of earlier British storytellers, even though the former were working from a medieval Continental tradition. We have no means of separating their invention from what is traditional.

If we look to the earliest traditions, evidence for Arthur's parentage is sparse apart from the Welsh genealogical tracts, which can hardly be relied upon. The bardic skill of imparting and memorizing a patron's lineage was one slow to fade, but the sixth century through the early medieval period was a time in which genealogical emendation and enhancement was quite an industry. It is normal to find the eponymous ancestor linked with Roman emperors, Celtic saints, and Arthurian battle lords with great impartiality. The resulting effect is similar to reading the list of Arthur's court in "Culhwch and Olwen." If we look to the patrilinear and matrilinear descents of Arthur (see figures 19 and 20), we note divergent traditions that predate the accepted family of Arthur derived from later sources in the French romances. Both of these simplified family trees derive from Welsh genealogical tracts.[12]

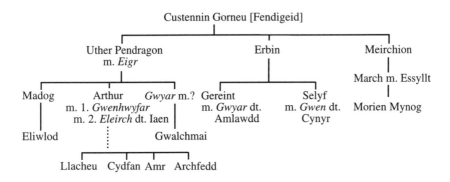

Figure 19. The patrilinear descent of Arthur. (Female characters are italicized.)

We see that Arthur's paternal grandfather is Custennin of Cornwall, later confused by Geoffrey and others with Constantine III, the man proclaimed emperor by the British troops in 407 C.E. Uther's brothers sire families which figure largely in Arthurian legend: Gereint, whom we know from the *Mabinogion* (see chapter 6), and March, the King Mark who marries Isolt, or Essyllt. Uther himself marries Eigr, or Igraine. This tradition gives them three children: Madog, of whom we hear nothing; Arthur; and a daughter, Gwyar, whose identity will prove to be of some interest (see figure 20).

Arthur marries Gwenhwyfar, according to all traditions, but, as can be seen in figure 19, he also marries Eleirch, by whom he has three sons and a daughter. Tradition speaks only of Llacheu, who is killed by Kay, and Amr, whom Arthur is responsible for killing, according to the earliest sources.[28, 87]

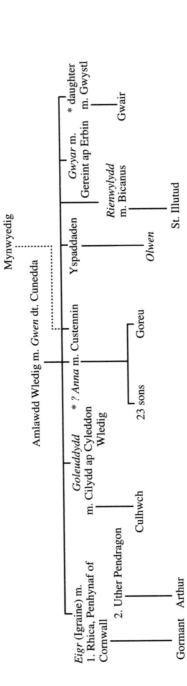

Figure 20. The matrilinear descent of Arthur. (Female characters are italicized; asterisks denote unnamed daughters.)

285

Figure 20 shows the six daughters of Amlawdd Wledig—a legendary character whose name, Amloth, seems to derive from the same root as that of Hamlet. Whoever he may have been, his daughters certainly seem to have been key figures in the sovereignty of Britain. This genealogy, largely derived from a twelfth-century life of St. Illtud—here a cousin of Arthur—shows Eigr (Igraine) marrying Rhica, the chief elder or counselor of Cornwall, rather than the more usual Gwrleis (Gorlois). We have already met Goleuddydd in chapter 6 of *Mabon*, along with her mysterious unnamed sister who marries Custennin ap Mynwyedig, a man ousted by Yspaddaden. Rienwylydd is the mother of St. Illtud. Gwyar—a different woman from Gwyar, daughter of Uther and Eigr—marries Gereint. A second unnamed sister marries Gwystl, the hostage; their son, confusingly called Gwair, is one of the knights whom Peredur encounters in the forest and whom he believes to be angels.

A glance at figure 21 will show that Geoffrey had linked his Arthur with the imperial line of Constantine III. Arthur's sister is called not Gwyar, but Anna, and she is married to Loth or Lot, of whom we'll learn more in the section Queen of the North, below.

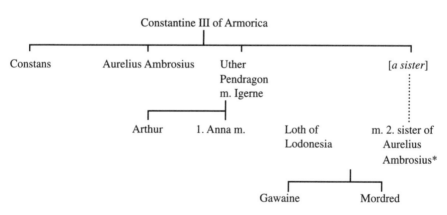

*This is an error on Geoffrey's part. Instead of "sister of Aurelius Ambrosius," this should read "sister of Arthur."

Figure 21. Arthur's family tree according to Geoffrey of Monmouth

There is doubtless much in these family trees which is fantastic and unhistorical, but despite the many interpolations created by well-meaning genealogists, they show certain traditional consistencies. Uther and Eigr are always Arthur's parents. Arthur has a sister. He always marries Gwenhwyfar. He is always uncle to Gwalchmai or Gawain.

Yet what can be gained from this accumulation of traditions? We are able to see Arthur's relationship with his cousins and nephews, those knights who will play so great a part in the stories associated with him and who will often stand in the place of the king as his champions. But for Arthur's relationship with Sovereignty we must look beyond genealogy to the complex webs of his sisters:

> He is a King crouned in Fairie,
> With sceptre and with his regally
> Shall resort as Lord and Soveraigne
> Out of Fairie and reigne in Britaine;
> And repaire again the Round Table.
> By prophesy Merlin set the date,
> Among Princes King incomparable,
> His seate againe to Caerlion to translate,
> The Parchas sustren sponne so his fate,
> His Epitaph recordeth so certaine
> Here lieth King Arthur that shall raigne againe.[23]

This verse by Lydgate emphasizes the manner in which Arthur is seen mythologically: He is a king aided by the Otherworld and his fate is administered by the mystic sisterhood of women, the Parchas Sustren, or the Parcae, who represent Sovereignty and the land.

This tradition, which neatly ties together the beginning and ending of Arthur's career, is founded mostly in Breton-influenced *enfances* (childhood stories) now lost to us but still perceptible in the childhood of Lancelot, whereby the hero becomes the foster son of a powerful otherworldly woman who endows him with supernatural gifts, powers, and objects. We find traces of this in the English Arthurian text of

Layamon, in which the elves are attendants at Arthur's birth and his body is finally received by Argante, queen of Faery.[43] Three fays are said to attend Arthur's birth and give him gifts in the Second Continuation of *Perceval*.[134] We see, too, traces of this tradition in Malory, where Arthur is endowed by the Lady of the Lake with Excalibur and its magical scabbard of invulnerability.[25]

Within British tradition there is no such fostering story, though Igraine seems to revert to the otherworldly queen archetype in Chrétien's *Perceval,* in which she appears as the queen of the Castle of Maidens, which is visited by Gawain. Within this otherworldly castle, where many women await the coming of a great champion to restore their rights, we see a vast, collective Sovereignty assembled. Three royal women administer the place: Ygerne (Igraine/Eigr), Arthur's mother; Morcades, who appears in later tradition as Ygerne's daughter and Gawain's mother; and Clarrisant, Gawain's sister. Although Gawain liberates the castle and thus becomes its lord by right, he does not recognize these women at all and is astonished when told who they really are:

"The white-haired queen [is] . . . King Arthur's mother." "By the faith I owe God and His power, as far as I'm aware, King Arthur has had no mother for a long time, not for a good sixty years, to my knowledge, and even for much longer than that."

"Yet it's true, sir; she is his mother. When his father Utherpendragon was laid to rest, it came about that Queen Ygerne came to this country bringing with her all her treasure . . . And I'm sure you saw the other queen, that tall, handsome lady who was King Lot's wife and . . . the mother of Gawain."[7]

It would seem that Ygerne has established herself on the Island of Women or in the Land of Youth, in the manner of the Celtic immrama stories on which this incident is clearly based, for one of the conditions of the champion who overcomes all obstacles to become its master is that he has no leave to depart from the castle again. The same thing happens to Maelduin and Bran when they reach the Land of Women.[162]

Arthur's ancestry aligns with this tradition in *Parzival*, where von Eschenbach describes Arthur's great-grandmother as being called Ter de la Schoy (the Joy of the Land), a faery from the land of Feimurgan, (Morgan le Fay).[40] So Arthur's ancestry is shown to be otherworldly and perhaps intimately related to Sovereignty.

As for Igraine—Eigr herself—like Modron, she represents a Daughter of Branwen, one of the great matriarchs of the Island of the Mighty. In Malory it is Igraine's daughters by Gorlois—"the famous Cornwall sisters," as T. H. White calls them—whose dynastic marriages secure the sovereignty of their mother's line in Britain, a role we will examine in the next section. But earlier tradition clearly identifies Igraine as an otherworldly woman, or a representative of Sovereignty, able to retreat to her unearthly "fastness." The attempt to give Arthur a faery godmother or foster mother is a persistent tradition.

The custom of fosterage was strong among the Celts. A child of good birth would be fostered within a noble household and raised with that family, thus enforcing ties of tribal obligation and reducing the likelihood of feud between those families. The foster mother would suckle her fosterling with her own children, thus making them brothers and sisters. In Malory, Kay becomes Arthur's foster brother after Uther's death, when Merlin ensures Arthur is fostered with Sir Ector of the Forest Sauvage.[25] But in Arthur's case we need to see if there is any likelihood of his fosterage by a representative of Sovereignty, for this mythos is very potent.

Within Celtic tradition the archetypal foster mother is the goddess Brighid, whose cult became subsumed in that of St. Brigit. This powerful figure was a territorial goddess particularly worshiped in Britain by the Brigantes, a tribe living in the north Midlands, hence her other name of Brigantia. Irish apocryphal tradition credits St. Brigit with fostering none other than Christ himself, and many commentaries give her goddesslike titles: *mathair mo rurech,* "mother of my lord," and *oen mathair Maicc Rig mair,* "the unique mother of the Great King's Son."[58] In some senses these titles are true, for such was the ancient goddess's power that her mythos and attributes passed entire into the cult of the Christian saint. Brighid was the mother of the gods and patron of the queenly arts of smithcraft and poetry as well as of women. It was logical that St. Brigit reflected these abilities.

In Brighid we see traces of the Goddess of Sovereignty, sponsoring her chosen candidate from his very birth, giving him to drink of her bountiful wisdom by laying him at her own breast. The apocryphal story of St. Brigit's fosterage of Christ must be seen in this light. As the goddess of the old dispensation, she fosters the god of the new faith, giving him a stake in the otherworldly consciousness of all British and Irish believers by a process quite natural and harmonious, for he is her Mabon, quite as much as any other of her foster sons.

If there was ever any story relating Arthur's fosterage by Sovereignty under the aspect of Brighid/Brigantia, we do not know of it. The fact that the Dark Age Arthur, presumed to have lived between 470 and 527 C.E., was contemporaneous with the historical St. Brigit of Kildare (470–523 C.E.) does not necessarily count for anything. However, the identity of the true Sovereignty of Britain may lie within her jurisdiction.

We have seen how Sovereignty sets tests for her champions. Arthur is not exempt from her scrutiny. In order to be secure in his kingship, he needs to perform two important deeds: He must openly welcome the cailleach aspect of Sovereignty in order to transform his kingdom and he must successfully obtain the hallows, which confirm his kingship. If we look to assorted legends and levels of tradition, we do indeed find evidence of both tests.

Arthur is the primary Grail winner, a fact which is not at all clear from later tradition. His descent into Annwfn may be classed with the other great redemptive acts usually associated with gods and heroes. He enters Annwfn in order to secure the cauldron of Pen Annwfn, according to the ninth-century poem "Preiddeu Annwfn" (*Mabon,* chapter 6). This cauldron combines all the primal aspects that surface later in the Grail stories: It is a life-giving vessel, it provides prodigious amounts of food to the courageous possessor, and it bestows wisdom. Like the rest of the hallows, it is a withdrawn part of the mythological regalia of Sovereignty, who appoints her guardians and posts many obstacles in the way of those who seek the hallows to prevent them from being received by the unworthy.

The poem tells us of the cauldron being warmed by the breath of nine maidens or muses. These are the archetypal guardians of the cauldron/Grail. The three-times-three sisterhood, the chorus of sibyls who keep the vessel, is an Underworld harmonic of the Goddess of Sovereignty herself; that much can be deduced from the evidence of the later Grail legends. We have only to look at "Peredur" to find that the nine witches of Gloucester are responsible for wielding yet another of the hallows, the spear, and that they enable Peredur to gain his manly training in weapon skills after the old Celtic fashion of women warriors who teach heroes. We have already noted the dichotomy in this story—that the witches hinder the Grail quest but actively help its eventual champion. This ninefold sisterhood represents the same harmonic as the ninefold muses of the cauldron.

Arthur's right to the cauldron is a royal and mystical one—he succeeds to Bran's ancient guardianship of this hallow. But there is another possibility raised by Welsh genealogical tracts: that Arthur's right is also an ancestral one. Independent genealogies trace both Arthur's maternal and paternal lines back to Bran ap Llyr Llediath, Bran the Blessed himself.[2]

The ninefold sisters never allow any of the hallows to fall into the hands of unworthy heroes, however well descended, and it is only by great toil and loss of men that Arthur is able to obtain the cauldron at all. Finding and maintaining the hallows is no sinecure, for any champion soon finds out that there are strings attached: Any king who falls out of harmony with his land and its people is likewise out of harmony with Sovereignty, who hides her fair face and assumes the garment of wasteland—a major theme of Grail literature.

It is interesting that the repositioning of the Grail legends tells us much about Arthur's unfolding role within tradition. The events of the earliest story, told in "Preiddeu Annwfn," undoubtedly occurred quite early in Arthur's reign. By the time of the later Grail romances we find that the stories occur towards the end of it. Arthur's kingdom is in disarray in these romances; part, if not all of it, has fallen into wasteland. His early prowess and reputation are obliterated by the ever-present menace of disorder, ruin, and mismanagement. This is especially so in *Perlesvaus*, where Guinevere begs Arthur to reestablish his early glory by attending to the state of his soul. It is on her advice that he retreats to the Chapel of St. Augustine in the forest and there, during many adventures both supernatural and mundane, he experiences a vision.

He has a vision of the Virgin in which she presents her own child as the offering at Mass. But as Arthur gazes on this scene, he sees the child turn into the crucified Christ, bleeding from his hands and feet. After admitting his own lack of responsibility towards his kingdom, Arthur hears a voice:

> Arthur of Britain, you may truly rejoice in your heart that God has sent me to you. He commends you to hold court as soon as possible, for the world, which has suffered much harm because of you and your neglect of great deeds, will now profit most greatly from your action.[29]

At the sound of this Arthur's heart is filled with joy—perhaps that very Joy of the Court that results from the successful endeavors of Sovereignty's champion.

This episode is crucial to an understanding of Arthur's role and shows his active involvement in maintaining his sovereignty, which is at risk through his own inaction. At the bidding of Guinevere, who, as we shall see, is the representative of Sovereignty, he rides into a perilous place, putting his person at risk. There he is granted the vision of the Blessed Virgin and her Son. And though the text tells us that the wasteland and the wounding of the Fisher King are caused by the unworthy knight (Perlesvaus, or Perceval), it is Arthur himself who has caused much suffering.

The mysterious voice is unidentified, though is clearly intended to be angelic at the very least, if not the voice of the Virgin herself, to whom, during the Middle Ages, was ascribed the special patronage of England, called the Dowry of Mary. The reproof of Arthur is very similar to the reproof that Perceval receives from the Black Maiden in other texts. Clearly the storyteller responsible for *Perlesvaus* understood the harmonic theme underlying the earlier traditions of Arthur's Grail questing, whereby the king himself must quest for the gifts of Sovereignty. This quest was lost sight of almost entirely in the later stories, where the Grail is pursued by Arthur's champions, not the king himself.

Although Arthur has, in *Perlesvaus,* temporarily fallen out of harmony with Sovereignty, he is reconciled to her and is able to hear her voice once more. This is very significant if we return briefly to the Amangons story (chapter 9): Because of Amangons's rape of the damsels of the wells, no one is able to hear "the voices of the wells." This telling phrase indicates the articulation of the land itself in the heart of the rightful king. We will recall that, in that story, Arthur and his knights are also unable to hear the voices of the wells, although they are well intentioned towards the damsels. This silence is broken in *Perlesvaus* when Arthur hears the voice of the Virgin herself. Interestingly, Arthur likewise hears the voice of Ragnell singing to the lute's accompaniment. Hearkening to the voice of the land is an essential skill for the Pendragon.

It was said earlier that there is no parallel tradition within Arthurian legend concerning marriage to Sovereignty, but this is not strictly true. Elements remain within the Arthurian corpus which are intriguing and indicative of earlier traditions. If we look to Uther's kingship, we find interesting traces of something called the custom of the Pendragon. This appears first in Chrétien's *Erec and Enid,* where it is called the custom (or the honor) of the white hart. Anyone who is able to win the head of the white hart is permitted to kiss the fairest of the maidens at court. Arthur judges Enid to be the most beautiful damsel there and says:

It's the business of a true king to uphold the law, truth, good faith, and justice . . . I do not wish the traditional custom to lapse which my family habitually observes . . . Whatever may become of me, I must safeguard and uphold the practice of my father Pendragon.[7]

Arthur then asks the opinion of the court, who unanimously accord the kiss of the white hart to Enid, whom Arthur kisses, saying: "My sweet friend, I give you my love in all honesty. I shall love you with all my heart without baseness or impropriety.[7]

And thus we hear from Arthur's own lips the vows that a king makes to Sovereignty, whose representative is Enid at this point. We have dealt at some length in chapter 6 with the implications of "Gereint and Enid," where we see on how many complex levels the Sovereignty motif is repeated. This same theme is taken up in *Lanzelet*, in which we hear again of the chase for the white hart and the kiss, but here there is slight variation: "And then the king was to take by right, and as it became him, a kiss from the most beautiful woman; that was his reward. His father Uther Pendragon instituted this custom; and his son has maintained it ever since."[42]

It is the king, not his champion, who awards this honor, we note. Perhaps here we have some relic of the king's marriage with the land. Certainly this is a Celtic custom which may have been present once within the earliest Arthurian oral traditions but which Chrétien and von Zatzikhoven have chosen to ennoble in their courtly language. We have only to look at Irish tradition for confirmation of the custom of the Pendragon. In "The Birth of Conchobar" we read: "Every Ulsterman rendered Conchobar a great honour [sending] his daughter to lie with Conchobar on the first night that he was her first husband."[105] We further discover that Conchobar Mac Nessa, Cú Chulainn's king, was under a geis to sleep with every bride on her first night of marriage. This causes considerable problems for Cú Chulainn and he is sent on an errand to hunt some game for his king while Conchobar sleeps in the same room as Cú Chulainn's wife, Emer. A druid also sleeps in the same room to restrain the king's sexual activity, and honor is satisfied without Conchobar breaking his geis.[135]

Submerged somewhere in this is the tradition of Arthur's marriage with the land. Enid is but one representative of Sovereignty. But there is yet one more telling example which we may call up to add to our knowledge. The long-neglected story of Gawain's marriage with Ragnell has recently been rediscovered by a wider readership, both feminist and folkloric, but it is still seldom noted that though Gawain weds Ragnell, it is Arthur who first encounters her. Following is my direct retelling of the circumstances of this marriage:

Arthur encounters a fearsome knight called Gromer Somer Joure, who lays a geis on Arthur to find within a twelvemonth what it is that women most desire. It is perhaps not insignificant that Arthur is hunting for a wild stag when he meets his adversary. Confiding his task to Gawain, the two of them try to amass suitable answers to this riddle. It is Gawain, his nephew and *tanaiste*, to whom Arthur turns and whom, eventually, he implicates in the events that will fall out.

Just like the kings of Celtic tradition, Arthur meets a hideous hag while on his quest. She knows his thoughts and offers him the answer in return for Gawain as her husband. Arthur promises to do his best and Gawain obliges him by agreeing to marry the woman. The answer is given by Ragnell and supplied by Arthur to Gromer as the riddle's solution:

"Our desire is to have sovereignty over the most manly of men." And so Arthur overcomes Gromer, who appears to represent the Provoker of Strife archetype in this story. Amid great lamentation, Gawain is married to Ragnell, though the king's life is no longer at risk. Alone in their chamber, Ragnell demands a kiss, at least. "I will do more than kiss you," Gawain says, "and before God."

She turns into a beautiful maiden—but there is a catch. Gawain may have her fair by day, for his honor at court, and foul by night; or foul by day, to his dishonor, and fair at night for his delight. He bids her choose and by so doing answers the riddle again, for she exclaims: "I would have been transformed until the best man in England married me and gave me sovereignty over his body and his goods."[78]

The original Sovereignty story is here shared between Gawain and Arthur: Arthur's life and kingdom are preserved by Gawain's sacrifice of his will to Ragnell in a medieval denouement to the primal Sovereignty theme.[163]

And so we discover that Arthur indeed stands in intimate relationship with Sovereignty on many levels. He is successful in finding the hallows and in some measure encounters the Dark Woman of Knowledge, Sovereignty in her cailleach aspect. He knows and accepts his fated part in the marriage of king with land.

But for the most part, Arthur's chief encounters with Sovereignty are with the women in his own family, particularly his sisters, and, of course, his wife. It is to these women that we turn next.

Queen of the North

During the lifetime of Uther, Arthur's father, a supernatural event takes place in the skies over Britain on the evening of the death of Ambrosius:

> At that time appeared a star, which was seen of many. [It] shone marvellously clear, and cast a beam that was brighter than the sun. At the end of this beam was a dragon's head, and from the dragon's mighty jaws issued two rays. One of these rays stretched over France, and went from France even to the Mount of St. Bernard. The other ray went towards Ireland, and divided into seven beams. Each of these beams shone bright and clear, alike on water and on land.[43]

Calling Merlin to him, Uther demanded some explanation of this wonder. Merlin announced the death of Ambrosius, Uther's brother, and interpreted the comet thus:

> The dragon at the end of the beam betokens thee thyself, who art a stout and hardy knight. One of the two rays signifies a son born of thy body, who shall become a puissant prince, conquering France and beyond the borders of France. The other ray which parted from its fellow betokens a daughter who shall be Queen of Scotland. Many a fair

heir shall she give to her lord, and mighty champions shall they prove both on land and sea.[43]

According to Geoffrey and Wace, this daughter is called Anna. She is the prototype for the half sister that tradition will later give Arthur in the shape of Morgause.

In the accretions of Arthurian tradition we see an interesting development in Arthur's sisters or half sisters. This development may be summarized as shown in figure 20. We can see how one full sister gradually becomes several half sisters. Consistently, however, the sister or half sister of Arthur is always the mother of Gawain. We also note that it is Chrétien who is responsible for Arthur's relationship with Morgain.[52]

The importance of Arthur's sister or sisters may not be immediately apparent. We must return to our first concepts of Sovereignty in order to see the connection, recalling that the primal concept of Sovereignty involved the matriarch of a tribe; she was the priestess or royal woman whose blood conferred sovereignty. From her descendants might be drawn the rulers of the tribe. In this regard we can see Eigr, or Igraine, and her many sisters as the manifestation of this concept. All the descendants of Eigr hold prime positions in the Arthurian cycle, so that while Arthur leaps into prominence as the main focus of the stories, Eigr's daughter likewise follows a royal destiny.

Whether this daughter is called Anna, Gwyar, Morcades, or Morgause is not a matter of great import. In all instances this woman marries Loth of Lothian (Lleu ap Cynfarch), a character to whom Geoffrey of Monmouth imputes great strength and loyalty to the throne of the Pendragons. It is into Loth's care that Uther places his kingdom before Arthur is acknowledged as king.[10] In this we can see the working out of the old Celtic kingship and the explanation of the strong tradition of distrust between Arthur and his Orkney nephews in later legends. For Arthur is not the only possible heir of his line: His sister bears the same blood he does and thus her descendants have an equal right to the throne. The sevenfold rays of light emanating from the prophetic comet do indeed become Arthur's champions, but do not, as in Geof-

Source	Name of Sister(s)
Welsh genealogical tracts	Gwyar, daughter of Uther and Eigr
Geoffrey of Monmouth	Anna, daughter of Uther and Igerne
Birth of Arthur (fourteenth-century manuscript)	Gwyar and Dioneta, daughters of Gwrleis and Eigyr
Chrétien *(Erec and Enid)*	Morgain and an unnamed woman, mother of Gawain
First Continuation of *Perceval*	Morcades, wife of Loth, mother of Agravain, Guerrehes, Gaheriet, Mordred, and Clarissans
Robert de Boron *(Merlin)*	Two unnamed girls, wed by Loth and Urien, and Morgain, all daughters of Igerne and Gorlois
Vulgate Cycle	Blaisine, Brimesent, Morgain, and one unnamed daughter
Malory's *Morte d'Arthur*	Morgause, Elayne, and Morgan, daughters of Igraine and Gorlois

Figure 22. Arthur's sister(s) in Arthurian tradition

frey's version of the episode, become the heirs to the throne of Britain.

If any woman stands to inherit the title Daughter of Branwen, then it is Arthur's sister. This archetype, discussed in chapter 8, is the basis for all those women who are the great matriarchs of the Island of the Mighty; they are the sovereignty-bestowing mothers of the royal line whose queenship is mystical rather than actual. If one glances at the texts in which the variously named sisters of Arthur appear, it will be seen that they are anything but passive, yea-saying women; rather they exemplify the energies of Sovereignty in being initiators, arch-conspirators, and sometimes actual enemies of the order of things.

It is, of course, the nephews of Arthur, Gwalchmai and Medrawt (or Gawain and Mordred), who spectacularly effect the outcome of

Arthur's reign. In the earliest texts both men have very different roles: Gwalchmai is Arthur's champion and faithful warrior in the service of Sovereignty rather than the blundering, obstinate Gawain of Malory's story, while Medrawt is the abductor of Gwenhwyfar and the thief of sovereignty rather than the incestuously begotten child whose death by exposure in an open boat is decreed by Arthur in the later stories.[87] The original men are, in their natures, more like Nissien and Efnissien of the Second Branch story, "Branwen, Daughter of Llyr": one is fair and compassionate, the other is embittered and unforgiving. But there are other *Mabinogion* parallels lying within this tradition which we have yet to lay bare.

Arthur's sister becomes, by her marriage to Loth, queen of the north—a position of great power strategically, for whoever holds the north guards the northern borders of the realm and may easily foment rebellion or muster troops against the king. But what of Loth himself?

He seems to have been a formidable figure, having a venerable tradition behind him. Geoffrey calls him "a valiant soldier, mature both in wisdom and age,"[10] to whom Uther gave his daughter, Anna, as a reward for his prowess in leading the British army, and to whom he entrusted the care of the kingdom during his illness. As Geoffrey tends to ignore female characters, we hear little of Anna herself, but she would seem to be much younger than her husband.

Loth's name runs throughout Celtic tradition in one form or another. A. C. L. Brown suggests that it has been inherited by Arthurian tradition from the Irish Fomorian leader's mother, Loth Luamnach, which means "destruction of the active." In the *Book of Invasions,* the name Loth occurs twice, appearing the second time as Loth, the grandfather of the Fir Bolg. Both the Fomorian and Fir Bolg peoples were considered to have been ugly, dark, misshapen, and evil. This tradition, in which a former race comes to represent negative aspects, the country aligned with barbarians or even devils, is common in both historical and mythological terms. Brown points out that Loth seems to inherit certain mythological titles: He is called the king of Lothian and Norway in

Geoffrey, while in the *Perceval* of Chrétien he is called king of Orkney—an appellation which continues into later tradition. Lothian is the area above Hadrian's Wall, between Galloway and Gorre in Arthurian legend. Mythically Norway is known as Lochlann, in Celtic tradition—literally the "land overseas"—and it is associated with the Land of the Dead. Orkney itself has accumulated much of the same reputation, both from its association with the classical name for Hades, Orcus, and an aboriginal tradition concerning the burial of the dead upon Orkney.[58]

To summarize this, we may posit Loth as a latter-day king of the dead who marries a young, sovereignty-bearing woman, whose children will have as much right to the throne as do Arthur's. If we look to parallel British tradition, which drew upon oral records as well as interpolating much of Geoffrey's work, we find, in Triad 70, that Loth becomes Lleu ap Cynfarch. Moreover, his brothers are none other than Urien, husband of Modron (herself a daughter of the king of Avalon), and Arawn, whom we met in "Pwyll, Prince of Dyfed" as king of Annwfn, the British Underworld. A glance at figures 23 and 24 will show that Lleu marries not Anna, daughter of Uther, but Gwyar, daughter of Eigr and Gwrleis, which may represent a tradition earlier than that of Geoffrey's *History*.[10]

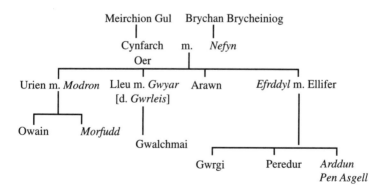

Figure 23. Descent of Lleu (Loth) ap Cynfarch according to Triad 70. Urien and Efrddyl are twins, as are Owain and Morfudd, while the children of Efrddyl are triplets. (Female characters are italicized.)

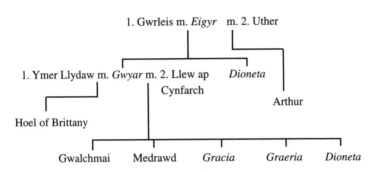

Figure 24. The relationship of Arthur and Gawain according to *Birth of Arthur*.
(Female characters are italicized.)

Loomis further suggests that Loth's underworldly antecedents may not end there. He posits that Loth is derived from or analogous to Lleminawc, the man who appears twice in British tradition: once in "Culhwch and Olwen," where he is described as the great-uncle of Arthur who comes from overseas, and once in the "Preiddeu Annwfn" and the later part of "Culhwch and Olwen" relating to the theft of the cauldron.[22] In this episode Lleminawc seizes Caledfwlch (Excalibur) and wields it with great skill, the suggestion being that this deed helped Arthur get the cauldron of Pen Annwfn.

The implications of this identification are immense. The "Preiddeu Annwfn" represents one of the earliest recorded traditions about Arthur which we may take to be authentic and uncontaminated by French romanticizing. It represents Arthur as entering Annwfn for the purpose of reiving the cauldron of Pen Annwfn, the king of the Underworld, and it is Lleminawc who helps him achieve this. In later traditions, from Geoffrey onwards, Arthur is acclaimed king on the death of Uther, but it is Loth who has held the kingdom during Uther's declining years and who enables him to gain his rights within the kingdom. Loth is therefore an enabling hero, in earlier tradition: one who helps Arthur to maintain his sovereignty within Britain. And it is to this man that Arthur's sister, or half sister, is married.

Loomis further suggests that the wars between Arthur and the Roman general Lucius Hiberius, described by Geoffrey, can be correlated with the later *Huth Merlin* text in which Arthur wars with Loth.[92] Such divergences show the meandering of the tradition until it reaches Malory's full-blown account of the enmity between the family of Loth and Morgause and Arthur.[15]

There is an ancient sovereignty pattern within this story, possibly stemming from the unique Pictish sovereignty custom of electing kings according to whether their mothers were sovereignty-bearing women, usually the sister of the king. By marrying Arthur's sister, Gwyar/Morcades/Morgause, Loth might automatically be seen, under this old pattern, as the rightful Pendragon of the matrilinear line. This would explain the enmity and friction that explodes time and again in the Arthurian-Lothian relationship: an enmity that is neutralized between Arthur and Gawain, his favorite nephew, but is exacerbated between Arthur and Mordred.

Which brings us back once more to the queen of the north and the fate of her children, so lyrically and prophetically announced by the comet. There have been many examples of women being used as political cement in history, but Arthur's sisters or half sisters, along with the other women appearing in the Celto-Arthurian cycles, occupy a different kind of role. Whether we wish to call this lady Anna, Gwyar, Morcades, or Morgause does not matter, for she retains her inalienable power of sovereignty inherited either from Eigr (or Igraine), as the representative of Sovereignty, or from Uther, as the Pendragon. Once ensconced in the north she plays her own game—a royal and often crafty one—against her brother. Traditions vary on this point, but she is seen to employ two forms of opening play: She either accepts supporters or champions who will advance her own cause as royal woman or else she jockeys her children into positions of power, urging on their efforts to displace their uncle, Arthur.

If we look closely at this activity of hers, we perceive that perhaps there is a single archetype here who has three aspects: a seemingly passive princess who accepts the husband chosen for her; a queen determined to set herself on the throne of Britain to be the prime Sovereignty of that land; and a queen mother who ceaselessly, tirelessly supports her children, particularly her sons' claims to sovereignty. If we return to figure 22, in which we see one sister of Arthur becoming three half sisters, we are dimly aware of how the threefold Sovereignty has become embedded in Arthurian tradition as the three Cornwall sisters, Elayne, Morgan, and Morgause, who correspond exactly to the threefold royal women outlined above.

Elayne marries Nentres of Garlot, an insignificant husband for an almost invisible woman in Malory. So thick on the ground are the Elaines of Arthurian tradition that even the writers of the romances themselves became confused. Yet we may recall the laudable figure of Elen, royal Helen of the Ways, as our prime archetype of the royal, sovereignty-bearing princess, as well as the daughter of King Pelles, another Elaine, whose fate is to become Guinevere for a night in order that she might compel the reluctant Lancelot to help her conceive the future Grail finder, Galahad. Both women submit to their fate, yet both gain a mystical triumph on behalf of the land. These are the true Daughters of Branwen, whose hearts are set on the well-being of the land and its people. Theirs is not a personal life but a redemptive one, a sacrifice which is often repellent to feminist politics, but which is nevertheless demanded at an otherworldly level by the Goddess of Sovereignty.

The second sister, Morgan, is, in Malory, married to Urien, though as we have seen in chapter 4, her antecedents are often quite other. She becomes, in later tradition, the chief enemy of Arthur, her half brother, whom she tricks with her magic wiles. This deterioration of the archetype is a feature of later tradition, where the romancers were at their furthest remove from the primal images of their craft. Morgan—who may also be Morgain, Morgen, or Modron—behaves like the hallows queen; she represents the Sovereignty of the Land, and the hallows are rightfully wielded at her behest and by her champions. But later writers have aligned her more nearly with the cailleach, the Dark Woman of Knowledge, in keeping with Morgan's earlier role as queen of Avalon, and have assigned her a more mundane role as Arthur's half sister. Chrétien, perhaps, achieves the nearest amalgam of these two roles in his *Perceval*, in which a thinly disguised Morgan appears as the proud damsel. This character is not quite a Black Maiden, though she shares certain attributes with women such as Luned of Owain (see Chrétien, lines 8286–8648).[7]

This character's name, L'Orguelleuse de Logres, is interesting in that there is some scholarly debate as to whether the original name for Britain's Sovereignty translated into a more rational French title. We know from Irish tradition that Ireland's Sovereignty calls herself Eriu or Ireland. It has been argued that Britain's Goddess might well have been named Logres and that the French writers made this into L'Orguelleuse, the proud damsel. Whether or not this can be proved, it is intriguing, for the Goddess of Sovereignty should indeed be the pride of the land, jealous of its welfare.

The third sister, Morgause—also called Morcades, a name derived from both Morgan and the Orkneys (Orcades), which she rules with Loth—represents the queen mother aspect of the threefold Sovereignty. She fights for the cause of her children in later tradition, though Malory causes her to sleep with Arthur in order to conceive Mordred incestuously. Although this theme of incest seems, at first sight, to be part of a later tradition, there remains the ancient concept of reenforcing the royal bloodline by intermarriage of brother and sister, which existed in Egypt and among other peoples in early times. The incestuous union of Arthur and his sister is a persistent subtextual tradition, even in the earlier cycles, where the sister, however named, is the mother of both Gawain and Mordred, though not of any other children.

What is the meaning of this threefold archetype in the light of Sovereignty? In order to answer this, we must go deeper into this very tradition. We may well find some startling resonances between Arthurian and Celtic tradition; in the following text, the most significant one being that Arthur's sister desires, above all things, to be seen and known as a virgin. It is worth bearing in mind that an unmarried woman, in medieval times, preserved her property rights on her own behalf. If she married, then those rights were transferred to her husband or sons. Beneath this understanding is the original foundation of Sovereignty herself—proud, single, independent, and determined to keep her realm intact. In the interweaving of the triple Sovereignty archetype which Arthur's sisters betray, we may well find ourselves back at the roots of one of the prime stories of the *Mabinogion*.

The following fragmentary story, "Les Enfances Gauvain,"[27] is from a French poem written in the early thirteenth century. It relates the birth and conception of Gawain, and its contents are substantially the same as the twelfth-century Latin romance *De Ortu Waluuanii* (The Rise of Gawain), ably translated by Mildred Leake Day.[9] The seeds for both versions lie in Geoffrey, but in the case of "Les Enfances Gauvain," there may be tangled references to "Math, Son of Mathonwy."

We may use the clues from *The Rise of Gawain* to fill in the lacunae of "Les Enfances Gauvain" (indicated in brackets) to give the following summary:

[Uther took hostages for the good behavior of his subjects. One of these was Lot, nephew of the king of Norway. Lot and Uther's daughter grew enamored of each other so she became pregnant.] Morcades then went to her brother Arthur, requesting that she retire to the Castle of Bel Repaire, accompanied only by her handmaid, her squire—who was in fact Lot—and a small household, the porter to admit only such persons of known respect or Arthur himself. Arthur assented and seven months later, Morcades was delivered of a son, Lot assisting at the birth. Had circumstances been otherwise, she would have been glad to raise the boy herself, but she decided that she could not lose the reputation of being a virgin.

Nearby lived a wise knight called Gauvain the Brown who often sent game from his hunting to Morcades and whose handmaid he longed to marry. The latter refused him. Lot and Morcades decided that they would have to be rid of the child and requested the handmaid to take the boy away secretly. However, Gauvain accosted her as she was stealing away with the child and, knowing it could not be hers, he asked to be allowed to take care of it, for he was without wife, child, or heir. The handmaid promised to wed Gauvain as soon as the child was baptized and Morcades had prepared his sending away. [She had arranged for merchants to take away the boy and raise him with care.] Gauvain baptized the boy by his own name and took special care of the richly embroidered shawl and other precious things betokening his birth. Gauvain also put a letter in a chest and wrapped it in the shawl before putting it and the little Gauvain into a barrel. This was to be thrown into the sea.

[Little Gauvain is found/stolen by a fisherman who brings him up.] The fisherman takes Gauvain to Rome on pilgrimage, during which the chest is opened and the truth is known. Up until this time, the fisherman has called Gauvain nothing but *beau fils* (good son). Gauvain is subsequently adopted by the pope as his nephew, and he keeps the boy's possessions against the day he will be made a knight.

Meanwhile, Morcades preserved her secret from all, especially the king. She consented to attend Arthur's wedding to Guinemar (Guinevere) at Dinasdaron. Guinemar spent all her time with Morcades, delighted with her company. Gauvain the Brown marries the handmaid.

Little Gauvain was now twelve years old and was made a knight on St. John's Day—a day sacred to both Christians and pagans. He was successful in all passages of arms and was never taken prisoner. The emperor of the Roman Empire died without heirs [and Gauvain was proposed as his successor].[9]

It is here that the fragment breaks off. *The Rise of Gawain* goes on to relate the adventures of the young Gawain and how he came to Arthur's court and was at last named and recognized. The fragmentary "Les Enfances Gauvain" is the work of a French romance writer, but it nevertheless reveals some interesting features native to British tradition.

Arthur's sister is Morcades, a single, independent woman who demands her own household and gives birth to her lover's child in secrecy in order to preserve her reputation as a virgin. Although the text makes it unclear whether or not Lot eventually marries Morcades, he remains a shadowy figure, disguised as her squire. She relinquishes her own child, endowing him with objects that will enable him to be named, armed, and supported in later life, but consigns him, via her handmaiden, to the sea. So far the tale is likely enough, but the interpolation concerning the fisherman and the pope is clearly derived from the famous medieval legend of Pope Gregory, who was similarly conceived—in incestuous circumstances—and thrown into the sea.[8] This interpolation rendered successive tradition more receptive to the idea of Arthur and his sister or half sister incestuously conceiving a son, which indeed happens in Malory, though the child is Mordred, not Gawain. Yet this is in itself significant.

There seems to be an underlying story struggling to break out here, but it is one which can be only tentatively filled in. If we compare figures 25 and 26, we will see a very rough similarity between two key stories: those of Arianrhod and of Gwyar/Morcades/Anna, Arthur's sister. Both women are born of great matriarchs who have important dynastic marriages. Both have half brother(s). Both have two sons, usually said to be twins. The isolation of both women—Arianrhod at Caer Arianrhod and Morcades at Bel Repaire—and the fact that one of their children is thrown into the sea and that the fatherhood of that child is questionable all betray a subtextual pattern that is more than coincidental. What we see here is the fertility of mythological tradition, as one set of characters inherits the archetypal characteristics of another set.

It would be wrong to try to make more of this beyond merely pointing out the parallels, but it does help us locate Arthur's sister in the directory of British archetypes, and it also suggests her role within the framework of Sovereignty. Arianrhod's role in "Math, Son of Mathonwy" (see *Mabon*, chapter 5) is notably equivocal, and the resulting story in which she appears leaves us with a correspondingly confused picture of her—the storyteller paints her as sulky, independent,

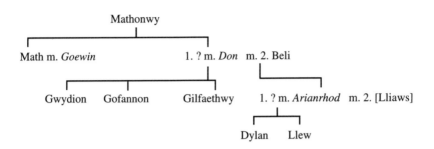

Figure 25. Arianrhod's family. (Female characters are italicized.)

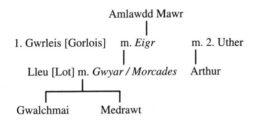

Figure 26. Morcades's family. (Female characters are italicized.)

two-faced, unloving, passionate, vindictive, and unforgiving. The confusion has been wrought by trying to force a goddess archetype into the framework of a human woman.

Arianrhod is primarily a hallows queen, one whose empowerment will make kings famous, one who holds the balance of the land. But she is set against her half brother Gwydion, with whom, possibly, she has an incestuous relationship. Arianrhod is the royal woman whose blood makes her children royal in turn. The dynastic conflict between her and Gwydion should not, therefore, exist—but it does. Like the Queen of the Turning Wheel (see chapter 7, page 204), Arianrhod is outraged at being pregnant: Her intrinsic sovereignty is at risk if she accepts either Dylan or Llew as her child. Dylan is fostered by Math, his great-uncle (who corresponds to Gauvain the Brown in "Les Enfances Gauvain"), and Llew is fostered by his father/uncle, Gwydion (in much the same way that Arthur promotes Gawain in every version of the legend).

Dylan is, of course, lost at sea, but Llew grows up to oppose, and be opposed by, his mother. Arianrhod's anger arises from not being chosen to be royal footholder—a post which requires that the candidate be a virgin. Similarly, it is the appearance of Morcades's virginity that is at stake when she retires to Bel Repaire, but her secret eventually comes to light with the return of Gauvain. The teller, however, has lost the impetus for this tale, failing to understand the underlying subtext that makes Morcades a royal woman like Arianrhod. Both women refuse to name or arm their sons or choose wives for them. This alone indicates where the mythological trail has led us. These are the conditions or geasa placed by Sovereignty upon the candidate for kingship. If he is successful in overcoming them and winning himself a name, arms, and a wife, he is found worthy and welcomed by Sovereignty in one of her many forms. Morcades/Morgause's two children and those of Arianrhod conform to very similar archetypal patterns. Mordred is the child whom Arthur causes to have cast into the sea, according to Malory.[25] Arthur realizes too late that he and his sister Morgause have begotten a child and orders that all children born on May Day be cast adrift in an open boat. Only Mordred survives, as fate dictates in many mythologies, leaving Arthur and his conscience with the reputation of Herod slaughtering the Innocents.

Gawain's career is quite different. His upbringing is rarely disputed: He is Lot's son, loyal to Arthur, often headstrong but always sensitive to the vocation of Sovereignty, whom he defends and champions. Thus Mordred is the Thief of Sovereignty and Gawain her champion, much as Efnissien and Nissien are thief and champion in "Branwen, Daughter of Llyr" (see *Mabon*, chapter 3). The two men, one dark and one light, are the twins of mythological conflict. And indeed there may be a tradition, now lost, which made them twins. If we refer to figure 23, we will see that twins run in Lleu's family. Because tradition is adamant in making Gwalchmai and Medrawt the sons of Arthur's sister, it is possible that they are indeed the children of one birth.

As we will see in the section The Flower Bride's Farewell, below,

Mordred, and not Gawain, is responsible for the final ruination of Arthur's kingdom. Within the mythological pattern it seems that both men are necessary: one to build up Logres, the other to tear away the old administration. Following our parallels with Dylan and Llew, it is interesting to note that Gawain, like Llew, marries an otherworldly woman (or rather a series of them), although there is no trace of the old geis against marrying a woman of earthly stock. He espouses Ragnell, a type of Loathly Lady or Black Maiden; in other stories he encounters faery women and has children by them. The ubiquitous title "solar hero" has been attached to Gawain quite as often as it has been to Llew, for he is knighted on St. John's Day, midsummer, and his strength is correspondingly more effective at midday. Mordred, on the other hand, as we shall see, involves himself in the abduction of Gwenhwyfar, the royal sovereignty-bearing woman of Arthur's reign.[175]

Thus we see that Arianrhod's and Morcades's seeming heartlessness in abandoning their sons is part of a larger pattern. We see that the king's sister occupies the place of Sovereignty, even within medieval Welsh retelling and French Arthurian romance. It is also appropriate that the symbolism of both women is so consonant: Caer Arianrhod is the Welsh name for the Corona Borealis, the crown of the north; while Arthur's sister, in all her appellations, remains queen of the north, proclaimed by a comet as a mother of champions.

But sisters—those of kings included—find the severest rivalry when the king marries. Yet in the case of Gwenhwyfar, even the most ardent supporter of Sovereignty must acknowledge the right to her queenship, for she is possessed of all the attributes of the Flower Bride. Layamon's *Brut* richly describes Arthur's assembly at Caerleon and shows how Arthur's sovereignty is upheld by the four kings of the Island: Cador of Cornwall, the king of Scotland, and the kings of North and South Wales. Guinevere is likewise attended by:

> four chosen queens; each bare [sic] in the left hand a jewel of red gold,
> and three snow-white doves sate on their shoulders; [these] were the

four queens, wives of the kings who bare in their hands the four swords of gold before Arthur, noblest of kings.[43]

In this most Saxon version of a British legend, we see the fourfold Sovereignty attendant upon Gwenhwyfar—those same four queens who will later bear to Avalon the most famous of Sovereignty's consorts.

The Flower Bride's Farewell

Gwenhwyfar, or Guinevere, is probably established in all minds for all time by now as the one who caused the Round Table to fall, particularly since Malory's and Tennyson's versions of the Arthurian legend were printed. She inherits the beauty and sovereignty-bestowing power of the Flower Bride, but also the reputation that attends this role—that of the fickle, unfaithful, and deceiving woman. In Triad 80, she is thus appended to the three unfaithful wives of the Island of Britain: "And one was more faithless than those three: Gwenhywfar, Arthur's wife, since she shamed a better man than any of the others."[38]

When earthly women inherit the role of Flower Bride, storytellers assume the worst and portray a veritable Delilah. Gwenhwyfar's later appearances within the Arthurian legend certainly attest to this treatment. But in the mythic schema, the Flower Bride is portrayed as being totally amoral, for she alone bestows sovereignty upon her chosen champion, selecting and discarding her candidates with impunity. This is what makes the marriage of Blodeuwedd to Llew so unendurable, for Blodeuwedd the Flower Bride is captured by the magic arts of Math and Gwydion to serve their purposes, brought from the Otherworld and fixed in a form wrought of flowers. The choice belongs to the Flower Bride, not to any man, no matter how wise or accomplished. The Flower Bride is not a mortal woman but an appearance of Sovereignty, and we should not be surprised to find that Gwenhwyfar was originally of otherworldly origin.

We have noted that Sovereignty has her three aspects, appearing as Flower Bride or sovereignty-bestowing maiden, sovereign queen, and admonitory hag or Loathly Lady. The division of a deity into such a triplicity was a common aspect of Celtic understanding; three could be part of an indivisible unity to the Celtic mind just as the Three Persons of the Trinity could be to the Greek mind. In Triad 56 we find a triple Gwenhwyfar:

> *Three Great Queens of Arthur's Court:*
> *Gwenhwyfar daughter of Cywryd Gwent,*
> *and Gwenhwyfar daughter of Gwythr ap Greidawl,*
> *and Gwenhwyfar daughter of Gogfran the Giant.*[38]

The meaning of this obscure triad has puzzled scholars. Are three separate women intended? Was there an extant tradition of Arthur marrying three women so identically named? Had traditional stories become so inextricably mixed that the collator of the Triads juxtaposed what he saw as a single tradition?

We are not helped much by the dearth of material relating to any of the fathers of these Gwenhwyfars. Rachel Bromwich suggests that Gwent perhaps be emended to Kent—not necessarily the county, but the title.[38] Of Gwythyr we have already heard, for he fights with Gwyn ap Nudd for the possession of Creiddylad, another Flower Bride and, according to this triad, perhaps also Gwenhwyfar's mother.[169] Of Gogfran the Giant, we have only the popular rhyme recorded by Sir John Rhys, which tells us about "Gwenhwyfar, daughter of Ogfran the Giant, bad when little, worse when big."[139]

Hidden beneath the detritus of tradition is a tempting but perhaps implausible pattern of a succession of Flower Brides, all representatives of British sovereignty, who are the mystical mothers or predecessors of Gwenhwyfar.

The three fathers of Gwenhwyfar mentioned above may each resonate with a single tradition concerning a sovereignty-bestowing woman having a giant relative, a story we have already encountered within "Branwen, Daughter of Llyr," who is called one of three great ancestresses of the Island of Britain. Gwynn Jones's translation of the

Mabinogion gives us Branwen as "one of the Three Matriarchs."[24] In some measure Branwen is indeed the very first in a long line of women who become Daughters of Branwen in a mystical sense, for they bear the sovereignty-bestowing blood of Britain.

Gwythyr ap Greidawl is, of course, the suitor of Creiddylad, the other great Flower Bride of British historical tradition. Creiddylad is none other than Cordelia, the daughter of Lear, one of three sisters. It is interesting that Cordelia and Branwen have been confused with each other—might this confusion be significant? In Gough's additions to Camden (in the 1789 edition), the following gloss is given to the grave of Branwen on the banks of the Alaw in Anglesey: "We have a tradition that the largest cromlech in this country is the monument of Bronwen, daughter of King Leir, who is said to have begun his reign about the year anno mundi 3105."[38] This confusion is interesting because it was Cordelia who buried her father in an underground chamber near the river Soar in Leicestershire. The grave was dedicated to the two-faced god Janus, and it was the meeting place of craftsmen, who would commence a new piece of work at that site at the turning of the old year. In Geoffrey, Cordelia succumbs to grief and kills herself.[10] In "Branwen, Daughter of Llyr," Branwen dies of grief at Bran's wounding, which is also Britain's devastation. Cordelia is also briefly queen in her own right. Branwen is a daughter of Llyr; Cordelia is a daughter of Leir—both Llyr and Leir are variants of the ancestral god of the sea.

The last father of Gwenhwyfar, Cywryd Gwent, or Kent, is the most puzzling character. But we may make an inspired guess and relate him to the tradition concerning Fflur. It is known only that Fflur's father was called Ugnach Gorr, or Dwarf. Fflur herself is loved by Caswallawn and stolen away by Julius Caesar. If we turn to Geoffrey's historical tradition once more, we find that Cassivelaunus's nephew, Androgeus, is created Duke of Kent. (Cassivelaunus is Geoffrey's version of Caswallawn.) Androgeus betrays his uncle to Julius Caesar after Cassivelaunus has ravaged Kent. Perhaps we have here a part of the lost Fflur cycle?[163] Interestingly, Cassivelaunus lays waste Androgeus's lands in much the same way that Gwyn ap Nudd does to the captives of Gwythyr's army. We also note that in "Branwen, Daughter of Llyr" it is Caswallawn who devastates Britain while Bran is in Ireland rescuing Branwen.

It is therefore possible that Triad 56 represents a hidden tradition concerning the Flower Bride. Although three men's names are given as fathers of Gwenhwyfar, the traditional lore hidden in each of these lines concerns the Daughters of Branwen, the women who represent the sovereignty of Britain in mythical/historical tradition: Branwen, Creiddylad/Cordelia, and Fflur. Gwenhwyfar's role as Arthur's queen has always been rather mysterious, but this triad enhances her status as a person in her own right.

Gwenhwyfar's name is related to the Irish *siabair,* meaning "phantom," "spirit," or "faery." In the Ulster cycle we see that the daughter of another prime representative of Sovereignty, Queen Medbh, has a similar name—Finnabair, meaning "white phantom."[38]

The earliest Welsh poets do not mention Gwenhwyfar at all. Indeed, the first mention of her being Arthur's wife appears in the *Vita Gildae*[21] by Caradoc of Llancarfan and in Geoffrey's *History.*[10] This is not to say that Gwenhwyfar did not exist in a prior tradition in her own right; we have only the evidence that has come down to us. What becomes clear is that she was originally an otherworldly queen whom Arthur steals for his bride, a figure like Rhiannon of Welsh or Etain of Irish tradition.

The many attempted abductions of Gwenhwyfar as outlined in figure 27 (page 315) attest to this lost tradition of Arthur's queen as the Flower Bride. Even when, in the later stories, Guinevere loses her otherworldly status, storytellers substitute a false Guinevere, as in the *Vulgate* text,[33] to help maintain her otherworldly persona in the stories. Arthur's real wife is lost or abducted and a substitute Guinevere lives with him, without his awareness that she is false. I shall not attempt to tell the stories of each abduction, for these are so complex and so various that they would require a book of their own. Instead I direct you to

K. T. G. Webster's study *Guinevere: A Story of Her Abductions*[156] or any of the related texts in the bibliography.

The proto-story of Gwenhwyfar's abduction is found in the *Vita Gildae,* in which Melwas of the Summer Country abducts her to his kingdom in the region of Glastonbury, where she lies hidden among the marshes. Arthur, described as a tyrant, besieges the place and prepares to make terrible war until the conciliatory services of Gildas the Wise cause Melwas to render Gwenhwyfar to Arthur once more.[21, 80] We have already noted that in early tradition Arthur is called a Red Ravager of Britain (see chapter 2).

This story, with a few variations, is substantially followed in Chrétien's "Chevalier de la Charette"[7] and Malory's *Morte d'Arthur,*[25] in which Lancelot rescues Guinevere from Meleagant and Meliagrance, respectively. In Malory we note that Guinevere is abducted while out Maying with her unarmed knights.

Wace's *Roman de Brut*[43] and Geoffrey's *History*[10] follow another tradition concerning Gwenhwyfar's connection with Mordred, which, as we have already noted (see chapter 7, note 6), is referenced in the triads. Arthur gives Britain into the joint regency of Mordred, his nephew, and Guanhumara (Guinevere) while he goes off on a campaign against the Romans. However, Guanhumara lives adulterously with her nephew-in-law, who seizes the crown in Arthur's absence. There follows the last battle of Camlann and the consequent deaths of Arthur and Mordred, and Guanhumara enters a convent in Caerleon.

More shocking, Wace makes Mordred Guinevere's brother and tells us that Mordred loved her secretly before becoming regent. Interestingly, Wace and Geoffrey interpolate the hoary tradition about Rome demanding tribute from Britain, so that Arthur is forced to go and fight the Romans, thus leaving Britain and Guinevere alone, though in Mordred's keeping. This seems to hark back to the Fflur/Caswallawn/Julius Caesar story once more. Mordred, as Arthur's nephew and (in Celtic terms) his *tanaiste,* seizes Guinevere, who, as Flower Bride, represents Britain's sovereignty.

Text	Date (C.E.)	Abductor
Vita Gildae	1130	Melwas of the Summer Country
History of the Kings of Britain	1136	Mordred, Arthur's nephew
Chevalier de la Charette	1160s	Meleagant
Lanzelet	1190s	Valerin
Roman de Brut	1155	Mordred, Guinevere's brother
Yder	1220	Yder
"Gereint and Enid" century	thirteenth	[Edern]
Diu Cröne	1230s	Gasozein
Vulgate Cycle	1220s	false Guinevere's men and Lancelot
Livre d'Artus century	thirteenth	Urien, Lot, and Galehot
Perlesvaus century	thirteenth	[Madeglans of Oriande]
De Ortu Waluuanii century	twelfth	[Gawain]
Durmart century	thirteenth	Brun de Morois
Morte d'Arthur	1470	Meliagrance and Lancelot

Figure 27. The abduction of Gwenhwyfar/Guinevere as Flower Bride. Bracketed names indicate potential abductors.

We will recall our discussion of Triad 54, which tells how Medrawt (Mordred) takes the food and drink from Arthur's court, drags Gwenhwyfar from her throne, and strikes her. This tradition seems related to the theme of his theft of the sovereignty of Britain. Related to this is Triad 53, which tells of the three harmful blows to the Island of Britain, the first of which is the striking of Branwen by Matholwch. The second blow is that which "Gwenhwyfach struck upon Gwenhwyfar: and for that cause there took place afterwards the Action of the Battle of Camlan."[38]

Gwenhwyfach appears only once within ancient British tradition, in "Culhwch and Olwen" as the sister of Gwenhwyfar. Triad 84 further tells that the Battle of Camlann is caused by a quarrel between the two. Because there is no extant tradition of Gwenhwyfar having a sister, we are faced with two possibilities: Either we have here a tradition concerning Arthur's queen and the false Guinevere, as discussed above, who appears in much later sources, or Gwenhwyfach is not a sister but a brother of Gwenhwyfar. Yet Gwenhwyfach is said to be Gwenhwyfar's sister in "Culhwch and Olwen."

Triad 54 tells us quite clearly that Mordred strikes the queen, an act attacking Arthur's sovereignty. Following Mordred's theft of Arthur's kingdom and wife, the Battle of Camlann ensues. This makes sense of Triad 53, above, if we substitute Mordred's name for that of Gwenhwyfach. We may find some help in the popular Welsh rhyme "Gwenhwyfar, daughter of Gogfran the Giant: bad when little, worse when big."[139]

In the name Gwenhwyfach, the last syllable is a mutated form of *bach*, or "little." In the name Gwenhwyfar the last syllable might once have been *fawr*, a mutated form of *mawr*, or "big." We are left with the three Gwenhwyfars again or, rather, a tradition which speaks about two of them.

Out of this tangle we may draw the following conclusion: Gwenhwyfar is a woman firmly in the role of Flower Bride, who, as we have seen, is both warm and loving as well as cunning and faithless when she chooses. This dual nature has been polarized into two characters, as we have seen in both the countess and Luned in Owain and the witches of Gloucester and the empress in Peredur. The Flower

Bride can indeed be a beautiful, gift-bestowing maiden, as is Guinevere at the beginning of Arthur's reign; but she partakes also of the nature of the Loathly Lady, the hag, the Dark Woman of Knowledge, the multiple forms adopted by Sovereignty time and again in her testing of the king. It is this nature which Guinevere adopts at the conclusion of Arthur's reign, when she discards her former husband and seeks a new champion.

Alongside Mordred we find numerous other abductors or potential abductors of Gwenhwyfar/Guinevere. Most of them are not significantly attached to the British tradition at all, but are the invention of French or German storytellers; all, however, derive from the general tradition relating to the Flower Bride's otherworldly abduction.

We have already noted the residual traces of this tradition in "Gereint and Enid": Edern may once have been an actual abductor in a proto-version of the story. There exists a corroborative text in the shape of *Yder*.[92] It tells how Yder (Edern) leaves his mother and grandmother in order to discover the whereabouts of his father, Nuc (Nudd). At Caruain he falls in love with a Queen Guenloie and immediately sets out to prove his manly prowess in a series of adventures. These include the overcoming of Arthur in knightly combat, the rescue of Arthur's queen, Guenievere, from a bear's attack, and the finding of his father. Guenievere provokes Arthur's jealousy by proclaiming that if she were to marry again, she would choose Yder. Yder succeeds in defeating two giants and bringing back their knife, according to Guenievere's command as a condition of their marriage, and Yder and Arthur's queen do indeed marry.

This strange story gives us two Guineveres and provides the Flower Bride with a lover whose father is the king of the Underworld. Gwyn ap Nudd, as we have seen, is one of the prime combatants for Creiddylad's hand. His son, Yder—or Ider, as he is called in William of Malmesbury's *De Antiquitate Glastoniensis Ecclesiae*—is further credited in that chronicle with the defeat of three giants near Glastonbury.

Glastonbury Tor, according to the Life of St. Collen, is the entrance to Gwyn ap Nudd's realm. It is also the place where Gwenhwyfar is abducted by Melwas.[21, 87]

Our pursuit of the tradition of Guinevere as Flower Bride is proving fruitful. But what do we make of the similarly named women Guenloie and Guenievere in Yder's story? Like the wife of Arawn and Rhiannon, it is possible that these two ladies share an identity. Both are called queens, and the storyteller describes Queen Guenloie in a manner suggesting that she is really intended to be Arthur's queen, for she harps on Arthur's prowess.

We note that the later Arthurian texts rarely show Arthur in action. He remains a figurehead seated at the Round Table, a crowned sovereign whose knights fight on his behalf and champion the king's justice. But when Guinevere is threatened, things change. It is only in the last flowering of the Arthurian legends, in Malory, that Arthur is content merely to sit and let justice take its course with his faithless wife by having her burned. Many of the earlier texts show him to be concerned enough to fight for her himself.

We also note that Guenievere sets Yder on a hallows quest for the giant's knife, which is much like the sword of light which Cai and company steal from Wrnach the Giant in "Culhwch and Olwen." What emerges in many texts is that Guinevere shows a marked preference for her would-be abductor.

Durmart, a thirteenth-century French romance, also features Ider (Yder). In a way similar to Gereint's, he champions Guinevere, who has been seized by Brun de Morois (possibly a figure related to both the Brown Earl and Earl Limwris in "Gereint and Enid"). When Brun swears that he will not force the queen while the sun shines, indicating that he is of otherworldly stock, we once more gain some insight into the nature of the light and dark combatants.

Figure 27 indicates in brackets potential abductors—that is, knights who show a marked interest in Guinevere but who do not actually abduct her in their respective stories. In each of the texts in which they are featured, we see traces of a prior liaison, as in *Yder* between Guenievere and her would-be abductor. In *De Ortu Waluuanii* (The Rise of Gawain), we find Guinevere remarking to Arthur that a better knight than he is on his way to court, one who will send her tokens. This is none other than Gawain, who overcomes Arthur, significantly, at a ford.[9]

In *Perlesvaus,* a Percival variant, Guinevere, like Enid in "Gereint and Enid," criticizes Arthur for his inability to keep a strong court and provokes him to seek adventures by which he might win glory. He is further admonished by a maiden similar to both Luned and the Black Maiden of "Peredur." Guinevere's role is strangely altered in this text, but in such a way that her role as Sovereignty of Britain is enhanced. While on a pilgrimage to Avalon, Arthur wins a crown and war horse in combat. It is awarded with the following words:

> "Sire, you have won . . . this golden crown and this war horse, for which you should rejoice indeed, so long as you are valiant enough to defend the land of the finest lady on earth, who is now dead."
>
> "To whom did the land belong?" asked the king. "And what was the name of the queen whose crown I see?"
>
> "Sire, the king's name was Arthur, and he was the finest in the world, but many people say that he is dead; and the crown belonged to Queen Guinevere, who is now dead and buried."[129]

Guinevere is indeed dead, from grief at her son's death and from worry over Lancelot's safety, for this text makes her the mother of Loholt, or Llacheu, slain by Kay. Here the sovereignty of Britain is Guinevere's gift.

Later on in the story, Madeglans of Oriande comes to court demanding that Arthur yield the Round Table and the sovereignty to him because he was Guinevere's nearest kinsman, and, now that she is dead, Arthur is no longer entitled to it. Madeglans likewise bids Arthur to renounce Christianity and marry Madeglans's sister, Jandree, and in return he may be permitted to remain king.

There is no text which presents Guinevere's sovereignty-bestowing role more clearly. The land and the crown are entirely derived from her. Her death, which is substituted for an abduction in *Perlesvaus,* is the occasion of the otherworldly kin coming to claim their rights on her behalf.

Diu Cröne, a German text by Heinrich von dem Tülin, establishes Guinevere's otherworldly provenance beyond doubt. Guinevere provokes Arthur, as in *De Ortu Waluuanii,* when she finds him huddling over a fire on a cold winter's day, saying that he was never so enduring as the knight who rode at the ford of Noirespine dressed only in a silk shirt. She describes this knight with warm appreciation, and Arthur sets out to find him. Arthur learns that the strange knight is the otherworldly Gasozein, who claims Guinevere as his own, for nocturnal spirits destined her to be his mistress when she was born. He accuses Arthur of having stolen her and they prepare to fight a duel, but it is decided to leave the matter to Guinevere's judgment. Her indecision is ended by Gasozein's abduction of her. Gawain eventually rescues her.[39] This story is related to Marie de France's *Lai d'Espine.*[26]

We have already noted Guinevere's abduction by Valerin in *Lanzelet.* The *Livre d'Artus* is a mangled tale in which duplications of incidents tirelessly occur, including several abductions of Guinevere by Urian, Lot, and Galehot. Guinevere's lover in this text is Gosengos, and he implies that she has had many lovers whom she has treated badly. (A similar complaint is made by the Sumerian Gilgamesh, when the goddess Inanna demands his love!)

This leaves only the *Vulgate Cycle* and its false Guinevere. The curious duplication of characters in this text probably arises as a result of the dual nature of the Flower Bride. Storytellers likely reasoned that Arthur's queen could not bear the burden of such a reputation and transferred to another character the queen's apparent wickedness. Much the same happens in the Tristan legend in which Tristan, upon arriving in Brittany after having been banished from Isolt, Mark's queen, takes up with another Isolt, who is eventually responsible for his death.[81]

In the *Vulgate Cycle,* Guinevere's father, Leodegran, and his queen beget the real Guinevere, and Leodegran and his seneschal's wife beget the false Guinevere. It is the false Guinevere who arranges for her half sister's abduction after her wedding to Arthur and substitutes herself as his new bride. She is discovered, however, and is banished. In the "Prose Lancelot," part of the *Vulgate Cycle,* it is Lancelot who is at first deceived by the false Guinevere, and then Arthur becomes the subject of her deception.[33] A distant echo of this scenario is found in Lancelot's bedding of Elaine, Pelles's daughter, while under the impression that she is Guinevere.[25] This might indeed have been the solution to Triad 53, specifically addressing the blow struck by Gwenhwyfach upon Gwenhyfar, had the "Prose Lancelot" and Triad 53 not been at such a remove from each other in terms of the date of their transmission. Here, Lancelot's tryst with Elaine (whom he believes is Guinevere) results in the conception of Galahad. In the later texts it is the quest for the Grail that empties the Round Table of its worthy knights, and the guilty love of Guinevere and Lancelot that brings the action to the Battle of Camlann. In one sense Elaine, as the false Guinevere, does indeed strike the real Guinevere a terrible blow, for it is Elaine who conceives the Grail winner, an honor which is denied the real Guinevere.

We can see that Guinevere's most famous abductor, Lancelot, appears as such only in the later texts, as in Malory, where he rescues the queen from burning at the stake. Though not the sole abductor in this tradition, having been fostered by the Lady of the Lake, he certainly succeeds to the role of otherworldly lord.[42]

There is one tale which tells of Guinevere's role as Flower Bride passing on to her daughter: the fragmentary folk ballad "King Arthur and King Cornwall." In this song, Guinevere provokes Arthur to search for the Round Table, whose provenance is known to the queen. Arthur rides out with some of his knights, disguised as a pilgrim, and comes to the castle of King Cornwall. There he hears a story about himself which gives him cause for dismay. King Cornwall relates:

Seven yeere I was clad and fed,
In Litle Brittaine, in a bower;
I had a daughter by King Arthur's wife,
That now is called my flower.
For King Arthur, that kindly cockward,
Hath none such in his bower.[64]

The apparent lack of issue from the marriage of Arthur and Guinevere (his sons are all by other women; see figure 19, page 283) testifies to the rupture of the king and his Sovereignty, though not to the point of ending the influence of either, for their roles are inherited by other characters in other times.

The career of Guinevere, however, marks the Flower Bride's farewell in British tradition, for she represents the final manifestation of Sovereignty's distinct maiden aspect within Britain's mythic history. She is still remembered in May revels and seasonal rites where, with her crown of flowers and virginal smock, she smiles down from every May Day float in the person of every little May queen. There are few who remember, as they watch the combat of the May king with his opponent, that the prize was once more than the honor of being king for a day—that the Flower Bride brought as her dowry the Sovereignty of Britain.

The Anastasis of Arthur

Arthur's interaction with Sovereignty is nowhere more apparent than in the days leading up to his departure from Logres. Few storytellers have been willing to speak of the death of Arthur, a tradition extended to all of royal blood in many parts of the world today. In modern Ghana, for instance, the people assert, "Ordinary people die and are dead. But the king is never dead. He is still alive. We do not talk of the death of the king."[62]

And so does the early Welsh poetic cycle *Stanzas of the Graves* state: "Anoeth bid bet y Arthur,"[44] or "difficult to conceive a grave for Arthur." For this reason I have drawn upon the Greek liturgical form *anastasis,* and have thus titled this section The Deathlessness of Arthur.

Arthur's encounters with Sovereignty in stories of the early tradition are mainly lost to us. All that is possible here is to use the obscure signposts of fragmentary stories to trace the mythological path leading to the well-documented later Arthurian tradition. We have seen how Arthur drinks from the white draft of fostering, as well as from the red draft of lordship; now is the time for him to drink of the dark draft of forgetfulness, after which his earthly kingdom of Logres is laid aside in exchange for the realm of the Goddess of the Otherworld, the Royal Virgin of Avalon herself.

Throughout his life Arthur encounters many aspects of Sovereignty: his mother, foster mother, sisters, wife, and the many unspecified damsels who come to seek his help in guarding the land. At the point of his departure he encounters them all at once in a single dream, which serves as a recapitulation of his life and relationship with the land.

This episode occurs in a single source: the *Alliterative "Morte Arthure,"* a fifteenth-century Middle English prose romance in the tradition of Geoffrey of Monmouth, rather than in a French romance. It predates Malory and, though it represents a rather late tradition, it does present us with one of the fullest encounters of Arthur and Sovereignty.

It opens with Arthur dreaming he is in a wood in a lovely valley. He sees descending from the sky a richly dressed woman, bedecked with jewels and with a crown upon her head. She whirls a wheel with her hands. In the center of this wheel is a kingly throne and clinging to the outer rim are six kings, each of whom bewails being enthroned. She welcomes Arthur, saying that she alone has been responsible for the honor he has won in battle. She seats him on the throne, combs his hair, and then gifts him with three items: a diadem; an orb symbolizing Arthur's sovereignty over the land; and a sword, which is Arthur's own. Entering an orchard, she bids the boughs bend low and present Arthur with apples, and tells him to eat as many as he chooses.

Then she went to the well, by the woodside,
That welled up with wine and wondrously flowed.
She caught up a cupful and covered it fairly,
And bade me drink deeply a draft to herself.[3]

[MY TRANSLATION]

But at midday her soft mood changes and she whirls the wheel, crushing Arthur violently.

A philosopher duly interprets Arthur's dream as being one of Fortuna. The six men are six of the Nine Worthies (Alexander, Hector, Julius, Judas Maccabaeus, Joshua, and David), to whom will be added Charlemagne, Godfrey de Bouillon, and Arthur himself.[3]

The figure of Fortuna enjoyed a new lease on life during the Middle Ages. She had previously been a popular goddess among the Romans, particularly among soldiers, who frequently set up shrines to both Fortuna and Victory. The question here is whether the depiction of Fortuna in *Alliterative "Morte Arthure"* has any relationship with our Sovereignty. Certainly she behaves like a Celtic Goddess: She empowers Arthur's kingship through his victory in battle; she gives him royal regalia and arms him; she commands apples to fall into his lap and is clearly mistress of the orchard; and, most significant, she gives him the red cup of lordship and bids him drink from it. While the concept of the Nine Worthies is a medieval one, the succession of the Pendragons is not.

As we saw in *Mabon* (chapter 9), the wheel turns inexorably so that there are always a king, his tanaiste (in this case, Mabon), and his predecessor (in this case, Uther). Yet the symbol of the wheel is not usually a goddess emblem among the Celts, but instead is wielded by Taranis, the god of thunder. Our story depicts a woman who is not merely a genius of the spring, but is instead, just like Sovereignty, a queenly character whose influence empowers kings. Nor is this the only appearance of Fortuna in the Arthurian legends.

We saw in chapter 9 that the Grail derives, in part, from the vessel that Sovereignty guards, whether a well, a spring, or a cauldron. In the thirteenth-century *Perlesvaus*, Gawain encounters many adventures on his quest to recover the Grail to the kingdom of Logres. He is the first to seek it, at the behest of the bald maiden of the cart and her two female companions, who have come to Arthur's court to request his help in healing the Wounded King and the wasteland. While following these maidens, Gawain comes upon a fountain with a golden vessel hanging from it. As he reaches to touch it, a voice tells him: "You are not the good knight who is served from the vessel and cured by it."[29] He then sees a priest approach, bearing a foursquare golden cup, which he rinses and then fills with the contents of the fountain cup. After this the three maidens appear:

> . . . all draped in white robes with white drapes to cover their heads; one of them carried bread in a vessel of gold, another brought wine in a vessel of ivory, and a third bore meat in a vessel of silver. They came up to the golden vessel . . . and in it they placed their offerings. And after waiting a while at the foot of the pillar, they began to walk back, but as they went, *it seemed to Sir Gawain that there was but one of them.*[29] [my italics]

Later Gawain comes to the Castle of Enquiry, where a hermit explains the wonders he has seen. The bald maiden is Fortuna, who has lost her hair because a knight has not yet asked the Grail question that will heal the land and the Wounded King. Her cart is Fortuna's Wheel, and her two maiden companions are dressed, one in fine clothes and one in poor garb, to signify the changing patterns of fortune. But when Gawain asks at the fountain for an explanation of the three white-robed maidens who have appeared, the hermit enigmatically replies: "Of that . . . I will tell you no more than you have heard . . . for no one should reveal the secrets of the Saviour; they should be kept secret by him to whom they are entrusted."[29]

This passage helps us clearly to associate Fortuna with Sovereignty in the person of the bald maiden, the genius of the land whose beautiful hair will not be restored until the Grail question is asked by a knight who will become not only the Grail winner but also the champion of Logres. The three mysterious and very Celtic maidens who appear at the fountain bearing vessels filled with food and drink seem to have strayed from one of the immrama, the otherworldly voyages of Maelduin or Bran mac Febal.[162] The hermit implies that these maidens are at the center of the Grail cult; his silence is as cryptic as his comment about the "secrets of the Saviour." We may conclude that here, perhaps, is the meeting place of the Christian mysteries of the Grail and the original damsels of the wells whom we met in the story of Amangons from *The Elucidation* (see chapter 9).

Interestingly, these three maidens appear to Gawain to be one woman—a highly significant factor, if we consider both Gawain's noted association with otherworldly women and the configuration of the archetypes of the Divine Feminine in Celtic culture. It is known that the native threefold goddesses depicted as the Matres, or Mothers, in Celtic Europe were intimately associated with the Roman cult of the Parcae, or Fates—also a threefold sisterhood.[168] While the fusion of Roman and British deities tended to produce sets of divine couples, such as Rosmerta, a native goddess of plenty, and Mercury, the Roman god of skill, certain goddesses remain unmatched, powerful in their own right.

At Corstopitum (Corbridge, Northumberland), two reliefs have been found of such goddesses. One shows a figure standing beside a vat with a dish or cup in her hand. The other shows two goddesses. The standing figure on the right has been identified as Fortuna, with cornucopia and rudder. The much larger one seated on the left holds an orblike object in her lap, while in her left hand is a scepter. Beside her is an altar with a bird upon it. At this site the goddess is invoked as Caelestis Brigantia, the Heavenly Brigantia.[142] Is it possible that the Sovereignty of Britain, as depicted in our selections from the Arthurian legends, could be this once mighty goddess of the native Britons—Brigantia, whose name means "high one" or "queen"?

We will recall that early tradition credits Arthur with bearing an image of the Virgin upon his shoulder at the Battle of Badon, and to this his victory is attributed (see chapter 1). This might indeed be so, but in the shifting associations of mythological archetypes, perhaps Arthur's spiritual allegiance was given to Sovereignty herself. To bring victory, Brigantia's name was invoked among both native tribes and Roman auxiliaries stationed in the British north. A relief found at Birrens depicts Brigantia with a mural crown that shows the crenellations of a fortress—she is a territorial goddess. In the relief she is standing on a globe, symbolic of victory and sovereignty, and is carrying a spear and wearing the gorgoneion of Minerva on her breast—the gorgon mask which is said to unman the enemy with its fearful glance. In this single depiction we see all the symbolism and aspects of Sovereignty, even down to the cailleach, or fearful aspect, assumed by the Black Maiden. It is not inconceivable that the fifth-century Arthur might have worn at the Battle of Baden a Roman cuirass on which the gorgoneion of Minerva was embossed.

Sir John Rhys has shown that the Welsh *brenhin*, or king, derives from the Celtic root word *brig*, meaning power, authority, or high esteem, all terms signifying sovereignty. The legendary judge of Ireland, Sencha, had a daughter called Brig whose duty it was to criticize and correct her father's judgments. This is a role we recognize from Sovereignty's aspect as Black Maiden, whose role it is to harangue her protégés. The goddess Brighid was also frequently called Brig.[140]

It is possible to further associate Brighid with the later appearance of Fortuna as Sovereignty. Brighid is primarily a goddess of nurture, whether of the growth and well-being of children or beasts or of the development of wisdom. To this day in Celtic countries, on the feast day of St. Brigit (Imbolc, February 1), people still make the Bride's Cross, a three- or four-spoked cross of rushes resembling a wheel. These emblems represent the sunwise power of the hearth's embers to spin, turn, and bring health to places where the emblems have been set up. We have already seen how Brighid mitigates the influence of the cailleach at this time of year (see page 262). Her mythos, whether of goddess or saint, speaks of power, wisdom, nurturing, and new beginnings. And so we may conceive the Celtic Goddess of Sovereignty.

But we should not forget that as an Irish three-form goddess, Brighid is associated with smithcraft and that her wisdom-in-battle aspect bestows victory upon her successful clients—which leads us to the last contender for the title of the Sovereignty of Britain.

Within the last days of his life, Arthur encounters the Lady of the Wheel: the aspect of the Goddess that governs the cutting of the thread, she who gathers to herself all those champions who have lived in her service—for she is the otherworldly mistress and she demands her tithe. As we might expect, Arthur puts Gwenhwyfar, the Flower Bride, behind him when the end is near. The Orkney clan, the sons of Morcades/Morgause, Gwalchmai and Medrawt, briefly take opposite roles in the conflict that stands between king and land, one championing the king, the other ready to wreak havoc. We note that Medrawt, in the early texts, attempts to steal the Flower Bride, thus becoming the Thief of Sovereignty (see chapter 6). It is Arthur's lot to encounter the Battle Goddess, the taker, the washer at the ford: Queen Dragon herself.

The earlier texts tell of Gwenhwyfar's abduction—whether willing or not—by Medrawt, which leaves Arthur without his representative of Sovereignty. But they also reveal that the Battle of Camlann is provoked by various incidents. One of these is shown in "The Dream of Rhonabwy," in which Iddawg, the Churn of Britain—so called because of his habit of stirring up trouble—carries a message of truce from Arthur to Medrawt and delivers it in such a way as to provoke the battle. In this instance, Iddawg appears to act as the Provoker of Strife, one of Sovereignty's henchmen whom she employs only when she is acting from her catabolic phase, breaking down the kingship in order to start again. The *Stanzaic "Morte Arthure"* tells us that the Battle of Camlann is also provoked by the appearance of an adder, which bites the foot of one of Mordred's company when both sides are observing

---

a truce. The man draws his sword to slash at it, and inadvertently begins the conflict.[3] Here is the cailleach, Queen Dragon herself, in the form of the adder who comes out of the ground to bring the reign of winter upon the earth, and returns only at the festival of Brighid (see chapter 9).

And so the two champions fight: Arthur against Medrawt/Mordred, who is, according to different viewpoints, either Arthur's son or nephew or the young champion of Sovereignty herself.

> When Medrawd heard that Arthur's host was dispersed, he turned against Arthur, and the Saxons and the Picts and the Scots united with him to hold this Island against Arthur. And when Arthur heard that, he turned back with all that had survived of his army, and succeeded by violence in landing on this Island in opposition to Medrawd. And then there took place the Battle of Camlan between Arthur and Medrawd, and Arthur slew Medrawd, and was himself wounded to death.[38]

And so the story of Vortigern and Merlin Emrys (see chapter 2), in which the dragons are released from the foundations of Vortigern's tower, is to some extent recapitulated here: Medrawt is Vortigern come again—a man who allies himself with the enemies of Britain. But Merlin's prophetic insight is no longer available to Arthur. Standing in the wings is Morgan, the Battle Goddess, the otherworldly mistress ready to claim her lord from the field of the slain. The adder as well as the raven are her totemic beasts and, like the dragons released by Merlin, betoken the end and beginning of a phase of Britain's sovereignty.

We have to some extent anticipated this discussion in chapter 4, in which we dealt with Morgan in her aspect as Battle Goddess. Perhaps here we truly understand how the gwyddbwyll combat of the Pendragons with Sovereignty reaches its endgame.

Morgan's oldest and perhaps least understood role in Arthurian legend is that of otherworldly mistress and healer. When she first appears in Arthurian tradition in Geoffrey of Monmouth's *Vita*

Merlini[11] as Morgen, queen of the otherworldly realm of Avalon, she bears little trace of the curious, changeable creature later tradition will make of her. Instead, she is the mistress of her eight companion sisters; she is able to fly, shapeshift, and heal, and is a mistress of wisdom. All these attributes seem at odds with the malevolent Morgan of Malory.

We note, however, that she is one of nine sisters, a number we have seen previously:

- Nine muses who warm Pen Annwfn's cauldron
- Nine witches of Gloucester who help/hinder Peredur
- Nine sisters of Avalon

All three examples are from British tradition, but are consonant with European traditions of the Nine Korrigans of Brittany, a cell of priestesses whom Pomponius Mela describes as being called the Gallenciae.[134] This ninefold sisterhood is the multiplication by three of the threefold Goddess herself, which classical tradition represents as the Parcae, or Fates, but which in Celtic tradition remains firmly associated with the Matres, the Mothers.[168]

Morgan has been through so many transformations and shifts of emphasis that the welter of surviving material shows clearly the synthesis of the Goddess into a series of otherworldly women. It is only when these supra-mortal qualities are bestowed in later tradition on the very mortal figure of Morgan, Arthur's sister, that storytellers are reduced to explaining away such power by making her an enchantress. There is no space here to recapitulate this complex development, though there are excellent studies by Paton[134] and Harf-Lancner[79] in which this transference is made apparent.

Morgan retains many Celtic characteristics. She has been mostly replaced by the figure of the Lady of the Lake as a foster mother of heroes, but she is still there, submerged in Arthur's career, the otherworldly woman who endows him with his sword, the hallow by which he defends the kingdom of Logres. It is this very sword which is returned to the Lady of the Lake at the conclusion of Arthur's earthly life, for it belongs to Sovereignty and must be won again by every candidate for the kingship. The Lady of the Lake, although developed in the French romances, is clearly derived from Celtic models of the insular Goddess who rules over a land of women, the famous Tir na mBan of Irish traditional immrama. The Lady of the Lake also arms her young fosterling, as we find in Lancelot's story,[107] which is resonant of the Celtic woman warrior who trained her fosterling in arms and combat and then, having taught him all her skills, finally sent him out into the world with a worthy blade to assist him.

In her opposition to Arthur, Morgan displays characteristics of the Black Maiden: She acts as an irritant, becoming the nagging reminder of Arthur's oath to the land, to Sovereignty herself, and reminding him of his geasa. She is also jealous of her affianced champion, and as we have seen, when Arthur weds Gwenhwyfar, who is the manifest Sovereignty of Britain, Morgan extends her opposition to the queen herself. This opposition is usually rationalized in the romances by the history of Morgan having loved a cousin of Guinevere and the queen having stood strongly against the relationship.[134] As the Black Maiden, Morgan also takes lovers and rival champions, whom she sets in active opposition to Arthur, notably Accalon of Gaul, who briefly holds the sword of Sovereignty, Excalibur, before Arthur overcomes him.[25]

But it is perhaps as Battle Goddess, queen of ravens, that Morgan's chief Celtic characteristic is manifested. The Morrighan of Irish tradition, herself a triple-form Goddess, plays a key part in the changing of dynasties and the succession of the land to a new champion. This predecessor of Morgan declares who is victorious at the Second Battle of Mag Tuired, the great battle fought between Lugh and the Tuatha de Danaan against the occupying Fomorians. Thus "[she] proceeded to proclaim that battle and the mighty victory which had taken place, to the royal heights of Ireland and to its faery hosts and its chief waters and its river-mouths."[179]

In other words, she proclaims the land itself to be victorious, though Lugh and the Tuatha have fought successfully for the sovereignty. She goes on to prophesy the end of the world in an apocalyptic manner:

> *I shall not see a world that will be dear to me.*
> *Summer without flowers,*
> *Kine will be without milk,*
> *Women without modesty,*
> *Men without valor,*
> *Captures without a king.*[179]

Her role is analogous to that of the figure who appears at the end of Merlin's prophecies of the end the world: "The Moon's chariot shall run amok in the Zodiac and the Pleiades will burst into tears. None of these will return to the duty expected of it. Ariadne will shut its door and be hidden within its enclosing cloudbanks.[10]

Likewise Morgan appears to end the reign of the Pendragons, to make an end because she is the Lady of the Wheel, Fortuna herself, who turns the Wheel of the Pendragons. In her many aspects she has been everything except the Flower Bride—a role reserved for Gwenhwyfar. But now her time has come to take her consort home; time to checkmate the king piece on the gwyddbwyll board of the land.

Her last transformation is perhaps the most amazing to modern readers. She changes from being the chooser of the slain, the raven queen—an archetype found in many cultures predominantly in northwest Europe, from Ireland to Scandinavia—to being the healer goddess who will mend Arthur's wounds. In Malory, the most familiar version, she takes him away on a barge, accompanied by two other queens: the threefold Sovereignty incarnate. But the barge is only an ill-disguised otherworldly crystal curragh that bears ardent travelers to the Land of Women or the Blessed Isles, where time is not.

Among the mysteries of Sovereignty, the passing of the king into the land is the most profound. After his earthly career, worn out by toil in the defense of the land, the land restores him by means of its otherworldly fruit; its everlasting fountains restore his youth and strength until the time comes for the wheel to turn again, when he too will change from being lord of the Underworld, Pen Annwfn, to being the Goddess's fosterling, her Mabon once more.

The *Vita Merlini* describes Arthur's passage in the barque of the mysterious Barinthus, accompanied by Taliesin and Merlin, to Avalon, where Morgan will heal his wounds.[11] Another text, *Le Dragon Normand*, by Etienne de Rouen, slightly postdates this tradition and gives us fresh insight into the nature of Arthur's passing:

> *The grievously wounded Arthur requested healing herbs from his sister:*
> *These were kept in the sacred isle of Avalon.*
> *Here the eternal nymph, Morgan, helped her brother.*
> *Healing, nourishing and reviving him, making him immortal.*
> *The Antipodes were put under his rule. As one of Faery,*
> *He stands without armour, but fearing no fray.*
> *So he rules from the underworld, bright in battle,*
> *Where the other half of the world is his.*[134]

[MY TRANSLATION]

This text gives details not found in Geoffrey, notably the references above. Interestingly the whole poem is about sovereignty—the sovereignty of Brittany—and includes a correspondence between Arthur and Henry II in which King Henry becomes a vassal of King Arthur! We note that Arthur is king of the southern hemisphere, though this is clearly intended to mean the Underworld, that subterranean kingdom whose unearthly influence governs the sovereignty of the land. Arthur becomes Pen Annwfn, the Sleeping Lord.

The *Gesta Regnum Britanniae* confirms Arthur's relationship with Morgan, the royal virgin of Avalon:

At that same time when Arthur bequeathed the diadem of royalty and set another king in his place, it was she who brought him over there in the five hundred and forty-second year after the Word

became incarnate without the seed of human father. Wounded
beyond measure, Arthur took the way to the court of the king of
Avalon, where the royal virgin, tending his wound, keeps his healed
body for her very own and they live together. (*Mabon*, chapter 9)

And so Arthur is established in tradition as an otherworldly king,
and with Morgan at his side he administers the important business of
Britain's sovereignty. As the king who does not die, he is always potentially available to his land and its people.

Thus Arthur had himself borne to Avalon and he told his people that
they should await him and he would return. And the Britons came
back to Carduel and waited for him more than forty years before they
would take a king, for they believed always that he would return. But
this you may know in truth that some have since then seen him hunting in the forest, and they have heard his dogs with him; and some
have hoped for a long time that he would return.[32]

We have thus come full circle in our study of the *Mabinogion*, for
here is where we began, in the First Branch story of "Pwyll, Prince of
Dyfed": The king of Dyfed meets Arawn, Pen Annwfn, while out hunting and the otherworldly adventures begin. The extract above from the
Didot Perceval proclaims the ongoing mythological existence of a king
for whose return many have hoped.

Arthur, hunting in the forests of Brocéliande, that great forest
which once covered the land of Logres, still pursues his quarry—the
white hart, Sovereignty's own beast, which only the best of champions
can win for the most sovereign of ladies.

The names of the land are as various as the aspects of Sovereignty
we have met in this book. The calling of the Pendragon is a serious
undertaking, but it must follow that we understand the name of the
land, the name that has remained silently hidden. This quest has under-
lain this study. However we call her—whether Elen of the Dream Paths,
Brighid, Morgan, Gwenhwyfar, Rhiannon, Modron, or Arianrhod—
Sovereignty will never cease to call her own champion.

And what of those who stumble into the subterranean chamber where Arthur, the Sleeping Lord, lies awaiting the call? Will they find that the horn of awakening is, after all, the horn that restores the Court of Joy? By what empowerments will they find the sword within their hands, the cup raised to their lips? Only those who are attuned to the voices of the wells, the voice of Sovereignty herself, can ever truly know the land. But that is an adventure that awaits us all.

Appendix
The Wheel of the Year: King and Goddess

Given the welter of evidence for Sovereignty in Celto-Arthurian tradition presented in this book, figure 28, showing the Wheel of the Year upon which the major harmonics of Sovereignty and king have been placed, serves as a summation of the roles of both.

The center of the diagram shows a cross plaited from reeds, which is traditionally made in Ireland on St. Brigit's day (February 1). Each arm of the cross indicates one of the four major aspects of Sovereignty. This is superimposed upon an equilateral Celtic cross, each arm of which indicates one of the four major aspects of the king. The Goddess corresponds to the Celtic festivals; the king corresponds to the quarter days, or sun festivals.

The Celtic year begins at Samhain with the rule of the cailleach. In the depths of winter, when the sun is at its lowest in the sky, Mabon is born, remaining hidden until his epiphany or finding. It is during this time that the king is fostered secretly by the Dark Woman of Knowledge or cailleach and is taught battle skills by the Black Maiden, who appears at Oimelc or Imbolc, when the rule of the cailleach is challenged by her in the manner discussed in chapter 9. The young king, in order to be acceptable to Sovereignty, must become aware of the needs of the land he seeks to govern.

THE WHEEL OF THE YEAR: KING AND GODDESS

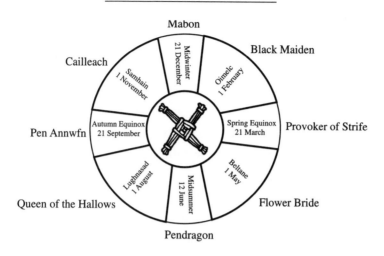

Figure 28. The Wheel of the Year

In so doing, he becomes a Provoker of Strife, stirring up trouble for the current king and spearheading resistance to a reign that has grown stale or corrupt. It is in this manner that he becomes the Champion of Sovereignty and proves worthy of the Flower Bride, Sovereignty's manifest representative, whom he marries. He may even be responsible for carrying her off as her abductor.

The Flower Bride is properly seen as the queen of May, and her time of manifestation is at Beltane. It can be seen from the diagram that this position is diametrically opposite that of the cailleach. On the Wheel of the Year, the young king has used the cailleach's knowledge to understand the needs of the land and has experienced the Goddess's transforming nature as she appears as Flower Bride. The land throws off its wasted appearance, which it affected during the previous reign of an unworthy king, and becomes fair once more. This is the land that the king marries.

As Pendragon, recognized king of Britain, the king is at his strongest at the time of midsummer, but in order to maintain his kingdom he must seek the gifts and empowerments of Sovereignty and ratify his union on a deeper level. The hallows are held by the queen of the hallows in her otherworldly castle. She appears at Lughnasad, the festival that in ancient tradition saw the *banais rigi*—the wedding of the kingship to the land. Throughout the long summer he seeks her gifts, eventually journeying into the regions of the dead, to the Underworld itself, to bring back the hallows. It is in this way that the king succeeds to his new role as Pen Annwfn, Lord of the Underworld, the Sleeping Lord who enters the realms of the cailleach to be reborn and remade. This transformation may take many turns of the wheel to effect, but the king is mythically tied to this wheel until his own deeds release him into the Otherworld, from whence he will come again.

Figure 28 shows the barest bones of a deeper pattern, which the reader is invited to uncover through reading, meditation, and personal revelation. The yearly cycle it represents may be enacted ritually, or made the focus of a reverent *anamnesis* (remembrance). It may also be combined with the many fragmented and partially restored texts exemplified in this book for the reconstruction of a more coherent cycle. The Arthurian Tarot[113] provides a visual summary of the major themes presented in this book.

Bibliography

Textual Sources

1. Bartrum, P. C. *Early Welsh Genealogical Tracts.* Cardiff: University of Wales Press, 1966.

2. ———. *Welsh Genealogies A.D. 300–1400.* Cardiff: University of Wales Press, 1974.

3. Benson, L. D., ed. *King Arthur's Death: The Middle English Stanzaic "Morte Arthure" and Alliterative "Morte Arthure."* Exeter: University of Exeter Press, 1986.

4. Best, R. L., ed. "The Adventures of Art, Son of Conn." In *Eriú* 3 (1906).

5. Bruce, J. D., ed. *Historia Meriadoci and De Ortu Waluuanii.* Baltimore: Johns Hopkins Press, 1913.

6. Chaucer, G. *Canterbury Tales.* Oxford: Oxford University Press, 1912.

7. Chrétien de Troyes. *Arthurian Romances.* Translated by D. D. R. Owen. London: Dent, 1987.

8. Cross, T. P. and C. H. Slover. *Ancient Irish Tales.* Dublin: Figgis, 1936.

9. Day, M. L. *The Rise of Gawain, Nephew of Arthur.* New York: Garland, 1984.

10. Geoffrey of Monmouth. *History of the Kings of Britain.* Harmondsworth: Penguin, 1966.

11. ———. *Vita Merlini.* Edited and translated by J. J. Parry. Champaign, Ill.: University of Illinois Press, 1925.

12. Gerald of Wales. *Journey through Wales.* Edited and translated by L. Thorpe. Harmondsworth: Penguin, 1978.

13. Gildas. *The Ruin of Britain.* Edited and translated by M. Winterbottom. London: Phillimore, 1978.

14. *The Gododdin.* Edited and translated by K. H. Jackson. Edinburgh: Edinburgh University Press, 1969.

15. Hartman von Aue. *Erec.* Translated by J. W. Thomas. Lincoln: University of Nebraska Press, 1979.

16. ———. *Iwein.* Translated by J. W. Thomas. Lincoln: University of Nebraska Press, 1979.

17. Joynt, M., ed. and trans. "Echtra Mac Echach Muigmedoin." In *Eriú* 4 (1910).

18. Kitteridge, G. L. "Arthur and Gorlagon." In *Philology and Literature* 8 (1903).

19. *The Laws of Hywel Dda.* Translated by M. Richards. Liverpool: Liverpool University Press, 1954.

20. "Life of St. Brigit." In *Lives of the Saints.* Edited by W. Stokes. Oxford: Clarendon Press, 1890.

21. "Life of St. Gildas." In *Lives of the Saints.* Edited by S. Baring-Gould. Edinburgh: Grant, 1877.

22. The *Mabinogion.* Edited and translated by J. Gantz. London: Penguin, 1988.

23. The *Mabinogion.* Edited and translated by Lady C. Guest. London: Ballantyne Press, 1910.

24. The *Mabinogion.* Edited and translated by G. Jones and T. Jones. London: Dent, 1976.

25. Malory, Sir T. *Le Morte d'Arthur.* Edited by John Matthews. London: Orion, 2000.

26. Marie de France. *French Medieval Romances.* Edited and translated by E. Mason. London: Dent, n.d.

27. Meyer, P. "Les Enfances Gauvain." In *Romania* 39 (1910): 1–31.

28. Nennius. *British History and Welsh Annals.* Edited and translated by J. Morris. Chichester: Phillimore, 1980.

29. *Perlesvaus.* Translated by N. Bryant. Cambridge: D. S. Brewer, 1978.

30. *"Sir Cliges" and "Sir Libeaus Desconus": Two Old English Metrical Romances Rendered into Prose.* Translated by J. L. Weston. London: David and Nutt, 1902.

31. *Sir Gawain and the Green Knight.* Translated by Rev. E. J. B. Kirtlan. London: Charles Kelly, 1912.

32. Skeels, D., ed. and trans. *"The Romance of Perceval" in Prose ("Didot Perceval")*. Seattle: University of Washington, 1966.

33. Sommer, H. O., ed. *The Vulgate Version of the Arthurian Romances*. Washington: Carnegie Institute, 1909–1916.

34. Stokes, W. "The Death of Muirchertach MacErca." In *Revue Celtique* 23 (1892).

35. Stokes, W. H. and Windisch, E. *Irische Texte*. Leipzig: Verlag con S. Hurzel, 1884.

36. Thompson, A., ed. *The Elucidation: A Prologue to the Conte de Graal*. New York: Publications of the Institute of French Studies, 1931.

37. Thorpe, L., ed. *Le Roman de Silence*. Cambridge: Heffer, 1972.

38. *Trioedd Ynys Prydein*. Edited by R. Bromwich. Cardiff: University of Wales Press, 1961.

39. Von dem Türlin, *Diu Cröne*. Edited by G. Scholl. Stuttgart: Bibliothek des Litterarischen Vereins, 1852.

40. Von Eschenbach, W. *Parzival: A Knightly Epic*. Translated by J. L. Weston. London: n.p. 1894.

41. ———. *Titurel*. Edited by C. E. Passage. New York: W. Frederick Ungar, 1984.

42. Von Zatzikhoven, U. *Lanzelet*. Edited and translated by K. T. G. Webster, with revisions by R. S. Loomis. New York: Columbia University Press, 1951.

43. Wace and Layamon. *Arthurian Chronicles*. Edited and translated by E. Mason. London: Dent, 1962.

44. Wilhelm, J. J. and L. Z. Gross. *The Romance of Arthur*. New York: Garland, 1984 and 1986.

General

45. Adler, A. "Sovereignty as the Principle of Unity in Chrétien's *Erec*." In *Publications of the Modern Language Association of America* 60, no. 4 (December 1945): 917–36.

46. ———. "Sovereignty in Chrétien's *Yvain*." In *Publications of the Modern Language Association of America* 62, no. 2 (June 1947): 281–305.

47. Anderson, A. O. "Gildas and Arthur." In *Celtic Review* 8 (1912–1913): 149–65.

48. Arden, J. and M. D'Arcy. *The Island of the Mighty*. London: Eyre Methuen, 1974.

49. Ashe, G. *Kings and Queens of Early Britain*. London: Methuen, 1982.

50. Barker, B. *Symbols of Sovereignty*. Newton Abbot: Westbridge Books, 1979.

51. Bartrum, P. C. "Was There a *British Book of Conquests?*" In *Bulletin of the Board of Celtic Studies* 23 (1968): 1–5.

52. Blaess, M. "Arthur's Sisters." In *Bibliographical Bulletin of the Institute of Arthurian Society* 8 (1956): 69–77.

53. Blake, W. *Poetry and Prose*. London: Nonesuch Library, 1975.

54. Breatnach, R. A. "The Lady and the King: A Theme in Irish Literature." In *Celtic Studies* 42 (1953): 321–36.

55. Brewer, E. *From Cuchullin to Gawain*. Cambridge: D. S. Brewer, 1973.

56. Bromwich, R. "Celtic Dynastic Themes and Breton Lays." In *Etudes Celtiques* 9 (1960–1961): 439–74.

57. Brown, A. C. L. "The Individual Character of the Welsh Owain." In *Romantic Review* 3 (April–September 1912): 143–72.

58. ———. *The Origins of the Grail Legend*. Cambridge, Mass.: Harvard University Press, 1943.

59. Bullock-Davies, C. "Lanval and Avalon." In *Bulletin of the Board of Celtic Studies* (n.d.): 128–42.

60. Byrne, F. J. *Irish Kings and High Kings*. London: Batsford, 1973.

61. Campbell, J. E. *Popular Tales of the West Highlands*. London: Wildwood Press, 1984.

62. Cannadine, D. and S. Price. *Rituals of Royalty*. Cambridge: Cambridge University Press, 1987.

63. Carmichael, A. *Carmina Gadelica*. Edinburgh: Scottish Academic Press, 1972.

64. Child, F. J. *The English and Scottish Popular Ballads*. New York: Dover Books, 1965.

65. Chotzen, T. D. "Le Lion d'Owein et Ses Prototypes Celtiques." In *Néophilologus* 18 (1932–1933): 51–58.

66. Corkery, D. *The Hidden Ireland*. Dublin: Gill and Macmillan, 1967.

67. Currer-Briggs, N. *The Shroud and the Grail*. London: Weidenfeld and Nicolson, 1987.

68. Curtin, J. *Hero Tales of Ireland*. London: Macmillan, 1894.

69. ———. *Irish Folk Tales*. Dublin: Talbot Press, 1944.

70. Eisner, S. *A Tale of Wonder*. Wexford: John English, 1957.

71. Ellis, T. P. "Urien Rheged and His Son, Owain." In *Welsh Outlook* 18 (1931): 121–23, 157–60, 183–85.

72. Evan, S. *In Quest of the Holy Grail*. London: Dent, 1898.

73. Frazer, J. G. *The Illustrated Golden Bough*. London: Macmillan, 1978.

74. Goetinck, G. W. *Perceval: A Study of the Welsh Tradition in the Grail Legend*. Cardiff: University of Wales Press, 1975.

75. Green, M. *The Celts and Their Gods*. Gloucester: Alan Sutton, 1986.

76. Gregory, Lady. *Gods and Fighting Men*. Gerrards Cross: Colin Smythe, 1970.

77. Grout, P. B., R. A. Lodge, C. E. Pickford, and E. K. C. Varty. *The Legend of Arthur in the Middle Ages*. Cambridge: D. S. Brewer, 1983.

78. Hall, L. B. *Knightly Tales of Sir Gawaine*. Chicago: Nelson Hall, 1976.

79. Harf-Lancner, L. *Les Fées au Moyen Age*. Paris: Librarie Honoré Champion, 1984.

80. Henken, E. R. *Traditions of the Welsh Saints*. Cambridge: D. S. Brewer, 1987.

81. Hill, J. *The Tristan Legend*. Leeds: University of Leeds Press, 1977.

82. Hull, E. "Old Irish Tabus or Geasa." In *Folklore* 12 (1901): 41–56.

83. Hyde, D. "The Well of D'yerree in Dowan." In *Great Fairy Tales of Ireland*. Compiled by M. McGany. London: Wolfe, 1973.

84. Jones, D. *The Roman Quarry*. London: Agenda Editions, 1981.

85. Jones, E. *The Bardic Museum*. London: A. Strahan, 1802.

86. Knight, G. *The Secret Tradition in Arthurian Romance*. Wellingborough: Aquarian Press, 1983.

87. Korrel, P. *An Arthurian Triangle*. Leiden: E. J. Brill, 1984.

88. Le Roux, F. and C. J. Guyonvarc'h. *La Souverainente Guerrière de l'Irelande*. Rennes: Ogam Celticum, 1983.

89. Lewis, C. S. *That Hideous Strength*. London: Bodley Head, 1945.

90. Lewis, F. R. *Gwerin Ffristial a Thawl Bwrdd*. Transactions of the Hon. Society of Cymmyrodrians, 1941.

91. Lloyd-Morgan, C. "Perceval in Wales: Late Medieval Welsh Grail Traditions." In *The Changing Face of Arthurian Romance*. Edited by A. Adams, et al. Cambridge: Boydell and Brewer, 1986.

92. Loomis, R. S. *Arthurian Tradition and Chrétien de Troyes*. New York: Columbia University Press, 1949.

93. ———. *The Grail: From Celtic Myth to Christian Symbol*. Cardiff: University of Wales Press, 1963.

94. ———. *Studies in Medieval Literature*. New York: Burt Franklin, 1970.

95. ———. *Wales and the Arthurian Legend*. Cardiff: University of Wales Press, 1956.

96. Luria, M. S. "The Storm-Making Spring and the Meaning of Chrétien's Yvain." In *Studies in Philology* 64 (1967).

97. Luttrell, C. *The Creation of the First Arthurian Romance: A Quest*. London: E. Arnold, 1974.

98. MacCana, P. "Aspects of the Theme of King and Goddess in Irish Literature." *Etudes Celtiques* 7 (1956): 76–114 and *Etudes Celtiques* 8 (1956): 59–65.

99. ———. *The Learned Tales of Medieval Ireland*. Dublin: Dublin Institute of Advanced Studies, 1980.

100. ———. *The Mabinogi*. Cardiff: University of Wales Press, 1977.

101. Mac Dougall, H. A. *Racial Myth in English History*. Montreal: Harvest House, 1982.

102. McKenna, E. L., ed. and trans. "Historical Poem VIII of Gofraigh Fionn O'Dilaigh." In *Irish Monthly* 47 (1919): 455–59.

103. MacNeill, M. *The Festival of Lughnasadh*. Oxford: Oxford University Press, 1962.

104. Macwhite, E. "Early Irish Board Games." *Eigse* 5 (1945): 25–35.

105. Markale, J. *Le Graal*. Paris: Retz, 1982.

106. ———. *King Arthur: King of Kings*. London: Gordon Cremonesi, 1977.

107. ———. *Lancelot et la Chevalerie Arthurienne*. Paris: Editions Imago, 1985.

108. ———. *Merlin l'Enchanteur*. Paris: Editions Retz, 1981.

109. ———. *La Tradition Celtique en Bretagne Armoricaine*. Paris: Payot, 1978.

110. Masefield, J. *Midsummer Night*. London: Heinemann, 1928.

111. Matthews, C. *Mabon and the Guardians of Celtic Britain*. Rochester, Vt.: Inner Traditions, 2002.

112. ———. "Mabon, Divine Celtic Child." In *The Second Book of Merlin.* Edited by Bob Stewart. Poole: Blandford Press, 1988.

113. Matthews, C. and J. Matthews. *The Arthurian Tarot.* London: HarperCollins, 1990.

114. Matthews, J. *An Arthurian Reader.* Wellingborough: Aquarian Press, 1988.

115. Matthews, J., ed. *At the Table of the Grail.* London: Watkins Publications, 2002.

116. Matthews, J. *Fionn Mac Cumhail.* Poole: Firebird Books, 1988.

117. ———. "The Grail Family." In *Avalon to Camelot* i, no. 3 (1983): 9–10.

118. ———. *The Grail: Quest for the Eternal.* London: Thames and Hudson, 1981.

119. Matthews, J. and M. Green. *The Grail-Seeker's Companion.* Wellingborough: Aquarian Press, 1986.

120. Matthews, J. and B. Stewart. *Warriors of Arthur.* Poole: Blandford Press, 1987.

121. Moncrieffe of That Ilk, I. and D. Hicks. *The Highland Clans.* London: Barier and Rockliffe, 1967.

122. Morduch, A. *The Sovereign Adventure.* Cambridge: James Clarke, 1970.

123. Morris, J. *The Age of Arthur.* London: Weidenfeld and Nicolson, 1973.

124. Newstead, H. *Bran the Blessed in Arthurian Romance.* New York: Columbia University Press, 1939.

125. Newstead, H. "The Joie de la Cort." In *Erec and the Horn of Bran. Publication of the Modern Language Association of America* 51 (1936): 13–25.

126. ———. "Perceval's Father and Welsh Traditions." In *Romanic Review* 36 (1945) 3–31.

127. Nitze, W. A. "Yvain and the Myth of the Fountain." In *Speculum* 30 (1955): 170–79.

128. O'Corráin, D. "Irish Origin Legends and Genealogy." In *History of Heroic Tale: A Symposium.* Edited by T. Nyberg. Odense: Odense University Press, 1985.

129. O'Donovan, J. *Miscellany of the Celtic Society.* Dublin, 1849.

130. O'Flaherty, W. D. *Women, Androgenes and Other Mythical Beasts.* Chicago: University of Chicago Press, 1980.

131. O'Rahilly, C. *Ireland and Wales.* London: Longmans, 1924.

132. Ovazza, M. "D'Apollon—Maponos a Mabonograin." *Actes du 14ième Congrès International Arthurian*. Rennes: Presses Universitaires, 1984.

133. Parry, T. *History of Welsh Literature*. London: Oxford University Press, 1955.

134. Paton, L. A. *Studies in the Fairy Mythology of Arthurian Romance*. New York: Burt Franklin, 1960.

135. Power, P. C. *Sex and Marriage in Ancient Ireland*. Cork: Mercier Press, 1976.

136. Proctor, C. *Ceannas nan Gáidheal*. Sleat: Clan Donald Lands Trust, 1985.

137. Rees, A. and B. Rees. *Celtic Heritage*. London: Thames and Hudson, 1961.

138. Reinhard, J. R. *The Survival of Geis in Medieval Romance*. Halle: Max Niemayer Verlag, 1933.

139. Rhys, J. *Welsh and Manx. Celtic Folklore*, vol. 2. London: Wildwood House, 1980.

140. ———. *The Hibbert Lectures: Lectures on the Origin and Growth of Religion as Illustrated by Celtic Heathendom*. London: Williams and Morgate, 1888.

141. Rolt-Wheeler, F. *Mystic Gleams from the Holy Grail*. London: Rider (n.d.)

142. Ross, A. *Pagan Celtic Britain*. London: Routledge and Kegan Paul, 1967.

143. Scott, R. D. *The Thumb of Knowledge*. New York: Columbia University Press, 1930.

144. Sheppard, O. *The Lore of the Unicorn*. London: Allen and Unwin, 1967.

145. Sims-Williams, P. P. "Some Functions of Origin Stories in Early Medieval Wales." In *History of Heroic Tale: A Symposium*. Edited by T. Nyberg. Odense: Odense University Press, 1985.

146. Spaan, D. B. "The Otherworld in Early Irish Literature." Ph.D. diss., University of Michigan, 1969.

147. Stafford, G. *Pendragon*. Albany: Chaosium, 1985.

148. Stewart, R. J., ed. *The Book of Merlin*. Poole: Blandford, 1987.

149. Stewart, R. J. *The Mystic Life of Merlin*. London: Arkana, 1986.

150. ———. *The Prophetic Vision of Merlin*. London: Arkana, 1986.

151. Sturm, S. "Magic in the Bel Inconnu." In *Esprit Créateur* 12 (1972).

152. Tolstoy, N. *The Quest for Merlin*. London: Hamish Hamilton, 1985.

153. Van Duzec, M. *A Medieval Romance of Friendship: Eger and Grime*. New York: Burt Franklin, 1963.

154. Van Hamel, A. G. "The Game of the Gods." In *Archiv fur Nordisk Filogi* 6 (1934): 218–42.

155. Vansittart, R. *The Dark Tower*. London: Macdonald, 1965.

156. Webster, K. G. T. *Guinevere: A Story of Her Abductions*. Turtle Press, 1951.

157. Weston, J. *From Ritual to Romance*. New York: Doubleday, 1957.

158. Williams, R. *The Lord of the Isles*. London: Chatto and Windus/Hogarth, 1984.

159. Wood, D. *Genisis*. Tunbridge Wells: Baton Press, 1985.

160. Wyatt, L. "Goddess into Saint: The Foster Mother of Christ." In *The Golden Blade*, 1987.

Related Publications

161. Bradley, M. Z. and D. Paxson. *Priestess of Avalon*. New York: Viking, 2001.

162. Matthews, C. *Celtic Book of the Dead*. London: Connections, 1999.

163. ———. *Celtic Love*. San Francisco: HarperSanFrancisco, 1999.

164. ———. *Celtic Spirit*. San Francisco, HarperSanFrancisco, 1998.

165. ———. *Celtic Wisdom Sticks*. London: Connections, 2001.

166. ———. "Princess Diana: Flower Bride and Queen of Hearts." In *Mythological Europe Revisited*. Edited by Fons Elders. Brussels: VUB University Press, 2000.

167. ———. *Sophia: Goddess of Wisdom, Bride of God*. Wheaton: Quest Books, 2000.

168. ———. "The Spells of Women: Ninefold Sisterhoods in Celtic Tradition." In *The Celtic Seer's Sourcebook*. Edited by John Matthews. London: Cassell, 1999.

169. ———. "The Three Gwenhwyfars." In *Within the Hollow Hills*. Edited by J. Matthews. Edinburgh: Floris Books, 1995.

170. ———. "The Voices of the Wells: Celtic Oral Themes in Grail Literature." In *At the Table of the Grail*. Edited by John Matthews. London: Watkins Publications, 2002.

171. Matthews, C. and J. Matthews. *The Encyclopedia of Celtic Wisdom*. London: Rider, 2001.

172. ———. *Ladies of the Lake*. London: HarperCollins, 1992.

173. Matthews, J. *Celtic Shaman*. London: Rider, 2001.

174. ———. *Celtic Totem Animals*. Glastonbury: Gothic Image, 2002.

175. ———. *Sir Gawain, Knight of the Goddess*. Wellingborough: Aquarian Press, 1990.

176. ———. *Song of Taliesin*. Wheaton: Quest Books, 2001.

177. ———. *Taliesin: The Last Celtic Shaman*. Rochester, Vt.: Inner Traditions, 2002.

178. Matthews, J. and C. Matthews. *The Encyclopedia of Celtic Myth and Legend*. London: Rider, 2003.

For more details about courses, events, and books by the author, please visit www.hallowquest.org.uk, or write to Caitlín Matthews, BCM Hallowquest, London WC1N 3XX, United Kingdom, enclosing a self-addressed envelope and three international postage-paid coupons.

Index

Because many of the characters listed below exist in both Celtic and medieval Arthurian tradition, often with differing characteristics, some have entries under separate names. (e.g. Gawain and Gwalchmai). Other entries are cross-referenced (e.g., Kay. *See* Cai) to indicate that the natures of these personae are substantially consistent throughout both traditions.